GOD AND THE ETHICS OF BELIEF

Philosophy of religion in the Anglo-American tradition experienced a "rebirth" following the 1955 publication of *New Essays in Philosophical Theology* (eds. Antony Flew and Alisdair MacIntyre). Fifty years later, this volume of new essays offers a sampling of the best work in what is now a very active field, written by some of its most prominent members. A substantial introduction sketches the developments of the past half-century, while also describing the "ethics of belief" debate in epistemology and showing how it connects to explicitly religious concerns and to the topics of the individual contributions. These topics include the relationship between God and the natural laws; the metaphysics of bodily resurrection; the role of appeal to "mystery" in the religious life; the justification of both theistic belief generally and more specific doctrinal beliefs; and the social-political aspects of religious faith and practice.

Andrew Dole is Assistant Professor of Religion at Amherst College.

Andrew Chignell is Assistant Professor in the Sage School of Philosophy, Cornell University.

God and the Ethics of Belief

New Essays in Philosophy of Religion

Edited by

ANDREW DOLE
Amherst College

ANDREW CHIGNELL
Cornell University

CAMBRIDGE UNIVERSITY PRESS
Cambridge, New York, Melbourne, Madrid, Cape Town, Singapore, São Paulo

Cambridge University Press
40 West 20th Street, New York, NY 10011-4211, USA

www.cambridge.org
Information on this title: www.cambridge.org/9780521850933

First published 2005

Printed in the United States of America

A catalog record for this publication is available from the British Library.

Library of Congress Cataloging in Publication Data

God and the ethics of belief : new essays in philosophy of religion / edited by Andrew Dole,
Andrew Chignell.
p.   cm.
Includes bibliographical references and index.
ISBN 0-521-85093-2 (hardcover)
1. Christianity – Philosophy.   I. Dole, Andrew, 1966–   II. Chignell, Andrew, 1973–   III. Title.
BR100.G62   2005
210 – dc22   2004027948

ISBN-13   978-0-521-85093-3 hardback
ISBN-10   0-521-85093-2 hardback

To Nicholas Wolterstorff

Contents

Contributors

William Alston is Emeritus Professor of Philosophy at Syracuse University.

Robert Audi is Professor of Philosophy and David E. Gallo Professor of Business Ethics at the University of Notre Dame.

Andrew Chignell is Assistant Professor in the Sage School of Philosophy at Cornell University.

Keith DeRose is Professor of Philosophy at Yale University.

Andrew Dole is Assistant Professor of Religion at Amherst College.

John Hare is Noah Porter Professor of Philosophical Theology at Yale Divinity School.

Derk Pereboom is Professor and Chair of Philosophy at the University of Vermont.

Alvin Plantinga is John A. O'Brien Professor of Philosophy at the University of Notre Dame.

Philip L. Quinn was John A. O'Brien Professor of Philosophy at the University of Notre Dame.

Richard Swinburne is Nolloth Professor of the Philosophy of the Christian Religion Emeritus at the University of Oxford.

Peter van Inwagen is John Cardinal O'Hara Professor of Philosophy at the University of Notre Dame.

Nicholas Wolterstorff is Noah Porter Professor of Philosophical Theology Emeritus at Yale Divinity School.

Linda Zagzebski is Kingfisher College Chair of the Philosophy of Religion and Ethics at the University of Oklahoma.

Acknowledgments

Our sincere thanks are owed to a number of people who helped make this project possible. First and foremost, we thank our contributors, many of whom presented drafts of their essays at a conference in New Haven in 2002 and subsequently revised or, in some cases, completely rewrote their papers. We are also grateful to Robert M. Adams and Michael Della Rocca for helping us to arrange the conference and to the Ernst Cassirer Fund at Yale for providing financial assistance.

For valuable advice on the introduction, we thank Marilyn McCord Adams, Robert Audi, Jesse Couenhoven, Matthew Halteman, John Hare, Basil Mitchell, Philip Quinn, and Stephanie Wykstra. For his guidance and general suffering during the time it took to bring the project to completion, we thank our editor at Cambridge, Andy Beck. For her excellent work on the index, our gratitude goes to ShawnaKim Lowey-Ball. And for generous support of various sorts, Andrew Chignell wishes to thank the Cornell branch of the Telluride Association.

Sadly, Philip Quinn passed away unexpectedly while this project was going to press. Those who had the pleasure of knowing Phil will agree that the philosophical world is much better off for the contribution that he made – through his writing, through his administrative work at the American Philosophical Association, and through his gracious personal interactions with many of us. We are honored to be able to publish one of his last papers as the final piece in this volume.

Finally, we are extremely pleased to dedicate this volume to Nicholas Wolterstorff on the occasion of his stepping down from full-time teaching at Yale. Nick has been a colleague or teacher of many of the contributors, a mentor to the editors, and a friend to all. He has exemplified a level of devotion to his community, to his students, and to the life of the mind that is almost impossible to match. We have little doubt that he will continue to do so, even in "retirement."

In *Reason within the Bounds of Religion*, Nick wrote that "if the activities of the scholar are to be justified, that justification must be found ultimately in the contribution of scholarship to the cause of justice-in-shalom. The vocation of the scholar, like the vocation of everyone else, is to serve that end." We present this volume to him with great affection and in the firm belief that his own career as a writer and teacher has indeed served that end.

The Ethics of Religious Belief: A Recent History

ANDREW CHIGNELL AND ANDREW DOLE

We begin with some truth in advertising: our title's *and* is really the logician's *inclusive or*. In other words, not all the essays in this book are strictly about God *and* the ethics of belief (where "the ethics of belief" refers to a specific research program in epistemology). Rather, some are mainly about God, whereas others are about God and belief; some focus on the ethics of belief, whereas still others are about *both* God and the ethics of belief. Most were first drafted for a 2002 conference in honor of Nicholas Wolterstorff upon his retirement from teaching; thus, the range of topics reflects his research interests as well as those of the authors.

The subtitle echoes the title of an edited volume published exactly fifty years ago: *New Essays in Philosophical Theology*.[1] The goal of that volume was to offer a sampling of a newly active research program in analytic philosophy, a program that the editors referred to as "philosophical theology" rather than "philosophy of religion" because of the latter term's association in those days with Hegelian thought.[2] The first *New Essays* dealt with religious topics of philosophical interest ranging from the nature of God and the rationality of theism to the metaphysical possibility of an afterlife and the status of religious language. This volume, likewise, provides a snapshot of the field – fifty years along – and addresses many of the same topics. Because Hegel's grip on the term has loosened in the interim, we have reverted to "philosophy of religion."

In what follows, we will first characterize the "ethics of belief" debate in epistemology, and then discuss how it relates to questions about *religious* belief and practice in particular. This will set the stage for a brief sketch of the history of philosophy of religion since *New Essays*, and of how these essays fit into it. We will conclude with a description of each essay individually and make a case for including them all under the rubric of the ethics of belief *broadly* construed.

THE ETHICS OF BELIEF

Narrowly construed, the ethics of belief debate revolves around the issue of whether there are norms governing our various practices of belief formation and, if there are, whether they are genuinely *moral* norms or norms of some other sort. Is it always *wrong* (or irrational, or impractical) to hold a belief without having sufficient evidence for it? Is it always *right* (or rational, or prudent) to hold beliefs on the basis of evidence, and to withhold them in the absence of evidence?

The *locus classicus* is an essay called "The Ethics of Belief" by William Kingdon Clifford – the nineteenth-century philosopher/mathematician whom William James dubbed "that delicious *enfant terrible*" of doxastic abstemiousness. In epistemological circles, Clifford is chiefly remembered for two things: a story and a principle. The story is that of a shipowner who is planning to sell tickets for a transatlantic voyage. It strikes him that his ship is old, and doubts creep into his mind about its seaworthiness. Knowing that repairs would be costly and cause a delay, he manages to push these doubts away and form the "sincere and comfortable conviction that his vessel is thoroughly safe and seaworthy." He sells tickets, bids the passengers farewell, and then quietly collects the insurance money when the ship goes down in a mid-Atlantic squall.

According to Clifford (who himself once survived a shipwreck, and must have found this behavior particularly deplorable), the owner in this case is "verily guilty of the death of those men" because even though he sincerely believed that the ship was safe, "he had no right to believe on such evidence as was before him." After making this diagnosis, Clifford changes the example: the ship doesn't meet a watery demise, but rather makes it safe and sound into the New York harbor. Does that affect the shipowner's culpability with respect to his belief? "Not one jot," says Clifford: he is equally guilty – equally blameworthy – for having believed something on insufficient evidence. Then Clifford gives us his famous principle: "It is wrong always, everywhere, and for anyone to believe anything on insufficient evidence."[3]

In his response to Clifford, James famously sniffs at the impracticable stringency of this principle, plumping instead for the more liberal policy that we often have the "right to believe" even when we lack sufficient evidence (and even when we *know* that we lack it).[4] In places, James goes further and suggests that in certain cases, it is not merely permitted but *positively commendable* or even *rationally required* that we believe on insufficient evidence.[5] He concludes by upbraiding Clifford for his demurral about religious belief in particular:

When I look at the religious question as it really puts itself to concrete men, and when I think of all the possibilities which both practically and theoretically it involves, then this command that we shall put a stopper on our heart, instincts, and courage, and *wait* – acting of course meanwhile more or less as if religion were *not* true – till doomsday, or till such time as our intellect and sense working together may have raked in evidence enough, – this command, I say, seems to me the queerest idol ever manufactured in the philosophic cave.[6]

Although the phrase "ethics of belief" may be of Clifford's coinage, there were obviously ethics of belief well before the nineteenth century. Descartes says in the *Meditations* that when forming a judgment, "it is clear by the natural light that perception of the intellect should precede the determination of the will." In the search for certain knowledge (*scientia*), at least, there is an obligation to withhold assent from any proposition the truth of which is not clearly perceived by the intellect.[7] In other contexts, it may be both appropriate and advantageous to hold a mere "opinion" (*opinio*) whose truth is not clearly and distinctly perceived. Even then, however, we need to have some sort of evidence before giving our assent: "Though we cannot have certain demonstrations of everything, still we must take sides, and in matters of custom *embrace the opinions that seem the most probable*, so that we may never be irresolute when we need to act."[8]

Locke is at least as stringent: in the search for scientific knowledge as well as in other contexts, he says, it is to "transgress against [one's] own light" to believe on insufficient evidence or to fail to proportion one's degree of belief to the amount of evidence that one has. In his discussion of the concept of "Faith," Locke writes:

He that believes without having any Reason for believing, may be in love with his own Fancies; but neither seeks Truth as he ought, nor pays the Obedience due to his Maker, who would have him use those discerning Faculties he has given him, to keep him out of Mistake and Errour. He that does not this to the best of his Power, however he sometimes lights on Truth, is in the right but by chance and I know not whether the luckiness of the Accident will excuse the irregularity of his proceeding.[9]

To believe without good reason or evidence is not only to misuse one's faculties and risk error, says Locke; it is also to violate a God-given duty to follow the dictates of reason. Given his divine command theory of moral rightness, it looks as though, for Locke, the duty to follow evidence is a *moral* as well as an *epistemic* one.[10]

This brings out an important point: there are different *kinds* of obligation that govern our practices generally, and there are also different *kinds* of obligation that govern our practices of belief-formation in particular. The ethicist of belief will typically try to specify which kinds, if any, he or she means to ascribe to us. Clifford and Locke claim that the question of whether one has done one's doxastic best is not only an epistemic but also a moral question. In other words, they think that to violate an epistemic norm is, by implication, to violate a moral norm.[11] Others claim that there are *only* epistemic norms in the neighborhood of belief. Consider this injunction from Kant, for instance:

Friends of the human race and of what is holiest to it! Accept what appears to you most worthy of belief after careful and sincere examination, whether of facts or of rational grounds; only do not dispute that prerogative of reason which makes it the highest good on earth, the prerogative of being the final touchstone of truth.[12]

Although there is a whiff of a merely hypothetical imperative here (if you want to get to truth, then you should follow your evidence), in general for Kant it is the *categorical* and *epistemic* imperative to be reasonable that should lead us to be evidence followers. To "think for yourself" and "free yourself from the self-incurred tutelage of others" is the epistemic duty of every enlightened subject.[13] It is an offense against reason – a degrading capitulation to cognitive heteronomy – to do otherwise.

A third general type of norm relating to our practices of belief formation is *pragmatic* or *prudential*. In some cases, it is the better part of wisdom to believe that *p* even in the absence of sufficient evidence for *p*. In other cases, it is pragmatically *necessary* to believe that *p* in order to accomplish some worthy goal. For example: Suppose you would like to retain a good relationship with your teenage son, and you are aware that this requires believing the best of him whenever possible. You have no conclusive evidence either for or against the proposition that he turns your house into an opium den of Edwardian proportions when you are away (he claims that he has recently taken up meditation, and that the funny smell when you come home is just incense). Because you think that your relationship will be seriously damaged if you come to think of your son as a hardcore opium user, you would violate a pragmatic norm if you were to go ahead and believe that he is.

The types of norms governing belief are often taken to be related, and in at least two ways. First, they may be conceptually or theoretically connected: That there is a *pragmatic* norm to follow evidence may serve as a premise in an argument to the effect that there is also an *epistemic* norm to follow evidence. And, as we saw with Locke and Clifford, that there is such an epistemic norm may be the basis for an argument that there is an analogous *moral* norm.[14] Second, the norms may conflict. The pragmatic norm that advises you to believe that your son is not turning the house into an opium den may eventually conflict with the epistemic norm to follow your olfactory evidence. A full-blown ethics of belief will say something about the connections between types of norms, and will also tell us which sorts of situations the various norms govern and what to do when norms conflict.

The type of theory that ascribes to rational people the obligation to *follow their evidence* when forming beliefs often goes by the name *Evidentialism*. Given that there are different kinds of obligation, there will also be different versions of Evidentialism: at the very least, we can distinguish pragmatic, epistemic, and moral versions. In general, it is incumbent on Evidentialists to specify the sorts of norms they are putting forward, as well as to provide some account of what can count as evidence (is it only propositional attitudes, or is there also non-doxastic evidence?), what it means to "have" evidence, and what the support relations between evidence and a belief are like. These issues are exceedingly complex, but it is not obvious that any of them can be the basis of a fatal objection to all forms of Evidentialism.[15]

Another major issue in the ethics of belief debate has to do with whether or not acts of belief formation are in any way under our control. If an act is not voluntary in at least *some* sense, it is hard to see how anyone could be genuinely *blameworthy* for having performed it. In response to this objection from "doxastic involuntarism," some ethicists of belief have developed accounts of *indirect* ways in which belief-formation can count as voluntary and thus be susceptible to moral evaluation.[16] Others take the objection to motivate a shift of focus away from belief and toward other positive propositional attitudes that are by definition voluntary – "acceptances," for instance.[17] Still others seek a position that supports talk of obligations on belief while absorbing the (putative) empirical datum that much belief-formation is not under the control of the will.[18]

THE ETHICS OF BELIEF IN PHILOSOPHY OF RELIGION

It should be clear from this brief survey of the ethics of belief debate in epistemology that the positions on offer will have implications for speculative metaphysical and religious belief formation. That's because metaphysical and religious doctrines often refer to entities that are empirically unavailable (deities, causal connections, wills, souls, possible worlds, universals), and the question naturally arises of how we can locate evidence for beliefs about such exotica. The shipowner's belief has nothing to do with the supersensible, of course, but it is clear in later parts of the essay that Clifford's principle is primarily targeted at *religious* belief that is not formed on the basis of sufficient evidence.[19]

Locke, too, explicitly emphasizes religion when discussing the import of his version of Evidentialism. *Pace* Clifford, Locke thinks that there *is* good evidence for belief in God, and thus that such belief is (when based on that evidence) both permitted and commendable.[20] Those unfortunate working-class folks who don't have much time, Locke says, may be excused from across-the-board duties to check their evidence. But they should at least use their Sabbaths to consider the evidence for their beliefs about "matters of maximal concernment."

Besides his particular calling for the support of this life, everyone has a concern in a future life, which he is bound to look after. This engages his thoughts in religion; and here it mightily lies upon him to understand and reason right. Men, therefore, cannot be excused from understanding the words, and framing the general notions relating to religion, right. The one day of seven, besides other days of rest, allows in the Christian world time enough for this (had they no other idle hours) if they would but make use of these vacancies from their daily labour, and apply themselves to an improvement of knowledge with as much diligence as they often do to a great many other things that are useless.[21]

Locke builds these claims about the duty to seek evidence for religious belief into his overall Evidentialist picture. By contrast, another early ethicist of belief, Blaise Pascal, takes religious belief as a primary focus. His famous "wager" argument (which is actually a last-ditch effort to encourage theism in his readers if all else fails) says that such belief is *pragmatically* justifiable even without sufficient evidence. Thus Pascal's is an anti-Evidentialist position, at least when it comes to pragmatic norms governing religious belief formation. He also offers advice about how to overcome the apparently involuntary nature of belief (use indirect methods to generate belief in God, he says, such as going repeatedly to Mass and taking holy water). And, of course, it is this proto-pragmatist line that James takes up in developing an *apologia* for religious belief in his response to Clifford.[22]

Whereas philosophers up through the nineteenth century worried most about the moral, epistemic, and pragmatic *justification* of belief, early twentieth–century philosophers focused primarily on questions about the *meaning* of the propositions believed. The dreaded "verifiability criterion of meaning" championed by many logical positivists claimed (in some of its versions) that statements that are neither *analytic* nor *empirically verifiable* are, strictly speaking, meaningless. An implication of this doctrine is that there is not much semantic room for synthetic judgments about supersensible entities.[23]

This strict verificationism had important ramifications for the ethics of belief. Theories of meaning are often and quite naturally accompanied by implicit epistemic, moral, or pragmatic principles according to which we should shun statements that are deemed meaningless by the theory, and verificationism was no exception. But the implicit status of such principles sometimes obscures the fact that they aren't *entailed* by the relevant theory of meaning. Clearly it *would* be pointless and irrational to try to accept statements like "All mimsy were the borogoves, and the mome raths outgrabe" or "Colorless green ideas sleep furiously." But even a strict verificationist might admit that though religious statements are equally meaningless from a cognitive point of view, something of pragmatic or moral value is expressed by them that isn't expressed by the foregoing balderdash.

The arch-positivist A. J. Ayer, for example, does not dispatch religious (and ethical) language as *mere* nonsense in his twentieth century classic, *Language, Truth, and Logic*. It *is* nonsense for Ayer, of course, but it also has an important "emotive" function distinct from the "descriptive" functions of ordinary and scientific language.[24] Perhaps a cognitively meaningless statement like "Mine eyes have seen the glory of the coming of the Lord" succeeds in expressing courageous hope for an amelioration of the human condition, or defiance in the face of our own finitude, or an affirmation of our absolute dependence on something that transcends our cognitive grasp. If so, says Ayer, then it may be pragmatically or morally valuable to utter this statement in various contexts; it may even be important for some of us to try to accept it if possible. And this may be true even though from an *epistemic* point of view, the statement is a miserable nonstarter.

THE FIRST *NEW ESSAYS*

Logical positivism and the verificationism underpinning it collapsed around mid-century.[25] This development, too, had important implications for the ethics of belief, and for the ethics of religious belief in particular. Indeed, the story of the "revival" of philosophy of religion within the Anglo-American tradition in the latter part of the century is in part the story of the reopening of lines of inquiry that had been blocked by the positivists. The publication of *New Essays* is viewed by many as a watershed in this process, decisively inaugurating a postpositivist period in the philosophical treatment of religion. As we will see below, however, *New Essays* was in fact more of a transitional document than an articulation of something entirely new.

In the preface to *New Essays*, editors Antony Flew and Alisdair MacIntyre explicitly deny that their contributors could be considered logical positivists "if this is taken, as it is and should be, to imply a toeing of the party line of the now defunct Vienna Circle."[26] But while the verifiability criterion is nowhere advanced with full confidence, positivism's deep influence on the collection is unmistakable.[27] One of the most prominent vestiges in *New Essays* is the shared assumption that religious language presents a particularly acute philosophical problem. None of the authors adopts Ayer's response to the problem exactly, but many pursue the project of salvaging an important but nondescriptive function for such language.

The most widely anthologized of the pieces from the collection – the "University discussion" among Antony Flew, R. M. Hare, and Basil Mitchell – is typical in this regard. In his part of the discussion, Flew substitutes Karl Popper's "falsifiability criterion of meaning" for the verifiability criterion, and then argues that because there is no fact or discovery or event that religious people would take to falsify their creedal statements, those statements don't succeed in asserting anything.[28] Hare responds by suggesting that religion consists not in "systems of assertions" that can be falsified by evidence, but rather in the articulation of a *blik* – a view of the world (like the conviction that nature is regular) that determines what counts as evidence and whether certain evidence is admitted, and so is not itself defeasible by evidence.

Similarly, Thomas Macpherson, reflecting on the closing pages of Wittgenstein's *Tractatus*, classifies religion as simply "the inexpressible" and notes that "perhaps positivistic philosophy has done a service to religion. By showing, in their own way, the absurdity of what theologians try to utter, positivists have helped to suggest that religion belongs to the sphere of the unutterable."[29] Flew concludes the volume in the same Wittgensteinian spirit, arguing that if the semantic and logical problems inherent in talk of "surviving death" cannot be resolved, then we must simply accept the Tractarian doctrine that "death is not lived through. Outside the visual field nothing is seen, not even darkness: for whatever is seen is within the visual field. When we are dead nothing is experienced, not even emptiness: for there is no one to experience. For each of us 'the world in death does not change, but ceases.'"[30] If we cannot make empirical sense of talk of the afterlife, Flew is saying here, then we must conclude that no substantive claims – and hence no claims about personal survival – are made by such talk.

This makes it clear, again, that although the editors of *New Essays* announced their departure from positivism, the verdicts expressed by the contributors turn out to be in substantial agreement with those of their predecessors. Still, *New Essays* also contains early strains of three new and distinct themes in the analytic treatment of religion – themes that would become prominent over the half-century to follow.

PHILOSOPHY OF RELIGION SINCE *NEW ESSAYS*

Further Problems concerning Religious Language

The first theme, the one most discernable within *New Essays* itself, retains the positivists' focus on language but abandons their strict criteria of meaning. The theme is expressive of the broader mid-century movement in analytic philosophy that is sometimes called "linguistic analysis."[31] Two years after *New Essays*, Basil Mitchell described that movement as follows:

Philosophers who adopt this approach (they are sometimes called "Linguistic Analysts") differ from the Logical Positivists in this characteristic way: in place of the dogmatic assertion that those statements alone have meaning which are empirically verifiable, they ask the question – of any class of statements – "what is the logic of statements of this kind?" that is to say, "how are they to be verified, or tested or justified? What is their use and function, what jobs do they do?"[32]

In the late 1950s, this kind of linguistic analysis was applied to theological utterances, and a "religious language obsession"[33] seized many philosophers of religion over the two subsequent decades. The obsession was most acute in Britain; this was due in part to the powerful influence of Wittgenstein there and in part to the prominence of a distinct "Oxford school" of linguistic analysis.[34] Many of the Wittgensteinians, then as now, tended to follow the positivists in denying that religious language makes substantive claims about the world (a tendency that earned this movement the sobriquet "therapeutic positivism"[35]). Members of the Oxford school, on the other hand, tended to engage in detailed analysis of religious language of the sort Mitchell describes, in an attempt to understand the various functions that such language serves. An account of the actual functions or uses of religious language, it was thought, could itself provide a guide to its meaning.[36]

A pervasive assumption in work from this period is that since questions about meaning are logically prior to questions about its truth or justification, the latter cannot profitably be pursued until the former are settled. Thus the American philosopher William Blackstone argued in 1963 that:

[u]ntil the content of a belief is made clear, the appeal to accept the belief on faith is beside the point, for one would not know what one has accepted. The request for the meaning of a religious belief is logically prior to the question of accepting that belief on faith or to the question of whether that belief constitutes knowledge. This point the philosophical analysts have driven home with a vengeance.[37]

The prevalence of this way of thinking led to the so-called Problem of Religious Language becoming a staple in textbook and classroom surveys of philosophy of religion, and often being treated as *the* major problem in the field. By the early 1970s, however, this model no longer enjoyed unquestioned dominance. Wittgensteinians were slowly being marginalized in analytic philosophy as a whole, and Oxford-style linguistic analysis suffered both from the deaths of J. L. Austin and Ian Ramsey and from ongoing attacks on the idea that linguistic meanings are stable enough to support anything like an analytic-synthetic distinction.[38] Although philosophy of language has remained a core area of analytic philosophy, the last thirty years have witnessed its transformation from "first philosophy" into one area of specialization among others. Alternative types of philosophy of religion slowly emerged from under the shadow of linguistic analysis, largely as a result of this development in the field of philosophy more generally.

The conviction that it makes sense to speak of *the* Problem of Religious Language also eventually came under attack by philosophers who had themselves been working on it. Blackstone, for example, professed to be following the positivists and the later Wittgenstein in his initial investigations into the nature and status of religious language.[39] The results of his work, however, tended to highlight the multifarious character of such language: "Sentences which perform a religious function," Blackstone wrote, "are of many different kinds. They include descriptions, predictions, explanations, exclamations, exhortations, prayers, questions, ejaculations, blessings, historical statements, and autobiographical statements. There are also sentences, we have seen, which purport to refer to something outside human experience – something in principle unverifiable."[40] In the end, Blackstone largely agreed with the positivists in taking the latter sort of religious assertion to be cognitively meaningless. But like the linguistic analysts, he observed that there is a considerable variety of uses to which religious language is typically put; he also noted that there are *some* statements central to certain religions – "Pharaoh let the Israelites go," for example, or "Mohammad engaged in ministry in Mecca" – that undoubtedly *do* make claims about the world. Moreover, for many of these statements there *is* considerable (though not conclusive) evidence.[41] The worry that such observations raise should be obvious: the more that religious utterances are seen as performing a variety of very different functions – some of which are shared with nonreligious utterances – the more *the* Problem of Religious Language dissolves into a multiplicity of problems in the philosophy of language generally.[42]

Traces of the religious language obsession and its aftermath can still be detected in contemporary philosophy of religion, and in at least two ways. First, as mentioned above, there is an ongoing tradition of reflection on religion that takes its cues from Wittgenstein's "Lectures on Religious Belief," "Remarks on

Frazer's 'Golden Bough,'" and "Culture and Value." Typical of this movement is a focus on religious language games and "forms of life" as cultural-linguistic entities, and a repudiation of the notion that religious utterances make genuine "descriptive" claims about the world in the way that everyday and/or scientific utterances do. Although the leading lights of this movement were analytic philosophers (Wittgenstein himself, Norman Malcolm, D. Z. Phillips), most of the people currently working in that field are now in departments of religious studies or divinity. This is largely due to the fact that the focus on social history, interpretation, and cultural forms in the academic study of religion (as well as its strong anti-metaphysical bias) makes it more hospitable than contemporary analytic philosophy to the neo-Wittgensteinian program.[43]

Another result of the move away from a focus on language in analytic philosophy of religion was the slow return to optimism about substantive metaphysics. The fact that the positivist program had faltered, together with the fact that subsequent linguistic analysts were able to open up a place for religious language that was not wholly "emotive," allowed for a return to traditional discussion of the *entities* referred to by such language. Talk of the nature and attributes of God conceived as a genuine metaphysical entity, for instance, began to supplant discussions of the nature of "God-talk" and its capacity to refer. Not everyone has celebrated this development or shares the new metaphysical optimism (the neo-Wittgensteinians, for instance, are very much opposed to it). But it is a visible trend, and metaphysics is now a much more important subfield in philosophy of religion than is the study of language. As a result, no full-bore treatments of religious utterance have been included in this volume (although Alston's contribution is somewhat in this vein); instead, it opens with a section on substantive metaphysical questions about the nature of God, freedom, and immortality. Still, the postpositivist program just described – with its suggestion that some objects of theological speculation are tractable to descriptive language – was clearly an important precondition of the projects pursued here.

Problems concerning Rationality

The second thematic trajectory in *New Essays* leads away from a preoccupation with language and towards a re-engagement with older lines of thought in philosophy of religion. C. B Martin's "A Religious Way of Knowing" and Alasdair MacIntyre's "Visions," for example, are both concerned with the question of whether certain types of experience can provide evidence for religious beliefs. Flew's "Divine Omnipotence and Human Freedom" raises objections to the free-will defense to the problem of evil, and advocates John Stuart

Mill's position that the problem of "reconciling infinite benevolence and justice with infinite power in the Creator in such a world as this" is impossible.[44] Finally, Patrick Nowell-Smith's "Miracles" deals with the question of whether events for which no scientific explanations are forthcoming provide evidence for the existence of a supernatural order. These essays are thus concerned with evaluating the *rationality of religious beliefs* through examining either the *evidence* for them or their *logical compatibility* with one another and with commonsense and scientific knowledge.

Two years after the publication of *New Essays*, Ronald Hepburn offered a succinct articulation of the central issue in this region: "If we are convinced that Hume and Kant and their successors have once and for all refuted the arguments of rational apologetics, we are faced with a choice between agnosticism (or atheism) and the discovery of an alternative method of justifying belief."[45] Worries about the justification or rationality of religious belief were thus seen as an inheritance of the Enlightenment rather than of positivism. The success of the positivist program would have rendered Hume's and Kant's criticisms of rational apologetics otiose, of course, but in the wake of positivism's demise and outside the ambit of the later Wittgenstein, material of this sort once again received serious consideration.

Hepburn's remark suggests that there was a general consensus that "Hume and Kant and their successors" had discredited traditional theistic proofs.[46] Such a consensus has, in fact, never existed; on the contrary, the adequacy of the Humean and Kantian objections has been debated – sometimes quite hotly – over the past half-century. Quite a few theistic arguments enjoyed favorable attention from prominent philosophers during that period: a case in point is Norman Malcolm's widely influential reconstruction in 1960 of the Anselmian ontological argument – a reconstruction that had, according to Malcolm, the twin merits of remaining untouched by Kant's criticisms and of being sound.[47] Another example is the design argument which, though often thought to have been maimed by Hume and given the deathblow by Darwin, has received a latter-day resuscitation in the form of the so-called fine-tuning argument.[48]

Thus, even during (and certainly after) the period when linguistic analysis was dominant, questions regarding the rationality of religious belief were beginning to receive significant attention from philosophers (even those who were primarily focused on linguistic issues[49]). And because the traditional theistic arguments have their roots in the history of philosophy, many of these philosophers started engaging materials from that history. As a result, the decline of the Problem of Religious Language went hand in hand not just with the return of metaphysics, but also with a revival of serious interest in the history of philosophical discussions of religion (which paralleled a revival of serious interest in the history of philosophy generally). The second section of this volume includes three essays that exhibit the ongoing importance that questions concerning rationality and justification have in contemporary philosophy of religion.

The Advent of "Christian Philosophy"

A third important thematic trajectory coming out of *New Essays* is only hinted at within the collection itself. In his reply to J. N. Findlay's contention that theism is no longer a viable option for those who have a "contemporary philosophical outlook," A. C. A. Rainer noted that not all of those who think of themselves as "contemporary" agree. In a prophetic vein, Rainer wrote:

But supposing that there were a consensus of contemporary thinkers about the theological implications of their interpretation of logic, or that the negative implications for theology of this interpretation had been demonstrated, what should the believer do? Accept the result without demur, and apply to a psycho-analyst for help in adjusting himself emotionally to a godless world? Not if he were a philosophical believer. It would be his responsibility, rather, to direct discussion onto the adequacy of the interpretation of logic assumed by contemporary thinkers. Precisely what form this interpretation should take is, and will continue to be, a matter for debate on purely logical and epistemological grounds. A critical examination of the presuppositions of thought and communication will help to clarify theological as well as scientific and philosophical thought.[50]

Here Rainer anticipates an approach to philosophy of religion that, though scarcely visible at the time, would come to characterize one of the more energetic parts of the field within an academic generation. The movement now referred to under the rubric "Christian philosophy" (the term, of course, has a much longer history[51]) emerged rather quietly during the 1960s and 1970s in Britain and the United States, and it was only toward the end of this period that references to a "revival" of philosophy of religion began to appear in the literature.[52] In its early stages, this movement was largely concerned with defending theism against a variety of philosophical objections. A hallmark of the approach was to direct critical attention to the assumptions motivating such objections – assumptions that, although often taken for granted by their proponents, could be seen as "matter for debate" on philosophical grounds. Rainer's injunction to the philosophical believer to question the "interpretation of logic assumed" by her opponents was thus a harbinger of what became a common strategy.

It's true of course, that philosophically tinged "apologetics" could be found in earlier theology – particularly in the Reformed tradition.[53] But "Christian philosophy" originated within the discipline of philosophy proper. Many of the prominent figures in this movement were trained in the nonreligious academic climate of the 1950s and 1960s. A common theme in subsequent descriptions of the period is that the pronouncements against the intellectual viability and interest of religion seemed in many cases to stem from a kind of allergic reaction to all things religious, rather than from well-grounded conviction.[54] Some of these younger religious philosophers thus spied an opportunity to turn the philosophical tools with which they had been equipped against what they saw as the secular biases of their own discipline. The goal, however, was emphatically *not* to traffic in fundamentalist apologetics or anti-intellectual fideism. Rather, it was to solicit a seat at the seminar-room table for philosophers who were explicitly committed to both reason and faith.

The example of Nicholas Wolterstorff (to whom this volume is dedicated) is emblematic in this regard. Wolterstorff was trained at Calvin College as an undergraduate, and then at Harvard, where he wrote a dissertation on Alfred North Whitehead. He soon turned away from process philosophy, however, in order to work on developing religion-friendly arguments in analytic metaphysics and epistemology. In an essay called "Can Belief in God Be Rational If It Has No Foundations?" he de-emphasized direct arguments for theism and instead took issue with the claim that the burden of proof in controversies concerning the existence of God rests squarely on the theist. Wolterstorff argued instead that in some cases, theistic belief can be "immediate" (i.e., based on no evidence at all) and yet still count as rational. This anti-Evidentialist suggestion – that "a person's being in the situation of believing immediately that God exists represents no failure on his part to govern his beliefs as well as can rightly be demanded of him" – struck many readers as outrageous. But it galvanized some to continue exploring the assumptions that had made philosophical atheism or agnosticism seem superior.[55]

Other participants in the movement took this idea one step further by challenging the thought that only claims acceptable to believers and nonbelievers alike could be used, without argument, as philosophical resources in public debate. Many saw nothing amiss in taking traditional religious doctrines as premises in philosophical arguments, and thereby explicitly locating the starting point for their projects "within" the religious sphere.[56] The distinction between "philosophy of religion" and "philosophical theology" slowly evolved to accommodate this development: it now rests on whether the premises of the arguments involved are supposed to be available to everyone (philosophy of religion) or just to those already located in a doctrinal tradition (philosophical theology).[57]

Within "Christian philosophy" there are more specific movements that are affiliated with particular denominations or theological traditions. The movement known as "Reformed Epistemology" is perhaps the most prominent of these. The Dutch theologian Abraham Kuyper is commonly cited as the intellectual grandfather of the movement, and the philosopher William Harry Jellema, who taught for thirty years at Calvin College and influenced many members of the movement, is considered its immediate forebear. The term "Reformed Epistemology" was not coined until 1980 or so, but even during the 1960s, scholars influenced by Jellema published a number of pieces that were important antecedents both of this movement and of "Christian philosophy" more generally.[58]

Reformed Epistemology itself is not easily defined (Keith DeRose simply calls it "that Alston-Plantinga-Wolterstorff stuff" in his contribution to this book), but it seems safe to say at least two things about it. First, it is primarily aimed at defending theistic belief against charges that it is impermissible, unjustified, or irrational. The later, more ambitious, and more controversial varieties also try to show that theistic or even specifically Christian belief is positively justified or warranted. Second, Reformed Epistemology bears little resemblance to classical Reformed theology: many of its leading practitioners are libertarians about free will, reject Calvin's doctrines of original sin and eternal damnation, and have little use for Reformed theories of predestination. (Many are universalists.)

The Roman Catholic tradition has also played a major role in the development of "Christian philosophy." In the early part of the recent century, philosophy in the Catholic tradition was predominantly Thomist in its orientation, and tended to view both the Continental and analytic (then largely positivist) traditions with suspicion. The second half of the century, however, saw expansion by explicitly Catholic philosophers into both major traditions (and, to a lesser extent, into the tradition of American pragmatism).[59] Some of them began to engage the philosophy coming out of the Reformed school, and thus to give Christian philosophy a more latitudinarian and ecumenical character.[60]

One tradition that has not been as visible as it might within recent philosophy of religion is liberal Protestantism. Although many philosophers of religion are Protestants of this sort, there has been little effort to develop a self-consciously "liberal" wing of the field. This is unfortunate, because the liberal Anglican, Lutheran, and Wesleyan traditions (for instance) arguably have as much to offer by way of philosophical resources as the Reformed and the Catholic traditions. Moreover, the pluralistic and ecumenical tendencies of liberal Protestantism would make a philosophy based in it *much* more palatable to nonreligious philosophers than some of the more conservative strains of Christian philosophy. Evangelical Protestants and Mormons, by comparison, have been very proactive, even founding their own journals and professional societies in recent years.[61]

In addition to the contributions of Christian philosophers, analytic philosophy of religion has also benefited from people working in other religious traditions, and in the other "Abrahamic traditions" (Judaism and Islam) in particular. Of course, these traditions have always been home to eminent scriptural scholars, theologians, and philosophers, but the explicit incorporation of the tools of analytic philosophy is (as it is within Christianity) a novel development. There has also been much discussion among philosophers of the problems raised by religious pluralism, discussions that have led in turn to debates about the place of religion in the public sphere and the social-political aspects of religious belief and practice. Some aspects of the latter debates are discussed in our third group of essays.

Obviously we have not tried to survey the entire field in what follows, or even to include samples of each of the active subfields.[62] That choice was motivated partly by concerns about thematic unity and partly by the desire to honor Wolterstorff, whose own recent work has been in metaphysics, epistemology, and social-political philosophy. In effect, then, we have followed the example of the first *New Essays*, and offer this volume as an updated sampling of the work being done in a few (albeit very important) parts of a large and varied field.

THE PRESENT ESSAYS

The book is divided into three main sections. Essays in the first section are concerned with metaphysical topics in the philosophy of religion; essays in the second deal with epistemology proper; and essays in the third address social-political issues. Each group of essays, however, can be seen as part of a discussion of the "ethics of religious belief" broadly construed. The Metaphysics group considers questions of coherence: Are the concepts involved in religious beliefs (God, the soul, the afterlife) intelligible, and do they refer to metaphysically possible entities? If not, then those beliefs will be ruled out by the (largely uncontroversial) epistemic obligation not to hold beliefs involving incoherent or unintelligible concepts. The Epistemology group deals directly with questions about the epistemic norms governing religious belief. The essays in the Social-Political section address the communal aspects and ramifications of religious belief and practice. Issues about the role of religious belief in social and political relations, particularly in a global context, are perhaps closest to being Lockean "matters of maximal concernment" for philosophy of religion at present and comprise an area of new interest and growth in the field. In the current political climate, it may be there – in the area of social and political thought – that reflection on the ethics of religious belief bears some of its most important fruit.

Metaphysics: God and Creatures

In the first essay ("Can God Break the Laws?"), Alvin Plantinga argues that theistic belief is not in any essential tension with a commitment to the fundamental project of natural science, where the latter is conceived as the attempt to discover and describe the natural laws. Plantinga does this by suggesting, not that there are no such laws, but rather that we can still think in terms of laws even if, as some theists claim, God is able to operate in special ways within nature. We simply have to view the natural laws themselves as statements of the "ordinary policy" guiding God's action in the world, rather than the "extraordinary policies" that God might adopt in the course of special intervention. Subscription to the project of natural science is thus not in conflict, at least in this respect, with sympathy for supernaturalism.

Linda Zagzebski ("Sleeping Beauty and the Afterlife") also seeks to demonstrate the compatibility of contemporary commitments (in this case, about the validity of causal laws and the essentially embodied nature of human persons) with traditional religious doctrines (in this case, about the afterlife). Although the survival of embodied persons after death might require a miraculous intervention of some sort, Zagzebski's thought-experiment-*cum*-fairy-tale is intended to show that there is no *conceptual* barrier to thinking that such survival is metaphysically possible.

Derk Pereboom ("Free Will, Evil, and Divine Providence") considers the nature of divine agency in the world as well. Starting with the assumptions that freedom is not compatible with determinism and that we are *not* free,[63] his goal is to argue that there is still room for accepting religious doctrines that appear at first face to require commitment to genuine human freedom. Pereboom focuses in particular on some perennial questions about God's relation to evil. His central and controversial claim there is that all events are directly willed by God. Events that appear to be evil are willed by God in order to promote a greater good (a good that may, however, be epistemically inaccessible).

William Alston's essay ("Two Cheers for Mystery!") falls squarely on the borderline between metaphysics and epistemology. His main thesis is that taking seriously the otherness and mysteriousness of the divine – as encapsulated in one or another version of what he calls "the Divine Mystery Thesis" – can be combined with saying and thinking things about God that are "close enough to the truth" to be a useful guide in the religious life. Alston is thus opposed to those who claim that the mysteriousness of the divine – and the resulting inadequacy of our religious concepts – prevent us from ever speaking truthfully about God. One of Alston's assumptions here is that rationally acceptable theistic belief can be based on "mystical" experiences and, conversely, that God is the sort of being that can put in an appearance – albeit of a nonstandard sort – to the intellectual faculties of normal human beings. This draws on the argument Alston articulated in his seminal work, *Perceiving God*.[64]

Epistemology: God and the Ethics of Belief

The second section of the book focuses directly on questions about the rationality of religious belief. Richard Swinburne ("The Probability of the Resurrection") is sympathetic to the Evidentialist picture of rationality (though not the vestigial positivism) we find in the first *New Essays*. The Evidentialist challenge to religion, again, says that because the available evidence for important doctrines is woefully inadequate, religious belief is epistemically irrational (think of Bertrand Russell in this regard, who remarked that if he were to survive death and confront God in the afterlife, he would defend his unbelief by saying, "Not enough evidence, God, not enough evidence!"). Although many philosophers have since argued that the Evidentialist standard of adequacy is inappropriate for evaluating epistemic rationality, Swinburne claims that the standard is by and large appropriate and, strikingly, that the evidence in favor of not only theism generally but also the death and resurrection of Christ is very strong. Given Swinburne's assumptions about the relative probabilities of the case, which he makes a case for here, it turns out that the likelihood of someone like Jesus of Nazareth being raised by God from the dead is in fact very high. Indeed, although he stresses that it is impossible to give precise values to the probabilities of most theories or hypotheses, Swinburne claims that when we assign *artificially* precise (but still quite defensible) values to various theological hypotheses, the probability of the resurrection turns out to be an eye-popping 97%! Here we see, then, an extension of Plantinga's and Zagzebski's efforts to show that it is metaphysically possible for God to intervene in nature and to do so by resurrecting a person from the dead. This is not only metaphysically possible, according to Swinburne – it is in fact *very likely* to have happened already.

Peter van Inwagen ("Is God an Unnecessary Hypothesis?"), by contrast, is explicitly anti-Evidentialist.[65] In this paper, he considers the claim that religious belief operates as an explanatory hypothesis of some set of data, and that it has been supplanted by more economical naturalistic hypotheses. Van Inwagen claims not only that those naturalistic explanations are inadequate to explain the relevant data set, but also that theism is rarely accepted as an hypothesis anyway. On the contrary, theistic belief is more like belief in the existence of external material objects, or other minds, or the intellectual equality of the sexes. These are beliefs for which (van Inwagen says) it is notoriously difficult to state conclusive arguments or provide adequate evidence; most people simply find themselves accepting such beliefs, even though they can cite no cogent or compelling arguments for them. Still, these beliefs are not (we all agree) irrational, and something similar can be said about belief in God. Most religious people do not prefer theism on the basis of the fact that it is, as an hypothesis, the best explanation of a certain data set. It may be, as van Inwagen says, a "hard-wired illusion," but it is not an hypothesis, and, *a fortiori*, not an unnecessary hypothesis.

Finally, Keith DeRose ("Direct Warrant Realism") continues in the same vein by describing and partially defending an anti-Evidentialist way of thinking about the structure and rationality of belief in general. DeRose takes his cues from Thomas Reid, the eighteenth-century Scottish philosopher and *éminence grise* behind many contemporary defenses of "Direct Realism" about both perceptual and religious belief. But DeRose rejects the Direct Realist claim (which is also typical of many Reformed Epistemologists) that perceptual and religious beliefs can obtain warrant *sufficient* for knowledge without enjoying some positive coherence with other beliefs that the subject holds. DeRose's "Direct Warrant Realism" says that beliefs get *some* of their warrant directly when produced by appropriate perceptual or religious belief–forming mechanisms, but they only get warrant *sufficient for knowledge* when additional warrant is "transmitted" to them by way of positive coherence.

Social-Political Philosophy: God, Ethics, and Belief

The third group of essays takes up questions about the interpersonal and socio-political aspects of religious belief. Robert Audi ("The Epistemic Authority of Testimony and the Ethics of Belief") continues the previous section's emphasis on the rationality of religious (among other sorts of) belief, but emphasizes the role that *social* or *communal* testimony plays. It is not the case (*pace* many in the Evidentialist tradition) that, in order to be rational, testimony-based beliefs require independent support from other justified beliefs about the reliability of the source and the likelihood of the testified proposition to be true. Rather, Audi argues (also following Reid) that a plausible theory of testimony will make sense of what is often our absolute dependence on others in our social and political communities – a dependence that comes without these adjacent supporting beliefs. Moreover, testimonial chains as a whole need not be weaker than their weakest link, and this is true even if the chain extends indefinitely and without any outside corroboration. This general theory of testimony underwrites Audi's final conclusion that some religious beliefs based on scriptural and/or communal testimony can be rationally acceptable within a sophisticated ethics of belief.

John Hare's essay ("Kant on the Rational Instability of Atheism") is part historical exegesis of Kant, and part positive recommendation for contemporary moral philosophers. His goal is to breathe new life into Kant's claim that there is a place within a proper ethics of belief for theism based not on epistemic but rather on *moral* and *social* considerations. We have a "need" for religious belief, Hare's Kant says, in order to make sense of the demands placed on us by the moral law, and to ground an ongoing commitment to morality in the public as well as the private sphere. Atheists, by contrast, are at a disadvantage in that their commitment to moral principles is rendered "rationally unstable" by their inability to meet that need. They will thus be less likely (or at least less motivated) to seek to promote the Kingdom of Ends.

Nicholas Wolterstorff ("Does Forgiveness Undermine Justice?") engages contemporary ethical and political theory more directly by articulating some fundamental tenets of what he calls "a single, unified account of justice and human rights."[66] The account is "unified" in that it characterizes both divine justice and human justice, divine rights and human rights. The essay thus connects with the issues about the relationship between divine and human agency that were raised in the first section of this collection. Wolterstorff's primary focus is the concept of forgiveness and the rights and duties that it involves. His aim is to characterize forgiveness in a way that makes sense both of our basic intuitions and of the Scriptural account of the way in which God "forgives" those who have faith in him.

Finally, Philip Quinn ("Can Good Christians Be Good Liberals?") critically examines what he calls "Christian liberalism" in the "Johannine tradition" of John Locke and John Rawls. According to Quinn, people in this tradition (including Wolterstorff) neglect the fact that there are *two* major traditions of liberalism in Western political theory and, by drawing on only one of them, significantly impoverish their accounts. Quinn himself tries to correct for this neglect by sketching an account of liberalism that is both friendly to religion and yet not based in the language of rights and distributive justice.

Quinn's is the most forward-looking of all the essays here, commending to religious people a theory that has genuine application in the contemporary political context. In conclusion, we wish to reiterate our own convictions that this area of reflection holds a great deal of promise for the continued flourishing of the "new" philosophy of religion, and for its ability to make a positive contribution outside the academy. It may be that philosophers, especially those who understand and participate in religious traditions, have a crucial role to play in defending liberal institutions and their commitment to tolerance in the face of the threats posed by individuals, groups, and governments operating in the name of God and religion. Quinn himself was inspired by this vision, and intended to spend part of the remainder of his career writing about these issues (sadly, he passed away as this volume was going to press). He opens his contribution with a quotation from Wolterstorff which encapsulates the vision. We think it fitting to conclude our Introduction with that same quotation:

Yet we must live together. It is to politics and not to epistemology that we shall have to look for an answer as to how to do that. "Liberal" politics has fallen on bad days recently. But to its animating vision of a society in which persons of diverse traditions live together in justice and friendship, conversing with each other and slowly altering their traditions in response to their conversation – to that, there is no viable alternative.[67]

NOTES

1. Antony Flew and Alisdair MacIntyre, eds., *New Essays in Philosophical Theology* (London: SCM Press, 1955).
2. Flew and MacIntyre, *New Essays*, x.
3. W. K. Clifford, "The Ethics of Belief," in *The Ethics of Belief and other Essays*, ed. Timothy J. Madigan (Amherst, NY: Prometheus Books, 1999), 77.
4. James called his response to Clifford *The Will to Believe*, but later said that this sounded too voluntaristic. In fact, he said, the essay should have been called "The Right to Believe" thus emphasizing that the debate was over deontology rather than psychology.
5. Cf. James, *The Will to Believe* (New York: Dover, 1956), 11: "Our passional nature not only lawfully may, but must, decide an option between propositions, whenever it is a genuine option that cannot by its nature be decided on intellectual grounds."
6. Ibid., 30.
7. René Descartes, "Meditations on First Philosophy," in *The Philosophical Writings of Descartes*, vol. II, trans. and eds. J. Cottingham, R. Stoothoff, and D. Murdoch (New York: Cambridge University Press, 1984), 41. See also Rule 2 of the *Rules for the Direction of the Mind* in vol. I, 10ff.

8. Descartes, Letter to Elizabeth, 15 Sept. 1645, in *The Philosophical Writings of Descartes*, vol. III, trans. and eds. J. Cottingham, R. Stoothof, D. Murdoch, A. Kenny, 267, our emphasis. Cf. *Discourse on Method*, vol. I, 123.
9. John Locke, *An Essay Concerning Human Understanding*, ed. Peter H. Nidditch (Oxford: Clarendon Press, 1975), 687–8.
10. This is the way that Wolterstorff interprets Locke in his *John Locke and the Ethics of Belief* (New York: Cambridge University Press, 1996). It may also be possible to read Locke as claiming that epistemic obligations arise simply out of reflection on the nature of our faculties and their proper use, and that they are *not* also moral obligations. Martha Bolton has suggested this in conversation with Andrew Chignell.
11. It is worth noting, without going into the details here, that the moral norm to follow evidence can be spelled out in different ways. Clifford seems to have thought of it as wholly deontological, and formulates his principles in terms of permissions and requirements. A distinct but related Evidentialist tradition thinks in terms of "intellectual virtues" instead – what guides us, on such a view, is the more general goal of becoming the sort of cognitive agent who would not believe on insufficient evidence.
12. Immanuel Kant, "What Does it Mean to Orient Oneself in Thinking?" in *Gesammelte Schriften*, vol. 8 (Königlich-Preussischen Akademie der Wissenschaften zu Berlin, 1902), 146; and in Kant, *Religion and Rational Theology* trans. and eds. Allen Wood and George di Giovanni (New York: Cambridge University Press, 1996), 18.
13. Immanuel Kant, "What is Enlightenment?" in *Gesammelte Schriften* 8:33–42 and *Practical Philosophy* trans. and eds. Mary Gregor and Allen Wood (New York: Cambridge University Press, 1996), 11–22.
14. The latter sort of argument would presumably go like this:

> (P1) We have an epistemic obligation not to believe on insufficient evidence;
> (P2) We have a moral obligation to uphold our epistemic obligations;
> (C) Thus, we have a moral obligation not to believe on insufficient evidence.

This keeps the kinds of obligations conceptually distinct while forging a strong link between them in the form of (P2). For an argument that Clifford himself didn't have a clear distinction between moral and epistemic obligations in mind, and thus didn't really defend (P2), see Susan Haack, "'The Ethics of Belief' Reconsidered" in *The Philosophy of Roderick M. Chisholm*, vol. xxv of *The Library of Living Philosophers* ed. Lewis E. Hahn (Chicago: Open Court, 1997).
15. Recent defenders of versions of Evidentialism include Allen Wood, Richard Feldman, Earl Conee, and Jonathan Adler. See Wood, *Unsettling Obligations: Essays on Reason, Reality, and the Ethics of Belief* (Stanford, CA: CSLI Publications, 2002); Feldman and Conee, "Evidentialism," *Philosophical Studies* Vol. 48 (July 1985): 15–34; Feldman, "The Ethics of Belief," *Philosophy and Phenomenological Research* Vol. LX, No. 3 (May 2000): 667–95; and Adler, *Belief's Own Ethics* (Cambridge, MA: MIT Press, 2002). See also Conee and Feldman's new collection, *Evidentialism: Essays in Epistemology* (New York: Oxford Press, 2004).
16. See, for example, Michael Stocker, "Responsibility Especially for Beliefs," *Mind* Vol. 91, No. 363 (1982): 398–417, and Richard Feldman, "The Ethics of Belief," esp. p. 675 ff.
17. See L. Jonathan Cohen, *An Essay on Belief and Acceptance*. (Oxford: Clarendon Press, 1992); Michael Bratman, "Practical Reasoning and Acceptance in a Context," *Mind* Vol. 101, No. 401 (Jan 1992): 1–15.

18. See Feldman, "The Ethics of Belief," and Adler, *Belief's Own Ethics*, especially chs. 1–3.

19. Clifford goes on to discuss religious beliefs such as the Muslim's that "there is one God and we shall live forever in joy or misery," or the Buddhist's that "there is no God and we shall be annihilated by and by if we are good enough." Clearly these are stalking-horses, at least in part, for the Christian beliefs that were prevalent in Clifford's own nineteenth century context (Clifford, "The Ethics of Belief," 85).

20. See John Locke, *The Reasonableness of Christianity: as Delivered in the Scriptures*, ed. J. C. Higgins-Biddle (Oxford: Clarendon Press, 1999). Also see *Essay*, Book IV, chapter 18, 688ff.

21. John Locke, *Conduct of the Understanding*, ed. Thomas Fowler (Oxford: Clarendon Press, 1881), section 8. Clifford, likewise, quotes someone protesting with respect to an important belief, "'I am a busy man; I have no time for the long course of study which would be necessary to make me in any degree a competent judge of certain questions, or even able to understand the nature of the arguments.'" Clifford's riposte: "Then he should have no time to believe" ("The Ethics of Belief," 78).

22. See Blaise Pascal, *Pensées* (Paris: Mercure de France, 1976). The most recent major English translation is *Pensées and other Writings*, trans. and ed. Honor Levi (New York: Oxford University Press, 1995). For a discussion of the connection to William James, see Jeff Jordan, "Pascal's Wagers," *Midwest Studies in Philosophy* 26 (2002): 213–23.

23. C. J. Misak, *Verificationism: Its History and Prospects* (New York: Routledge, 1995), especially chapter 2.

24. A. J. Ayer, *Language, Truth and Logic*, (London: Gollancz, 1936), ch. 6.

25. This is much too simple, of course. But there was, in any case, a major and sustained attack on positivism around mid-century. One of the most influential briefs against it, Carl Hempel's "Problems and Changes in the Empiricist Criterion of Meaning," was published in 1950 in *Revue Internationale de Philosophie* 4, 11 (1950): 41–63. For more of the story, see Misak's *Verificationism*.

26. Flew and MacIntyre, *New Essays*, ix.

27. A fact that led some later commentators to claim that in some of the essays, there was "an insufficiently critical acceptance of a positivistic view of meaningfulness." See the introduction to *Rationality, Religious Belief, and Moral Commitment* eds. Robert Audi and William Wainwright (Ithaca: Cornell University Press, 1986), 10.

28. Flew explains his view as follows: "[O]ne way of trying to understand (or perhaps it will be to expose) [a religious person's] utterance is to attempt to find what he would regard as counting against, or as being incompatible with, its truth. For if the utterance is indeed an assertion, it will necessarily be equivalent to a denial of the negation of that assertion. And anything which would count against the assertion, or which would induce the speaker to withdraw it and to admit that it had been mistaken, must be part (or the whole) of the meaning of the negation of that assertion. And to know the meaning of the negation of an assertion, is as near as makes no matter, to knowing the meaning of that assertion. And if there is nothing which a putative assertion denies then there is nothing which it asserts either: and so it is not really an assertion." Flew and MacIntyre, *New Essays*, 98.

29. Thomas Macpherson, "Religion as the Inexpressible," in Flew and MacIntyre, *New Essays*, 140–1.

30. Antony Flew, "Death," in Flew and MacIntyre, *New Essays*, 272. Flew is citing Wittgenstein, *Tractatus Logico-Philosophicus*, 6.431 and 6.1411.

31. Some historians of the period identify an intermediate stage ("logical empiricism") between logical positivism proper and the period of "linguistic analysis." See, for example, Jerry Gill, *Ian Ramsey: To Speak Responsibly About God* (London: George Allen & Unwin Ltd., 1976), 21 ff.

32. Basil Mitchell, *Faith and Logic: Oxford Essays in Philosophical Theology* (London: George Allen & Unwin, 1957), 5.

33. Peter Byrne, "Contemporary Philosophy of Religion in Britain," in *Perspectives in Contemporary Philosophy of Religion*, eds. Tommi Lehtonen and Timo Koistinen (Helsinki: Luther-Agricola-Society, 2000), 11.

34. For a contemporaneous assessment of the differences in method between "Oxford philosophy" and what has come to be known as "neo-Wittgensteinianism," see J. O. Urmson, "The History of Analysis" in *The Linguistic Turn*, ed. Richard Rorty (Chicago: University of Chicago Press, 1967), 294–311.

35. Urmson mentions Gilbert Ryle, John Wisdom, and Friedrich Waismann as early practitioners of "therapeutic positivism" (Urmson, "The History of Analysis," 299). There are now, of course, many different versions of neo-Wittgensteinianism on the market. The most visible current example of Wittgenstein-inspired critiques of "realism" about religious language is found in the work of D. Z. Phillips. See, for example, "Where We Are: at the Mercy of Method," in his *Recovering Religious Concepts: Closing Epistemic Divides* (London: MacMillan, 2000), 1–15.

36. Examples of this approach are Willem F. Zuurdeeg's *An Analytical Philosophy of Religion* (1956); Richard Braithwaite's *An Empiricist's View of Religion* (1955); the work of Ian Ramsey, displayed in both his early *Religious Language* (1957) and the posthumous *Christian Empiricism* (1974); and the papers by R. M. Hare collected in *Essays on Religion and Education* (1992).

37. William Blackstone, *The Problem of Religious Knowledge: The Impact of Contemporary Philosophical Analysis on the Question of Religious Knowledge* (Englewood Cliffs, NJ: Prentice-Hall, 1963), 2.

38. See, most notably, W. V. O. Quine, "Two Dogmas of Empiricism," in *From a Logical Point of View: Nine Logico-Philosophical Essays* (Cambridge, MA: Harvard University Press, 1953).

39. Blackstone, *The Problem of Religious Knowledge*, 4.

40. Ibid., 166.

41. Ibid., 166. For another influential argument from the same period to the effect that "descriptive" truth-claims *are* often made within religious discourse, see William Christian, *Meaning and Truth in Religion* (Princeton, NJ: Princeton University Press, 1964).

42. Jerry Gill sees Ramsey's work in leading in exactly this direction as well; see his *Ian Ramsey*, 44.

43. See, for example, Norman Malcolm and Peter Winch, *Wittgenstein: A Religious Point of View?* (Ithaca, NY: Cornell University Press, 1995); Fergus Kerr, *Theology after Wittgenstein* (Oxford: Blackwell, 1986); D. Z. Phillips, *Wittgenstein and Religion* (New York: St. Martin's Press, 1994), and George Lindbeck, *The Nature of Doctrine: Religion and Theology in a Postliberal Age* (Westminster: John Knox Press, 1984).

44. Flew and MacIntyre, *New Essays*, 144f.

45. Ronald Hepburn, "Poetry and Religious Belief," in *Metaphysical Beliefs*, ed. Alisdair MacIntyre (London: SCM Press, 1957), 89.

46. Claims to the effect that Hume and Kant had a decisively negative effect on religious speculation have persisted to the point where they are something of a commonplace. In 1988, Tom Morris commented on the prevalence of such views within theological circles in particular: "In a strange way, [Hume and Kant] have become the unlikely patron saints of current academic theology, as the popular appraisal of their work has shifted the whole theological enterprise into its now common non-metaphysical directions.... But we rarely, if ever, see an account of precisely which arguments... are supposed to have accomplished the alleged demolition of cognitivism, and exactly how they may be supposed to have had that effect." Morris, "Introduction," in *Philosophy and the Christian Faith*, ed. Thomas Morris (Notre Dame: University of Notre Dame Press, 1988), 3.

   Wolterstorff, similarly, responds as follows to the charge that historical ignorance accounts for the fact that some philosophers continue to discuss the sorts of issues which Kant (for example) is supposed to have resolved: "[T]he situation is not that we have failed to consider the Kantian alternative, and are consequently still wandering around in unenlightened naiveté; the situation is rather that we have considered the Kantian arguments and found them wanting." Wolterstorff, "Analytical Philosophy of Religion: Retrospect and Prospect," in *Perspectives in Contemporary Philosophy of Religion*, eds. Lehtonen and Koistinen, 160. With regard to Kant, see John Hare's essay in the present volume.

47. Norman Malcolm, "Anselm's Ontological Arguments," *Philosophical Review* 69 (Jan. 1960): 41–62.

48. For recent overviews of this debate, see Neil Manson, ed., *God and Design: The Teleological Argument and Modern Science* (New York: Routledge, 2003), and Niall Shanks, *God, the Devil, and Darwin: A Critique of Intelligent Design Theory* (New York: Oxford University Press, 2004).

49. In his preface to *The Justification of Religious Belief* (London: MacMillan, 1973), Basil Mitchell notes that "this book was originally to have been entitled *The Language of Religion* but at an early stage, like some characters in fiction, it took on a life of its own, and assumed a different subject which in turn dictated a different title" (vii).

50. A. C. A. Rainer, "Can God's Existence be Disproved?" in Flew and MacIntyre, *New Essays*, 71.

51. Many of the early modern philosophers used the term, for instance. In the early twentieth century, it typically referred to a movement in Roman Catholic circles led by Émile Bréhier, Étienne Gilson, Jacques Maritian, and Maurice Blondel. For a further summary of the history of "Christian philosophy" (and an argument against construing the movement too narrowly), see Jorge J. E. Gracia, "Does Philosophy Tolerate Christening? Thomas Aquinas and the Notion of Christian Philosophy," in *Philosophy of Religion for a New Century: Essays in Honor of Eugene Thomas Long*, eds. Jeremiah Hackett and Jerald Wallulis (Dordrecht: Kluwer, 2004) 37–61.

52. For example, in 1972, Charles Conti cited "the present revival of interest in philosophical theology" as a reason for issuing a collection of essays by Austin Farrer. See Conti ed., *Reflective Faith: Essays in Philosophical Theology* (Grand Rapids, MI: Eerdmans, 1972), ix.

53. In a survey of early "Philosophy and Reformed Theology," Colin Brown focuses on the work of Cornelius Van Til, Karl Barth, and Francis Schaeffer. Brown, *Philosophy and the Christian Faith* (London: Tyndale Press, 1969), 245–67.

54. This aspect of academic culture at mid-century is mentioned in several places by contributors to Tom Morris, ed., *God and the Philosophers* (New York: Oxford University Press, 1994).

55. Wolterstorff, "Can Belief in God Be Rational If It Has No Foundations?" in *Faith and Rationality*, eds. Alvin Plantinga and Nicholas Wolterstorff (Notre Dame: University of Notre Dame Press, 1983), 176. In addition to *Faith and Rationality*, another book from the mid-80s which showcased the growing prominence of the "new" philosophy of religion was *Rationality, Religious Belief, and Moral Commitment*, eds. Robert Audi and William Wainwright (Ithaca, NY: Cornell University Press, 1986).

56. For a good example of contemporary work that takes certain tradition-specific doctrinal claims not as *problems* requiring a philosophical defense but as *resources* for solving other philosophical problems, see Marilyn McCord Adams' work on the problem of evil, in particular, *Horrendous Evils and the Goodness of God* (Ithaca, NY: Cornell University Press, 1999). Adams deploys doctrines specific to the Christian tradition against the problem of evil, rather than staying within the bounds of "restricted standard theism." She defends this practice at length in Adams, "Problems of Evil: More Advice to Christian Philosophers," *Faith and Philosophy* 5 (April 1988): 121–43. Wolterstorff also defends it in his debate with Robert Audi in *Religion in the Public Square* (Lanham, MD: Rowman and Littlefield, 1996).

57. Given this usage, and given the contents of the essays that follow, a completely accurate (if completely unwieldy) title for the present volume would be *God and/or the Ethics of Belief: New Essays in Philosophy of Religion and/or Philosophical Theology.*

58. See, for example, Wolterstorff's essay in the 1964 *Festschrift* for Jellema (Plantinga ed., *Faith and Philosophy* [Grand Rapids, MI: Eerdmans,1964]); Plantinga's *God and Other Minds* (Ithaca, NY: Cornell University Press, 1967); and Arthur Holmes's *Christian Philosophy in the Twentieth Century* (Nutley, NJ: Craig Press, 1969).

59. For an informative survey of Roman Catholic philosophy during this period, see Arthur Madigan, S. J., "Catholic Philosophers in the United States Today: A Prospectus," *Occasional Papers of the Erasmus Institute* (2001–2), 1–24. Thanks to Philip Quinn for this reference.

60. There is even a collection of essays by Catholic philosophers responding to Reformed Epistemology: Linda Zagzebski, ed., *Rational Faith: Catholic Responses to Reformed Epistemology* (Notre Dame, IN: University of Notre Dame Press, 1993).

61. The Evangelical Philosophical Society was founded in 1974 and publishes the biannual journal *Philosophia Christi.* The Society for Mormon Philosophy and Theology was founded in 2003; it currently sponsors an annual meeting and the electronic journal *Element.*

62. One important subsection of the field that we have had to neglect entirely here is the Continental part. For an overview and discussion, see Philip Goodchild, ed., *Rethinking Philosophy of Religion: Approaches from Continental Philosophy* (New York: Fordham University Press, 2002), especially the essays by Goodchild and Matthew C. Halteman.

63. Assumptions defended in his recent *Living without Free Will* (New York: Cambridge, 2001).

64. Alston, *Perceiving God* (Ithaca, NY: Cornell University Press, 1991).

65. See his assault on Clifford's Principle in "It Is Wrong, Everywhere, Always, and for Anyone, to Believe Anything upon Insufficient Evidence," in *Faith, Freedom, and Rationality: Philosophy of Religion Today*, ed. Jeff Jordan (Lanham, MD: Rowman and Littlefield, 1996).

66. One that he articulates at more length in a forthcoming book, *Justice: Divine and Human*.

67. Nicholas Wolterstorff, *John Locke and the Ethics of Belief* (New York: Cambridge University Press, 1996), 246.

PART ONE

METAPHYSICS: GOD AND CREATURES

1

Can God Break the Laws?

ALVIN PLANTINGA

Documents beginning with "it gives me great pleasure to..." ordinarily enjoy all the sincerity of *Dear* in *Dear IRS*. This case, however, is different; it really does give me great pleasure to contribute an essay to a volume dedicated to Nicholas Wolterstorff. He and I have been friends and colleagues (sometimes at a bit of a distance) for more than 50 years. I have learned much from him, and admire him enormously. No one has done more to enhance the renewal of Christian philosophy in the twentieth century. I'm delighted to take part in this project and am grateful to the editors for making it possible.

This paper is part of a larger project investigating a number of connected topics, all of them centering around the relation between God and the world, the notion of God's acting in the world, and the question of how properly to conceive the connection between scientific statements about the world and theological or religious statements about God's relation to the world and action in it. In this present bit of the project, I am interested in particular in the question of the relation between the laws of nature, if indeed there are any such things,[1] and the ways, if any, in which God can act in the world. I'll be particularly interested in a fascinating argument by Sydney Shoemaker for the conclusion that the laws of nature are necessary in the broadly logical or metaphysical sense; if this is true, then perhaps God's possibilities of action in the world are severely limited.

SPECIFYING THE QUESTION

A common contemporary thought is that God does *not* act in the world (or at any rate doesn't act in any way that goes beyond creating it and then conserving it in existence). Oddly enough, this opinion is rather popular among theologians, in particular theologians prepared to revise traditional Christian belief in one way or another. Thus, for example, Rudolf Bultmann:

The historical method includes the presupposition that history is a unity in the sense of a closed continuum of effects in which individual events are connected by the succession of cause and effect.

This continuum, furthermore,

cannot be rent by the interference of supernatural, transcendent powers.[2]

Here it looks as if Bultmann thinks God not merely does not, but *cannot* act (the continuum cannot be rent . . .) in this closed continuum of effects. John Macquarrie agrees:

The way of understanding miracle that appeals to breaks in the natural order and to supernatural interventions belongs to the mythological outlook and cannot commend itself in a post-mythological climate of thought . . . The traditional conception of miracle is irreconcilable with our modern understanding of both science and history. Science proceeds on the assumption that whatever events occur in the world can be accounted for in terms of other events that also belong within the world; and if on some occasions we are unable to give a complete account of some happening . . . the scientific conviction is that further research will bring to light further factors in the situation, but factors that will turn out to be just as immanent and this-worldly as those already known.[3]

So does Langdon Gilkey:

. . . contemporary theology does not expect, nor does it speak of, wondrous divine events on the surface of natural and historical life. The causal nexus in space and time which the Enlightenment science and philosophy introduced into the Western mind . . . is also assumed by modern theologians and scholars; since they participate in the modern world of science both intellectually and existentially, they can scarcely do anything else. Now this assumption of a causal order among phenomenal events, and therefore of the authority of the scientific interpretation of observable events, makes a great difference to the validity one assigns to biblical narratives and so to the way one understands their meaning. Suddenly a vast panoply of divine deeds and events recorded in scripture are no longer regarded as having actually happened. . . . Whatever the Hebrews believed, *we* believe that the biblical people lived in the same causal continuum of space and time in which we live, and so one in which no divine wonders transpired and no divine voices were heard.[4]

Now what, precisely, are these theologians thinking, and why are they thinking it? Begin with the traditional Christian and theistic picture of the world.

First, God is a person, one who has both knowledge and aims or ends, and can act on the basis of his knowledge to achieve his ends. Second God is all-powerful, all-knowing, and wholly good. God has these properties essentially, and indeed necessarily: he has them in every world in which he exists, and he exists in every possible world. (Thus God is a necessarily existent concrete being, and the only necessarily existent concrete being.) Third, God has created the world. Of course this leaves a lot of latitude and a lot of unanswered questions: Did this creation take place in time? Does this imply that the world has not existed for an infinite stretch of time? How much of this creation did he do directly, and how much by way of intermediaries? These and other questions in the neighborhood are fascinating, but not directly relevant to our inquiry. Fourth, according to classic Christian and theistic belief (as opposed to deism), God conserves, sustains, and maintains in being this world he has created; without his providential preservation and sustenance, the world would disappear like a candle flame in a high wind. Indeed, some, including Thomas Aquinas, go even further: every causal transaction that takes place is such that God performs a special act of concurring with it; without that concurrence, the transaction could not take place.[5] Fifth, God does these things *freely*; he doesn't have essentially the property of having created the world, or of sustaining it or some part of it in existence.

Returning to the theologians quoted above: what they mean to say, I believe, is compatible with God's creating the world and sustaining it in the fashion just outlined. What then do they mean to deny? This continuum, says Bultmann, "cannot be rent by the interference of supernatural, transcendent powers"; according to Macquarrie, a "way of understanding miracles that appeals to breaks in the natural order and to supernatural intervention belongs to the mythological outlook and cannot commend itself in a post-mythological climate of thought"; and according to Gilkey, "contemporary theology does not expect, nor does it speak of, wondrous divine events on the surface of natural and historical life." What these thinkers claim, then, to a zeroeth approximation, anyway, is that *God does not perform miracles* (construed in traditional fashion) and that God does not *intervene* in the operation of the world he has created, or, what is perhaps the same thing, *act outside* the natural order in the world. But how shall we think of miracles? And what is this notion of God's *intervening* in his creation? As to the second, given the theistic idea that God constantly supports his creation, so that without his constant upholding and preservation, it would simply disappear, drop out of existence, the idea of his intervening, or worse, "interfering" (as Bultmann suggests), is at best inappropriate. Acting in a world that is such that its continued existence demands your constant activity is hardly "intervening," let alone "interfering with." What is really involved here? How can we state the matter more effectively?

That is not an easy question. In the Christian tradition, there are two fundamentally different strands of thought on this point. First, there is *occasionalism*: here the basic idea that what God has created, at least apart from human and other persons, is *causally inert*. And although human and other persons can be causally active, their causal activity is limited to a certain control over their own interior or mental life: I can decide, for example, to raise my arm; this decision is the occasion for God's then raising it (thus "occasionalism"). Hence there are no so-called secondary causes (apart from human and other persons). It is not the case, literally speaking, that billiard ball A's hitting billiard ball B causes B to roll off, or that the high winds caused the trees to be uprooted, or that the explosive's detonation caused the building to implode. What actually happens, in cases like these, is that billiard ball A rolls toward B, reaches a position of spatial juxtaposition with it, and then God causes the second billiard ball to roll off; there is the movement of air masses, the high wind, and then God causes the trees to be uprooted; the explosive detonates, and then God causes the resulting chain of events issuing in the building's imploding. (I've described these situations macroscopically, in terms of the behavior of billiard balls, buildings and trees, but presumably (in principle) they could also be described in microscopic detail.) The exception would be the sort of causal activity involved in a created person's intellectual and volitional activity. I will to raise my arm; my willing is the occasion of God's causing my arm to rise; I do not myself cause my arm to rise; God does that. But God does not cause the event consisting in my willing to raise my arm. *I* cause that event, just as I sometimes cause such events as my considering whether seven plus five equals twelve, my thinking about Vienna, and the like.[6]

The other main line of thought calls for the reality of secondary causes. On this view of the matter, God creates creatures with causal powers; these creatures are secondary causes, God being the primary cause. Of course this thought may be construed and developed in a variety of ways. Perhaps causal power is located at and restricted to elementary particles (among the current candidates for this office are electrons, quarks, and gluons), what happens at higher levels in some way supervening on what happens at the elementary level. Perhaps, on the other hand, higher level creatures – animals, plants, the sun, people – have causal powers that are not reducible to the causal powers of elementary particles; perhaps, indeed, these creatures have causal powers that do not supervene upon the causal powers of elementary particles; perhaps, in fact, there *aren't* any elementary particles, and perhaps also, as some scientific antirealists would claim, there aren't any such things as electrons, quarks, and gluons (whether or not they are elementary). In any event, on this view there are secondary causes, and not all causal power is exercised by God.

Occasionalism is perhaps the neater and cleaner of the two; the problem with secondary causation is the nature of this creaturely causality. What *is* this causation? And what kind of necessity (if any) goes with it? When God says "Let there be light," there is light; indeed, *necessarily*, when God says "Let there be light," there is light. Here the necessity is just metaphysical or broadly logical necessity, the same kind that is enjoyed by the truths of logic and mathematics.[7] But what about the necessity that is supposed to go with creaturely causation? Suppose the cause does its thing; it is still possible, one thinks, that the effect may fail to occur. God, for example, could suppress the effect. Still, *some* kind of necessity seems to be involved here: *what* kind? This is a difficult question; fortunately it is not one we need to try to answer.

Now suppose we return to our present question: Bultmann, Gilkey, and others declare that God does not intervene in the world he has created and does no miracles: how shall we think of divine intervention and miracle? What is it they are denying? On the occasionalist account, divine intervention and miracle would be no more than God's treating the stuff of his creation in a way different from the way in which he ordinarily treats them. Ordinarily, when a person tries to walk on water, he sinks; ordinarily water does not turn into wine; ordinarily, a dead person does not come back to life; if God had always treated the stuff he has made in the way he ordinarily does, life, one thinks, would never have arisen from nonliving matter. On special occasions, however, God may treat these things differently, so that water is changed into wine, or a human person succeeds in walking on water, or rises from the dead. Of course there are traps here: what, exactly, constitutes God's "acting in the same way?" Is just any improbable event – say my drawing a particular bridge hand – a matter of God's treating what he has created differently, not going on in the same way? Well, no, but then what is it for God to act in a special way? Recalling our Wittgenstein, we know that there are pitfalls in this notion of going on in the same way, and hence in that of acting specially. Still, the idea is clear enough for present purposes: in any event, God's going on in the same way precludes such things as his changing water into wine or directly creating the first living beings.

On the secondary causes view, miracle or "intervention" also requires that God treat what he has made in a special way: he temporarily suspends the ordinary active power of what would otherwise be a cause, or the ordinary passive power of what would otherwise be an effect, himself causing something else to occur. Of course this can go on in several ways: God might fail to support the cause in existence, so that it no longer exists; or he might fail to concur with what would otherwise have been the causal transaction in question; or he might confer special passive powers on some entity involved in the effect. On the secondary causes view, perhaps we can make sense of the idea of a way the world works when God acts in the world only to conserve it and its parts in being (and possibly concur in causal transactions). A miracle or intervention then occurs when God does something beyond conservation (and perhaps concurrence). Both of these pictures of divine special activity cry out for analysis; but there is no time, here, for that. Still, both pictures are initially coherent and reasonably clear, if woefully underdeveloped. And in the case of each, intervention and miracle are to be understood in terms of God's acting in a special way, treating some of his creatures differently from the way in which he ordinarily treats them. Of course, this is necessary but not sufficient for miracles. To be miraculous, one might think, an event must also be in some way revelatory of God or his purposes or intentions. Thus, Christians think, Jesus performed miracles, signs, and wonders to show that he really did come from God and to validate his teaching.

Well then, what reason do those revisionist theologians give for their contention that God does no miracles and never intervenes in the workings of his world? As engaging an answer as any is Tillich's: "Miracles cannot be interpreted in terms of supranatural interference in natural processes. If such an interpretation were true, the manifestation of the ground of being would destroy the structure of being; God would be split within himself."[8] Moving to something a bit less Delphic, we note that Macquarrie and Gilkey, in the quotations above, unite in declaring that the reason is that, nowadays, in this modern and postmythological age, we just don't think that God intervenes in his creation. Gilkey adds that theologians, because they belong to the modern world, can't help themselves: they "can scarcely do anything else," he says; this thing is bigger than either one of us. But of course the fact that quite a few people nowadays[9] reject divine special activity in the world or even can't help themselves, simply find themselves compelled, somehow, to reject it, is interesting as sociological commentary, but hardly a reason for supposing that such activity does not in fact occur.

A marginally more compelling reason is suggested by Macquarrie: "the traditional conception of miracle," he says, "is irreconcilable with our modern understanding of both science and history," because "science proceeds on the assumption that whatever events occur in the world can be accounted for in terms of other events that also belong within the world," which would leave no room for special divine activity. Well, perhaps this is marginally better, but it still doesn't come to much. Perhaps science or scientists proceed on a certain assumption: it doesn't follow that the assumption in question is true, or even that those who proceed on it believe that it is. (No doubt some think it is a useful assumption on the basis of which to conduct inquiry, whether or not it is true.) Is it Macquarrie's idea that the very practice of science requires the practitioner to reject the idea (for example) of God's raising someone from the dead? Of course the argument form

If X were true, it would be inconvenient for science;

therefore,

X is false

is less than maximally compelling. We aren't just given that God has arranged the universe for the comfort and convenience of the American Academy of Science, much as he no doubt admires it. To think otherwise is to be like the drunk who insisted on looking for his lost car keys under the street-light, on the grounds that the light was better there. (In fact it would go the drunk one better: it would be to insist that because the keys would be hard to find in the dark, they must be under the light.) But why think in the first place that one would have to embrace this semideism in order to do science?

Here I can be brief; William Alston has already proposed a compelling argument for the claim I propose to support, namely that believing that God has done and even still does miracles isn't any kind of impediment at all to pursuing science.[10] As he points out, there isn't the faintest reason to think I couldn't sensibly believe that God raised Jesus from the dead and also engage in medical research into, say, Usher's syndrome or multiple sclerosis, or ways of staving off the ravages of arthritis. What would be the problem? That it is always *possible* that God should do something different, thus spoiling my experiment? But that *is* possible: God is omnipotent. (Or do we have here a new antitheistic argument? If God exists, he could spoil my experiment; nothing can spoil my experiment; therefore . . .) No doubt if I thought God *often* or *usually* did things in an idiosyncratic way, so that there really isn't much by way of discoverable regularities to be found, *then* perhaps I couldn't sensibly engage in scientific research; the latter presupposes a certain regularity, predictability, stability in the world. But that is an entirely different matter. What I must assume in order to do science is only that *ordinarily* and for the *most* part, these regularities hold.[11] This reason, too, then, is monumentally insufficient as a reason for holding that God never acts specially in his world.

SHOEMAKER AND THE LAWS OF NATURE

Kripkean Considerations

The above reasons for thinking God never acts specially in his creation, there-fore, are somewhat less than wholly conclusive. Is there a better reason? Well, here's a suggestion: perhaps God never acts specially in his creation because he *can't*. For perhaps *determinism* is true: perhaps whatever happens is de-termined by what has already happened: wouldn't this preclude special di-vine action? Because this threatens to be both imprecise and uninformative, suppose we follow Peter van Inwagen and state determinism as follows: the complete state of the universe at any time t, conjoined with the natural laws, entails the complete state of the universe at any other time t^*.[12] Here there are various restrictions that have to be laid on the notion of a complete state of the universe at a time (in particular, the state of the universe at a time t cannot explicitly include such states of affairs as *Clinton's resigning the presidency at t^**, for t^* different from t); See van Inwagen (pp. 59–60) for some of these restrictions.

Now suppose we briefly consider the laws of nature; and here again, van Inwagen is a good guide. Although it isn't easy to say just what it is to be a law of nature, at the least, we ordinarily take them to impose limits on our technology. We can do many wonderful things: for example, we can fly from Paris to New York in less than four hours. No doubt our abilities along these lines will continue to expand; perhaps one day we will be able to travel from Paris to New York in less than four minutes. Even so, we will never be able to travel to the nearest star in less than four years. That is because c, the velocity of light, is an upper limit on the relative velocity of one body with respect to another.[13] That it *is* such an upper limit, we think, is a natural law. But the distance to the nearest star is such that if I were to travel there (in a spaceship, say) in less than four years, my velocity with respect to the earth would have to exceed that limit. And if, indeed, this restriction on the relative velocities of moving objects *is* a law of nature, we won't be able to manage that feat, no matter how good our technology. The laws of nature, therefore, place a constraint on what we can and cannot do. However, theists don't ordinarily think *God* is subject to the same constraints; they ordinarily think it is God who imposes or sets these laws for the cosmos, and he can undo them, or act contrary to them if he pleases. Perhaps I cannot build a spaceship that will travel faster than light with respect to the earth; but God can cause a spaceship to achieve any velocity he pleases.

But now suppose the laws of nature, whatever precisely they are, are necessarily true in the metaphysical or broadly logical sense. (In what follows, when I use the term *necessary*, I'll mean *necessary in the metaphysical or broadly logical sense*, but will suppress that qualifier.) Then not even God can act contrary to them; not even God can cause to be actual some state of affairs precluded by a law of nature. If it is a law that no objects have a relative velocity greater than *c*, and if that law is necessary, then not even God can cause there to be a pair of objects whose relative velocity is greater than *c*. Suppose, therefore, both that determinism is true, and that the laws of nature are necessary. Then any state S_1 of the universe *entails* any other state S_2 of the universe.[14] And then, so it might seem, God cannot act in the universe at all. Now God is indeed omnipotent, but this omnipotence does not include the ability to cause to be actual a state of affairs that is impossible. God can create the universe, complete with its laws. But once the universe is in place, so it seems, there is no further action he can take with respect to it. Each state entails each succeeding state; there is no room, it appears, for his action.

So it appears; but is it in fact true? Does determinism, together with the proposition that the laws of nature are necessary, entail that God doesn't act specially? No. For perhaps the laws entail propositions of the following sort:

if conditions $C_1, \ldots C_n$ hold at t^*, then at t^* God does A[15]

where A is something special, like raising someone from the dead. Determinism thus construed doesn't preclude special divine action. What it *does* preclude is *free* divine action. For suppose God does A at t. All previous states of the universe – for example, S^* – entail that God does A at t. But S^* is outside God's control, in the sense that there is no action A^* he can perform at t such that his performing A^* entails that S^* did not hold at t^*. For t^* is prior to t; and not even an omnipotent being can perform an action at t that entails that S^* did not hold at t^*. (Thus, for example, not even God now has the power to perform an action that entails that Abraham did not exist; it's too late for that.) If God does A at t, therefore, it isn't possible for him to refrain from A at t; and that's sufficient for his not doing A freely at t.

So if (a) determinism is true, and (b) the laws of nature are metaphysically necessary, then it is not possible for God to act freely in the universe. But each of (a) and (b) is at least moderately counterintuitive in its own right. Their conjunction, furthermore, is wildly counterintuitive: for it entails that the state of the universe at my birth either entails that I will have a glass of wine tonight, or else it entails that I will not have a glass of wine tonight; and that, I take it, is incredible. But are there perhaps reasons for thinking the conjunction of (a) and (b) true? Reasons strong enough to overcome the initial implausibility of their consequences? For purposes of this paper, I shall leave determinism aside and focus just on (b): is there reason to think that (b) is true, that the laws of nature are indeed necessary?

There is more than one argument for this conclusion, but perhaps the most interesting is offered by Sydney Shoemaker. In a paper published nearly 25 years ago,[16] Shoemaker argued for the position that laws of nature are necessary; more recently, he has revised and simplified the argument.[17] I wish to take a look at the argument as it appears in this most recent and presumably most authoritative guise. Shoemaker begins by invoking Kripke:

Kripke . . . argued that the class of truths deserving this label [i.e., the label of being necessary] is much larger than had traditionally been supposed. And, in his most radical departure from the traditional view, he held that many of these truths have the epistemic status of being a posteriori. One important class of these truths included statements of identity, such as "Hesperus is Phosphorus" and "Water is H_2O." Another included statements about the essences of natural kinds, such as "Gold is an element" and "Tigers are mammals." (pp. 59–60)

Fair enough: but how does it bear on the question of whether the laws of nature are necessary? As follows:

The source of resistance [to the idea that the laws are necessary] that most immediately leaps to mind lies in the fact that we can easily imagine what it would be like to experience a world in which the laws are different. We can imagine conducting crucial experiments and having them come out differently than they do here. And as Hume reminded us, we can imagine bread failing to nourish, water failing to suffocate, and so on. (p. 61)

It is as a response to this resistance, says Shoemaker, that Kripke's views are relevant. How, exactly?

But, of course, in the sense in which we can imagine these things we can imagine analyzing gold and finding that it is not an element, analyzing water and finding that it is not H_2O, dissecting tigers and finding that they are reptiles, and so on. Most philosophers are now persuaded, by Kripke's arguments, that such imaginings are no real threat to the claim that it is necessary that gold is an element, that water is H_2O, and that tigers are mammals. (pp. 61–2)

Now here I think Shoemaker has gone awry; I doubt that these Kripkean claims offer aid and comfort to the thesis that the laws of nature are necessary. Let me explain. Kripke's principal thesis here is that natural kind terms – *tiger, water, gold* – function as *rigid designators*; they are not, for example, as Frege or Russell might have thought, disguised descriptions.[18] Although there is a certain amount of controversy about the notion of rigid designation, what is clear is that the thesis in question is a *semantical* thesis, a thesis about the meaning or function of certain words. But then, of course, it is not, just by itself, of direct relevance to the question of which *propositions* are necessary or contingent; what it *is* relevant to is the question of which propositions get expressed by which *sentences*. What it is relevant to is the question of which propositions get expressed by sentences containing those natural kind terms.

Accordingly, consider the sentence:

(1) Tigers are mammals.

The idea is that in those distant pre-Kripkean times, we thought that (1) was contingent, that is, expressed a contingent proposition; it seemed easy enough to see that tigers could have turned out to be reptiles – just as, for example, whales turned out to be not fish but mammals. Now what Kripke got us to see, if he's right, is that terms like *tiger* function in a way different from what we originally thought. We had thought *tiger* was synonymous with some conjunction of predicates, perhaps something like *large, carnivorous, feline animal with a striped back and white underside whose range is much of Asia.*[19] If that is how the term is to be understood, then (1) expresses a proposition in the neighborhood of:

(2) All large carnivorous feline animals with striped back and white underside whose range is most of Asia are mammals

which is clearly contingent if true. Even if it is true, it could easily have turned out to be false. (Compare whales.)

By way of a judicious selection of examples, however, Kripke gets us to see (if he's right) that the term *tiger* does not in fact function in the suggested way. It is instead a "rigid designator" whose meaning is fixed ostensively, by something like *is of the same kind as* that (pointing to a tiger) or *is of the same kind as the large, carnivorous, feline animals with striped back and white underside whose . . .* If this is the way the term functions, then the sentence (1) expresses a proposition like:

(3) Everything that is of the same kind as the large, carnivorous, feline animals . . . is a mammal.

Perhaps more perspicuously, we could put this proposition as follows: consider the kind exemplified by those large, carnivorous, feline animals and call it *K*:

(4) Every example of *K* is a mammal.

So (1) expresses the same proposition as (3) and (4). But the proposition expressed by (3) and (4) is at least arguably necessary. Here is the argument. First, it may be hard to say precisely what natural kinds are, but perhaps we can begin like this:

(5) K is a natural kind only if (a) it is not the case that there is a number n such that it is necessary that there be more or fewer than n examples of K and (b) K is such that necessarily, whatever has it, has it essentially.[20]

The next step is to note that kinds, which are of course properties, entail other properties: for example, so the suggestion goes, the kind *tiger* entails the property *being mammalian,* so that necessarily, anything that is of the kind *tiger* is mammalian.[21] Obviously, however, it is necessary that if a thing has a property P essentially, then it has essentially any property entailed by P. Hence it is necessary that all tigers have essentially the property of being mammals. But if it is necessary that tigers have this property essentially, then it is necessary that they have it; hence the proposition expressed by (3) and (4) is necessary. But, so the claim goes, the proposition expressed by (1) is the proposition expressed by (3) and (4); hence the sentence (1), contrary to what we originally thought, expresses a necessary, not a contingent, proposition. And something similar goes for such other kinds as gold and water. We come to see, perhaps contrary to what we originally thought, that such sentences as:

(6) Water is H_2O

and

(7) Gold has atomic number 79

really express necessary rather than contingent propositions.

So what Kripke does, if he's right, is get us to see that a sentence like (1) ordinarily expresses the proposition expressed by (3) and (4). What he gets us to see, if he's right, is what propositions are in fact expressed by sentences like (1), (6), and (7). Of course, this is not, so far, to get us to see that some proposition we thought to be contingent is in fact necessary; it is instead to get us to see that some sentence we thought expresses a contingent proposition in fact expresses one that is necessary.

But then it is initially problematic or misleading to say, as Shoemaker does, that what Kripke showed us is that "the class of truths deserving this label [i.e., the label of being necessary truths] is much larger than had traditionally been supposed." It isn't that Kripke identifies some class of propositions and shows us that, contrary to what we had traditionally supposed, these propositions are necessary. No: the propositions he refers us to – propositions of the same sort as (3) – were not previously thought to be contingent but now seen or shown to be necessary. It wasn't that, ante-Kripke, we thought that animals of the same kind as *that* (pointing to a tiger) could have failed to be mammalian. It's rather that we weren't clear (assuming Kripke is right) about what proposition is in fact expressed by the sentence (1). What he does do is argue that some *sentences* we thought expressed certain contingent propositions in fact express noncontingent propositions.[22]

Whether or not Shoemaker is misleading here, our next question is this: how do these Kripkean considerations apply to natural laws? What would be the lesson to derive from Kripke about natural laws? The analogous moral – the moral analogous to that in the case of *tiger, water,* and *gold* – would be to make very sure we get the right proposition before us in trying to determine whether natural laws are necessary or contingent. Let's suppose that Newton's so-called Law of Universal Gravitation is indeed a law:

$$(NL)\ F_g = \frac{G\,mm'}{r^2}$$

where F_g is the gravitational force between any pair of particles, m and m' are their masses, and r is the distance between them. G is a universal constant whose numerical value depends on the units in which force, mass, and length are expressed. What (NL) says, obviously, is that:

(NL) Every particle of matter in the universe attracts every other particle with a force directly proportional to the product of the masses of the particles and inversely proportional to the square of the distance between them.[23]

To state it more simply, note that (NL) can properly be seen as a universal proposition predicating of each particle of matter a certain complex property: being such as to attract every other particle with a force of a certain kind. Call this property G. Then (NL) says that:

(8) Every material particle has G.

But if Kripkean considerations are relevant here, there will be two propositions plausibly associated with (8). On the one hand, there is:

(8*) Everything that plays the material particle role (whatever the nature of those things) has G

and on the other hand there is:

(8**) Everything of the same kind as the things that play the material particle role has G.

If the analogy with the *tiger*, *water*, and *gold* cases hold, the idea would be first, that (8*) is contingent (there are possible worlds in which what plays the material particle role does not have *G*), second, that (8**) is necessary (it is necessary that things of the same kind as the things that actually do play the material particle role have that property essentially), and third, although it is easy to think of (8) as expressing (8*), the fact is it expresses (8**).

But here a problem confronts Shoemaker. In the case of (5), (6), and (7), we are indeed inclined, to at least some extent, to think the proposition in question necessary. Things of the same kind as *that* (pointing to a tiger) are plausibly thought to be essentially mammalian (and it is also plausible to suppose that nothing of that kind could fail to be essentially mammalian); the stuff that actually does play the water role – that is, H_2O – could not have failed to be H_2O;[24] although some substance distinct from gold could have played the gold role, the substance that does (plausibly) couldn't have had a different atomic weight. But we don't have any such inclination in the case of (8**). For consider those particles that are of the same kind as the particles that play the material particle role: we have no intuition to the effect that such particles have *G* essentially, or even have essentially the property of conforming to an inverse square law. At any rate *I* have no intuition of that sort. If we think about the matter at the micro level, at the level of the current candidates for the post of being elementary particles, we have very little by way of intuition at all. The world of electron, quark, and gluon, if indeed there is such a world, is so strange and eerie that we have no idea at all about whether these items, if items they be, have *G* essentially. At the macroscopic level – the level of everyday objects – we do indeed have intuitions, but our intuitions do not support Shoemaker's thesis. Here our intuitions, for whatever they're worth, are that, for example, there could be a pair of material objects composed of just the material of which they *are* composed, that did not attract each other according to an inverse square law, or that a pair of objects that actually exist, composed of the very stuff they are composed of – Earth and Venus, for example – could have attracted each other with a force differing from that with which they do in fact attract each other. These intuitions, I think, are weak but nonnegligible – although I must concede that here we may be close to the border between seeing that something is possible, on the one hand, and failing to see that it is impossible, on the other.

As far as I can see, therefore, these Kripkean considerations do not support Shoemaker's case; if anything, they cut mildly against it. Kripkean considerations enjoin us to make sure we have the right proposition in mind – (8**) as opposed to (8*); but once we do have the right propositions in mind, it is not the case (contrary to the way things stood with *tiger*, *water*, and *gold*) that this proposition seems to be necessary. Indeed, this proposition seems, if perhaps only dimly, to be contingent.

Shoemaker's Argument

Now I suspect Shoemaker begins with these ideas from Kripke in order to soften us up, perhaps getting us to discount our initial intuitions, or at least take them a little less seriously. I've been arguing that these Kripkean ideas do not in fact serve that function; in particular, they don't serve to exhibit some propositions such that we are initially inclined to think them contingent but after appropriate Kripkean consideration see that they are necessary. In any event, however, Shoemaker also has a direct argument for the conclusion that the laws of nature are metaphysically necessary:[25]

It seems to me a general feature of our thought about possibility that how we think that something could have differed from how it [is] in fact is closely related to how we think that the way something is at one time could differ from that way that same thing is at a different time. In possible world jargon, the ways one and the same thing of a given sort can differ across worlds correspond to the ways one and the same thing of that sort can differ at different times in the same world. (p. 63)

The principle proposed here, which is also the first premise of the argument, seems to be something like:

(9) For any object x and any property Px has, if it is not possible that x have P at one time and fail to have it at another, then P is essential to x.

How does this apply to the case before us?

But now consider the case of properties. Different things can be true of a property at different places and at different times. E.g., the frequency of its instantiation can be different, and it can be coinstantiated with different properties insofar as this is compatible with the laws. But it cannot be governed by different laws at different places or at different times. Applying again the principle that constraints on intra-world variation are also constraints on inter-world variation, we get the conclusion that the same property cannot be governed by different laws in different worlds. Since I take it that the causal features of properties are features they have in virtue of the laws that govern their instantiation, this is equivalent to my claim that the causal features of properties are essential to them. And it implies that causal necessity [the sort of necessity displayed by the laws of nature] is a special case of metaphysical necessity. (p. 70)

Here the idea is that a property P can itself have different properties at different times; still (and this is the second premise of the argument), no property can be governed by a given law at one time but not be governed by that law at some other time:

(10) It's not possible that there be a property *P* and a law *L* such that *L* governs *P* at one time but not at another.

The conclusion deduced from (9) and (10), then, is:

(11) For any property *P* and any law *L* that governs *P*, *P* has essentially the property of being governed by *L*.

Thus, for example, the property *being a material object* or *materiality* has the property *being such that its instantiations exemplify G*. Further, it is a *law* that material objects have *G*, and hence a law that materiality has the property in question. But a property "cannot be governed by different laws at different places or at different times." Hence [by (9)], materiality has essentially the property *being such that its instantiations exemplify G*. And hence (given the necessary existence of properties) the proposition:

(8) All material objects exemplify *G*

is a necessary truth.

What shall we say about this argument? Well, we might note initially with respect to (9) that there are plenty of pairs of objects and properties $<O,P>$ such that *O* can't have *P* at one time and fail to have it at another, but where it is also clear that *O* does not have *P* essentially. For example, there is the property *being the first dog to be born at sea*: Consider Rex, the lucky dog that has it. Obviously Rex can't have this property at one time but lack it at another; equally obviously, it is not essential to him. Rex could have failed to have this property, and would have, had his mother never taken an ocean voyage. Clearly there are as many properties of this sort as you like: *being six feet tall at the age of fourteen, being mean-tempered at some time or other, being born in 1950, wearing a tuxedo on December 31, 1999, living through the Second World War*, and the like.

Now Shoemaker is aware of such examples:

This principle [(9)] needs to be qualified, as Randy Clarke pointed out to me. The property of being the child of someone who has visited Paris is not one that one can have and then lose; but it is one that one can have in the actual world, but not have in some other possible world. The principle is meant to apply only to non-historical properties; it says that where a non-historical property is not one that a given sort of thing can have and then lose, it is not one that a thing can have in the actual world and fail to have in some other possible world. (footnote 9, pp. 75–76)

Still, even if he is aware of examples of this sort, Shoemaker's response to them is at best a bit underdeveloped. What, exactly, or even approximately, are *historical* properties? That's not a trivial question, and Shoemaker makes no attempt whatever to answer it. Returning to (8), however, the idea would have to be that *conforming to (8)* is not a historical property. Perhaps Shoemaker thinks part of the difference between that property and those clearly historical properties is that the latter involve a historical reference – a reference to specific times, or time intervals, or historical events, or something of the sort.

However that may be, I think we can see that Shoemaker's argument fails, and can do so without entering this question of the nature of historical properties. First, what is the reason for believing (10), that is, for thinking that it's not possible that a property be governed by a law at one time but not at another? Shoemaker says only that "Since laws are supposed to hold timelessly, or omnitemporally, we can be sure that the properties that figure in laws retain the same causal features over time" (pp. 65–6) and "it [a property] cannot be governed by different laws at different places or at different times" (p. 70).[26] Laws are propositions (presumably universal propositions); some propositions are true at one time but not at another (e.g., the proposition *there are automobiles* is true now but wasn't true 150 years ago); but laws are true at every time if true at any. It is also plausible (though not essential for my argument) to think that a law is a *true* proposition. If so, we can say that the property *being a law* entails the property *being true omnitemporally* – that is, at every time. It is therefore necessarily true that for any proposition Q:

(12) If Q is a law, Q holds omnitemporally.

Thus consider (8), that is, Newton's law: (8) is a law only if it holds omnitemporally; and because (8), we are supposing, *is* a law, it holds omnitemporally. Of course it doesn't follow that (8) has *essentially* the property of holding omnitemporally. For all we know so far, (8) could perfectly well have been true at one time but not at another. What follows is only that if it *had* been true at one time but not at another, it would not have been a law. If this is so, however, we can state (10), the second premise of Shoemaker's argument, more exactly:

(10*) Necessarily, for any property P and proposition Q, if Q is a law and Q governs P, Q governs P omnitemporally.

Again, (10*) has at least the initial appearance of truth; at any rate, I do not propose to contest it.

But now we can see that the argument is unsound; more precisely, we can see that (9), the first premise of the argument, is false. Suppose we had a decent analysis of the concept or property of being a law; presumably it would have the following form:

(13) Q is a law if and only if Q is a proposition that meets condition C and is true omnitemporally

where C includes whatever properties a law must display in addition to omnitemporal truth: *being a universal proposition*, and *supporting (the appropriate) counterfactuals*, perhaps, or *mentioning no specific place or time*, or *being what science discovers*, or whatever. Now given (13), we can easily see why (10*) is true. First, *being a law* entails *being omnitemporally true*; so necessarily, if Q is a law and governs a property P, Q governs P omnitemporally, that is, Q is omnitemporally true. Now any property governed by a proposition Q that is a law has the property *being governed by Q and being such that Q is a law*. Thus materiality has the property *being governed by (8) and being such that (8) is a law*. This is a property it has, and one that it cannot have at one time and not at another: if (8) is a law, it follows that it is true at every time, and hence governs materiality at every time.

According to (9), however, the first premise of Shoemaker's argument, it follows that materiality *has essentially* the property *being governed by (8) and being such that (8) is a law*. And this is dubious *in excelsis*. We can see this as follows. First, consider the notion of a *weak* law; a weak law is just any universal proposition that is omnitemporally true. Suppose, for example, the proposition

(14) All Buicks are within 10,000 miles of a large city

is in fact omnitemporally true; then (14) is a weak law. But then the property *being a Buick* has the property *being governed by (14) and being such that (14) is a weak law*. Furthermore, *being a Buick* cannot have this property at one time but not at another. According to (9), therefore, it has this property essentially – in which case (14) is a necessary truth. But of course it isn't: clearly it's perfectly possible that some automobile could get transported to the moon, let's say, where there aren't any cities for it to be within 10,000 miles of. Weak laws can't be true at one time but not another; so properties can't be governed by a weak law at one time but not at another, but it doesn't follow for a moment that if a property is in fact governed by a weak law, then it has essentially the property of being governed by that law, so that the weak law is a necessary truth. And in this regard laws *simpliciter* are just like weak laws.

Say that $O(P)$, the *omnitemporal transform* of a property P, is the property of having P omnitemporally. Then it is not possible that I have an omnitemporal transform at one time but not another; that is, it is not possible that I have $O(P)$, for some property P, and have it at one time but not another. Thus consider the property *lives in Königsberg* and call it K. Obviously one can't have $O(K)$ at one time but not another; it is a necessary truth that anyone who has $O(K)$ at any time has it at every time. But equally obviously it fails to follow that anyone who has $O(K)$ has it essentially. For anyone who has $O(K)$ essentially has K essentially; but no one, not even Kant, can have K essentially. Under what conditions is it the case that a thing has essentially $O(P)$, for some property P? Well, only if it has P essentially, of course; but also only if its having P entails its having $O(P)$:

(15) For any object x and property P, x has $O(P)$ essentially only if it is not possible that x have P but lack $O(P)$.

(15) is obvious: a thing has a property essentially only if its having that property is entailed by its having *any* property.

Now return to (13) above, and note that the property *being a law* is the omnitemporal transform of *being a proposition that meets C* (where C is the property that together with *being omnitemporal* is sufficient for *being a law*). This means that the property *being governed by Q and being such that Q is a law* is the omnitemporal transform of *being governed by Q and being such that Q meets C*. Accordingly, the former will be essential to a property that has it only if it is entailed by the latter. Specified to the present case, what this means is that materiality has the property *being governed by (8)* essentially only if the property *being governed by (8) and being such that (8) meets C* entails the property *being governed by (8) and being such that (8) holds omnitemporally*. And this, in turn, will be true only if

(16) (8) meets C

entails

(17) (8) holds omnitemporally.

But it doesn't. It certainly seems that (8) could meet C – that is, be a true universal proposition that makes no reference to specific times and places, supports the relevant counterfactuals, and the like – but fail to hold omnitemporally. Perhaps, for example, it didn't hold during the very early history of the universe; and perhaps at some time in the future, it will fail to hold. In any event, it certainly seems *possible* for it to fail to hold. Just as a person could exemplify *living in Königsberg* but fail to exemplify its omnitemporal transform, so a property can exemplify *being governed by a proposition that has C* but fail to exemplify the omnitemporal transform of that property. And hence (9), the first premise of Shoemaker's argument, appears to be false. It seems entirely possible for a thing to have accidentally a property that it can't have at one time but not at another; and it seems entirely possible for a property to be governed by a law without *essentially* being governed by that law. With respect to the case in question: it seems entirely possible for a property such as materiality to have accidentally the property *being governed by (8) and being such that (8) is a law* even if it is not possible for it to have that property at one time and not at another.

GOD AND NECESSARY LAWS

Even though Shoemaker's argument fails, it is of course still possible (epistemically possible) that some or all of the laws of nature are in fact necessary. Further, it is possible that they are necessary for roughly Shoemakerian reasons: it could be that the properties governed by these laws have essentially the property of being governed by them. Return, once more, to (8), Newton's law: perhaps *materiality* has essentially the property of being governed by (8), in which case (8) would be necessarily true. What can we say of this suggestion, and how, if at all, would it limit God's action in the world?

Suppose we begin by turning to the so-called fine-tuning argument for theism.[27] The fundamental constants of physics – the speed of light, the gravitational constant, the strength of the weak and strong nuclear forces – must apparently have values that fall within an extremely narrow range for life to be so much as possible. If these values had been different even minutely (if, e.g., the gravitational constant had been different by one part in 10^{40}), habitable planets would not have developed and life (at least life at all like ours) would not have been possible.[28] Thus Carr and Rees:

The basic features of galaxies, stars, planets and the everyday world are essentially determined by a few microphysical constants and by the effects of gravitation.... several aspects of our Universe – some which seem to be prerequisites for the evolution of any form of life – depend rather delicately on apparent 'coincidences' among the physical constants.[29]

According to Brandon Carter, "If the force of gravity were even slightly stronger, all stars would be blue giants; if even slightly weaker, all would be red dwarfs;"[30] under these conditions, he says, there would probably be no life. So, probably, if the strength of gravity were even slightly different, habitable planets would not exist. Stephen Hawking adds that the existence of life also depends delicately upon the rate at which the universe is expanding: " . . . reduction of the rate of expansion by one part in 10^{12} at the time when the temperature of the Universe was 10^{10} K would have resulted in the Universe's starting to recollapse when its radius was only $1/3,000$ of the present value and the temperature was still 10,000 K"[31] – much too warm for comfort. He concludes that life is possible only because the universe is expanding at precisely the rate required to avoid recollapse. Similar considerations apply, apparently, to the weak and strong nuclear forces.

All this clearly suggests a Designer who intended the existence of living creatures, and eventually rational, intelligent, and morally significant creatures such as we like to think of ourselves as being. This is not the place to investigate the cogency of the argument;[32] what is relevant here is that these suggestions by Hawking, Carter, Carr, Rees, and others seem clearly possible, and clearly presuppose that the gravitational constant and the other fundamental physical constants could have displayed different values from the ones they do display. Indeed, the suggestion goes much further: that these constants have the values they do have is not merely not necessary; it is, we might say, maximally contingent, in the sense that there are very many, perhaps infinitely many, other possibilities that seem to be equally good candidates for the job. The gravitational constant could have displayed very different values; but then *materiality* could have obeyed a law quite different from (8); so Newton's law is at best contingently true. Now, suppose this is true: doesn't that mean that Shoemaker is mistaken and that at any rate, *this* law of nature is not necessary in the broadly logical sense?

Perhaps not. The idea is that in other possible worlds, the strength (call it S) of the gravitational force is different from what it is in fact. But are we just given that matter, in these other possible worlds, is the same stuff we enjoy in α, the actual world – matter$_\alpha$, as we might call it? Surely not; it is open to a partisan of necessary laws to hold that matter$_\alpha$ has essentially the property of displaying the strength it does display. In other possible worlds, perhaps G is replaced by some other constant; but in those worlds, Shoemaker might contend, what plays the matter role is not matter$_\alpha$, but stuff of a different kind. This stuff is related to matter$_\alpha$ in the same way as water – that is, the stuff that plays the water role on Earth – is related to Putnam's XYZ, the stuff that plays that role on Twin Earth. Matter has essentially the property of conforming to Newton's law; in those worlds where G is replaced by some other value, what plays the matter role is not matter$_\alpha$.

Well, suppose so. But then what about (8) itself: would it be necessary, or contingent? (8) speaks of the property *materiality*: but what property *is* that? Is it *materiality*, a property had only by material particles in α? If so, sentence

(8) expresses a necessary truth. Or is it instead the property *plays the material particle role*, a property exhibited by matter$_\alpha$, but also, in other possible worlds, by whatever plays the material particle role in those worlds? If it's *that* property, then (8) expresses a contingent truth. The question here is whether the laws of nature involve only *infima species*, species that do not themselves play the role of determinable to lower-level species, or whether, on the other hand, a law can involve properties that stand to other specific properties as determinable to determinant. Can natural laws involve properties such as *being an animal*, *being a mammal*, and *being an ungulate*? Can natural laws involve such a property *P* even if some of the determinable properties falling under *P* are not exemplified? If so, some, at least, of the laws will presumably not be necessary. But perhaps it is open to the partisan of necessary laws to say that the laws must contain only *infima species* such as *materiality*, not higher-level properties such as *plays the material particle role*, which can be exhibited by particles quite different from those that display *materiality*. Then it is open to him to hold that the laws of nature are indeed necessary, even if those fine-tuning considerations are in fact possible.

The objection from the fine-tuning argument, then, is not wholly conclusive; but there is another objection from *responses* to the fine-tuning argument. One kind of response is offered by "inflationary" scenarios: in the very early history of the universe, so they say, enormously many, perhaps infinitely many, subuniverses were spawned;[33] these subuniverses are causally isolated from each other and display many, perhaps infinitely many, different combinations of values for the fundamental physical constants. In a second kind of scenario, our universe began in a big bang some 10 to 15 billion years ago; it will eventually collapse, resulting in a "big crunch," which will lead to another big bang and another subuniverse, and so on, the physical parameters being reset at random during each big crunch. This process has been going on for all eternity; hence the precise values of the physical constants displayed in *our* subuniverse were bound to arise at one point or another, and indeed bound to arise infinitely many times. Perhaps "there has been an evolution of worlds (in the sense of whole universes) and the world we find ourselves in is simply one among countless others that have existed throughout all eternity."[34] These scenarios are said to blunt the edge of the theistic fine-tuning argument; for if all or even very many of the possible distributions of values over the physical constants get displayed in one or another subuniverse, it is not surprising that the particular distribution we see should get displayed; and it is equally unsurprising that it should get displayed in a subuniverse in which there are such living, intelligent creatures such as we ourselves to behold it.

We need not look into the question of whether this is an adequate response to the fine-tuning argument;[35] what is of interest to us presently is that in these scenarios, it isn't just that in *other* possible worlds we find other distributions of values for the fundamental constants, we find such different distributions right here in α, the actual world. True, these distributions are in different subuniverses, different parts of the actual world; but all the subuniverses do in fact exist, and they all exist in α, the actual world. These inflationary suggestions may be highly speculative, but they do seem to be at least epistemically possible, there is no reason we can easily see for supposing that they are not possible in the broadly logical sense.

But then consider *materiality* again. We have been supposing that this property is really materiality$_\alpha$, a property essential to the things that play the material particle role in α. But if any of these inflationary scenarios are possible, there are different distributions of values of the physical constants in different localities – in different subuniverses – in α. But then Newton's law holds for some subuniverses, but not for others; it isn't necessary after all, since it is not essential to materiality to be governed by (8). Indeed, (8) is not so much as true: it holds for some subuniverses but not others.

Even here, however, the partisan of necessary laws need not be without a reply. We imagined him simply claiming that what plays the material particle role in other possible worlds – those other possible worlds that display different distributions of values across the physical constants – is not what plays that role in α, the actual world; and the things that play that role in α – material particles – do indeed have essentially the property of conforming to (8). Why can't he take this strategy one step further? What plays the material role in *our* subuniverse, he may say, is not the same sort of thing as what plays that role in those subuniverses displaying a different distribution of values over the physical constants. Matter$_\alpha$ – whatever plays the matter role in α – has a multiple character: many different kinds of material particles would play this role, a different kind for each subuniverse displaying a different distribution of values. Materiality$_\alpha$ is not an *infima species*; that honor is reserved for such properties as *materiality$_n$*, a property had essentially by the particles that play the material object role in subuniverse n. The natural laws, he may repeat, involve only *infima species*; but then Newton's law would concern only matter$_n$ and govern only *materiality$_n$*. That proposition, however – the proposition that *materiality$_n$* conforms to Newton's law – would then be necessary.

Well, this may be getting a bit far-fetched, but suppose it is all true. And now suppose we return to the question with which this inquiry began: is it possible for God to act in the world? Theists hold that God has created the world and conserves it in being; perhaps he also concurs in causal transactions; is it possible for him to act in other ways as well? According to the negative reply, God can only create and sustain; necessary natural laws governing the behavior of the stuff he creates do the rest. But now we must think about *conservation* principles: principles to the effect that this or that quantity – angular momentum, mass, energy, mass/energy, whatever – is conserved. Among the laws, so we are told, is the proposition:

(18) In any closed system, mass/energy is conserved.

Now (18) is a law, we may suppose, only if it is true, and true omnitemporally. But according to theism, whether (18) is true or omnitemporally true depends on God's continuing to sustain the things he has made. If he were to withdraw this support from an object in the world – the moon, say – it would go out of existence, disappear like your breath on a frosty morning. This could be so without any flow of energy across the borders of a system – the solar system, say – containing it. But God's conserving the moon in existence is a free act on his part; it is entirely within his power to continue to preserve the moon in existence, but also, if he sees fit, to withdraw that support and permit it to cease to exist. And just as God is free to allow the things he has created to cease to exist, so he is free to create new things, and indeed new kinds of things. He could create additional elementary particles or, for that matter, a full-grown horse if he so desired. He could create matter of a kind different from matter$_\alpha$, if it is possible in the broadly logical sense that there be matter of a kind different from matter$_\alpha$. Whether (18) is a law, therefore, depends on God's free activity. Hence (18) is not a necessary truth; if indeed it is a law, it follows that some laws are not necessarily true.

We might note parenthetically that if these conservation laws are indeed laws, then, given that they depend on God's future free action a law will be a so-called soft fact about the present or past. Given such a law, note still further that it is possible for there to be things you and I can do such that if we were to do them, that law would not have been a law. For it is possible for there to be something you can do such that if you were to do that thing, then God would act in such a way that the law in question would not have been a law. In this way, it is possible that we human beings have counterfactual power over some of the laws of nature.[36]

Returning to the question of God's action in the world, we have seen conservation laws will not be necessary if theism is true. But it is epistemically possible for Shoemaker laws – laws that depend on certain properties having essentially the property of being such that their instances conform to certain universal propositions – to be necessary. And now consider the Shoemakerian response to the claim that, possibly, the matter of α, the actual world, displays different values for the fundamental constants in different subuniverses: the response, we recall, was that α would then display many different *kinds* of matter, a different kind for each different distribution of the values over the fundamental constants. Each kind of matter, further, has essentially the property of conforming to a particular distribution of values over those constants; and for any kind k of matter, there will be distribution d of values such that the proposition:

(19) Materiality$_k$ displays distribution d

is a law, and is also necessarily true.

But then how, if at all, is God's activity constrained? Well, of course he will be unable to create matter$_k$ that doesn't conform to distribution d; he could no more do this than create a material object that is both round and square. But what about the sorts of cases we were initially concerned with – changing water into wine; creating life specially; preserving people thrown into a fiery furnace from being burned; causing a dead man to return to life; accelerating a spaceship to a velocity, with respect to earth, greater than c; and all the rest? The conclusion, I think, is that the necessity of the Shoemaker laws, if indeed there are some, gives us no reason so far to think God is unable to act in these special ways. We can see this as follows. Suppose we grant (what is far from obvious) that (a) the matter of α or of our subuniverse essentially conforms to the laws to which it does conform, and (b) those laws are such that if the matter of α or of our subuniverse conforms to them, then in α or our subuniverse, there will be no events of the kind mentioned above – no special acts of God, as we might call them. It wouldn't follow that God could not act specially in those ways; for it is, of course, open to God to create matter of a different character from the matter our subuniverse actually displays. And perhaps, if he did this, and appropriately replaced a bit of the one kind of matter by a bit of the other, the result would be water being instantaneously transformed into wine, living beings suddenly appearing where there had been none before, someone's being restored to life after being dead, and so on. So it isn't at all clear that the necessity of Shoemaker laws constrains God's activity in the world in a relevant way.

Of course there are a thousand questions that arise here, and a thousand questions that cry out for answers: they will have to cry unanswered, at least for the moment. My present conclusion is that (a) Shoemaker's argument for the necessity of laws is unsuccessful, and (b) even if the Shoemaker laws are necessary, that fact need not relevantly constrain God's action in the world. So neither Shoemaker's argument nor the necessity of Shoemaker laws, if they are necessary, gives us reason to discount our original intuitions to the effect that it is entirely possible for God to act specially in the world.[37]

NOTES

1. For a powerful argument for the conclusion that there are not, see Bas van Fraassen, *Laws and Symmetry* (Oxford: Oxford University Press, 1989).

2. *Existence and Faith*, ed. Schubert Ogden (New York: Meridian Books, 1960) 291–2. Writing 50 years before Troeltsch, David Strauss concurs: "all things are linked together by a chain of causes and effects, which suffers no interruption." *The Life of Jesus, Critically Examined* (Philadelphia: Fortress Press, 1972), sec. 14. (Quoted in Van Harvey, *The Historian and the Believer*, (Champaign, IL.: University of Illinois Press, 1996), 15.

3. *Principles of Christian Theology*, 2nd ed. (New York: Scribner, 1977), 248.

4. "Cosmology, Ontology and the Travail of Biblical Language," reprinted in *God's Activity in the World: the Contemporary Problem*, ed. Owen C. Thomas (Chico, CA: Scholars Press, 1983), 31. See also, e.g., Gordon Kaufman, "On the Meaning of 'Act of God,'" in his *God the Problem* (Cambridge: Harvard University Press, 1972), 134–5.

5. One might suspect this requirement of concurrence is just a matter of paying God metaphysical but empty compliments; why add this requirement to all the rest? One possibility is that conservation is a matter of sustaining a substance in existence, while concurrence is a matter of conserving a particular causal power in the conserved substance. Another possibility, one that no doubt was not foremost in the minds of the medievals, is that concurrence may be useful with respect to the so-called pairing problem alleged to afflict substance dualism: when I will to move my arm (given that I am an immaterial substance), why is it that the arm of one particular body (mine) moves, rather than the arm of some other body?

6. Descartes' view on this matter is perhaps best thought of as a limited occasionalism: all causal power belongs to God and other spirits, with finite spirits like us being granted a limited causal influence in the world of matter.

7. As well, of course, as many others that are not neatly systematized in the way mathematics and logic are: for example, *there aren't any things that do not exist, nothing has any properties – not even nonexistence – in possible worlds in which it does not exist*, and (according to classical theism) *there is such a person as God.*

8. *Systematic Theology* vol. I (London: Nisbet, 1953), 129.

9. Although Gilkey et al. vastly overestimate the number; see my "Two or More Kinds of Scripture Scholarship," *Modern Theology* (April 1998), and chapter 12 of my *Warranted Christian Belief* (New York: Oxford University Press, 2000).

10. See his "Divine Action: Shadow or Substance?" in *The God Who Acts: Philosophical and Theological Explorations*, ed. Thomas F. Tracy (University Park: Pennsylvania State University Press, 1994), 49–50.

11. As Alston argues in the article just cited.

12. In *An Essay on Free Will* (Oxford: Clarendon Press, 1983), 65. Here I take the complete state of the universe at a time to be a *state of affairs*, and extend the notion of entailment in the obvious way so that it can relate states of affairs to each other as well as to propositions. Alternatively, we can follow van Inwagen and leave the ontology of states or the universe indefinite, speaking instead of the (or, a) proposition that *specifies* the state of the universe at a time.

13. Strictly speaking, what is precluded is not relative velocities greater than c (for perhaps tachyons aren't precluded) but acceleration of one body relative to another from a velocity less than c to one greater than c.

14. By the principle that if A & B entail C, and B is necessary, then A entails C.

15. Here I was helped by a conversation with Carl Gillett.

16. "Causality and Properties," in *Time and Cause*, ed. Peter van Inwagen, (Dordrecht: Reidel, 1980).

17. "Causal and Metaphysical Necessity," *Pacific Philosophical Quarterly* 79, 1 (March 1998): 59–77. (Page references to Shoemaker are to this article.)

18. At any rate, descriptions that do not express properties that constitute *essences* of the denotata.

19. Alternatively, the term might be thought to be a cluster term, so that it applies to things that have most (or a weighted most) of the above properties.

20. Compare the account of individual essence in my book *The Nature of Necessity* (Oxford: Clarendon Press, 1974), 72. A consequence: whatever lacks K lacks it essentially.

21. Could it be that a properly formed tiger should suffer a serious accident, the result of which it was no longer a mammal? Presumably *being quadrupedal* is also entailed by the kind *tiger*; and clearly a tiger could lose a leg or two. But perhaps *being a mammal*, unlike *being a quadruped*, is a property a mammal can't come to lack: *being a mammal* is the property of displaying a certain sort of construction *if properly formed, non-defective*. A mammal could then come to lack that sort of construction, but would not thereby come to lack the property of being a mammal. For the sake of simplicity, I'll assume that this is in fact true; what I say can easily be reformulated in such a way as to accommodate the falsehood of this assumption.

22. Of course not everyone is prepared to distinguish propositions from sentences. Those who do not make that distinction, however, will presumably be able to make an equivalent distinction by noting the difference between coming to see that a sentence is necessary in virtue of discovering that it doesn't mean what one thought it did, and coming to see that it is necessary without learning anything new about its meaning.

23. As stated in F. W. Sears and M. W. Zemansky, *University Physics*, 3rd ed. (Reading, MA: Addison-Wesley Publishing Co., 1964), 103. I abstract from difficulties such as that it's not at all clear that the current candidates for the ultimate constituents of matter are indeed particles, or that if they are, they can sensibly be thought of as *objects* or substances. I also abstract from the questions whether there *are* any such things as electrons, quarks, and gluons, as currently described, and whether current science is committed to the existence of such things.

24. And of course this isn't due merely to the way H_2O is being selected for attention here – i.e., as H_2O. The first dog to be born at sea, we think, could indeed have failed to be the first dog to be born at sea, and would have failed to be so had her mother never taken an ocean voyage.

25. Shoemaker has another argument as well, one I won't comment on here. For incisive critical comment on this other argument, see Dean Zimmerman, "Shoemaker's Argument for His Theory of Properties," *Facta Philosophica* 2 (2000): 271–90.

26. This is the familiar idea that part of what it is to be a *law* is to hold at all times if at any. But why? Couldn't it be that there are different laws during different cosmic epochs?

27. For a solid presentation of this argument, see Robin Collins, "A Scientific Argument for the Existence of God: The Fine-Tuning Design Argument" in *Reason for the Hope Within*, ed. Michael Murray (Grand Rapids, MI: William B. Eerdmans Publishing Co., 1999), 47, and "Evidence for Fine-Tuning," in *God and Design: The Teleological Argument and Modern Science*, ed. Neil A. Manson (New York: Routledge, 2003), 178–99.

28. See Paul Davies, *Superforce: The Search for a Grand Unified Theory of Nature* (New York: Simon and Schuster, 1984), 242.

29. "The Anthropic Principle and the Structure of the Physical World," *Nature*, 1979, 605.

30. "Large Number Coincidences and the Anthropic Principle in Cosmology," in *Confrontation of Cosmological Theories with Observational Data*, ed. M. S. Longair (Dordrecht: D. Reidel, 1974), 72.

31. "The Anisotropy of the Universe at Large Times" in Longair, 285.

32. For a defense of the argument, see Collins, "A Scientific Argument."

33. Perhaps by virtue of so-called vacuum fluctuations; see Quentin Smith, "World Ensemble Explanations," *Pacific Philosophical Quarterly* (1986): 82.

34. See Daniel Dennett, *Darwin's Dangerous Idea* (New York: Simon and Schuster, 1995), 177. Dennett's use of "universe" here corresponds to my use of "subuniverse."

35. Collins argues (cogently in my opinion) that it is not in "A Scientific Argument," 60ff.

36. See my "On Ockham's Way Out" in *Faith and Philosophy* 3 (July 1986): 235–69.

37. My thanks to David Vander Laan, Tom Crisp, Marie Pannier, Ray Van Arragon, Erik Wielenberg, Matt Davidson, Jan Korditschke, Mike Rea, and Bruce Gordon.

2

&

Sleeping Beauty and the Afterlife

LINDA ZAGZEBSKI

The christian doctrine of the resurrection of the body is philosophically vexing. Considering that philosophers have no trouble describing scenarios in which it is problematic whether some person in the near future is me, it is no wonder that the problem of whether I will exist in the far distant future taxes our imaginative and conceptual resources beyond the limit. Nonetheless, many of us like to test the limit. The following story is set in the Middle Ages and freely uses some of the philosophical resources of the time, particularly the work of Aquinas, but most of the arguments and conclusions are not those of any actual medieval philosopher. The scientific knowledge of the protagonists is also premodern (although small bits of matter are called molecules in the narrative). The story can be read as an extended thought experiment describing something that *could* happen compatible with the following rules: (1) In the story, the bodies of the deceased must come back to life long after death. (2) The story may make no reference to an omnipotent deity or to a supernatural realm or to souls that can exist detached from bodies. (3) The story must alter what we know about the laws of nature as little as possible compatible with the above.

A MEDIEVAL TALE

At the christening of Princess Aurora, a wicked fairy appears and puts a curse on the baby in a fit of pique over not being invited to the festivities. She proclaims that the little girl will one day prick her finger on a spinning wheel and die. The good fairies present have sufficient magical power to alter the curse, but not to eliminate it entirely. They say that she will not die, but will fall asleep for a hundred years. One might think that the curse and its alteration amount to the same thing, but perhaps not. That is one of the things we will investigate.

The princess' distraught parents destroy all the spinning wheels in the kingdom, but on Aurora's sixteenth birthday, the wicked fairy lures her to the top of a tower in the castle, where the fairy is spinning on a wheel that makes an enchanting sound. Aurora is curious because she has never seen a spinning wheel, and as she approaches, she falls under the spell of the music, dancing closer and closer to the wheel, whereupon she pricks her finger and falls into a deep sleep. Since the good fairies cannot wake her, they cast a sleeping spell on the entire castle. Every living creature falls asleep on the spot. The good fairies then make a tall, dense hedge of sharp thorns grow around the castle so that the inhabitants are undisturbed in their slumber. From time to time, princes from faraway kingdoms hear the legend of the sleeping princess and attempt to get through the hedge, but they all fail. (It is no accident that all of them are guys the princess would not be interested in anyway.) At the end of a hundred years, Prince Charming appears, makes it through the hedge with the aid of the fairies, and awakens Sleeping Beauty with a kiss. At that instant, everyone else awakens and no one realizes that a hundred years have passed. The very same humans and animals who fell asleep a hundred years before continue their lives exactly where they left off.

How do the good fairies accomplish this feat?

Maybe they have sufficient magic to stop all causal processes. Perhaps they freeze the food, the animals, and the humans. To be on the safe side, they probably should put everything in cryonic suspension. The entire castle with all its contents could be enclosed in a giant block of ice. But maybe the fairies do not want to do that, or maybe there is some reason why it will not work. If freezing is not an option, they will have to do something to prevent the food from spoiling, the wood from rotting, the plants and animals from aging and dying. And they will have to do something about the fact that the animals are not taking in food and water. This does not strike me as an easy task. After all, the fairies did not create the world. I assume they are embodied beings themselves. They have magical powers that permit them to rearrange natural phenomena, but their powers are limited by nature – loosely interpreted, of course.[1]

The fairies must either prevent the causal processes of nature from occurring or figure out a way to reverse the effects of those processes. One option might be to continuously replace each individual molecule. That seems tedious, but within the capabilities of a fairy. Assuming the fairies replace all the molecules, does that change the castle or anything in it? I think not, assuming that there is literally no change except a change of molecules. (Whether that is possible is an issue to which we will return.) Nor does it matter if the material particles are replaced gradually or all at once. Some philosophers have the intuition that an object is more likely to survive the replacement of parts if the process is gradual than if the same number of parts were replaced very rapidly. My conjecture is that there are two explanations for this intuition, neither of which has anything to do with the replacement of molecules *per se*. One is that in the non-magical world a large proportion of the physical parts of a physical object cannot be rapidly replaced without destroying what Aristotle calls the form of the object, whereas a gradual change of physical parts does not compromise the object's form to any significant degree. A car is still a car while the tires are being changed or the radiator is being changed, and so on, but if the car is taken apart and every part changed, there is no form of a car for a time, and hence, no car. Second, in many thought experiments involving change of parts, the parts replaced have fairly intricate form themselves – for instance, the engine of a car or the keyboard of a computer. In these cases the thought experiment describes not only a removal and change of the matter of an object, but also a removal and change of the form of some of the parts necessary for the functioning of the whole. I think, then, that the worry is not about the change of matter, but about the change of form that accompanies the change of matter. Of course, Aristotle says there is no matter without some form, so even a change of one molecule includes some change of form. But I think we do not worry about that when the object is of sufficient size and complexity that a molecular change makes no difference to the form of any functioning parts, although the judgment is obviously difficult to make in many cases. Some objects have only meager form to begin with – say, a rock – and there is a fine line between changing the form of an insignificant part and altering the form of the whole.

In fact, there may be no line at all. Aquinas maintains that an artifact is a collection of substances conjoined by an accidental form. It has no substantial form. Each of its parts retains its own form while part of the artifact. So a computer would have only an accidental form and its keyboard would retain its accidental form while functioning as part of the computer, and the substances that are parts of the keyboard would retain their substantial form. In contrast, a living organism has a single substantial form that organizes the substance into a single living body. No part of a substance is a substance while it is a component of a larger whole that is a substance even if it would be a substance when not a component of the whole.[2] A living organism is thus a single substance with one substantial form. In the case of animals and humans, the organism is a living body. The substantial form of a living body is a particular.[3] It is what makes the body live and function as a thing of its kind. It configures the matter of the body in a distinctive way, causes the organs of the body to function in the way they function for that species, and is that in virtue of which the organism lives and grows in characteristic ways. It causes the animal to have the characteristic consciousness of an animal – sensation. If it is human, it causes it, in addition, to have the characteristic conscious powers of humans – reasoning and will (and Aquinas should add, I think, characteristic human emotions). Something is identical to a particular substance S just in case it has the particular substantial form of S.[4] In contrast, because artifacts have no substantial form but are a compilation of parts, each of which retains its form when part of the artifact, they do not have determinate persistence conditions.[5]

The fairies are well acquainted with the concept of a form. The Daisy Fairy, who has undertaken a study of Aquinas, argues that the project of keeping in existence the living bodies within the castle differs from the project of keeping artifacts in existence. That means, she says, that they should be wary of applying their intuitions about the identity of artifacts to the identity of living organisms. To do so is to use harder cases in an attempt to illuminate easier cases. The rest of the fairies are not sure that the identity of an artifact is any harder to figure out than the identity of an animal, but they agree that the problems differ and that this complicates their task. It may be harder to keep some kinds of objects in existence than others, and they will not always know when they have succeeded. In the case of some kinds of objects, there may not even be a fact of the matter as to whether they have succeeded.

Now suppose that the good fairies are busy and decide at the outset that they will replace all the molecules of the castle and everything it contains once a week. Again, let us assume they are able to do this without changing anything in the form of the objects in the castle except the form of the molecules themselves. They pluck out each molecule successively and zap a qualitatively identical one in its place almost simultaneously. As far as I can see, that does no damage to the identity of the objects whose molecules the fairies replace. It is still the same castle, same inhabitants, same food on the table, same dog sleeping under the table by the roast beef. In some cases, the molecule replaced may have changed during the week, in which case it must be replaced by a molecule qualitatively identical to the way it was one week before. But presumably, the fairies prefer that the objects do not change very much before they replace their molecules. If so, because some objects change more rapidly than others, and change of molecules threatens the identity of some objects more than others, they settle on a scheme of changing the molecules of the food on the table very frequently, the molecules of living organisms fairly often, the molecules of the table less often, and the molecules of the rocks very infrequently.

There is another way the story could go that I think we should take seriously. Suppose that in the case of living things it turns out not to be possible to replace every molecule without altering the form of the whole. Suppose that while replacing the molecules of the sleeping dog, all seems to be going well until suddenly the dog dies. The fairies do not understand what they did to cause the animal's death and quickly backtrack, replacing the last molecule removed with the original, whereupon the dog revives. They discover that they are able to replace most but not all of a living body's molecules without destroying the body's form, but they are not able to figure out in advance which ones are necessary and which are not. It is not even clear whether there are particular molecules necessary or a certain proportion of the original molecules necessary, or whether instead their action in replacing the molecules has some undetectable physical consequence that destroys the organism's form. But let us assume that enough molecules can be replaced to keep the organism alive for a hundred years.

What do the fairies do with the molecules they remove from the castle? Maybe they just add them to their stockpile of molecules – far away, of course. (They do not want Prince Charming running into a pile of molecules on his way to the castle.) Once they have removed the molecules of some object in the castle, such as the king's throne, then if they have the time and the inclination, they might find it fun to fashion a qualitatively identical throne in some remote place using the same molecules. The Lilac Fairy warns that this would create a problem because if the throne assembled in the remote place is identical with the original throne, then there are two thrones identical to the original, and that is impossible. Most of the fairies decide that their original intuition stands. If they pluck out each molecule of the throne and immediately replace it without changing the form of the throne, the throne that results is the same throne on which the king has been sitting. The throne assembled in a remote place has a different form (recall that a form is a particular), even though it has (at least most of) the same molecules as the original.

The Rose Fairy observes that some artifacts survive being taken apart and reassembled in a different place, such as a large lamp that was sent from a distant castle, but the Iris Fairy argues that even in such cases, it is doubtful that it is the identity of matter that makes it the same artifact. Rather, we think that the form of some artifacts permits the artifact to be disassembled; the form does not require a constant unity of parts. This leads to further discussion, and at the end, the fairies take the tentative position that what makes an object that exists at one time identical to an object that exists at another time is identity of form, and identity of matter is required only if and when it is not possible to change the matter without changing the form. But they also decide to heed the Daisy Fairy's warning that artifacts may not have determinate persistence conditions, so there may be no answer to the question of which throne is the original throne and which artifacts survive disassembly.

Suppose now that the good fairies are so busy that they do not have time to change the molecules very often. So they let the food spoil, the hair and fingernails grow, and the sleeping bodies age a few weeks before they replace the molecules. Then they replace them with newer molecules that make the food wholesome again and the animal bodies exactly as they were at the time the spell was cast. Surely the bodies are the same bodies, the plants are the same plants, the food is the same food. If you doubt this, then we can suppose the fairies use a process that reverses the deterioration process. The natural causal process that began just after the spell was cast is reversed until everything is exactly as it was at the beginning of the Great Sleep. If each object and living thing maintains its identity while it gradually deteriorates, surely it maintains its identity while it reverse-deteriorates.

Suppose, however, that the rosebush by the castle door dies before the fairies can prevent it. The fairies consider this a serious problem because most of them think that now that rosebush is no longer in existence. They agree with the Lily Fairy, who proposes that to be this rosebush is to have a certain life, to be a certain *living* organism. So a dead rosebush is not the rosebush that existed on the same spot before it died. The Tulip Fairy adds that if a rosebush is just a living organism of a certain kind, then a dead rosebush is not literally a rosebush at all.[6] Some of the fairies are not sure that they agree with that, but they agree that the dead rosebush is not numerically identical to the rosebush that used to live on that spot. The castle is now missing an item, and if they want everything in and around the castle when Sleeping Beauty awakens to be identical to everything that existed when she fell asleep, they are going to have to bring that very same rosebush back into existence. Is that possible? It is possible, I propose, if it is possible to bring into existence a rosebush that is a continuation of the same life as the previous rosebush. If so, perhaps the task is not much more difficult than it was before the bush died. If the process of reverse-deterioration works while the bush lives, I don't see why it cannot work soon after the bush dies. If the causal process can run backwards, it can do so whether or not the bush dies in the interim. Granted, the death of a living thing results in rapid changes in the configuration of matter (which the fairies say is produced by its substantial form), but in this case, those changes have not progressed very far, so if they are reversible, the bush can live and bloom again.

To say that the numerically identical rosebush exists as the result of such a process commits us to saying that there can be gaps in the existence of a living thing. I am not averse to such a commitment. In the nonmagic world, we do not see reverse causal processes, much less reverse causal processes that reverse the process of going from life to death. But if we did, I think we would say that the rosebush came back to life, not that a new rosebush came into existence. If the rosebush exists when and only when a certain substantial form exists, then there can also be gaps in the existence of a substantial form.

The problem of bringing the rosebush back to life and the case of the reassembled throne may suggest that spatial continuity is more important than temporal continuity. One reason for thinking that the throne that is assembled from the throne molecules in a different place is a different throne is that the throne does not exist in the spaces between the castle and the new location, even if the throne is reassembled so rapidly that there is no temporal gap. On the other hand, a consideration in favor of the judgment that the revivified rosebush is the same rosebush is that it comes back to life in the same place even though there is a temporal gap in its existence. But we must be careful about drawing this conclusion. If identity of substantial form is necessary and sufficient for the identity of a living organism, spatial or temporal continuity is relevant only insofar as such continuity is a condition (or perhaps just an indication) of identity of an object's form. With the rosebush, even though the substantial form is gone once it dies, the dead bush has some form. There is something in that space that is related both to the bush that used to live on that spot and the bush that comes to life. But another reason we would think it is the same bush is that the causal process through which the dead bush goes from death to life simply reverses the process through which the living bush went from life to death. I do not think we can say which of these reasons is the more salient without looking at further cases.

Now let's make the situation harder. Suppose the fairies are so busy that they do not notice that the king has died. This is a real problem because they certainly do not want Sleeping Beauty waking up to find out that her father died on her birthday. The king is a human person and the fairies assume that a human person is an individual human animal, a living human body.[7] Hence, the king is a living human body. This is not to say that the fairies believe the king is a bunch of body cells. To be a living human body is to be informed matter. Because the king is dead, the informed matter that used to exist on the throne is no longer there. The king's corpse is not the king for the same reason that the dead rosebush is not the rosebush. The king no longer exists in the castle where he is supposed to be. In fact, the fairies conclude that he no longer exists at all, just as the rosebush no longer exists once it dies.

Because the powers of the fairies do not extend beyond nature, they have no direct contact with heaven or any realm outside of space and time, nor can they maneuver human souls into the matter of this world. If we use Swinburne's analogy of the soul as a lightbulb and the brain as a socket, they cannot plug the lightbulb into the socket.[8] So the fairies hope that Swinburne's analogy is inaccurate. If the king has a soul that left his body, they are not going to be able to find it. But maybe their task is not much harder than it was with the dead rosebush. As long as the king's body is mostly intact, if they can rejuvenate the cells of the dead body by replacing them with healthy cells, perhaps he will live again. This might work if we assume that there is a connection between the form of the dead body and the substantial form that exists when the individual cells are revivified, and that assumption is as plausible for the king as for the rosebush. But on the view we are considering, the body that comes alive is the king's body if and only if it is matter informed by the king's substantial form.

The Azalea Fairy is skeptical that the plan will work. At death, the king's substantial form is completely gone, and what is left is a corpse with a different form.[9] If that corpse is revivified, by what right can they claim that the newly living body has the same substantial form the king had before death? Revivifying his corpse may not be sufficient to bring *him* back to life.

The fairies discuss this possibility for a while. The Lily Fairy argues that because they agree that the king just *is* his living human body, any way to make his body live again makes *him* live again, although the Azalea Fairy points out that that does not solve the problem because the dispute is over what counts as *his* body. After considerable discussion, the fairies conclude that it is the king who lives again if they can make his body live again, and it is likely that they can make his body live again if they replace the decaying cells before the configured matter of the body has deteriorated very much. As with the rosebush, the considerations in favor of this judgment include the fact that spatial continuity is preserved and the process that makes a king come to life is the same causal process that led to the king's death, only in reverse.

The Lily Fairy proposes that they apply the same identity criterion to a human body as to a rosebush: a living human body at t_2 is identical to a living human body at t_1 just in case the body at t_2 is a continuation of the same life as the body at t_1. The fairies agree with this criterion, but the Tulip Fairy points out that it is not very illuminating because the issue they are debating is whether the revivified body of the king is a continuation of the same life as before the king's death. The intuitions of most of the fairies is that it is.

Notice that the continuation-of-life criterion does not preclude a gap. A life may include the occasional temporal gap as long as it is the same life before and after the gap. If so, and if the fairies are sufficiently busy, the plants and animals in the castle may die many times and be rejuvenated many times as long as their lives continue after the gap.

Now suppose the fairies are very busy indeed, flying around trying to out-wit the Evil Fairy. Suppose they wait 99 years and 364 days. By that time, the bodies are no longer sleeping, they are dead and decomposed, and the derelict castle is in serious disrepair. In this case, it is not merely a question of replac-ing molecules one by one because it is not just the substantial form of each living thing that has changed. Most of the accidental forms have changed too, although the matter is presumably around somewhere. Is reversing the causal process sufficient to bring back into existence the very same castle, the same rosebush, the same food on the table, the same dog, the same king, queen, and courtiers, and the same Sleeping Beauty? Possibly, but this is the sort of situation most of us find conceptually difficult. The fairies agree that the task is hopeless unless they can count on the truth of the principle that it is possi-ble that there are gaps in the existence of an individual living thing. The gaps that are most plausible are short ones, not because there is any metaphysical difference between short and long, but because there is a causal connection between the living thing and the corpse, and it is more plausible to think that the process is reversible as long as some form remains in the corpse. Still, they agree that there is no metaphysical prohibition in principle to there being gaps in the existence of a living thing.

The Lilac Fairy then proposes that they accept the following principle:

Lilac's principle: Necessarily, a replica or duplicate of a person S is not identical to S.[10]

In support of her proposal, the Lilac Fairy argues that if a person is replicated once, it is possible for her to be replicated twice, but if replication is sufficient for identity and it is possible to be replicated twice, it would be possible that there are two beings identical to the original person. But it is not possible that two persons are identical to one. Hence, a process of replication or duplication does not result in a person identical to the person replicated.[11]

The Tulip Fairy is not convinced. "Of course two persons cannot be identical to one," she remarks, "but that does not rule out identity by replication. It just means that at most, one person resulting from replication has the substantial form of the original person and is thus identical to the person replicated. Because a substantial form is a particular, there will never be two replicas of a person with equal and maximally strong claims to identity with the person replicated. The person we are looking for is the one with the right substantial form. There can never be more than one, so it does not matter what physical process keeps the form in existence. Replication cannot be ruled out."

The rest of the fairies nod in agreement, but then the Lilac Fairy worries that there are many processes that result in *apparently* equal claimants to identity to some object, and how are they to know which one is the actual continuer of the existence of the original object? Not only replication but bifurcation has this problem. The road leading to the castle bifurcates a quarter mile from the castle gate. The king's deck of cards fell on the floor one day, and half was recovered by one servant and the other half by another. Not realizing that the other servant had the rest of the cards, each of them secretly added enough cards to the ones he had to make a full deck, thereby resulting in two decks of cards with an apparently equal claim to identity to the original deck. It seems obvious, the Lilac Fairy says, that processes of bifurcation resulting in two strong and apparently equal claimants to the identity of an object do occur.

"But those are artifacts," replies the Daisy Fairy, "and there really *is* a problem of conditions for their persistence because they have no substantial form. Some simple substances, such as worms, divide also, and in those cases, it is most reasonable to say that neither one has the substantial form of the original.[12] But maybe the substantial form of a more complex living thing is more resilient. Possibly it can survive replication or bifurcation."

"But how are we to tell which of two competitors has the right substantial form?" asks Lilac. It is not enough for us to *be* successful at bringing Sleeping Beauty and all the castle's inhabitants back to life; we want to *know* or at least have good reason to believe that we have been successful."

"I don't think we can tell for sure when we have been successful, but surely we can often tell when we have failed," remarks the Lily Fairy. "The substantial form of a living thing is not a mysterious entity whose presence or absence is undetectable. We observe its effects. The most obvious of these is the way in which a bunch of matter is configured. It is the substantial form that configures it in that way, gives the organism life, and in the case of animals, makes it conscious. The particular bodily configuration and particular consciousness of an individual animal are the result of its particular substantial form. So if we try to bring Sleeping Beauty back to life by a process that results in a very different bodily configuration or a consciousness that is not distinctively hers, we will know that we have failed."

The Daffodil Fairy notices that in less than an hour, a hundred years will have passed since the beginning of the Great Sleep, so they had better act quickly. For lack of a better idea, they use the same procedure they used earlier: they reverse the causal process. They need to rely on the principle that there can be gaps in the existence of a living thing, but they have not had time to discuss whether there can be gaps in the existence of the nonliving things in the castle, and some of the fairies worry that they have lost their chance to bring back the numerically identical castle with all its furnishings. But they are willing to let that worry slide because it is the living things in the castle that are most crucial. The Lilac fairy agrees to the plan because a reverse causal process is not duplicable. They then reverse the process, and to their great joy, Sleeping Beauty, the king, queen, courtiers, and servants, as well as all the plants and animals, come back to life. At least, to all appearances, they are exactly the same, and all the humans in the castle seem to have the right memories and psychological characteristics.

"Well, at least we don't know that we have failed," says the Lily Fairy. "I hope we have succeeded." I think the hope is justified.

Now let's look into the future, after the fairy tale normally ends. Suppose that the fairies successfully keep everything in existence for a hundred years by whatever means. Sleeping Beauty wakes up, marries Prince Charming, and they live together happily until their deaths. Meanwhile, the thorn hedge is removed by the fairies, but another one is built around the castle and environs so that the castle with the fields and villages around it is sealed off from the rest of the world. A thousand years go by. (The fairies live a long time.) Eventually, the fairies become curious about Sleeping Beauty's castle and they decide to go and see how her descendants are faring. To their disappointment, they find out that all living things within the thorn hedge have died. No plants, animals, or human beings remain, and the castle itself is a ruin. During the time since the Awakening, not only have all the plants and animals that inhabited the castle during the period of the Great Sleep died, but their bodies have decayed and their molecules have become parts of new substances – new plants, new animals, new human beings – which subsequently died and their molecules recycled through further substances. Eventually, the last living thing died. The fairies are distressed because they would like to see Sleeping Beauty and all the other inhabitants of the castle live again. Is there anything they can do to make that happen?

It is much less clear that reversing the causal process will work this time because many of the molecules that were once components of Sleeping Beauty's living body have at later times been components of the bodies of other living things, including other human beings. In fact, it is possible that all of the molecules that were components of her body at the time of her death were eventually components of the bodies of other living things, even many living things at different times. If the fairies reverse the causal process all the way back to the way it was a thousand years before, at best they will have brought Sleeping Beauty back to life, but they will have done so at the expense of simultaneously bringing back to life her descendants and the descendants of the other living things known to her in the castle on the day of her sixteenth birthday.

After considerable discussion, it turns out that most of the fairies are ambitious enough to want to attempt to bring back to life everyone who ever lived in the castle. The Azalea Fairy maintains that the idea is foolhardy. "Far better to bring a few people back to life than to try to bring back everyone and fail," she says. But the other fairies insist on trying, although they admit that the reverse causal process will not work. The Daisy Fairy (whom you may recall is fond of the work of Aquinas) reports on Aquinas's answer to the problem of what happens on the day of the general resurrection to the body of a cannibal who eats nothing but human flesh: " . . . it is not necessary . . . that whatever has been in man materially rise in him; further, if something is lacking, it can be supplied by the power of God. Therefore, the flesh consumed will rise in him in whom it was first perfected by the rational soul."[13] This suggests, she says, that some of the material particles of the resurrected body are those that the body had during life, but it is not necessary that it have all or even very many of the particles it had at any time during life, and missing particles can be replaced. The Rose Fairy agrees and reminds the other fairies that when they substituted molecules during the Great Sleep, they were assuming that there are few material particles necessary for the identity of a human body. If that is the case, why should they pay so much attention to using a process that ends up with the same body cells as Sleeping Beauty had at the end of her life? If the same molecules were not necessary for the hundred years she was sleeping, why should they be necessary now?

"But how else can we proceed?" asks the Azalea fairy. "We changed molecules when we knew, or at least had good reason to believe, that we were keeping the substantial form intact. But we have no idea how to get the substantial form back except by reversing the process that destroyed the form in the first place."

"Aquinas's comment on cannibals gives me an idea," says the Daffodil Fairy. "Let us begin a reverse causal process, starting by reconfiguring the matter of the most recently deceased animals and plants. Then we proceed backward, adding new molecules to fill in gaps when needed to bring back to life a creature some of whose molecules at the time of its death are now in use by a creature whom we have already brought back to life. We will need to add more and more molecules as we go backward, and of course the molecules making up the plant and animal organisms brought back to life will not be the same as those that made up the plants and animals at the time of their death. We will have to be careful, though, because we discovered that sometimes replacing molecules results in a change of form, but we think we can tell when that happens and we have time to try many different arrangements."

The Lilac Fairy denies that the plan will work. "Any reverse causal process that uses some of the same molecules but not all in reconfiguring the bodies we intend to bring back to life can result in duplication. It is possible that whatever molecules are not used in reconfiguring the body of the last person who died can be put to use in configuring another body just like it. The process proposed by the Daffodil Fairy allows the possibility of more than one contender to identity with the original person. We will not be able to tell which one has the substantial form of the original, if either one of them does."

The fairies are distressed, but then the usually silent Iris Fairy speaks up. "This is the way I see our problem," she says. "We have agreed that identity of substantial form is both necessary and sufficient for the identity of a living organism like Sleeping Beauty. If her substantial form has either ceased to exist permanently or has an independent existence in a realm outside our reach, there is nothing we can do to bring her back into existence. We also know that a certain configuration of matter is not sufficient for her substantial form because we can easily configure more than one parcel of matter in that way, but her substantial form is a particular. We felt confident, or at least hopeful, that a precise reversal of the causal process worked, but why did we think that? It could not have been because we ended up with the same matter. We must have thought there was a connection between the substantial form of a living substance and such a process. But our reason for thinking that was pretty weak. We noted that the substantial form of a living organism persists while it undergoes material changes determined by normal causal processes, and so we conjectured that it would persist while undergoing the same processes in reverse. That made sense while the substantial form was still in existence, but once it had gone out of existence, we had to hope that each substantial form operates in nature in a way that distinguishes it from any other form. That was a big assumption because some philosophers think it is possible for two numerically distinct human beings to be indistinguishable in all their qualitative properties, both properties of their bodies and behavior, and properties of their conscious states and memories."

"I cannot agree with those philosophers," says the Lily Fairy. "At best, two substantial forms are indistinguishable from the outside, but surely they are distinguishable from the inside."

"There is no inside to a plant," remarks the Azalea Fairy.

"True, but the human beings are our primary concern. I think that one of the following options must be true:

(1) Like artifacts, human beings have no determinate persistence conditions. In particular, it can happen that for some human being S who exists at t and some human being S' who exists at t', there is no fact of the matter whether S is identical to S'.

"If (1) is true, there may be no fact of the matter whether we have succeeded in bringing back to life Sleeping Beauty and the other castle inhabitants. We have agreed in rejecting (1), but it is a possibility we should not forget.

(2) For any human being S at t and human being S' at t', there is a fact of the matter whether S is identical to S', but it may be a fact that is inaccessible to any mortal being, including S and S'.

"Now we can debate what it means to be accessible, and what we are to say about various situations in which we can imagine inaccessible identity conditions," continues Lily, "but I propose that (2) is false. Or more cautiously, we should operate as if it is false because otherwise we are operating in the dark. If so, the following must be true:

(3) For any human being S at t and human being S' at t', if S is identical to S', that fact is accessible to somebody, either to S and S' or to a careful observer of S and S'. If S is not identical to S', that fact is accessible to somebody, either to S and S' or to a careful observer of S and S'.

"If (3) is true, it will never happen that there are two equal and maximally strong competitors to identity to any person S. The presence or absence of S's substantial form is a fact about nature accessible to mortal beings who are themselves part of nature."

"Why do we have to choose between (2) and (3)?" asks the Iris Fairy. "Maybe we can usually tell whether the substantial form of some human S is identical to the substantial form of some human S', but perhaps there are exceptions. If so, (3) would be true for the most part and (2) would be false for the most part, but we need not go so far as to accept (3) unequivocally."

"Why don't we try the reverse causal process I proposed earlier and see what happens?" asks the Daffodil Fairy.

"But if the identity or nonidentity of some S and S' is accessible only from within their own consciousness, how are we to tell what has happened?" asks the Lilac Fairy. "As a matter of fact, I don't know how they can tell either. It's not as if S' at t' can go back in time to t and inhabit the consciousness of S to compare it with her own."

"I think it will be observable from the outside if it is a fact accessible to mortal beings at all," says the Rose Fairy. "But that's not really the point. I think we should stop worrying so much about how we are going to know whether to congratulate ourselves on success and spend more time trying to bring these people back to life." The rest of the fairies agree that it is time to take action.

There are many ways the story can go from this point. Here is one of them. The fairies proceed with the Daffodil Fairy's original plan. They start by reversing the causal process that led to the death and decomposition of the last remaining human being in the castle. When she comes back to life, she is delighted to be alive and seems to be the same person who died years before. They then continue working backward, adding new molecules to fill in gaps when needed to bring back to life a human being some of whose molecules at the time of its death are in use by those whom the fairies have already brought back to life. When they have been working for a while, they decide to experiment. They take half the molecules from the original body of Sleeping Beauty's great-great-granddaughter and make one body with that half and another body with the other half. But a curious thing happens when they both come to life. Only one of them is recognizable to family and friends as the woman she once was. They find the other one puzzling. Sometimes when they try this experiment, neither one seems to be identical to the original. Of course, this might happen most of the time or even all of the time. It could also happen that the fairies have to try thousands of times to bring one human to life who seems to be identical to one long deceased, using many alternative arrangements of molecules. But suppose that no matter how many times the fairies try the experiment, it never happens that there are two strong and equally plausible candidates for identity with the deceased. At most, one of them seems to be the person who once lived. The fairies do not understand why this is the case. But they can succeed in bringing a dead person to life without understanding whether and why they are successful. Their success need not have much to do with having a correct theory of personal identity. In fact, they do not even have to know exactly what physical process is sufficient to bring Sleeping Beauty to life, only that if there is one, and they have the time and the patience to try many alternatives, they might get lucky. Perhaps it would take thousands of years of attempts, maybe even millions, in which case we should hope that the fairies are *very* long-lived.

Accounts of an afterlife only aim at the possible, as they should, but some stretch credibility more than others. Of course, the extent to which an account is far-fetched depends on one's prior metaphysical positions, and accounts vary in their relative advantages and disadvantages. The partial account of personal identity and the afterlife given in this paper has some advantages over other accounts. The fairies do not have to find all the same molecules in order to bring back to life an individual human body. So they do not have the problem of two distinct persons competing for the same molecules. Nor do the fairies have to resort to making a replica.[14] I assume that the identity of a replica to the thing replicated is at best problematic. The fairies are not bifurcating Sleeping Beauty, a view that is problematic for the same reason as the replica theory.[15] The problems with bifurcation and replication exist as long as it is possible that a process of either kind results in two maximally strong claimants to identity to a person. Thought experiments in which such things happen are so common that we are used to thinking of those scenarios as possible. I am proposing that we do not actually know that any such thing is possible.

Further, the fairies do not face the problem that each person has a soul that could continually change while their bodies remain the same, a well-known complaint against traditional dualism.[16] Finally, the fairies do not have to take an allegedly subsistent individual form in a realm outside of the natural world and somehow inform it in new matter, as in the theory of Aquinas.

The account is intended to be neither materialist nor dualist in their contemporary senses. A substantial form is a particular, but it is not a substance capable of existence independent of the body. It has properties that no material base has, and it is compatible with the tale I have told that a substantial form is an emergent entity, but I have left the story of the origin of the substantial form untold.

CONCLUSION

There are two strands of thought about human persons that are in tension with each other and force us to make some hard choices. One is the motive to think of human persons as human organisms, part of the natural world. The other is the motive to think that an individual person is the sort of thing that is distinct from everything else in the world, including every other person, in a very strong sense. Unlike Aquinas's position on artifacts, a person has determinate persistence conditions. Furthermore, a person is not replicable or subject to any process that results in two equal and maximally strong claimants to identity to that person. The second motive is hard to reconcile with the first because duplication and bifurcation in the material world are ubiquitous. It is not surprising, then, that so many philosophers have been attracted to the idea that each person is distinct because of the possession of a soul that is outside the realm of the laws of nature. It appears, then, that we cannot have it both ways; we have to make a choice.

In this paper, I have suggested that it is possible we do not have to make the choice. Perhaps nature cooperates with the strong distinctness of persons as described above. There might be a substantial form that is a nonduplicable particular, but which cannot exist without informing matter. A particular person S exists when and only when S's substantial form informs some matter.

The narrative of this paper suggests further that a substantial form might be connected to the matter it informs in such a way that it exists when and only when there is a specific combination of molecules conjoined in a certain configuration. Possibly the specific material base that accompanies the substantial form of a person is itself nonduplicable, but it is repeatable. If it is repeatable, a person can come back to life. If it is nonduplicable, there will never be two maximally strong claimants to identity to the person who died. If a particular substantial form is tied to a particular material base by the laws of nature, then resurrection is compatible with the laws of nature.[17]

NOTES

1. For this reason, it will not do any good for the fairies to emulate Peter van Inwagen's proposal on death and resurrection in "The Possibility of Resurrection" (reprinted in *Immortality*, ed. Paul Edwards [New York: Macmillan, 1992] 242–6), attempting to move the castle and all its contents to some other region where they have better control over the environment, simultaneously replacing the real castle with a castle simulacrum. There is no other place where the fairies can control the castle any better than they can in its original location. And of course there is no need for a simulacrum if nobody can get through the hedge.

2. See Eleonore Stump, *Aquinas* (New York: Routledge, 2003), 40.

3. As Stump interprets Aquinas, what individuates Socrates is a particular substantial form, a view I am using in this paper. But Aquinas also thinks that a substantial form of a human being is *this* substantial form in virtue of the fact that it configures *this* matter (see Stump, 49). I am not using the latter part of Aquinas' view in this paper, nor am I using his position that the substantial form of a human being subsists – continues to exist after death.

4. According to Aquinas, substances and artifacts do not exhaust the class of things. A severed hand is neither a substance nor an artifact. See Stump, 42.

5. According to Eleonore Stump, Aquinas has no principled way to draw the line between a change of matter that is just an alteration in the artifact and a change of matter that changes the identity of the form of the whole so that the original form, and consequently the original artifact, no longer exist. See Stump, 59.

6. Aquinas thinks that when we apply names of the living body and its parts to the dead body and its parts, we use the words equivocally. A dead body is not literally a human body because at death, the substantial form of the body is replaced by a different, nonanimating form. See Stump, 194–5.

7. I do not mean to say, of course, that the defining features of personhood are captured by this identity. If there are nonhuman persons, then human and nonhuman persons have something in common that has nothing to do with being a human animal. The features that make something a person (e.g., subjectivity, capacity for emotion, thought, and action) probably accompany some feature of being a living human body, but I will discuss these features in this paper only in passing.

8. Richard Swinburne, *The Evolution of the Soul* (Oxford: Oxford University Press, 1986), 310f.

9. To say that some form remains is not to say that some part of the substantial form remains after death, according to Aquinas, because the substantial form is a particular that is entirely gone. But there is in place of the animating substantial form of the substance a form that configures its matter for a while.

10. I assume that a replica and a duplicate are the same thing, except that I tend to call something a duplicate when that which it duplicates is still in existence. If not, I usually call it a replica. I don't think my usage is unusual, but if it is, my discussion of replicas can be suitably altered.

11. Derek Parfit argues that identity is not what matters to survivorship. See "Why Our Identity Is Not What Matters" in *Personal Identity*, ed. Raymond Martin and John Barresi (Oxford: Blackwell Publishing, 2003), 115–43; reprinted from Parfit, *Reasons and Persons* (Oxford: Oxford University Press, 1984).

12. Aquinas maintains that when a worm divides, two substances result from one. Neither one is identical to the original worm. See Stump, 41.

13. *Summa Contra Gentiles* IV.81.13.

14. A well-known replica account is given by John Hick in *Philosophy of Religion*, 3rd ed. (Englewood Cliffs, NJ: Prentice-Hall, 1983).

15. Dean Zimmerman, "The Compatibility of Materialism and Survival: The 'Falling Elevator' Model," *Faith and Philosophy* 16, 2 (1999) 194–212.

16. This complaint appears in many places, but see "The First Night" in John Perry, *A Dialogue on Personal Identity and Immortality* (Indianapolis: Hackett, 1978).

17. I thank Ray Elugardo, Monte Cook, Andrew Dole, Andrew Chignell, Brian Leftow, and William Hasker for discussion of the issues of this paper and comments on previous drafts.

3

Free Will, Evil, and Divine Providence

DERK PEREBOOM

Traditional theists in our environment, and christians in particular, tend to endorse libertarianism about free will, according to which we have the free will required for moral responsibility, free will of this sort is incompatible with determinism, and determinism is false. Divine determinism is nonetheless well represented in the history of traditional theism – and by "divine determinism" I mean to specify the position that God is the sufficient active cause of everything in creation, whether directly or by way of secondary causes such as human agents. This position is either obviously or arguably held by Augustine, Luther, Calvin, Descartes, Spinoza, Leibniz, and Schleiermacher, among others. Yet despite the historical prominence of this view, there is an obvious and compelling reason for rejecting it. The consequence that God is the sufficient active cause of all the evils that occur threatens to make divine determinism unconscionable from the very outset. Now if an available alternative were the position that we have libertarian free will, that God is not omnipotent, and that there are evil forces in the universe, other than mere willings, against which God needs to *struggle*, then one can see why rejecting the determinist perspective would seem attractive. Yet even if this Zoroastrian alternative remains the de facto position of some, it is outside the bounds of traditional Christian, Jewish, and Islamic orthodoxy. But affirming libertarianism while retaining a commitment to divine omnipotence, although attractive indeed, is not obviously and decisively superior to certain options open to the divine determinist. At least so I shall argue.

For some theists, an important motivation for accepting the libertarian view of free will has been that the doctrine of eternal damnation is difficult to reconcile with determinism, and divine determinism in particular. In addition, libertarianism promises a solution to the problem of evil, and this yields another motivation. However, libertarianism has also been thought to pose a threat to divine providence, God's beneficent governance of the world. But this last problem would be solved by Molinism, according to which God can know what every possible libertarian free creature would choose in every possible circumstance, and then with this knowledge, God is able to direct the course of history with precision.[1] Indeed, it would seem that all things considered, from the point of view of theological desirability – setting aside considerations of plausibility – libertarianism supplemented by Molinism is without equal. But both libertarianism and Molinism are controversial positions. What if they were, in the last analysis, false? Is the fate of Christian theism tied to the truth of these two positions? One possibility that appears to be gaining currency is that libertarianism is true and Molinism is false, and as result, divine providence is relatively weak; Thomas Flint calls this position "openism." But what if libertarianism itself is false (I don't think we can take for granted that it isn't)? Would Christianity thereby be rendered implausible?

MORAL RESPONSIBILITY AND THEISM

The most prominent trend in traditional Calvinism, and more broadly, in the Augustinian strain in Christianity, maintains a strong doctrine of divine providence. In the hands of some, the development of this doctrine includes the claim that God determines everything that occurs in creation. At the same time, another prominent trend in traditional Calvinism and Augustinianism has it that human beings are morally responsible for their sinful actions, and that they deserve punishment – even eternal damnation – by virtue of having acted sinfully. Together, these doctrines strongly suggest a theological compatibilism between moral responsibility and divine determinism. This theological compatibilism has historically been a concern to those raised in these traditions. From Molina and Arminius on, the most common avenue of disagreement has been to adopt a libertarian view of free will. (From here on, the term *free will* shall refer to libertarian free will, unless otherwise noted.) But another option, typically only hinted at, is to endorse hard determinism or a similar position, according to which determinism is true, and as a result, we are not morally responsible for our actions.[2]

A serious misgiving one might have about this view is that it would undermine the notions of sin, guilt, repentance, forgiveness, and gratitude so central to the ethical framework of traditional theistic religions. But there are good reasons to think that this worry is ultimately unfounded. What is claimed to be incompatible with determinism is moral responsibility. For an agent to be *morally responsible for an action* is for it to belong to the agent in such a way that he or she would deserve blame if the action were morally wrong, and he or she would deserve credit or perhaps praise if it were morally exemplary. The desert at issue here is basic in the sense that the agent, to be morally responsible, would deserve the blame or credit just because he or she has performed the action, and not, for example, by virtue of consequentialist considerations. It is commonly supposed that moral responsibility is an absolutely central ethical notion, so that morality itself stands or falls with it. In my view, this is a misconception.

First of all, note that being morally responsible is distinct from *behaving responsibly*, that is, behaving morally, and from *taking responsibility* for something – making a sincere commitment to a task in one's community, for example, or to care for someone. It is also different from the legitimacy of holding oneself and others *morally accountable*, where this amounts to the legitimacy of demanding that agents explain how their decisions accord with the moral point of view, and that they consider what their decisions reveal about their moral character and dispositions. The notions of behaving responsibly, taking responsibility, and moral accountability are independent of moral responsibility, and can survive without it.

Furthermore, absence of moral responsibility is compatible with our actions being good and bad, or right and wrong. By ordinary intuitions, the actions of a small child can be good or bad, right or wrong, before he or she qualifies as morally responsible. A legal analogy also indicates why this might be so. Suppose that someone has, unbeknownst to you, slipped a drug into your seltzer that makes you compulsively speed in your car – so much so that it causally determines you to speed. Suppose that an officer stops you as you are speeding on the freeway. Even if you are not blameworthy for speeding in this case, what you were doing was manifestly legally wrong. By analogy, moral wrongdoing is also consistent with the absence of blameworthiness. Even if an agent is not blameworthy for lying, it may still be wrong for him to lie.

But denying moral responsibility might be thought to threaten the attitudes of guilt and repentance, because these attitudes would seem to presuppose that we are blameworthy for what we have done. Here there is much at stake, for these attitudes lie at the core of the traditional theistic conception of the formation of moral and religious character, and of what it is to have the right relationship with God. Without guilt and repentance, an agent would be incapable of restoring relationships damaged because he or she has done wrong. He or she would be kept from reestablishing his or her moral integrity and the kind of relationship with God that these changes make possible. For other than the attitudes of guilt and repentance, we would seem to have no psychological resources that can play these roles. But giving up on moral responsibility would appear to undermine guilt because this attitude essentially involves the belief that one is blameworthy for something one has done. Moreover, if guilt is undermined, the attitude of repentance would also seem threatened, for feeling guilty is not implausibly required for motivating repentance.

However, imagine that you behave immorally, but because you do not believe that you are morally responsible, you deny that you are blameworthy. Instead, you agree that you have done wrong, you are saddened by your having behaved immorally, and you thoroughly regret what you have done. In addition, because you are committed to moral improvement, you resolve not to behave in this way in the future, and you seek the help of others in sustaining your resolve. None of this is threatened by giving up moral responsibility. Indeed, I suspect that given what is ordinarily meant by a sense of guilt, because moral sadness and regret are not undermined, the sense of guilt would thereby still count as legitimate.

Forgiveness might appear to presuppose that the person being forgiven is blameworthy, and if this is so, it would indeed be undermined if one gave up moral responsibility. But forgiveness has central features that would be unaffected, and they are sufficient to sustain the role forgiveness as a whole typically has in good relationships. Suppose a friend repeatedly mistreats you, and because of this, you have resolved to end your relationship with him. However, he then apologizes to you, in such a way that he thereby signifies that he believes he has done wrong, that he wishes he had not mistreated you, and that he is sincerely committed to refraining from the offensive behavior in the future. Because of this, you decide to renew rather than to end the friendship. None of this conflicts with giving up moral responsibility. The aspect of forgiveness that is undercut by the denial of moral responsibility is the willingness to disregard deserved blame or punishment. But if we were not morally responsible and did not believe we were, we would no longer need the willingness to overlook deserved blame and punishment to have good relationships.

Gratitude might well presuppose that those to whom one is grateful are morally responsible for beneficial acts, and for this reason, gratitude would be threatened. At the same time, certain aspects of this attitude would not be imperiled, and I contend that these aspects can play the role gratitude as a whole has in good relationships. Gratitude involves, first of all, thankfulness toward someone who has acted beneficially. True, being thankful toward someone often involves the belief that he or she is praiseworthy for an action. But at the same time, one may also be thankful to a toddler for some kindness, even though one does not believe he or she is morally responsible. Even more, one may be thankful to a friend whose beneficent actions proceed from deeply held commitments. The aspect of thankfulness could be retained even if the presupposition of praiseworthiness is rejected. Gratitude also typically involves joy occasioned by the beneficent act of another. But a rejection of moral responsibility fully harmonizes with being joyful and expressing joy when others are considerate or generous on one's behalf. Such expression of joy can bring about the sense of goodwill often brought about by gratitude, and so in this respect, abandoning moral responsibility does not produce a disadvantage.

What has traditionally been the greatest difficulty for divine determinism is the consequence that God is the cause of sin. Libertarians may hold that God does not cause sin at all (in the sense of actively bringing it about) but instead that free creatures cause it. Divine determinists have tried to avoid God's being the cause of sin by distinguishing different ways in which God determines our decisions, but I find all such attempts that I have encountered unpersuasive. A few, such as William Mann, advocate accepting all of the consequences (given compatibilist presuppositions) of the claim that God is the cause of sin.[3] Now both theistic compatibilists and hard determinists face this difficulty. But in an important respect, the problem is worse for compatibilism, for this position is threatened not only with the claim that God deterministically causes sin, but that God deterministically causes our blameworthiness and our being deserving of punishment. Of these, the hard determinist need countenance only that God causes sin, and not also our blameworthiness and our deserving punishment. For the hard determinist, sin has more of the features of natural evil than usually supposed, and as a result, God's causing sin is much more like God's causing natural evil as it is typically conceived.

SALVATION

Libertarian free will might seem to provide an especially crucial advantage to Christian theism in the area of soteriology. For the most widespread view as to how Christ's suffering, death, and resurrection save us is the standard substitutionary atonement theory, and it must be relinquished if moral responsibility is denied. On this theory, we deserve extensive punishment just by virtue of our sinful actions, and Christ, by his suffering and death, bears this punishment in our place. But if we do not deserve even blame, let alone punishment, just by virtue of our sinful behavior, then an essential component of this theory is false. One should note that this substitutionary theory has familiar problems of its own – even without concerns about free will, the retributive theory of punishment is not without its difficulties,[4] and the notion that retributive justice allows one person's punishment to count for another's is difficult to reconcile with ordinary moral intuitions. Moreover, other theories of Christ's atonement are consistent with this view. Among them is

Abelard's moral example theory, according to which Christ's obedience unto death serves as a motivating example for us to emulate. On Jürgen Moltmann's view, through Christ's suffering and death God manifests solidarity with us in our worst sufferings, thereby identifying with us in our most difficult and painful experiences.[5] As far as I can see, nothing in this position depends crucially on our being morally responsible. Or consider Richard Swinburne's position, according to which the perfect life of Christ is a gift that God gives us so that we can pay the compensation we owe for our wrongdoing.[6] It is not at all clear that any feature of this view conflicts with the denial of free will and moral responsibility.

Historically, perhaps the most effective reason for rejecting any sort of divine determinism and endorsing instead libertarian free will is the unconscionability of God's damning people to hell after determining them to sin. But another response is Schleiermacher's – to maintain the divine determinism and accept instead the doctrine of universal salvation.[7] Indeed, the best reading of the texts of the Christian scriptures might well be on the side of universalism. Here are a number of passages that count in its favor:

1. *Romans 5:18.* Therefore just as one man's trespass led to condemnation for all, so one man's act of righteousness leads to justification and life for all.
2. *Romans 11:32.* For God has imprisoned all in disobedience so that he may be merciful to all.
3. *I Corinthians 15:22.* For as all die in Adam, so all will be made alive in Christ.
4. *Colossians 1:19–20.* For in him [Christ] all the fullness of God was pleased to dwell, and through him God was pleased to reconcile to himself all things, whether on earth or in heaven, by making peace through the blood of his cross.

Universalism is an option for the Christian who is a divine determinist, and in my view, it is far from obvious that on the whole the scriptural texts count against this position.[8]

THE FREE WILL THEODICY

A potential drawback for the rejection of libertarianism is that it rules out the free will theodicy, which is often thought to be the most powerful defense we have of divine goodness in the face of evil. The free will theodicy in systematized form dates back at least to early Christianity and perhaps to Zoroastrianism, and remains the most prominent of all theodicies. In the most common version, God had the option of creating or refraining from creating libertarian significantly free beings – beings with libertarian free will that can make choices between right and wrong. A risk incurred by creating such beings is that they might freely choose evil and the choice might be unpreventable by God. Benefits include creatures having moral responsibility for their actions and being creators in their own right. Because the benefits outweigh the risks, God is morally justified in creating such significantly free beings, and he is not culpable when they choose wrongly.

But how plausible is this as a theodicy for the most horrible evils? If it isn't very plausible, perhaps not much is relinquished by accepting a view that rules it out. A familiar problem is that many of the more horrible evils would not seem to be or result from freely willed decisions. People being injured and dying as a result of earthquakes, volcanic eruptions, and diseases – including mental illnesses that give rise to unfree immoral choices – would not seem to result from freely willed decisions, and for this reason are standardly classified as *natural* as opposed to *moral* evils. But a further objection, raised by several critics, is that even if we have free will of the libertarian sort, and many of our choices are freely willed in this libertarian sense, the consequences of those decisions are preventable by God. In general, evil consequences are preventable effects of freely willed decisions.[9] Or, God might intervene earlier on in the process. Given the nature of libertarian free will, short of killing them or disabling their wills, God might not have been able to prevent the Nazi leadership from deciding to perpetrate genocide, but God could have nonetheless prevented or limited the genocide by, say, rendering the Nazi guns, trains, and gas chambers ineffective. One answer to this is Richard Swinburne's, that if God were to regularly prevent such evils in this way, then we would not fully understand the kinds of consequences our decisions could have, and this would have considerable disvalue. But, one might argue, God might have intervened earlier yet in the process by, for example, healing the bad effects of childhood abuse and trauma. Or rather than intervening, God might have designed us so that we were not nearly as vulnerable to experiences of this sort and, more generally, less vulnerable to the kinds of psychological problems that play a role in motivating evil decisions.

Swinburne has developed a thorough response to these sorts of objections. He argues that it is not just freely willed decision *tout court* that has the relevantly high intrinsic value, but two characteristics in addition: freely willed decision's accomplishing what the agent intended – what he calls *efficacious* free will – and freely willed decision's adjudicating between good and evil options, each of which genuinely motivate the agent – *serious* free will, in his terminology. Swinburne contends that it is serious and efficacious free will that has the intrinsic value high enough to justify God in sometimes not preventing the decidedly evil consequences of immoral decisions. His account is significant, for it does not avoid a proposal for the kind of value free will must possess to sustain the role in theodicy that so many believe it has. In his view, first of all, "the very fact of the agent having a free choice is a great good for the agent; and a greater good the more serious the kind of free will, even if it is incorrectly used." Moreover, an agent "is an ultimate source in an even fuller way if the choices open to him cover the whole moral range, from the very good to the very wrong." And indeed, "an agent who has serious and efficacious free will is in a much fuller way an ultimate source of the direction of things in the world" than one who does not.[10] Furthermore, in preparation for his theodicy, Swinburne contends that:

It is a good for us if our experiences are not wasted but are used for the good of others, if they are the means of a benefit which would not have come to others without them, which will at least in part compensate for those experiences. It follows from this insight that it is a blessing for a person if the possibility of his suffering makes possible the good for others of having the free choice of hurting or harming him; and . . . of choosing to show or not show sympathy . . . [11]

To illustrate the import of these claims for theodicy, Swinburne discusses the example of the slave trade from Africa in the eighteenth century. About this practice he writes, in what is by now a well-known passage:

But God allowing this to occur made possible innumerable opportunities for very large numbers of people to contribute or not to contribute to the development of this culture; for slavers to choose to enslave or not; for plantation-owners to choose to buy slaves or not and to treat them well or ill; for ordinary white people and politicians to campaign for its abolition or not to bother, and to campaign for compensation for the victims or not to bother; and so on. There is also the great good for those who themselves suffered as slaves that their lives were not useless, their vulnerability to suffering made possible many free choices, and thereby so many steps towards the formation of good or bad character.[12]

One problem for this line of thought is that it finds itself in opposition to strongly ingrained moral practice when horrible evil is at issue. First, as David Lewis points out, for us the evildoer's freedom is a weightless consideration, not merely an outweighed consideration.[13] When the slave traders come to take your children, and you are contemplating violent resistance, we do not expect you to consider the value of the slave traders' efficacious but immoral free will, which would be high indeed if value of this sort could have the role in justifying God's allowing the slave trade that Swinburne suggests it does. Moreover, if he is right, then when twenty slave traders have freely decided to try to take your children, ten times as much value of the sort he describes would be at stake as when there are only two, and there would be that much more reason not to resist. Moreover, all else being equal, there would be significantly less reason to harm in self-defense an opponent who appears to have free will then one who is known to be mentally ill and incapable of free decisions.[14] None of this has a role in our ordinary moral practice.[15]

A further problem for the free will theodicy is occasioned by Swinburne's view that to choose freely to do what is right, one must have a serious countervailing desire to refrain from doing what is right instead, strong enough that it could actually motivate a choice so to refrain.[16] Swinburne thinks that this point supports the free will theodicy, because it can explain why God allows us to have desires to do evil, and, by extension, why God allows choices in accord with those desires. But this claim rather serves to undermine the force of the free will theodicy as an explanation for many horrible evils. For we do not generally believe that the value of a free choice outweighs the disvalue of having desires to perform horribly evil actions, especially if they are strong enough to result in action. For example, the notion that it is more valuable than not for people to have a strong desire to abuse children for the reason that this gives them the opportunity to choose freely not to do so has no purchase on us. Our practice for people with desires of this sort is to provide them with therapy to diminish or eradicate such desires. We have no tendency to believe that the value of making a free decision not to abuse a child made in struggle against a desire to do so carries any weight against the proposal to provide this sort of therapy. Furthermore, were we to encounter someone with a strong desire to abuse children but who nevertheless resisted actively seeking to do so, we would not think that his condition has more value overall than one in which he never had the desire to abuse children in the first place. Moreover, I daresay that a significant proportion of people alive today – well over 90% – have neither intentionally chosen a horrible evil nor had a genuine struggle with a desire to do so – they have never, for instance, tortured, maimed, or murdered, nor seriously struggled with desires to do so. But we do not think that their lives would have been more valuable had they possessed such desires even if every struggle against them had been successful. Thus it is questionable whether God would allow such desires in order to realize the value of certain free choices. This aspect of Swinburne's theodicy may have some credibility with respect to evils that are not horrible, but much less, I think, when it comes to horrible evils. Here I would like to emphasize that if we thought free will did in fact have the proposed degree of intrinsic value, our moral practice would be decidedly different from what it is now – in ways that, given our moral sensibilities, we would find very disturbing.

I should note that some versions of the free will theodicy do not essentially require the libertarian version of free will. For example, Eleonore Stump argues that suffering from moral and natural evil contributes to a humbling recognition of oneself as having a defective will, which in turn can motivate one to turn to God to fix the defect in the will.[17] The defect in the will is that one has a bent toward evil, so that one has a diminished capacity to will what one ought to will. Now, as far as I can see, no feature of this account demands libertarian free will, nor even a notion of free will of the sort required for moral responsibility. Indeed, hard determinism can accommodate the causal process that Stump specifies. Nothing about this process, as she describes it, requires an indeterministic conception of free will, nor does it require that the agent be morally responsible, in this case praiseworthy, for turning to God on the occasion of suffering.

THE RETRIBUTIVE PUNISHMENT THEODICY

Another traditional theodicy that potentially requires libertarian free will is that God brings about or allows evil as punishment for sin. Now no feature of hard determinism per se rules out a deterrence theory or a moral education theory of punishment, but retributivism, as it is usually conceived, would be precluded. What is lost as a result? It is implausible to think that in William Rowe's example, the five-year-old girl deserves to be punished by being raped and beaten by virtue of anything she has done.[18] Does an ordinary person, never having committed a serious crime, and who is not in any other respect an extraordinary sinner, deserve to suffer from a lengthy, painful, and fatal disease as punishment for the wrongs he has done?[19] Our judicial system would regard punishment of this sort *for serious crimes* as monstrous. Imagine if we were to punish *murderers* by inducing such suffering – who would find that conscionable?

Someone might reply that because each of us deserves an eternity of torture, *a fortiori* each of us also deserves suffering of this sort. But because it is doubtful that anyone genuinely understands why we all might deserve punishment of this degree as a matter of retributive justice alone, this line of thought does not promise a plausible theodicy. Let me emphasize that even thinking of ordinary people as deserving a long and painful disease, for example, would constitute a serious revision in our moral practice, for in that practice, sympathy without reservation is the appropriate response.[20]

DOING AND ALLOWING

The libertarian view would appear to enjoy a considerable advantage precisely in making possible a theodicy for the consequences of freely willed evil decisions. For it need only grant that God allows these consequences, whereas divine determinism seems constrained to accept that God actively brings them about. When one envisions some particularly egregious past horror, it might be especially difficult to accept that God actively brought it about. I find it very difficult to reconcile myself to such particular claims. But is it any easier to reconcile oneself to the claim that God *allows* that specific horror? Suppose that you are subjected to abuse by someone who hates you. If the abuser had libertarian free will, then even though God did not actively bring about the decision to abuse you, God nevertheless allowed the consequences of this decision to occur while at the same time having the power to prevent them. In the divine determinist view, by contrast, God actively brings about these consequences. Factoring in providence, on the libertarian view, God allows the abuse to occur in order to realize a greater good, whereas on the determinist view, God actively brings it about in order to realize a greater good.

One should first note that although it is often held that actively bringing about or *doing* evil is prima facie morally worse than merely *allowing* evil, of course it is not as if allowing evil is generally morally permissible. Rather, in comparing the libertarian and determinist theological conceptions on this issue, the important question is this: Supposing that on the libertarian position God is justified in allowing evil consequences for the sake of some greater good, would it be morally worse for God actively to bring them about for the sake of that good? The answer to this question depends at least in part on the nature of the good to be realized. In some cases, God might well be justified in allowing the evil consequences, but not in actively bringing them about. By analogy, a parent might justifiably allow a child to play with matches, foreseeing that he might well incur a slight burn as a result, although it would be wrong for the parent to actively bring about that burn.[21] But consider, for instance, the purported good of retributively justified punishment where the evil consequences in question are actively brought about by agents other than God who are not appropriate authorities for inflicting the punishment at issue. If these evils are to be justified as retributive punishment, it would actually seem *better* for God actively to bring them about than merely to allow these other agents to do so. By analogy, if Lee Harvey Oswald did in fact kill John F. Kennedy, and if Oswald did deserve the death penalty, it would have been better for an appropriate authority to administer the penalty than for that authority to allow Jack Ruby to kill him. Assuming that God is an appropriate authority for punishment, it would then be better that God actively bring about some punishment than merely allow a person who is not an appropriate authority to do so.

Consider, furthermore, the good of soul building that John Hick discusses.[22] Suppose God knew that someone's character would be significantly improved morally if he suffered in a certain way, and that God would be justified in allowing the person to suffer on such grounds. Wouldn't God then also be justified in actively bringing about the suffering on those grounds? An apt analogy would seem to be that of say, Civil War surgery. Suppose the doctor knows that the patient will not survive unless he undergoes painful surgery. It is clearly not morally worse for the doctor to actually perform the surgery himself than it would be for him to allow another doctor to perform it.

Now indeed the intrinsic value of serious and efficacious free will would not be realizable if God actively caused rather than merely allowed the conse-quences of evil free decisions. But several key goods could be realized whether God actively brought about or merely allowed the suffering required for those goods, and for them it would appear at least as good for God to bring about the suffering as to allow it.

SKEPTICAL THEISM

What position on the problem of evil is open to the divine determinist? A nonretributive punishment theodicy is available, as is a modified form of the soul-building theodicy, as well as a version of Alvin Plantinga's theodicy, according to which sin and suffering are required for the greater good of the incarnation and atonement.[23] But rather than advocate a full-fledged theodicy, I prefer to side with skeptical theism, developed in recent times by Stephen Wykstra and William Alston, among others.[24] Skeptical theism claims that because of the limitations of our cognitive capacities, the nature of the good is or might well be beyond our understanding to such a degree that we should not expect to understand how it is that God's governance of the universe accords with divine goodness. Various problems for skeptical theism have been raised. To my mind, an especially serious one is that it might occasion further skeptical analogues and consequences that we would want to avoid. I shall argue that one main version of this threat is especially serious for possible goods that essentially involve libertarian free will, but not for certain possible goods that are independent of this sort of free will.[25]

The version of this challenge to skeptical theism on which I want to focus has been advanced by Bruce Russell, and it claims that this view will have skeptical consequences for our moral practice.[26] If the theist claims that there are goods not fully understood by us that could not have been realized had God prevented various horrible evils, and that God might well be justified in allowing these evils in order to realize those goods, then there might well be situations in which we fail to prevent evils of these kinds where we do no wrong. In fact, we may on some such occasions be obligated not to prevent these evils. Or at very least, on certain occasions we might have to give serious consideration to reasons not to prevent those evils when ordinary moral practice would not give serious consideration to such reasons. Let us call this *the challenge from skeptical consequences for morality.*

Now Alston, Daniel Howard-Snyder, and Michael Bergmann have replied to this objection by claiming in effect that in morally justifying our actions, we are limited to goods that we understand, whereas the possible goods the skeptical theist is adducing are at least to some degree beyond our understanding.[27] But this does not seem right; our moral justifications should not be limited to goods we understand – as Russell in fact argues. Let me amplify Russell's contention. Consider first an analogy to the skeptical theist's situation that features only human agents.[28] Fred assists doctors in a clinic that specializes, among other things, in a painful bone disease. He is careful to note what the doctors do to help the patients. Suppose that Fred has excellent reason to trust the doctors as thoroughly competent. The clinic stocks morphine as a painkiller, and Fred knows that if morphine were administered to the bone disease patients, their acute pain would be relieved. But the doctors never, in his experience, have given morphine to patients suffering from this disease, even though they, in his experience, have given it to other patients in the clinic. Fred has no inkling why they do not administer the morphine to the bone disease patients. However, for all he knows, they might have given it to such patients in certain circumstances in the past, although he has no reasonable guess as to frequency, and he has no idea of what these circumstances might be. One day, because of a hurricane, all the doctors are away from the clinic, but Fred is there. A patient is suffering from the bone disease, and Fred has the opportunity to administer morphine. It would seem that he has some significant moral reason not to do so.

Now consider the skeptical theist's analogous situation. Sue, a doctor, knows that there have been thousands of cases of people suffering horribly from disease X. She is a skeptical theist who believes that God is justified for the sake of goods beyond her ken in not preventing these thousands of cases of suffering (she trusts God in a way analogous to the way in which Fred trusts the bone specialists). Suppose that her belief in God is rational, and also that her belief regarding the God-justifying goods is rational. In addition, for all she knows, God in the past might have prevented people from suffering from this disease under certain circumstances, although she has no reasonable guess as to how often God might have done this, and she has no idea of what these circumstances might be. Now a drug that cures disease X has just been developed, and Sue is deciding whether to administer it. Sue's situation seems similar to Fred's: it would seem that insofar as Sue is rational in believing that God has significant moral reason to allow thousands of people to suffer from disease X, she has significant moral reason not to administer the drug that cures disease X – even if in the last analysis, she should administer the drug because the reasons she has to heal the sick and to relieve suffering are stronger.[29]

Stump raises an objection of this sort as a possible rejoinder to her "fixing the will" theodicy. She says "someone might object . . . that this solution to the problem of evil prohibits us from any attempt to relieve human suffering and in fact suggests that we ought to promote it, as the means to man's salvation." In reply, she argues that:

Because God can use suffering to cure an evil will, it does not follow that we can do so also. God can see into the minds and hearts of human beings and determine what sort and amount of suffering is likely to produce the best results; we cannot . . . Furthermore, God as parent creator has a right to, and a responsibility for, painful correction of his creatures, which we as sibling creatures do not have. Therefore, since all human suffering is prima facie evil, and since we do not know with any high degree of probability how much (if any) of it is likely to result in good to any particular sufferer on any particular occasion, it is reasonable for us to eliminate the suffering as much as we can. At any rate, the attempt to eliminate suffering is likely to be beneficial to our characters, and passivity in the face of others' suffering will have no such good effects.[30]

The analogy between Fred and Sue casts some doubt on some of these contentions. In Stump's view, the evil will can be cured through both moral and natural evil. To the extent that we are capable of bringing about moral evil and preventing natural evil, it would seem that we can indeed help to bring about the suffering that would cure the will. Moreover, our duty not to produce but rather to prevent suffering is in a sense not absolute; a doctor might actually be obligated actively to bring about suffering if it is required for the sake of a great-enough medical good. And even if we do not know with any high degree of probability whether suffering is likely to be beneficial, this fact would not all by itself remove the obligation to take this consideration seriously in moral deliberation. Still, as we shall now see, in a skeptical theist account, the good Stump adduces has an advantage over those that require libertarian free will.

There is a continuum of possible God-justifying goods that potentially serve the aims of skeptical theism, ranging from goods of which we haven't the least knowledge, through those of which we have some but nevertheless incomplete knowledge. As I have argued, skeptical theism does suggest a general threat to ordinary moral practice. However, of those goods of which we have some inkling, some would yield a more substantial threat than others. Consider the skeptical theist's claim that the following hypothesis is true for all we know: The intrinsic value of serious and efficacious free will justifies God in allowing certain horrible evils – whose point we cannot otherwise see. Weight given to this hypothesis would pose a clear and immediate threat to our moral practice. For we would have reasonable beliefs as to where this intrinsic value is to be found and how to secure it, and this would then give rise to certain prima facie obligations. For example, we could have a reasonable belief as to whether a slave trader was freely willing his aims, and we would have a prima facie obligation to take the intrinsic value of his serious and efficacious free will into consideration in deciding what to do by way of defense against him. But again, as Lewis remarks, the value of free will is now a weightless consideration for us, and thus we would face a disruptive effect on our moral practice.

Consider, in addition, the skeptical theist's claim that the following hypothesis is true for all we know: The value of retributive punishment justifies God in allowing certain horrible evils, whose point we cannot otherwise see. Suppose a skeptical theist were to suggest the hypothesis that ordinary people suffer from painful diseases as retribution for sinful inner lives.[31] It might well be that we are in no epistemic condition to tell whether any ordinary person's inner life merits suffering of this kind. But weight given to this hypothesis would give rise to reasons to abandon the unreserved sympathy we have for ordinary people who suffer from painful diseases. This, again, would constitute a clear and immediate threat to our moral practice.

But there are skeptical theist hypotheses regarding other goods of which we have some inkling, which would not yield such a clear and immediate threat, and the reasons are epistemic. Stump's proposal is a case in point. As she herself points out, it would never be reasonably clear to us when suffering would have the beneficial effect of motivating the agent to turn to God, nor how much would be required to have this effect. So in this case, the undermining threat to our moral practice would not be clear and immediate. The good of our identifying with God in suffering that Marilyn Adams discusses is like this as well. We would be completely in the dark, I would think, whether someone would be able to re-envision her suffering as a point of identification with God.[32] The same is true for the good of the incarnation and atonement that Plantinga adduces. Suppose we believed that God might well allow evils as a requirement for the atonement in particular, the purpose of which is to reconcile the world to God. We would have very limited knowledge as to where or to what degree such evils would be required. So on the assumption that this hypothesis is true, the threat of our moral practice being undermined is not clear and immediate. It must be acknowledged that even if for these sorts of goods the threat to moral practice is not clear and immediate, the prospect of realizing these goods might still occasion some loss of resolve to prevent suffering.[33] However, here a consideration raised by Swinburne, William Alston, and Steve Layman is pertinent, that the difference in powers and in authority between God and us, or facts about God's relation to us that derive from these differences, might have significant consequences for the justification of allowing or bringing about suffering.[34] For example, given God's epistemic capacities relative to ours, there are goods for the sake of which God's allowing or bringing about evil might well be justified whereas our doing the same would not. Accordingly, I would draw the following tentative conclusion: skeptical theism that adduces goods essentially involving libertarian free will gives rise to an especially serious version of the challenge from skeptical consequences for morality, although this is not the case for several prominent examples of goods that do not essentially involve free will.

DIVINE PROVIDENCE

Does divine determinism undermine the comfort and the meaning in life that a belief in divine providence potentially provides? The understanding that everything that happens is causally determined by God in accord with a divine plan for the world could indeed be a comfort to us. A problem one might raise for this conception is that any individual person would be participating in that plan without freely willing that participation – where freely willing participation includes not only choosing it without being determined to do so, but also adequately understanding in advance what one is participating in. But there is reason to hold that believing one has a role in a great divine plan, even if one does not freely will one's participation, could provide comfort in one's suffering and a sense of meaning for one's life. It is well known that during the early years of the Civil War, Abraham Lincoln's leading purpose was to preserve the Union, and not to end slavery.[35] But later he began to waver on this issue, and, what is more, to have a sense that God had a purpose for the war that he, Lincoln, did not initially have. A few years into the war he wrote:

I am almost ready to say this is probably true – that God wills this contest, and wills that it shall not end yet. By his mere quiet power, on the minds of the now contestants, he could have either saved or destroyed the Union without a human contest. Yet the contest began. And having begun, He could give the final victory to either side any day. Yet the contest proceeds.[36]

And then in 1864 we find Lincoln saying:

I claim not to have controlled events, but confess plainly that events have controlled me. Now, at the end of three years' struggle the nation's condition is not what either party, or any man, devised or expected. God alone can claim it. Whither it is tending seems plain. If God now wills the removal of a great wrong, and wills also that we of the North as well as you of the South shall pay fairly for our complicity in that wrong, impartial history will find therein new cause to attest and revere the justice and goodness of God.[37]

One's sense is that Lincoln's conception of the Civil War as a key component in God's plan to end slavery in the United States reconciled Lincoln to the evils of that struggle and gave it immense significance for him, despite the fact that he did not initially choose to fight the war for the reasons he came to believe God had for ordaining it, and thus even though at first he did not freely participate in the divine plan as he later conceived it.

But what about the suffering that God's plan might involve – suffering that given divine determinism, none of us endorse with free will? Would one's conviction that everything that happens is determined in accord with that plan nevertheless provide adequate comfort in suffering? According to the Stoic view, God determines everything that happens in accord with the good of the whole universe, and the nature of this good is incompletely understood on our part.[38] There is an all-encompassing divine plan, neither whose nature nor means of realization we understand very well if at all, but yet we can know that everything that happens is determined by God with an aim to the realization of that plan. One can reconcile oneself to the suffering in one's life by abandoning one's merely personal concerns – that is, one's ordinary human aspirations for personal survival, happiness, and success – by identifying with these divine aims. Descartes, in a letter to Chanut, eloquently expresses the Stoic idea (that is, if we take his reference to free will to be compatibilist). In this excerpt, he sets out "the path one ought to follow to arrive at the love of God:"

But if . . . we heed the infinity of his power, through which he has created so many things, of which we are the least part; the extension of his providence that makes him see in one thought alone everything that has been, is, shall be, and could be; the infallibility of his decrees which, although they do not disturb our free will, nevertheless cannot in any fashion be changed; and finally, if, on the one hand, we heed our insignificance, and if, on the other hand, we heed the grandeur of all created things, by noting the manner in which they depend on God and by considering them in a fashion that has a relationship to his omnipotence . . . meditation upon all this so abundantly fills the man who hears it with such extreme joy that, realizing he would have to be abusive and ungrateful toward God to wish to occupy

God's place, he thinks himself as already having lived sufficiently because God has given him the grace to reach such knowledge, and willingly and entirely joining himself to God, he loves God so perfectly that he desires nothing more in the world than that God's will be done. That is the reason he no longer fears either death, or pains, or disgraces, because he knows that nothing can happen to him save what God shall have decreed; and he so loves this divine decree, esteems it so just and so necessary, knows he ought so entirely to depend upon it, that even when he awaits death or some other evil, if *per impossibile* he could change that decree, he would not wish to do so. But if he does not refuse evils or afflictions, because they come to him from divine providence, he refuses still less all the goods or licit pleasures one can enjoy in this life, because they too issue from that providence; and accepting them with joy, without having any fear of evils, his love renders him perfectly happy.[39]

In Descartes's understanding, if one's love for God were of the right sort, one's identification with the aims of God would be so thorough that even if one could, one would not refuse one's own death or other personal suffering, because one understands them as proceeding from the decree of God.

In the Stoic conception, we should align ourselves with the divine perspective so that we will enjoy equanimity no matter what happens, even if the divine plan conflicts with the good as conceived from one's personal point of view. This vision seems a little glassy-eyed; one might doubt whether such a reason is sufficient to motivate many of us. As Thomas Nagel remarks, normally "one is supposed to behold and partake of the glory of God, for example, in a way in which chickens do not share in the glory of *coq au vin.*"[40] To consider an extreme case, if one believed in divine determinism and in eternal damnation, then one's comfort and sense of meaning might well be compromised, certainly in the case of the person who was convinced that he himself was eternally damned, but even for the believer who feels assured of his salvation. For then God's care for the universe would allow for God's deterministically causing the lives of certain persons to be endlessly miserable. The comfort that might result from believing that everything that happens is determined by a being with this sort of character would not, in my estimation, be unequivocal.[41]

However, what if the point of the divine plan were to reconcile everything – including every person – to God. The Christian scriptures state that this will happen through the incarnation and atonement of Christ. So what if:

Ephesians 1:8–10: [God] has made known to us in all wisdom and insight the mystery of his will, according to his purpose which he set forth in Christ as a plan for the fulness of time, to unite all things in him, things in heaven and things on earth?

And what if for each of us:

Romans 8:18: Our present sufferings are not worth comparing with the glory that will be revealed in us?

Then God would not determine any of us to a life of endless misery. Moreover, what if, as Marilyn Adams suggests, God is in the end good to every person by insuring each a life in which all of the suffering experienced contributes to a greater good within that very life?[42] Then it might even be, as Plantinga states it, that God would know that if I were able to make the decision whether to accept the suffering, and knew enough about the divine plan, and had the right affections, then I myself would accept the suffering.[43] Then each of us would say, by analogy with Lincoln on the Civil War, that the suffering was worth the result even if we did not in fact freely endorse either the suffering or the result.

CONCLUSION

So it may be that traditional theistic religion does not require libertarian free will. It might be that Molinism is theologically preferable, but I believe that there is a deterministic perspective that is not decidedly worse. At least, given our limited cognitive capacities and our lack of ability to understand divine purposes, we should not be confident in judging that the deterministic perspective is decidedly worse. It is indeed difficult for us to believe that God brings about the horrors of this world, but it is perhaps no less difficult to believe that God merely allows them, especially if, as I have argued, it is implausible that the goods that essentially involve free will can justify God's allowing these evils. But if we focused instead on the good that the traditional theistic religions view as the goal of history, then, despite initial appearances, a deterministic conception of the plan for realizing that good might well turn out to be as attractive as a Molinist alternative.[44]

NOTES

1. Luis de Molina, *Liberi Arbitrii cum Gratiae Donis, Divina Praescientia, Providentia, Praedestinatione et Reprobatione Concordia* (1595), tr. (of Part IV) A. J. Freddoso, *On Divine Foreknowledge: Part IV of the Concordia* (Ithaca, NY: Cornell University Press, 1988). For an excellent exposition and defense of Molina's position, see Thomas Flint, *Divine Providence: The Molinist Account* (Ithaca, NY: Cornell University Press, 1998).
2. Perhaps Friedrich Schleiermacher had hard determinist views, at least early in his career. I was made aware of this possibility by Andrew Dole's "Schleiermacher's Early Essay on Freedom," a paper he presented at a conference of the Society for Christian

Philosophers in Bloomington, Indiana, in September 2002. The manuscript version of Schleiermacher's essay has no title. It was originally published in excerpted form in Wilhelm Dilthey's *Leben Schleiermachers* under the title "Über die Frieheit des Menschen." In the *Friedrich Schleiermacher Kritische Gesamtausgabe* (Berlin: Walter De Gruyter, 1983), it appears as "Über die Frieheit" (KGA I.1, 1984, 217–357), which has been translated into English as *On Freedom* (Lewiston: Edwin Mellen Press, 1992).

3. William Mann, "God's Freedom, Human Freedom, and God's Responsibility for Sin," in *Divine and Human Action*, ed. Thomas V. Morris (Ithaca, NY: Cornell University Press, 1988), 182–210.

4. For my view on retributivism, see my *Living without Free Will* (New York: Cambridge University Press, 2001), 159–61. In this book I develop my more general perspective on free will and moral responsibility.

5. Jürgen Moltmann, *The Crucified God* (New York: Harper and Row, 1974).

6. Richard Swinburne, *Responsibility and Atonement* (Oxford: Oxford University Press, 1989).

7. Friedrich Schleiermacher, *The Christian Faith*, ed. Mackintosh and Stewart (Philadelphia: T&T Clark, 1928) 550–1.

8. See Keith DeRose's "Universalism and the Bible," on his website, http://pantheon.yale.edu/~kd47.

9. Steven Boër, "The Irrelevance of the Free Will Defense," *Analysis* 38 (1978): 110–12; J. L. Mackie, "Evil and Omnipotence," *Mind* 64 (1955): 200–12.

10. Richard Swinburne, *Providence and the Problem of Evil* (Oxford: Oxford University Press, 1998) 82–9.

11. Ibid., 103.

12. Ibid., 245.

13. David Lewis, "Evil for Freedom's Sake," *Philosophical Papers* 22 (1993): 149–72, at p. 155.

14. Mark Moyer made this point in conversation.

15. When this paper was presented at Yale University, Swinburne argued that only God has the authority to allow people to suffer intensely in order to secure the intrinsic value of free will, drawing on the analogy of parents and children. However, there is at least no epistemic problem here for us. There are epistemic reasons that nondoctors should refrain from performing painful operations on patients in order to secure medical goods. Nondoctors usually don't know enough to be successful at realizing medical goods by such means. But there is no analogous problem for allowing or causing people to suffer for the sake of securing the intrinsic value of serious and efficacious free will, for all adult human beings can typically understand well enough where that value is to be had, and how to secure it.

16. Swinburne actually makes a stronger claim than this: see his *Providence and the Problem of Evil*, 85–6.

17. Eleonore Stump, "The Problem of Evil," *Faith and Philosophy* 2 (1985): 392–423.

18. William Rowe, "The Evidential Argument from Evil: A Second Look," in *The Evidential Argument from Evil*, Daniel Howard-Snyder, ed. (Indianapolis: Indiana University Press, 1996), 262–85.

19. For an opposing perspective, see William Alston, "The Inductive Argument from Evil and the Human Cognitive Condition," *Philosophical Perspectives* 5 (1991): 27–67;

reprinted in *The Evidential Argument from Evil*, ed. Daniel Howard-Snyder (Indianapolis: Indiana University Press, 1996), 97–125, section V.

20. This general issue is raised in the ninth chapter of the Gospel of John, which begins as follows:

John 9:1–3. As he walked along, he saw a man blind from birth. His disciples asked him, "Rabbi, who sinned, this man or his parents, that he was born blind?" Jesus answered, "Neither this man nor his parents sinned; he was born blind so that God's works might be revealed in him."

21. Thanks to Andrew Chignell for this point and example.
22. John Hick, *Evil and the God of Love*, 2nd ed. (New York: Harper and Row, 1978).
23. Alvin Plantinga, "Supralapsarianism or *O Felix Culpa*," ms.
24. See, for example, Stephen J. Wykstra, "The Human Obstacle to Evidential Arguments from Suffering: On Avoiding the Evils of 'Appearance,'" *International Journal for Philosophy of Religion* 16 (1984): 73–94, and "Rowe's Noseeum Arguments from Evil" in *The Evidential Argument from Evil*, ed. Daniel Howard-Snyder, 126–50; also William Alston's "The Inductive Argument from Evil." These skeptical theist accounts were occasioned by William Rowe's "The Problem of Evil and Some Varieties of Atheism," *American Philosophical Quarterly* 16 (1979): 335–41. Immanuel Kant developed a version of this strategy in his late essay "On the Miscarriage of all Philosophical Trials in Theodicy," of which an English translation appears in *Religion within the Boundaries of Mere Reason and Other Writings*, trans. and eds. Allen Wood and George di Giovanni (New York: Cambridge University Press, 1998); see also my "Kant on God, Evil, and Teleology," *Faith and Philosophy* 13 (1996): 508–33.
25. I discuss skeptical theism in more detail in "The Problem of Evil," in *The Blackwell Guide to the Philosophy of Religion*, ed. William E. Mann (Oxford: Blackwell, 2004) 148–70, at 159–6.
26. Bruce Russell, "Defenseless," in *The Evidential Argument from Evil*, ed. Howard-Snyder, 193–205, at pp. 197–8.
27. Michael Bergmann, "Skeptical Theism and Rowe's New Evidential Argument from Evil," *Nous* 35 (2001): 278–96, Daniel Howard-Snyder, "The Argument From Inscrutable Evil," in *The Evidential Argument from Evil*, ed. Howard-Snyder, 286–310, at pp. 292–3.
28. I present an example of this sort in my "The Problem of Evil," 164–5.
29. Thanks to David Christensen, Michael Bergmann, and Daniel Howard-Snyder for discussions that helped formulate this example and that influenced what follows.
30. Eleonore Stump, "The Problem of Evil," 412–3.
31. See Alston, "The Inductive Argument from Evil," section V.
32. Marilyn Adams, *Horrendous Evils and the Goodness of God* (Ithaca, NY: Cornell University Press, 1999).
33. Thanks to Andrew Chignell for prompting this clarification.
34. Richard Swinburne, *Providence and the Problem of Evil*, 243; the comment by Steve Layman is in Daniel Howard-Snyder's "The Argument from Inscrutable Evil," 292; William Alston, "Some (Temporarily) Final Thoughts," in *The Evidential Argument from Evil*, ed. Howard-Snyder, 311–32, at p. 321.
35. Lincoln wrote to Horace Greeley: "My paramount object in this struggle is to save the Union, and is not either to save or destroy slavery. If I could save the Union

without freeing any slave I would do it, and if I could save it by freeing some of the slaves I would do it; and if I could save it by freeing some and leaving others alone I would also do that. What I do about slavery, and the colored race, I do because it helps to save the Union." (In Stephen B. Oates, *With Malice Towards None: The Life of Abraham Lincoln* [New York: New American Library, 1977], 340.)

36. Stephen B. Oates, *With Malice Towards None*, 343.

37. Stephen B. Oates, *With Malice Towards None*, 416. Lincoln wrote in the Second Inaugural Address of 1865:

> If we shall suppose that American slavery is one of those offenses which, in the providence of God, must needs come, but which, having continued through His appointed time, He now wills to remove, and that He gives to both North and South this terrible war as the woe due to those by whom the offense came, shall we discern therein any departure from those divine attributes which the believers in a living God always ascribe to Him? Fondly do we hope, fervently do we pray, that this mighty scourge of war may speedily pass away. Yet, if God wills that it continue until all the wealth piled by the bondsman's two hundred and fifty years of unrequited toil shall be sunk, and until every drop of blood drawn with the lash shall be paid by another drawn with the sword, as was said three thousand years ago, so still it must be said "the judgments of the Lord are true and righteous altogether."

38. I discuss these issues in "Stoic Psychotherapy in Descartes and Spinoza," *Faith and Philosophy* 11 (1994): 592–625.

39. Descartes to Chanut, Feb. 1, 1647, AT (*Oeuvres de Descartes*, ed. Ch. Adam and P. Tannery [revised edition, Paris: Vrin/C.N.R.S., 1964–76.]) IV, 608–9. The translation is from John J. Blom, *Descartes, His Moral Philosophy and Psychology* (New York: NYU Press, 1978): 206–7.

40. Thomas Nagel, "The Absurd," in *Mortal Questions* (New York: Cambridge University Press, 1979), 16.

41. What explains my disagreement with a large sector of the Christian theological tradition on this issue? By contrast with many in this tradition, for me it is highly unintuitive that divine determinism is compatible with the sort of retributivism that would justify eternal damnation.

42. Marilyn Adams, *Horrendous Evils and the Goodness of God*, 55.

43. Alvin Plantinga, "Supralapsarianism or *O Felix Culpa*," (ms.).

44. This paper benefited from questions and comments at the conference at Yale University at which it was first presented, and from discussions at the University of San Francisco and at the University of Minnesota, Morris. Thanks in addition to Michael Bergmann, David Christensen, Mark Moyer, Daniel Howard-Snyder, and the editors of this volume for helpful commentary.

4

∾

Two Cheers for Mystery!

WILLIAM ALSTON

I

One finds in contemporary Anglo-American analytic philosophy of religion what looks to be a considerable degree of confidence in human powers to determine what God is like; how to construe his basic attributes; and what his purposes, plans, standards, values, and so on are – and to determine these in some detail. I do not suggest that anyone thinks we can attain a *comprehensive* knowledge of God's nature and doings. But on many crucial points, there seems to be a widespread confidence in our ability to determine exactly how things are with God.

There are lively arguments as to whether God's being is temporal or atemporal; whether God is free in various respects – free to do wrong, free to either create something(s) other than himself or not, free to create something less than a best of all possible worlds; whether God has obligations; what the conditions are under which God permits suffering, for example, whether it is only on condition that the suffering is necessary for some good (or avoidance of evil) that outweighs it, or only on condition that it is necessary for a benefit to the *sufferer* that outweighs it; whether God undergoes emotional states, whether, for example, he is pained by human wrongdoing. The topic of divine knowledge is a particularly rich field for such investigations. Does God have foreknowledge of human free actions? Does God have "middle knowledge" – knowledge of what free choice a given human being would make in a certain possible situation? Is all of God's knowledge intuitive? Is it propositionally structured? To cite a controversy in which I have been involved, does God have beliefs? And so on.

These controversies are typically conducted under the assumption that our cognitive relation to God, our (best) modes of conceptualization of and thinking about God, are such as to make it possible for us to arrive at the exact truth on such issues. In this essay, I want to set this confidence against a quite different assumption – that God is inevitably so *mysterious* to us, to our rational capacities – indeed that he is the *supreme* mystery – that nothing we can think, believe, or say about him is *strictly* true of God as he is in himself. Let's call this the Divine Mystery Thesis (DMT). I will plump for giving divine mystery more recognition than it customarily receives in my cultural circle. But I must confess to a certain degree of ambivalence with respect to this alternative. Though I find impressive support for DMT, I find myself unwilling to write off all attempts to determine just what God is like. Hence, I will not offer a straightforward argument for DMT, much less seek to establish it conclusively. Rather, I shall suggest that there are grounds for taking it seriously as an alternative perspective. And my main concern here will be to explore how on this alternative our thought and talk about God in terms of our concepts (whose else?) can still be close enough to the truth about God to serve as a guide for our religious thought and behavior. Hence the title, a variant on E. M. Forster's *Two Cheers for Democracy*.

II

The first item on my agenda is to indicate some strands in the Christian tradition that favor the DMT. I don't mean to suggest that such support is limited to Christianity. But because the Christian tradition is what I am most familiar with, and because I am not concerned here with comparative religions, I will limit my specific references to that, much of which is easily generalizable to other theistic religions. And the most prominent nontheistic religions in the world today are much more unambiguously committed to the DMT.

1. My first point is a very general and basic one. I don't know whether it should be called a "strand in the Christian tradition," but it is a plausible way of thinking, and one that underlies the more familiar strands to which I shall turn momentarily. If we think about the relation of human cognitive powers to the absolutely infinite source of all that is other than itself, it seems reasonable to suppose that the former would not be in a position to get an account of the latter that is exactly correct, even in certain abstract respects. We have a hard enough time crafting a picture of the physical world, not to mention the mind and society, of the complete correctness of which we can be assured. How much less can we expect such a result when we turn our thoughts to an infinite source of all being? You may think that it is possible for God to come to our rescue and reveal to us certain truths about his nature, purposes, plans, activities, and so on. But given the way he has chosen to deal with us, in order to communicate with us, he has to use language we can

understand, and the conceptual limitations of such language is one form of the disability just suggested. "But if Jesus Christ is divine, the incarnate second person of the Trinity, don't some of his utterances completely come up to the mark?" This runs into the same problem of these utterances being couched in human language and thus subject to the same conceptual limitation. Though I find this line of thought plausible, I don't want to lay much stress on it, in comparison with the other supports I go on to mention.

2. Next there is the view, widespread in patristic and medieval theology, that God is absolutely simple. This is meant in a very strong sense, according to which there is no real distinction in God between different attributes, attitudes, and actions. This view can be found in Augustine, Anselm, Aquinas, and many others. As Aquinas trenchantly points out (*Summa Theologiae* (ST), I, 13 and elsewhere), this has the consequence that everything we can say about God, at least of a positive character, is more or less defective. All our propositional thought and speech is necessarily carried on by making distinctions – between subject and predicate, between different predicates that are applied to the same subject, and so on. You may object that this conclusion implies that the very premise on which it depends, that God is absolutely simple, is itself not strictly true. But the response lies in that saving qualification, "of a positive character." For the attribution of divine simplicity to God is thoroughly negative. It consists in denying each and every conceivable form of multiplicity in the divine being. A being in whom there is no real distinction between thoughts, actions, intentions, and attributes clearly presents a mystery to our faculties.

3. Another fertile source of the DMT is found in the puzzles, paradoxes, and insoluble problems to which theological thought seems so frequently to lead. In Christianity, the central doctrines of the Trinity and the Incarnation are signal cases in point. Despite strenuous efforts by the best minds, the explanation of how there can be only one God but three divine persons and how one and the same individual, Jesus Christ, can be fully human and fully divine seems to persistently evade our grasp. And moving to less distinctively Christian themes, there are the familiar paradoxes of omnipotence, of absolute goodness and freedom, and of divine omniscience and human free will. So strong has been the aura of mystery that pervades traditional Christianity that the movement of natural religion (explored in Hume's famous *Dialogues*) was impelled by a hunger for a form of religion in which everything would be clear and simple, well within the grasp of any normal human intellect.

For that matter, the problem of evil that even the natural religion of the eighteenth century could not escape, as Hume pointed out so acutely, spawns mysteries aplenty. Why does God allow such a massive human evil as the Holocaust (which is only an especially efficient item in the millennia-old succession of human massacres), not to mention the ravages of disease? Attempts have not been lacking to dispel the apparent mystery by constructing theodicies that make explicit why God has refrained from preventing such things. But despite the ingenuity of many of these attempts, none of them have commanded general assent, and Job still seems to many of us to exemplify the appropriate response to the question, one that leaves the mystery unresolved. My process theology friends will, of course, tell me that if I were to cease clinging to an unreasonable attachment to absolute divine omnipotence, the evil in the world would not seem so mysterious. And I must confess that if there were no other supports for DMT, I would take more seriously the simpler and neater approach of process theology to the problem. But in the light of those other supports, I am disinclined to go the process theology route.

4. Now I come to what I regard as the most convincing basis for taking divine mystery seriously – experiential acquaintance with God. And, as a preface to this, I need to take note of a fundamental difference between two ways of identifying God – the *descriptive* and the *experiential*. One can distinguish God from other objects of thought and speech by certain identifying attributes – first cause; being itself; absolute and infinite power, knowledge, and goodness; and the like. Or one can identify God as what is experienced by certain persons at certain times and places. The person(s) in question could be oneself, but it could also be historical figures – Moses, the prophets, and so on. This difference between these methods of identifying God makes itself felt in several ways.

The most important of these is in what is, and is not, up for grabs. On the descriptive approach, if God is identified as, for example, the infinitely good, knowing, and powerful being, then there can be no question that God is, for example, omniscient. If it turns out that we were talking about a being that isn't omniscient, that shows we weren't talking about God after all. On the experiential approach, by contrast, no divine attributes enjoy this sacrosanct status. If it should turn out that the being who spoke to Moses in the desert was not omniscient or perfectly good, it doesn't follow that it wasn't God who was speaking. It rather implies that God is different in certain respects from what we had supposed him to be.

To highlight this contrast, I have been speaking in terms of pure approaches. And it is, no doubt, more common for them to be combined. Even if one takes oneself to identify God as the being one has experienced at certain times, one typically also privileges certain descriptions. And even if one identifies God as the one and only absolutely perfect being, one might also take him to be identified as the object of certain experiences. But even if one feels complete confidence in both modes of identification, one of them may be more deeply rooted than the other. What happens if the person becomes convinced that certain identifications from the two modes do not pick out the same being? Which of the two contenders holds fast and which gives way? If the person reacts to such an eventuality by saying "I guess what I was aware of on those occasions wasn't God after all," it is the descriptive mode that is given priority. Whereas if the reaction is "I guess God isn't absolutely omnipotent after all," it is the experiential mode that is calling the shots.

Another important difference between the approaches is that the descriptive approach, but not the experiential, provides for a purely hypothetical discussion of the nature of God. If we can identify God by a set of essential properties, then we can use those properties to specify what God *would* be like *if* God exists. We can then engage in discussions of what else would be true of God, if there is such a being. For example, we can consider whether God, if such there be, would have complete knowledge of all future human actions. Indeed, what is undoubtedly the most widely commented-on discussion of this issue in twentieth century philosophy in English – Nelson Pike's "Divine Omniscience and Voluntary Action" – is conducted without assuming the existence of God. For another noteworthy example of the same phenomenon, consider the seminal article on the problem of evil by William Rowe – "The Problem of Evil and Some Varieties of Atheism," which has spawned a veritable mountain of responses, counterresponses, and so on. Rowe argues that if God were to exist, He would have prevented certain kinds of evil, examples of which do exist. Hence God does not exist. But no such license is enjoyed by those who identify God solely as an object of experience. For they have no way of telling what properties God has, much less what properties are essential to him, except by reflecting on experiences of God and coming to realize what kind of being God experientially reveals himself to be. And by choosing that starting point, they have blocked off any possibility of engaging in the exploration of the nature of God without assuming God to exist.

Let's return to the idea that there is experiential support for the DMT. Those whose most basic way of identifying God is experiential will naturally take the ways God appears to their experience or to the experience of others as the prime source of their view as to what God is like. And there is considerable support in the mystical and contemplative tradition of Christian spirituality for the view that God is, most fundamentally, a mystery to our understanding. I could cite many passages that make this point. Here is one from the enormously influential early medieval mystical theologian, Dionysius the Pseudo-Areopagite:

It [the Divine] is not soul or mind . . . it is not order or greatness or littleness . . . it is not immovable or in motion or at rest, and has no power; and is not power or light, and does not live and is not life ... nor is it one, nor is it Godhead or goodness ... nor does it belong to the category of nonexistence or to that of existence.[1]

One can hardly represent God as more mysterious than that! But lest one should get the impression that such sentiments are confined to long-dead white males, here are some bits from two more recent white males, only one of which is dead, and that for not so long.

First I turn to a Trappist monk who is the leading figure in the Centering Prayer movement, which is an attempt to present the Christian tradition of contemplative prayer in a contemporary dress, videlicet, Thomas Keating. In his book, *Open Mind, Open Heart*, he writes:

Contemplative prayer is the opening of mind and heart, body and emotions – our whole being – to God, the Ultimate Mystery, beyond words, thoughts and emotions.[2]

Our experiences of God ... are not God as He is in Himself. God as He is in Himself cannot be experienced empirically, conceptually or spiritually. He is beyond experiences of any kind ... Anything that we perceive of God can only be a radiance of His presence and not God as He is himself ... When the divine light strikes the human mind, it breaks down into many aspects just as a ray of ordinary light, when it strikes a prism, breaks down into the varied colors of the spectrum. There is nothing wrong with distinguishing different aspects of the Ultimate Mystery, but it would be a mistake to identify them with the inaccessible Light.[3]

Here is a similar passage from Keating's fellow Trappist, Thomas Merton:

Contemplation is, above all, awareness of the reality of the Source of our being. It *knows* the Source obscurely, inexplicably, but with a certitude that goes both beyond reason and beyond simple faith. For contemplation is a kind of spiritual vision to which both reason and faith aspire, by their very nature, because without it they must always remain incomplete. Yet contemplation is not vision because it sees "without seeing" and knows "without knowing." It is a ... knowledge too deep to be grasped in images, in words or even in clear concepts ... in the very moment of trying to indicate what it knows the contemplative mind takes back what it has said, and denies what it has affirmed. For in contemplation we know by "unknowing." Or, better, we know *beyond* all knowing or "unknowing."[4]

You may well wonder why the second passage from Keating was cited as an example of someone's taking God to be an ultimate mystery on the basis of experience of God. For Keating seems to be saying there that an experience of God does *not* reveal what God is in Himself. He even says that God "is beyond experiences *of any kind.*" But perhaps the next passage from Merton, though deliberately paradoxical, provides a corrective to this impression. The "experiences" Keating was speaking of are those taken by their subject to show God to have various features or aspects that we can grasp "conceptually," various distinct properties or attitudes or actions that we can notice, label, and file away. Whereas, Merton says, the knowledge of God one gets in contemplative "experience" is "knowing without knowing." As I say, that is deliberately paradoxical and elusive, and as purely negative as the earlier passage from Dionysius. But the following passage from *New Seeds of Contemplation* gives a more positive idea of the contemplative alternative to experience of the sort Keating was dismissing.

The living God, the God Who is God and not a philosopher's abstraction, lies infinitely beyond the reach of anything our eyes can see or our minds can understand. No matter what perfection you predicate of Him, you have to add that your concept is only a pale analogy of the perfection that is in God, and that He is not literally what you conceive by that term . . . If nothing that can be seen can either be God or represent him to us as He is, then to find God we must pass beyond everything that can be seen and enter into darkness. Since nothing that can be heard is God, to find Him we must enter into silence.

Since God cannot be imagined, anything our imagination tells us about Him is ultimately misleading and therefore we cannot know Him as He really is unless we pass beyond everything that can be imagined and enter into an obscurity without images and without the likeness of any created thing.[5]

But then, what sort of experience or knowledge do we attain when we do that? Merton goes on to say:

God cannot be understood except by Himself. If we are to understand Him we can only do so by being in some way transformed into Him, so that we know Him as He knows Himself. And He does not know Himself by any representation of Himself: His own infinite Being is His own knowledge of Himself and we will not know Him as He knows Himself until we are united to what He is . . .

The very obscurity of faith is an argument of its perfection. It is darkness to our minds because it so far transcends their weakness . . . The closer we get to God, the less is our faith diluted with the half-light of created images and concepts. Our certainty increases with this obscurity . . . And it is in the deepest darkness that we most fully possess God on earth, because it is then that our minds are most truly liberated from the weak, created lights that are darkness in comparison to Him; it is then that we are filled with His infinite Light which seems pure darkness to our reason.[6]

And so by a fundamental transformation in which the subject becomes united to God as much as is possible in this life, one has a taste of what it is like to know God as he knows himself. And this knowledge he realizes to be something radically different from any knowledge we can capture in our concepts and modes of thinking and speech. And this is what tells the contemplative that God is an ultimate mystery that can only be understood in this intuitive knowledge that is beyond images, words, and concepts.

Many similar testimonies could be cited from the millennia of the Christian contemplative tradition. The two twentieth-century figures I have been quoting have been most influenced by St. John of the Cross and the anonymous author of the medieval treatise *The Cloud of Unknowing*. But the themes illustrated by the above passages are omnipresent in the Christian mystical and contemplative tradition. And speaking of mysticism, one feature of what we might call extreme mysticism, in Christianity and elsewhere, is a claim that in the height of mystical experience, the human subject is merged in the divine object and loses its separateness. The more careful writers stress that it is not an ontological identity but what we might call a phenomenological identity. The communion is so intimate that the human subject loses its sense of distinctness from the divine. But be that as it may, the mystic is still an individual person ontologically distinct from God, as he or she realizes once again when he or she emerges from the mystical trance.

One may well ask why we should take the word of these contemplatives for the divine mystery. Why should we suppose that they are in the best position to tell us what God is like? I think the main reason is to be found in the spirituality of their lives, and in the character of their teaching concerning human life and concerning what constitutes the most complete human fulfillment. A documentation of this claim would run far beyond the limits of this essay.

I want to return to the point that I make no claim to have established the DMT. Doubts can be raised about all of the supports I have compiled. Even if our thought, belief, and talk about the divine generates puzzles and problems, the correct solutions to which are not clear to thinkers generally, it could still be reasonably supposed that correct, even generally accepted, solutions are not impossible. Moreover, one could agree that the Trinity, the Incarnation, and the problem of evil pose insoluble problems and still maintain that some strictly true statements can be made about God, thus rejecting the radical position of the DMT. As for the doctrine of absolute divine simplicity, it has been subjected to vigorous criticism more than once.[7] And the appeal to mystical experience is subject to familiar objections to claims of the probative value of religious experience generally – that subjects of such experience construct their experiences on the basis of antecedent beliefs, that explanations in terms of purely natural factors can be given for the experiences, and so on.[8] Nevertheless, I feel that the supports I have cited do show that the DMT is worthy of serious consideration, and that is the most I have been concerned to show here.

III

Now I come to the main problem of this essay, for which the portrayal of the DMT as a serious contender is a propaedeutic. Suppose we go along with the DMT for a moment, assume it so as to explore its implications. Does it require us to eschew any thought and talk of God? Must we be deprived of all guidance in our lives by considerations of what God is like, what his purposes and plans are, what destiny he has laid out for us, what requirements he makes of us, what he proposes to bestow on us under what conditions, and so on? That would be a severe deprivation indeed. And it is often remarked that even the mystics who engage in the toughest talk of divine ineffability, like the bit I just cited from Dionysius, do not practice what they might be supposed to be preaching. They are far from saying nothing positive and significant about God. Quite the contrary! They are among the most verbose and prolific of theologians. So we should not despair of finding some room for thought and talk of God that is of crucial importance for our lives, along with a proper appreciation of divine mystery. I will now consider how this might be managed.

A crucial point is that for the most part, the terms we use to speak of God are taken from our talk of creatures – terms like *purpose, plans, knowledge, love, command, forgive*, and so on. Even if, as the stress on mystery implies, these terms are not strictly true of God in just the same sense as that in which they are sometimes strictly true of creatures (else God could be captured in our conceptual nets), it seems plausible that there must be some *analogy* between human and divine purposes, plans, commands, forgivenesses, and so on. Why else use those terms rather than innumerable others? And the idea that talk of God is *analogical* has surfaced repeatedly in the Christian tradition and other traditions. But we must tread carefully here if we are not to lose the commitment to mystery. The crucial question is this: Are we in a position to specify just how divine knowledge, purpose, and so on are and are not similar to their human prototypes? If we were, then we would be able to frame concepts that contain all and only the points of commonality between divine and human purpose, and so, once again, we would be able to say things of God that are perfectly true, contrary to the DMT. To give divine mystery its due, we must recognize that we cannot whittle away at the creaturely terms until they contain only what is strictly true of the divine. We can, of course, go some distance in that direction. We can remove from terms such as *command* and *forgive* any implication that this is done by the use of vocal cords, and remove other semantic components of relevant terms that require a body. But the DMT requires that even when we have done everything we can to spruce up terms for speech about God, what we say is still not strictly true of God as it stands. As Aquinas says in *Summa Contra Gentiles*, I, 30, "there is in every name that we use an imperfection, which does not befit God."

So the only way to conform to both the constraints under which we are working is to use creaturely terms (purified as much as possible) in our thought and talk of God, while recognizing that they are not fully adequate to the task. That's easy to say, but the question that remains is how, given that less than complete adequacy, such talk can be an appropriate guide to our lives. That is the problem I want to make a start at tackling.

One Christian thinker I find to be very insightful on this issue is I. M. Crombie, in two essays from the 1950s, one in *New Essays in Philosophical Theology* (1955) edited by Antony Flew and Alasdair Macintyre, and one in *Faith and Logic* (1957) edited by Basil Mitchell. Crombie holds that "when we speak about God, the words we use are intended in their ordinary sense (for we cannot make a transfer, failing familiarity with both ends of it), although we do not suppose that in their ordinary interpretation they can be strictly true of him. We do not even know how much of them applies."[9] Thus Crombie leaves us wondering how we can suppose that we are saying anything reasonably determinate about God. Here is his answer to the challenge: "The things we say about God are said on the authority of the words and acts of Christ, who spoke in human language, using parable; and so we too speak of God in parable – authoritative parable, authorized parable; knowing that the truth is not literally that which our parables represent . . . trusting, because we trust the source of the parables, that in believing them and interpreting them in the light of each other, we shall not be misled, that we shall have such knowledge as we need to possess for the foundation of the religious life."[10] This is, of course, an extended use of *parable*, in which anything we say of God, even something so simple as "God wants us to have loving communion with him," counts as a parable. Though the words do not strictly apply, we have the authority of Christ (God incarnate) for taking them to be close enough to the strict truth about God to be an adequate guide to our relations with God and with our fellows.

Note that this resolution of the problem holds, at best, only for those who accept the authority of Christ; it is an account of the kind of meaning these statements can have for those within the Christian community and who recognize the kind of divine authority of which Crombie speaks. One who satisfies those conditions can have an assurance that what is being thought and said about God is close enough to the exact truth for our condition, even though in that condition vaunting theoretical aspirations cannot be satisfied. But because the problem we are considering does not arise only for orthodox Christians, it would be desirable to have a more generally applicable response. And, indeed, I think that Crombie's idea can be turned into something that is not tied to a particular religious orientation. Crombie's basic idea, we might say, is this: Where we are dealing with something we cannot cognitively grasp sufficiently to make statements that are strictly true of it, we may still manage something that is close enough to being strictly true to be a useful guide for our lives and, more specifically, for our interactions with the entity or entities in question. Of course, if we don't have Crombie's reasons for supposing that our ordinary talk and thought about God is close enough to being true for being a useful guide for our lives, then we will need some other reason for thinking so. But to specify other reasons would be to present a fully developed alternative to Crombie, something I am not concerned to do in this essay. My aim is only to delineate *possibilities* for finding an important place for ordinary talk and thought about God, even if none of it is strictly true of God. And for that purpose, what I just called "Crombie's basic idea" is sufficient, even if it is not further developed in a way that is neutral between different religious orientations.

So far, perhaps, so good. But even if we are reconciled to this stance of "this is the best we can do, and it suffices for our most basic needs in this life," we would like to have something more of a sense of how these not fully adequate ways of thinking and talking can be an effective guide for our lives. Here, some less puzzling examples of this sort of situation can be enlightening. I will present two for your consideration.

1. Let's think of my three-year-old grandson wanting to know what I do when I go to my office. Telling him "I work" doesn't completely satisfy his thirst for knowledge, and so I tell him that I "make things." "Like we do with blocks at preschool?" he replies. "Well, not exactly," I say, "but something like that. I don't build structures with blocks or anything else you can hold in your hands, but I do make things." Let's assume that this satisfies him, for the moment. Is he in possession of an adequate conception of the intellectual work that is involved in "making" a piece of philosophical writing, or constructing an argument for or a refutation of a position, or analyzing a concept, or preparing notes for a class? Obviously not. His attention has been directed to an activity with which he is familiar and told that what I do is something like that. He is in no position to specify exactly how what I do is like making play houses with blocks, though he has been told one way in which it is unlike; but at least he has come to realize that some kind of "making" is involved. This is a useful example of how one's grasp of a state of affairs can be more than zero,

even though it radically fails to be an adequate grasp of that subject matter. My grandson in this situation is in something like the position we are all in with respect to God according to the DMT. To be sure, my grandson has the potential of eventually coming to understand the kinds of making in which I engage in my office, whereas according to the DMT, all of us are permanently and irretrievably stuck in our inadequacy to grasp God as he is in himself. Still, this analogy does give some idea of how a cognitive grasp of a subject matter can be more than zero even though it is radically inadequate.

But you will undoubtedly complain that gaining this much knowledge of what I do in my office is a pretty thin case of giving my grandson a practical guide for (even a little bit of) his life. My second example will do better on that score, as well as dealing with *not strictly true modes of cognition* that characterize adults and are still useful for them.

2. It is a fundamental feature of sense perception that sense experience is a joint function of the objects perceived and of our ways of being perceptually affected by them. We cannot neglect either of these factors. Obviously the nature of the object makes some difference. Otherwise, everything we see at a given moment would look just alike. But we make a contribution too. We are not perfectly clear windows that admit an unadulterated grasp of the objective realities perceived. One and the same object looks different from different perspectives and distances, and in different conditions of our perceptual apparatus. And the same object appears differently to perceivers with significantly different perceptual faculties – differently to bats and birds and dogs and whales than to us.

Moreover, from the seventeenth century on, thinkers have been impressed with the way our contribution to perceptual experience is such as to make it a not wholly reliable guide to what perceived objects are like in themselves. Modern physics has enforced a distinction, among perceived qualities, between *primary* qualities that attach to physical objects as they are in themselves (size, shape, motion) and *secondary* qualities that do not, at least as they appear to our sensory experience. To take the most familiar example, our visual awareness of color presents it as something simple that is spread uniformly and continuously over the surface of visual objects. But with respect to a uniformly red disk, physical science recognizes no such quality of the disk itself. It depicts that object as made up of innumerable submicroscopic particles (none of which itself exhibits phenomenal color) separated by empty space. Moreover, phenomenal colors exhibit various interrelations – for example, the distinction between pure and mixed colors – that correspond to nothing in the external physical stimuli that give rise to color perception.

The bearing of this on our present concern comes into view when we ask about how to interpret ordinary attributions of color to perceived objects, such as "That leaf is yellow." There are several candidates. (1) The most obvious and naive understanding is the one we have just seen to be rejected by physical science: "There is a color spread continuously over the leaf surface, a quality of just the sort it visually appears to have." Call this the *phenomenal* understanding. (2) What we mean is that the leaf is such that, in the normal condition of visual perception, it produces in us an appearance of phenomenal yellow. That avoids conflict with science but at the cost of a considerable distance of the attributed property from the way the leaf visually appears. It also has what many philosophers regard as the disadvantage of making color appearance conceptually prior to what is attributed to the perceived external object. Call this the *dispositional* understanding. (3) We pin down the physical property that is responsible for the disposition in (2) and take "The leaf is yellow" to be attributing that property to the leaf. This has both the advantage and the first disadvantage of (2). And it substitutes for the second disadvantage of (2) one of its own. It seems to be impossible to specify any such property without making it highly disjunctive. Depending on conditions of vision, even those that would ordinarily be regarded as normal, there are a number of different physical states of the leaf that may lead to its looking yellow.

It is no part of my aim here to decide between these alternatives. The above is only designed to set up what I hope is an illuminating example of a not strictly true way of thinking and talking about objects that is, nonetheless, of great practical utility in guiding our dealings with them. For this purpose (1), the phenomenal construal, gives us just what we need. As we have just seen, thinking of the leaf as possessing yellowness as it appears to us visually, has, for good and sufficient reason, been ruled out as an accurate account of what the leaf is like in itself. But in spite of this, our visual discrimination of the colors of objects, taken neat without fancy theoretical transformations, are of enormous value in guiding our dealings with those objects. We get practically valuable information about the chemical nature of a solution by determining whether it turns a certain kind of paper from looking yellow to looking blue. What color a person's skin looks to be tells the physician something about that person's state of health. By seeing whether the grass looks green or brown, one is guided to water it or not. And so it goes in innumerable other cases. I submit that this is an excellent model for how a way of thinking and talking about a subject matter can be a highly significant guide to our interactions with it, even though it is not strictly true of it. To be sure, the analogy with my central topic is not perfect. In the present case, so far as anything I have said goes, it is in principle possible to substitute for the naive color attributions some that are strictly true, however inconvenient or even impossible it would be to do this in practice. But no analogy can be expected to hold in every respect. What I have sought from this one is an example of a construal of a subject matter that is of enormous practical usefulness even though it is not strictly correct.

IV

Let's see where this leaves us. I have suggested that there is enough support for the DMT to warrant taking it as a serious alternative, but not enough to establish it conclusively. If it is a serious alternative, it is worth considering whether it rules out any significant place for positive thought, belief, and talk about God, which, of course, would be carried on by applying our concepts to God. Clearly, the DMT rules out any such concept applications being strictly true. But in the last section, I gave some reason for supposing that such thought and talk may still be close enough to being strictly true to provide a useful guide for our lives, more particularly for the Christian form of life. This "close to being true" approach is only one of several possibilities for squaring significant thought and talk of God with the DMT. Others include *panmetaphoricism* (taking it all to be metaphorical rather than literal); Hick's religious analogue to Kant's view about the physical world, according to which our ordinary way of thinking of "The Ultimate Reality" in a particular religious tradition has the status of *phenomena*, the way the Ultimate appears to people in that tradition, rather than the status of *noumena*, the way the Ultimate is in itself; and Tillich's view that practically all conceptual talk of Being-Itself (Tillich's favorite term for the Ultimate Reality) is *symbolic* rather than being literally true of the Ultimate Reality. A thorough treatment of the problem would involve a critical examination of these alternatives as well, but that is a task that extends beyond the limits of this essay.

The previous paragraph is concerned with the problem of finding a way in which conceptual thought and talk about God could be an important guide to the Christian life, even if we accept the DMT as presented earlier in this essay. Here the DMT is left intact, whereas it is the usual view that applications of our concepts to God can be strictly true that is modified. But we can also consider ways in which the DMT might make some concessions without losing its basic thrust. For example, we might follow up the reference to "God as He is in Himself" in Keating and distinguish that from "God in His relations to creatures." In terms of that distinction, much of what is said and thought about God in Christianity and other theistic religions belongs in the latter compartment. That includes God's creative activity, his providential care for us, his plan of salvation for us, his promises to us, his requirements on us, and much else. All this could count as strictly true without running into conflict with the DMT, so long as the latter is restricted to God as he is in himself. To be sure, some fundamental Christian doctrines and convictions would be excluded from strict truth. Most obviously, the Trinity falls in this class. And so do the standard theistic attributes of omnipotence, omniscience, perfect goodness, and other forms of absolute perfection, so long as we take these as dispositions God would possess even if there were no creatures with respect to which they are exercised. But this weakening of the DMT would allow much of the heart of Christian belief to enjoy strict truth, and, for the rest, the earlier suggestion of "close enough to the truth" could be invoked. This is a response to the problem in which each side of the conflict gives up something but retains enough to make a distinctive contribution to the total picture.

NOTES

1. Dionysius, *The Divine Names and Mystical Theology*, 120.
2. Keating, *Open Mind, Open Heart*, 14.
3. Ibid., 17.
4. Merton, *New Seeds of Contemplation*, 1–2.
5. Ibid., 131.
6. Ibid., 132–5.
7. See, for example, Plantinga, *Does God Have a Nature?*
8. For discussion of these objections see, for example, Alston, *Perceiving God*, chapters 5 and 6.
9. Flew and MacIntyre eds., *New Essays*, 122.
10. Ibid., 122–3.

BIBLIOGRAPHY

Alston, William P. "Can We Speak Literally of God?" in *Is God GOD?*, ed. Axel Steuer and J. McClendon. Nashville, TN: Abingdon Press, 1981. 144–83.

Alston, William P. "Functionalism and Theological Language," *American Philosophical Quarterly* 22, 3 (1985): 221–30.

Alston, William P. "Divine and Human Action," *in Divine and Human Action*, ed. T. V. Morris. Notre Dame, IN: University of Notre Dame Press, 1988. 257–80.

Alston, William P. "Literal Talk of God: Its Possibility and Function" in *This Is My Name Forever*, ed. Alvin F. Kimel, Jr. Downer's Grove, IL: Intervarsity Press, 2001. 136–60.

Alston, William P. *Perceiving God: The Epistemology of Religious Experience*. Ithaca, NY: Cornell University Press, 1991.

Dionysius the Pseudo-Areopagite. *The Divine Names and Mystical Theology*, trans. C. E. Bolt. New York: Macmillan, 1920.

Flew, Antony and Macintyre, Alasdair, eds. *New Essays in Philosophical Theology*. London: SCM Press, Ltd, 1955.

Keating, Thomas. *Open Mind, Open Heart*. New York: Continuum Publishing, 1986.

Merton, Thomas. *New Seeds of Contemplation.* New York: New Directions Publishing Corporation, 1961.

Mitchell, Basil, ed. *Faith and Logic.* London: Allen & Unwin, 1957.

Pike, Nelson. "Divine Omniscience and Voluntary Action," *Philosophical Review* 74 (1965): 27–46.

Plantinga, Alvin. *Does God Have a Nature?* Milwaukee: Marquette University Press, 1980.

Rowe, William. "The Problem of Evil and Some Varieties of Atheism," *American Philosophical Quarterly* 16 (1979): 335–41.

∾

PART TWO

EPISTEMOLOGY: GOD AND THE ETHICS OF BELIEF

5

ॐ

The Probability of the Resurrection

RICHARD SWINBURNE

A central doctrine of the christian religion is that jesus Christ rose from the dead – which I interpret in the traditional way as "rose bodily" from the dead – on the first Easter morning. In this paper, I seek to investigate the question of what kind of historical evidence and how much of it we would need to establish it as probable that Jesus did rise bodily. For reasons of space, I cannot assess the details of the historical evidence here, but I have done so in a recent book.[1]

In assessing any historical hypothesis, we have to take into account three kinds of evidence. The first kind is the most obvious kind – the testimony of witnesses about and the physical data caused by what happened at the time and place in question. If it is suggested that John robbed a certain safe, then our obvious historical evidence is what witnesses said (about who was near the safe at the time in question, and where John was at that time), and physical data such as fingerprints on the safe, money found in John's garage, and so on. I shall call such evidence the posterior historical evidence. Insofar as the hypothesis is a simple one, and the posterior historical evidence is such as you would expect to find if the hypothesis at stake is true but not otherwise, that is evidence that the hypothesis is true. For example, if John robbed the safe, you would expect to find his fingerprints on it but would not expect to find them if he didn't; and in the absence of evidence for a hypothesis of the unreliability of witnesses, if John robbed the safe, you would expect any people who saw John at the time or were near the safe at the time to say that they saw John there, but would not expect them to say this if he didn't.

I stress here, as elsewhere in this paper and in everything else I have written, the crucial importance of its simplicity in assessing the truth of a theory. There are always an infinite number of possible theories in science, history, or any other sphere of inquiry, that are such that if they were true, you would expect to find the evidence that you do. John's fingerprints being on the safe, and the testimony of George to John's presence at the scene of the theft at the time of its occurrence, and John having a lot of money hidden in his garage, could easily be explained by Harry having planted John's fingerprints there for a joke, George telling a lie because he disliked John, and Jim having put the proceeds of a quite different robbery into John's garage. But, in the absence of further evidence, the theory that John did the crime is that most likely to be true, because it is the simplest in postulating that one person (John) doing one action (robbing the safe) caused in different ways the three pieces of evidence. Unless the simplest theory of data is that most likely to be true, no scientific theory would have any justification at all, for it is easy enough to invent an infinite number of theories that are such that they make the occurrence of the data probable but that disagree totally with each other in their predictions for the future. Unless there is something internal to a theory other than its relation to the evidence that makes it likely to be true, we must abandon all inquiry, and our clear convictions about what is evidence for what indicate that simplicity is that internal feature we regard as evidence of truth.

As well as the posterior historical evidence, we need to take into account general background evidence of how likely the hypothesis is to be true, independently of the detailed historical evidence. In my humble example, this evidence will be evidence of John's past behavior and the past behavior of other suspects that might, for example, support strongly (as its simplest explanation) a theory that John is not the sort of person to rob a safe, whereas George is just that sort of person. In that case, even if the posterior historical evidence is exactly what we would expect if John robbed the safe, but not quite what we could expect if George had robbed the safe, nevertheless we may rightly conclude that George is the most probable culprit.

In this example, the background evidence was fairly narrow – John or George's past behavior. But the joint influence of background evidence and posterior historical evidence operates where the background evidence is far more general. Suppose an astronomer observes through his telescope a certain pattern of bright dots that is exactly what you would find if these dots were the debris of a supernova explosion. It is right so to interpret them if your theory of physics, as best supported by all the other evidence available to the physicist – that is, the general background evidence – allows that supernovas can explode. But if your theory of physics says that supernovas cannot explode, then the hypothesis that one did on this occasion will need an enormous amount of detailed historical evidence (itself vastly improbable on any hypothesis of equal simplicity other than the hypothesis that it was caused by a supernova explosion) before we can regard that as probable – and if we do so regard it, we will have to regard the whole theory of physics that rules it out as itself improbable, given our new detailed historical evidence.

The general background evidence may indicate not simply that the postulated hypothesis is or is not likely to be true, but that it is likely to be true only under certain conditions – for example, that John is likely to rob safes when and only when financially broke, or that supernovae are likely to explode when, and only when, they reach a certain age. In that case, another kind of historical evidence will enter the equation, evidence showing that those conducive conditions were or were not present. That again will be strong insofar as it is such as you would expect to find if those conditions were present, and not otherwise (and insofar as the supposition of these conditions is a simple one). I shall call such evidence the prior historical evidence.

When we are dealing with a hypothesis H that would be not too improbable on one worldview T but would be immensely improbable on a rival worldview, the general background evidence will be all the evidence that is relevant to the probability of the different worldviews; and to the extent to which it supports most strongly the worldview T that makes H not too improbable, we need less by way of detailed historical evidence in order for the claim that H is true to be probable overall. The hypothesis that Jesus rose from the dead is of just this kind. For if there is no God, the ultimate determinant of what happens in the world is laws of nature, and for someone dead for thirty-six hours to come to life again is (with immense probability) a clear violation of those laws and so impossible. This is for the reason Hume gave – that all the evidence that some regularity operated on very many known past occasions is evidence that it is a law of nature, and so operated on this occasion too, and so Jesus did not rise. But if there is a God of the traditional kind, laws of nature only operate because he makes them operate, and he has the power to set them aside for a moment or forever.[2] Hence, if Jesus rose from the dead, God raised him up. So I shall treat the hypothesis that Jesus rose as equivalent to God raised Jesus. But if there is a God with the power to raise Jesus, he will only do so insofar as he has reason to do so; and, if he doesn't this Resurrection is not to be expected.

So to determine whether Jesus rose from the dead, it is not enough to investigate whether what I have called the posterior historical evidence (what St. Paul wrote, that the original text of Mark's gospel ended at 16:8, or what was written in the original text of Josephus's *Antiquities*) is the kind of evidence to be expected if Jesus rose, but not otherwise. One must also investigate whether general background evidence supports the worldview that there is a God of a kind able and likely to intervene in human history in this kind of way in this kind of situation, or whether there is no such God. And we must also investigate the prior historical evidence – that is, whether the nature and circumstances of the life of Jesus were such that if there is a God, he would be likely to raise *this* person from the dead. Insofar as our general background and prior historical evidence supports the view that there is a God who would be likely to raise Jesus from the dead, we shall need a lot less by way of detailed historical evidence in order for it to be overall probable on our total evidence that Jesus rose from the dead. Conversely, insofar as our prior evidence (background or historical) supports a rival worldview that there is no God (of the traditional kind) or that if there is such a God, he has no reason to intervene in human history in this kind of way, or that even if God does have such reason, Jesus was not the sort of person whom he would have brought to life again, we would need an immense amount of posterior historical evidence in order for our total evidence to make it probable that Jesus rose.

New Testament scholars, both those who do believe and those who do not believe that the Resurrection took place, are apt to make such statements as "I (unlike my opponents) am going to reach my conclusion solely on the basis of the historical evidence [and by that they mean what I have called the posterior historical evidence] and nothing else." If it *was* possible to do such a thing, it would be highly irrational – for it involves taking into account only part of the evidence. But it is not even possible to do this, for in order to reach a conclusion about whether your evidence makes it probable that the Resurrection did or did not occur, you need a view about how *much* posterior historical evidence is required to show this; and you can't have that without having a view about how likely such an event is to occur anyway – and that involves taking a view about whether there is a God and what he is likely to do. What New Testament scholars are apt to deny that they do, they in fact do implicitly, because in reaching a conclusion about the Resurrection they must take a view about how strong the posterior historical evidence needs to be.

I have argued at considerable length over many years[3] in favor of the view that the existence of a universe, its almost total conformity to natural laws, those laws being such as to lead to the evolution of human beings, those human beings having souls (a continuing mental life whose continuity is separate from the continuity of their physical life), the occurrence of various events in history, and millions of humans having experiences that seem to them to be of God, is evidence that makes probable the existence of God. In arguing thus, I have followed in the tradition of Jeremiah, the Wisdom literature, the Epistle to the Romans, Gregory of Nyssa, John of Damascus, Thomas Aquinas, John Duns Scotus, and innumerable other Christian thinkers. The kind of God such argument shows to exist, I claim, is omnipotent, omniscient, and perfectly good. Others have argued that this evidence, together with other evidence, such as the fact of pain and suffering, makes the existence of such a God improbable. This needs to be argued out, and that cannot be done here. But suppose the natural theologian is right that there is substantial positive evidence for the existence of such a God. In that case, clearly God could, if he so chose, raise Jesus from the dead. Hence, to the extent to which, in virtue of his goodness, he has reason to do so, it is probable that he would. God very seldom raises the dead (in their original bodies while others on Earth continue their normal life). Jesus would therefore need to be a very special sort of person for God to have reason to raise him. There might be various reasons why God would choose to raise Jesus, but I shall consider here only the reasons God would have if Jesus were God Incarnate – because, as we shall see later, given the evidence of the kind of life Jesus lived, he would only have raised him if he were God Incarnate. That is, I shall argue that in virtue of God's goodness, he had reason to become incarnate and live a certain sort of life, and that if he did, God had reason to raise him from the dead.

Theologians have always claimed that the main reason God would choose to become incarnate is to make atonement for human sins. They have produced their various theories of why humans need atonement, how they are unable to provide it for themselves, how God alone could provide it by becoming incarnate and suffering and dying, and how, thereby, God could make the atonement available to all who accepted God's action on their behalf. There is the theory that the death of God Incarnate would pay a ransom to the devil, or the theory that it would be a punishment vicariously suffered by God on our behalf, the theory that it would constitute God Incarnate paying compensation to God the Father for the wrong we have done, and the theory that the life and death of God Incarnate would constitute a sacrifice offered to God the Father on behalf of humans. God has no right to send anyone else to do such a formidable task (whatever its exact nature) on his behalf. He must act himself. These theories thus seek to explain why a good God might choose to become incarnate in such a way that he would be killed for leading a holy life. While leading this life, he would need to explain to us that that life was being led to redeem us from our sins. Then the Resurrection would constitute God's demonstration to us that the ransom or compensation had been paid, the punishment or the sacrifice accepted. For on all these views, humans need to accept and use this redemptive life and death. The Resurrection of someone dead for thirty-six hours would, as I have noted, be a violation of laws of nature, and this could only be done by him who keeps the laws of nature operative – God. Bringing to life someone killed for living a certain sort of life (and undergoing a certain sort of death) would thus constitute God's demonstration to us of his acceptance of that life as proper compensation, sacrifice or whatever, his signature on that life.

The second reason God would choose to become incarnate is a reason that would operate even if humans had not sinned. God made humans subject to pain and suffering of various kinds caused by natural processes. God, being perfectly good, would only have permitted this subjection if it served some greater goods. Theodicy seeks to explain what are the relevant greater goods[4] – for example, the great good of humans having the significant free choice of whether to cope bravely with their own suffering and show compassion to others who suffer. We humans sometimes rightly subject our own children to suffering for the sake of some greater good (to themselves or others) – for instance, making them eat a plain diet or taking some special exercise for the sake of their health, or making them attend a "difficult" neighbourhood school for the sake of good community relations. Under these circumstances, we judge it a good thing to manifest solidarity with our children by putting ourselves in somewhat the same situation – sharing their diet or their exercise, or becoming involved in the parent/teacher organization of the neighbourhood school. Indeed, if we subject our children to serious suffering for the sake of a greater good to others, there comes a point at which it is not merely good but obligatory to identify with the sufferer and show him or her that we have done so. A perfectly good God would judge it a good thing to share the pain and suffering to which he subjects us for the sake of greater goods – by becoming incarnate. Living a holy life, protesting against injustice under difficult conditions, is liable to lead to execution. God needs to have told or shown us that he is God Incarnate. In that case, his Resurrection would constitute God's signature on that teaching, and so show us that God has identified with our suffering.

And finally, we need better information about how to lead good lives in the future, and encouragement and help to do so. Humans can, and to some extent in the centuries before Christ did, find out for themselves what is right and wrong. But although the outlines may be discoverable, the details are not easy to discover – are abortion and euthanasia always wrong, or only wrong under certain conditions; are homosexual relationships sometimes permissible, or never; and so on – and in all these matters, humans are prone not to face the deliverances of their consciences. They need information. True, this could be provided through a revelation to some prophet without any need for incarnation. But moral information needs to be filled out by moral example – we need to be shown what a perfect life consists in, and that God has no right to tell anyone else to do for him. It would be good for this information to include encouraging information, for example, that God will take us to heaven if we trust him and fulfill his commandments. And it would be good if God gave us some extra help in leading the moral life – a community of encouragement, for example. Again, God raising someone killed for a certain teaching and living a certain life constitutes his signature on that teaching.

We now have three reasons why a good God might choose to become incarnate in such a way as to suffer and probably die, and how he would need to show us that it was he who had done this – which would be achieved by a supermiracle such as a resurrection. In my view, although it is quite probable that in virtue of his goodness, God might choose to become incarnate for the first and third reasons, he has no obligation to do so, and there are other (perhaps less satisfactory) ways of dealing with the problems to which his incarnation for these reasons would provide a solution. But in my view, given the extent of human suffering, our creator has an obligation to share it with us, and so it is necessary that he will become incarnate for the second reason.

So, if God did become incarnate in some human (let us call him a prophet) for the second reason and one or both of the other reasons, he would need to live a certain sort of life. To identify with our suffering and to provide an example for us, God Incarnate needs to live a good life in difficult circumstances, and a good but hard life ending in a judicial execution would certainly be that. To show us that he is God who has done this, he needs to show us that he believes himself to be God. To enable us to use his life and death as atonement for our sins, he needs to tell us that he is leading his life for this purpose. In order to make it plausible that he is preaching a revelation, he needs to give us good and deep moral teaching on how to live. And to make all this available to generations and cultures other than those in which he lived, he needs to found a church to teach humans what he has done and to apply to them his atoning life. So we have prior reason for expecting a resurrection, not of any human, but of a human about whose life our evidence is what we would expect if he had led a life of the above kind. The stronger the background evidence that there is a God whose goodness would lead him to become incarnate for the stated reasons, and the stronger the prior historical evidence that Jesus led the sort of life described above, the stronger reason we have for supposing that God would put his signature on it by a supermiracle such as the Resurrection.

Our historical evidence about the life and teaching of Jesus is, of course, not enormous in quantity, and requires careful sifting. My assessment of the balance of New Testament scholarship is that the evidence is such as we would expect if Jesus led a good and holy life, gave us good and deep moral teaching, and founded a church that did teach that he was God Incarnate who atoned for our sins. It is, I suggest, impossible to understand his forming a community of twelve leaders except as forming a new Israel, whether in the end he intended it to become independent from or merge back into the old Israel. New Testament scholarship is, however, divided about whether the evidence is such as one would expect if and only if Jesus proclaimed that his life and death was an atonement for sin; and on the whole, it claims that the evidence is not such as would be expected if Jesus taught his divinity. My own view is that the prior historical evidence is such as is to be expected with modest probability (say, $\frac{1}{4}$) if both these claims are true – that Jesus taught both his atonement and his divinity. But I am not arguing that here. My point here is that the stronger the prior historical evidence that the life and teaching of Jesus was of a certain kind, the more reason we have for expecting God to raise him from the dead.

Only in the light of the general background evidence and the prior historical evidence can we approach the sort of evidence that alone New Testament scholars normally consider relevant – the testimony of witnesses (or lack of it) about the appearances of the risen Jesus and the empty tomb, what I have called the posterior historical evidence. To this I would add the much neglected evidence of the universal celebration by the early church of the eucharist on Sundays. Here the question is – if Jesus rose, would one expect this amount and kind of testimony? If so, then of course, the evidence supports the Resurrection.

I now need to add one further piece of evidence to the prior historical evidence. This is that Jesus led the life he did, when there is no other known serious claimant (before or after Jesus) for satisfying either the prior or posterior requirements for being an incarnate God in any way as well as Jesus. By the prior requirements I mean living a good and holy life; giving us good, deep moral teaching; showing us that he believed himself to be God Incarnate and that he was making atonement for our sins; and founding a church that teaches the latter things. By the posterior requirements, I mean his life being culminated by a supermiracle, such as a resurrection from the dead. Other founders of great religions did, of course, live good lives, give deep moral teaching, and found churches – the Buddha, for example. But manifestly, the Buddha did not teach his own divinity, nor did Mohammad. And manifestly, neither of them taught that their lives atoned for our sins. There have been many modern messiahs who have claimed to be God, but they have not satisfied the other requirements – in particular, their lives have not been holy. And no great religion other than Christianity has made a claim to be founded on a supermiracle for which there is in any way the kind of detailed testimony that there is for the foundation miracle of Christianity (inadequate though that might seem to some). In making these points about other religions, I am not seeking to denigrate these religions – I am simply making the uncontestable historical point that they do not make the kind of claims (true or false) about their founders that Christianity makes about its founder. It is not on grounds of that kind that they seek our allegiance.

The relevance of this evidence is that it shows that either God became incarnate in Jesus for the reasons stated, or that (so far) he has not become incarnate for these reasons. Our reasons for expecting an incarnation would not have been fulfilled – but of course, they could always be fulfilled at a later time. Yet the nonexistence of any other plausible candidate for satisfying *either* the prior *or* the posterior requirements shows that the *coincidence* of the prior and posterior evidence (even if weak) in one candidate is an extremely unlikely event in the normal course of things – that is, unless God brought it about. But if God did not become incarnate for the stated reasons in Jesus but became incarnate in some other prophet or plans to do so in the future, it would be deceptive of him to allow the existence of the amount and kind of evidence of his incarnation (including proclaiming that he was atoning for our sins – which God should not allow others to do) in Jesus together with the amount and kind of posterior historical evidence that there is of his resurrection; it would be like leaving someone's fingerprints at the murder scene when he or she had not committed the murder, or spreading a rumor that someone had won a presidential election and therefore had the right to give orders to soldiers to kill when that person had not won the election. In virtue of his perfect goodness, God would not do that sort of thing. If God planned the coincidence in Jesus of the two kinds of evidence, then Jesus was God Incarnate; and it is very improbable that there would be this coincidence unless God planned it.

Having sketched in qualitative terms the kinds of evidence that need to be weighed in order to see whether it makes it probable that Jesus rose from the dead, I now proceed to show how we can weigh the different kinds of evidence together with the help of the probability calculus and more particularly with the help of the relevant theorem of that calculus, Bayes's theorem.[5] I express this theorem using the letters e, h, and k, which can represent any propositions at all; but we shall be concerned with it for the case in which e represents observed evidence (data), k represents "background evidence," and h is a hypothesis under investigation:

$$P(h|e \& k) = \frac{P(e|h \& k)\,P(h|k)}{P(e|k)}.$$

This theorem sets out in a formal way the factors that determine how observational evidence supports a hypothesis. $P(h|e \& k)$ may be called the posterior probability of h, that is, its probability on e as well as k. The theorem brings out that a hypothesis h is rendered probable by observational evidence e and background evidence k, insofar as (1) $P(e|h \& k)$ (the posterior probability of e) is high, (2) $P(h|k)$ (the prior probability of h) is high, and (3) $P(e|k)$ (the prior probability of e) is low. The first condition is satisfied to the extent to which you would expect to find e if h is true (given k). The second condition is satisfied to the extent to which h is simple and you would expect h to be true on background evidence alone. The third condition is satisfied to the extent to which $P(e|k)$ is not much greater than $P(e|h \& k) \, P(h|k)$; that is, you would not expect to find e unless h is true. Of course, when assessing the probability of a scientific or historical theory, one cannot give exact numerical values to all these terms – except in extreme cases. But we can give rough values to them – say, that some term has a high value or a low value or is greater than this term or less than that one – and that is often quite enough to give us some interesting results.

Now let k be the evidence of natural theology. Let e be the detailed historical evidence,[6] consisting of a conjunction of three pieces of evidence (e_1 & e_2 & e_3). Let e_1 be the prior historical evidence of the life of Jesus and e_2 the posterior historical evidence, such as the postcrucifixion testimony of witnesses about the Resurrection. Let e_3 be a further part of the prior historical evidence – that no other known prophet satisfied either the prior or the posterior requirements for being God Incarnate in any way comparable to the way that evidence (viz. e_1 and e_2) suggests that Jesus did. Let h be the hypothesis that Jesus rose from dead. Our interest is in $P(h|e \& k)$, the probability that Jesus rose from the dead (h), on the evidence of both natural theology (k) and the detailed history of Jesus and of other human prophets (e).

Bayes's theorem tells us that this probability is a function of the three elements. But these in turn, according to the calculus, are functions of other probabilities; and we must approach our result gradually. As we go along, I shall allocate certain values to these other probabilities (some for which I have argued in the present paper, others arbitrary ones from the point of view of the reader of this paper, but ones I believe to be roughly correct and for which I have argued elsewhere). I shall then point out that these values make h very probable on ($e \& k$), and that we would have to give some very different values to some of the probabilities to avoid that conclusion; and I leave the reader to reflect just how plausible that would be.

Let us represent by t, theism, the claim that there is a God of the traditional kind. $P(t|k)$ is the probability that there is such a God on the evidence of natural theology. Let us give this the modest value of $1/2$. Then let us represent by c, the claim that God would (sometime) become incarnate for two or three of the reasons sketched earlier, which would require a supermiracle at the end of that life to authenticate it as God's life (c for *chalcedonian incarnation*). Let us also give to $P(c|t \& k)$, the probability that if there is a God, he would become incarnate in the stated way, the modest value of $\frac{1}{2}$. The value you give it will measure the extent to which you are impressed by arguments for the probability or even necessity of an incarnation. You'll recall that my arguments suggest a much higher value. $P(c|k)$ is the probability on the evidence of natural theology that there is a God who becomes incarnate for those reasons. $P(c|k) = P(c|t \& k) P(t|k)$; given my suggested values, that is $\frac{1}{2} \times \frac{1}{2} = \frac{1}{4}$.

Now, initially, instead of e_1, e_2, and e_3, let us take the slightly different f_1, f_2, and f_3. f_1 is the evidence that the prior requirements for being God Incarnate are satisfied in one unnamed prophet (to the degree but not necessarily in the same way that they are in Jesus). f_2 is the evidence that the posterior requirements for being God Incarnate (that is, his life being culminated by a supermiracle) are satisfied in that same prophet (to the degree to which they are in Jesus). f_3 is the evidence that neither the prior nor the posterior requirements are satisfied to that degree in any other prophet. Now if c is true, if there occurs an incarnation, how probable is it that there will be evidence f, the conjunction $(f_1 \& f_2 \& f_3)$? I have argued that one would expect a God Incarnate to live a holy life, teach us deep moral truths, found a church teaching his incarnation and atonement, and himself teach that his life was an atonement and that he was divine. I have suggested that the kind of evidence we have about the life of Jesus is such as we would expect on the first three counts but possibly not on the last two. And perhaps if Jesus' life was culminated by a supermiracle such as the Resurrection, one would really expect rather more evidence of appearances and an empty tomb than one has. So what value shall we give to $P(f|c \& k)$? Let's be modest and call it $\frac{1}{10}$. So, given the evidence of natural theology, the probability that there is a God who becomes incarnate for the stated reasons and leaves us with evidence of the kind f that he has done so is

$$P(f \& c|k) = P(f|c \& k) P(c|k) = \frac{1}{10} \times \frac{1}{4} = \frac{1}{40}.$$

Now let us turn to $P(f|k)$. This equals {the probability, given k, that there is a God who becomes incarnate and leaves evidence of kind f} plus {the probability, given k, that either there is no God or he does not become incarnate and you still have f}:

$$P(f|k) = P(f \& c|k) + P(f|\sim c \& k) P(\sim c|k).$$

And because (as I have just argued) $P(f \& c|k) = P(f|c \& k) P(c|k)$, we can replace the first item on the right-hand side of the equation, thus yielding

$$P(f|k) = P(f|c \& k) P(c|k) + P(f|\sim c \& k) P(\sim c|k).$$

The first combined term on the right-hand side of the equation is the one we have just calculated and to which we have given the provisional estimate of $\frac{1}{40}$. What of the second term? $P(\sim c|k) = \frac{3}{4}$, given that (as we have provisionally assumed) $P(c|k) = \frac{1}{4}$ – because by an obvious axiom of the calculus, $P(c|k) + P(\sim c|k) = 1$. What next of $P(f|\sim c \& k)$? That is the probability that if there is no incarnation (because either there is no God or he does not become incarnate) and yet there is the evidence of natural theology, f still occurs. f, you recall, is as a whole evidence that one prophet satisfied both the prior and posterior requirements for incarnation, even though only one prophet in human history satisfied the prior requirements and only one prophet satisfied the posterior requirements to that degree. The probability of such a chance coincidence is enormously low, unless God so planned it. If God did plan this connection, it would have been deceptive of him if that prophet was not God Incarnate, for – if we assume a God with reason to become incarnate – the co-occurrence of the prior and posterior evidence would be taken as showing that. So let's say that $P(f|\sim c \& k) = \frac{1}{1000}$. So,

$$P(f|k) = \frac{1}{40} + \frac{3}{4} \times \frac{1}{1000} = \frac{103}{4000}$$

Then (by Bayes's theorem, substituting c for h and f for e)

$$P(c|f \& k) = \frac{P(f|c \& k)P(c|k)}{P(f|k)} = \frac{100 \times 4000}{4000 \times 103} = \frac{100}{103},$$

a number very close to 1. This represents the probability on the sort of evidence that we have about Jesus that God has or will become incarnate. But now our evidence is somewhat greater than f. It is the evidence e that the prophet whom f concerns is Jesus. It can hardly make any difference to the probability that f (with k) gives to c if we add to f who the prophet is, because all the relevant facts about Jesus are incorporated anyway into f. So,

$$P(c|e \& k) = P(c|f \& k) = \frac{100}{103}.$$

Now the probability of c on $(e \& k)$ will be virtually the same as the probability of h on $(e \& k)$. For if God becomes incarnate in such a way that his life needs to be culminated by a supermiracle, and there is only (given e) one serious candidate for this – the Resurrection – there must have been a resurrection. And given the evidence of the kind of life that Jesus led and that no one else has ever led that kind of life, it would have been deceptive of God to bring about the resurrection of Jesus unless Jesus was God Incarnate. So h is true if and only if c is true. Hence, by another obvious axiom of the calculus,

$$P(h|c \& k) = P(c|e \& k) = \frac{100}{103}.$$

The probability on our total evidence that the Resurrection occurred is something of the order of 97%. (If I'm wrong that the Resurrection would only have occurred if Jesus was God Incarnate, then of course, $P(h|e \& k)$ may exceed $P(c|e \& k)$.)

I have reached this high value despite attributing the rather low value of $\frac{1}{10}$ to the probability that if Jesus were God Incarnate, we would have the sort of detailed historical evidence about his life and purported resurrection that we do. To avoid my conclusion, if they leave the other probability values intact, an objector will have to lower this value to $\frac{3}{1000}$ before the posterior value of h falls below $\frac{1}{2}$. Alternatively, they will need to be much more dismissive of natural theology than I am. If, for example, they think that natural theology only gives a probability of $\frac{1}{51}$ rather than $\frac{1}{2}$ to the existence of God, or that there is only a probability of $\frac{1}{51}$ that if there is a God, he will become incarnate, it becomes marginally less probable than $\frac{1}{2}$ that God became incarnate in Christ. Or, to my mind implausibly, an objector might claim that it is not at all improbable (even if God is not responsible for it) that we should get this coincidence of evidence of a prophet satisfying the prior requirements and evidence of a prophet satisfying the posterior requirements in one prophet, even though for no other prophet has there been that quality of evidence that he or she satisfied either of the two requirements. But they would need to increase the value of $P(f|{\sim}c \& k)$ from $\frac{1}{1000}$ to above $\frac{1}{30}$ to get the posterior probability of h falling below $\frac{1}{2}$.

Sherlock Holmes made the famous remark: "When you have eliminated the impossible, whatever remains, *however improbable*, must be the truth."[7] If we gloss this a little (and ignore the issue of prior probability for the sake of a nice maxim), we get, "When you have eliminated what makes it very very improbable that we would have the evidence we do, whatever remains, even if it makes it very improbable that we would find the evidence we do, is very probably the truth." If you agree with me that the coincidence of the evidence we have of the satisfaction of the prior and posterior requirements is (barring divine intervention) very, very improbable, and the evidence of their coincidence (if God intervened to become incarnate and to rise from the dead) only very improbable, it follows that it is very probable that Jesus rose from the dead, and also that he was God Incarnate.

NOTES

1. *The Resurrection of God Incarnate* (Oxford: Clarendon Press, 2003).
2. Because this is a short paper, I am making the assumption that the only alternative to the view that laws of nature are ultimate is traditional theism. For an argument that alternatives involving many gods or a weak or morally imperfect god are far less

simple and so less probable than traditional theism, see my *The Existence of God*, 2nd
ed. (Oxford: Clarendon Press, 2004), chapter 5.

3. See my *The Existence of God* and the shorter *Is There a God?* (Oxford: Oxford University
Press, 1996).

4. For my theodicy, see my *Providence and the Problem of Evil* (Oxford: Clarendon Press,
1998), or – more briefly – *The Existence of God*, chapter 11.

5. For full discussion of the probability calculus and its application to measuring
how probable some evidence makes some hypothesis, see my *Epistemic Justification*
(Oxford: Clarendon Press, 2001), chapters 3 and 4.

6. The historical evidence may be described in broad, general terms or fairly precise
terms. By phrases such as "the kind and quantity of evidence" and "the degree" in
which requirements are satisfied, I had in mind a very broad-brushed description
of the evidence – e.g., "Jesus said some words on crucial occasions to the effect
that his life and death constituted an atonement and let his followers believe this,"
rather than that he said and they said exactly the words they did. Clearly on any
hypothesis, the former is going to be a lot more probable than the latter. Indeed, it is
a theorem of the probability calculus that if one proposition (a precise one) entails
another proposition (an imprecise one), the latter is always at least as probable and
normally more probable than is the former, on the same evidence. But it does not
matter just how precisely we construe the evidence. For whereas the probability of
just that evidence on the hypothesis that Jesus was God who rose from the dead will
be lower the more precisely the evidence is construed, it will be also lower in the same
proportion on the negation of that hypothesis. The two diminutions of probability
will thus cancel each other out.

7. A. Conan Doyle, "The Sign of Four," in *The Complete Sherlock Holmes*, vol. 1 (Garden
City, NY: Doubleday, 1930), 111, emphasis in the original.

6

⌒

Is God an Unnecessary Hypothesis?

PETER VAN INWAGEN

Summa theologiae, i, q.2, a.3 (the "five ways" article, the article whose topic is indicated by the heading "Whether God Exists") begins with two "Objections." Each of these objections is an argument. The first is a version of the argument from evil. The second is as follows:

Objection 2. It is, moreover, superfluous to suppose that what can be accounted for by a few principles has been produced by many. But it seems that everything we see in the world can be accounted for by other principles, without supposing God to exist. For all natural things can be accounted for by one principle, which is nature; and all voluntary things can be accounted for by one principle, which is human reason or will. Hence, there is no need to suppose that a God exists.

I will call this the superfluity argument. Here is a formulation of the essential point of the superfluity argument in language the modern mind may find more congenial than Thomas's talk of "principles":

The only reason we could have for believing in God would be that it was necessary to postulate his existence to account for some observed fact or facts. But science can explain everything we observe, and its explanations do not appeal to God or to any other supernatural agency. Hence, there is no reason to believe that God exists. That is to say, the existence of God is an *unnecessary hypothesis*.

(A parenthetical remark. Thomas's formulation of the argument proceeds from the premise that it is superfluous to posit God when everything we observe is explicable as either a production of nature or of the human will. Thus, the existence of the Connecticut River Valley is explained by an appeal to the action of impersonal forces, and the existence of Hartford by the action of, as it were, personal forces – but only human ones. Today, I suppose, everyone who was willing to grant that the existence of everything that was not the work

131

of human beings could be accounted for by the action of impersonal forces would also be willing to grant that human beings, and the human will and all its determinations, could be accounted for by the action of impersonal forces – just those impersonal forces whose modes of operation are the subject matter of science. For that reason, in restating the superfluity argument in modern language, I have allowed the statement "science can explain everything" to do duty for Thomas's "all natural things can be accounted for by one principle, which is nature; and all voluntary things can be accounted for by one principle, which is human reason or will.")

The conclusion of the argument from evil is the proposition that God does not exist. It is therefore easy to see why this argument counts as an "objection" to the position Thomas takes in the article "Whether God Exists": its conclusion is the logical contradictory of that position. But the conclusion of the superfluity argument is not the proposition that God does not exist. It is not even logically inconsistent with the proposition that God exists. The conclusion of the superfluity argument is that there is no need to suppose that God exists, or in the modern jargon, that the existence of God is an unnecessary hypothesis. I take it that Thomas was not confused on this point. I take it that he was well aware that the conclusion of the superfluity argument, unlike the conclusion of Objection 1, is not the proposition that God does not exist. I take it that by calling the superfluity argument an "objection," he meant only that its conclusion, if true, constitutes a serious objection to accepting the proposition that God exists.

The superfluity argument, in one form or another, is well known to present-day atheists. Several atheists in the analytical tradition in philosophy (I'm thinking primarily of Antony Flew and Michael Scriven[1]) have defended the position that, although it is true that the conclusion of the superfluity argument is not the proposition that God does not exist, the argument can be elaborated in such a way as to produce an argument for that conclusion. Others have defended a somewhat weaker thesis: that the premises of the superfluity argument imply that atheism is the only reasonable position as regards the existence of God. I want to begin by asking whether the argument, or some elaboration of it, supports atheism. But the main questions I shall address are these: Does the argument indeed show (and if so, in what sense?) that the existence of God is an unnecessary hypothesis? Does the argument support agnosticism?

Can the superfluity argument be elaborated in such a way as to produce an argument whose conclusion is "God does not exist"? We could, of course, turn the superfluity argument into an argument for that conclusion simply by adding a premise: If there is no reason to believe that something of a certain sort exists, if there is no need to postulate the existence of things of that sort, then nothing of that sort exists. But that premise wouldn't be very plausible. There is no reason to believe that there exist intelligent extraterrestrial beings within a thousand light-years of the earth. No observed phenomenon requires us to postulate the existence of such beings. If someone believes that there are such beings (and many do), we can correctly point out that that person has adopted an unnecessary hypothesis. But it hardly follows that no such beings exist. And there's really not much more to be said about this. There is no way to turn the superfluity argument into a plausible argument that is in the strictest sense an argument for the nonexistence of God – that is, an argument whose conclusion is that God does not exist.

Flew and Scriven reject this thesis. Insofar as arguments for its falsity can be found in their writings, they are all variants on what might be called the Santa Claus argument (or the Great Pumpkin argument). The idea is this: it is obviously irrational (for an adult) to believe in Santa Claus (or the Great Pumpkin or some other particular creature of childish fable); and when we think about the irrationality of such a belief, we see that it is due entirely to the fact that there is no evidence for the existence of Santa Claus (or the Great Pumpkin et al.). Here is a version of the argument that features Santa Claus:

Why do adults not believe in Santa Claus? Simply because they can now explain the phenomena for which Santa Claus's existence is invoked without any need for invoking a novel entity.... As we grow up, no one comes forward to *prove* that [Santa Claus] does not exist. We just come to see that there is not the least reason to believe he *does* exist.... Santa Claus is in the same position as fairy godmothers, wicked witches, the devil, and the ether.... the proper alternative when there is no evidence is not mere suspension of belief [in Santa Claus], it is disbelief. (Scriven, *Primary Philosophy*, p. 103)

This is wholly absurd. It is simply not true that the reason adults do not believe in Santa Claus is that there is no evidence for his existence. First, the fact, if it is a fact, that there is no evidence for the existence of x is no reason at all for believing that x does not exist. The case of the intelligent extraterrestrials shows this: there is no evidence for the existence of intelligent extraterrestrials within a thousand light-years of the earth, but, if there is also no evidence for their nonexistence, what it is rational to do is to suspend judgment about their existence, not to disbelieve in them. Secondly, it is flatly obvious that there is *no* "hypothesis" better supported by the evidence available to us than the hypothesis that there is no person with the properties children believe Santa Claus to have. (Well, maybe 'Something exists' and

'There are conscious beings' are better supported by the evidence.) If you want to collect a small part of the inconceivably vast body of relevant evidence in your own person, you have only to stay awake by the Christmas tree all through Christmas Eve and Christmas morning or collect testimony from parents about the source of the presents under the tree – or visit the North Pole. Although the parts of the world observable by six-year-olds look the way they would look if Santa Claus existed (the Santa Claus story has this feature by adult design), the parts of the world observable by adults do *not* look the way they would look if Santa Claus existed. And the same goes – or almost goes; the evidence isn't *quite* as strong as in the "Santa Claus" case – for fairy godmothers (and for witches if by 'witches' we mean women who in reality have, from the devil, the powers that some women have no doubt *believed* they had and had from that source). And the same goes – or almost goes; the strength of evidence is a few notches down from that of the "fairy godmother" evidence – for the ether (if the ether existed, the Michelson-Morley experiment would yield different results at different points in the earth's orbit, which it doesn't).[2]

If, as I have been maintaining, there is no way to turn the superfluity argument into a plausible argument whose conclusion is that God does not exist, it does not follow that the argument is useless to the atheist. Atheism can be supported by other arguments than arguments for the nonexistence of God in this strict sense. Atheism would, for example, be supported by an argument that showed that atheism was the *most reasonable* of the three available positions concerning the existence of God: atheism, agnosticism, and theism. An argument for this conclusion could be derived from the superfluity argument if we added to it the premise:

If there is no reason to believe that a certain thing exists, then it is more reasonable to believe that it does not exist than either to believe that it exists or to suspend judgment about whether it exists.

But, again, this premise is not very plausible. Consider once more the case of the nearby (by cosmic standards) intelligent extraterrestrial beings. Because there is no reason to believe that such beings exist, the premise we are considering implies that it would be more reasonable to believe that no such beings exist than to suspend judgment about whether they exist. But that doesn't seem right. Suppose there are neither good reasons for thinking that such beings exist nor good reasons for thinking that they don't exist. Then, presumably, the rational thing to do is to suspend judgment about whether they exist. In any case, it certainly isn't *more* reasonable to believe that they don't exist than to suspend judgment about their existence.

Some philosophers have tried to strengthen the conclusion of the super-fluity argument by adding the following principle to its premises:

If there is no reason to believe that a certain thing exists, and its existence is *highly improbable*, then it is more reasonable to believe that it does not exist than either to believe that it exists or to suspend judgment about whether it exists.

This principle does not seem right to me. I assign a very low probability to the thesis that there is an intelligent nonhuman species within a thousand light-years of the earth (and not simply because I think that there is no evidence that supports it; I have "positive" reasons for assigning a low probability to this thesis), and I think that there is no evidence for the existence of such a species. But I do not have the following belief: that there is no such species. And I do not think it would be reasonable for me to have this belief. What it would be reasonable for me to believe, in my view, is what I do believe, namely that the proposition that there is such a species has a very low probability. In any case, if we were to apply this principle to the question of the existence of God, we'd need some reason to think that the existence of God was highly improbable. Have we such a reason? What might it be?

Reasons for believing things, if they can be stated at all, if it is possible to put them into words, can be formulated as arguments. Is there a nontrivial argument for the conclusion that the existence of God is highly improbable? (There are, of course, trivial arguments for any conclusion.) Any valid argument whose conclusion was 'God does not exist' and the conjunction of whose premises was known to be highly probable would (in effect) constitute a nontrivial argument for the conclusion that the existence of God was highly improbable, and it is certainly a popular view that there are arguments with both these features. Suppose an atheist thinks that a certain argument for the nonexistence of God, "Argument X," proceeds from highly probable premises. That atheist might suggest that Argument X and the version of the superfluity argument we are now considering could usefully be employed together. Argument X by itself (given that the conjunction of its premises is highly probable but not certain) can lead those who have appreciated its force only to agnosticism[3] (the atheist might argue), but, if Argument X and the superfluity argument are employed together (the atheist might continue), the above principle entails that they can together establish the conclusion that atheism is a more reasonable position than agnosticism. But this suggestion represents the present version of the superfluity argument as functioning as an appendage to some other argument – as, essentially, completing the work that some other argument leaves unfinished. Has the argument any force in its own right, so to speak? It may be that some who employ the present version of the superfluity argument would say that it was just *evident* that the thesis that God exists was highly improbable, so evident that no argument was needed to establish its very low probability. I make bold to say that these people are just wrong. And, in any case, as I have said, the principle upon which the argument rests is doubtful. One simply cannot deduce from the premise that the truth of some proposition is highly improbable the conclusion that it is more rational to reject that proposition than to suspend judgment about whether it is true. Consider any proposition whose truth is known to be highly improbable but which is not known to be certainly false. (For example: the proposition that New York City will be destroyed by a huge meteorite at 11:23 P.M. on August 12, 2073.) If someone who is aware of this known probability does not accept the denial of that proposition (and, of course, does not accept the proposition itself), that person violates no norm of rationality. Let us, therefore, consider other possibilities.

Some philosophers have advanced arguments that are very much like Thomas's superfluity argument, but with the following premise added:

If there is no reason to believe that a certain thing exists, and that thing, if it existed, would be *very different from* the things we know about through experience, then it is more reasonable to believe that it does not exist than either to believe that it exists or to suspend judgment about whether it exists.

Because it seems reasonable to accept without further argument the thesis that God, if he exists, is very different from the things we know about through experience (I suppose sense experience is what is meant; I leave questions of religious or mystical experience aside), the revised argument may seem promising. I think, however, that the suggested new premise is, again, not very plausible. Consider the hypothesis that there are intelligent beings somewhere in the physical universe that are vastly different from us and from everything in our experience. (Wells's Martians wouldn't be different enough; I'm thinking of something like the intelligent cloud of intersiderial matter in Fred Hoyle's novel *The Black Cloud* or, a current favorite of science fiction writers, very flat beings inhabiting the surfaces of neutron stars.) There is no reason to think that intelligent extraterrestrial beings very different from us and from everything in our experience exist and no reason to think that they don't. Or, at any rate, let us assume that there is no reason of either sort. The proposed principle then tells us that it is more reasonable to believe that such beings do not exist than to suspend judgment about their existence. And that seems wrong. We should be wary of supposing that a thing's being very different from the things we know about is even a weak reason for supposing it not to exist. As the biologist J. B. S. Haldane – a staunch atheist – said (endorsing

Hamlet's well-known remark to Horatio), "Now my own suspicion is that the universe is not only queerer than we suppose, but queerer than we *can* suppose." A similar point was made by the dying atheist William Herrick Macaulay, who, when his pious sister (the novelist Rose Macaulay) suggested that he consider the possibility of God and an afterlife, replied, "Well, there's nothing so rum it might not be true." If we take 'queer' and 'rum' to apply to that which is vastly different from anything we're familiar with, these two quotations rather support my point.

We must conclude, I think, that there is no way to turn the superfluity argument into a plausible argument for the conclusion that atheism is the only reasonable position one can take as regards the existence of God. If it can indeed be established that there is no reason to believe in the existence of God, the most that can be got out of this premise is – unless, in addition to having no reason to believe that God *does* exist, we also have some reason to believe that God does *not* exist – that we should be agnostics, that we should suspend judgment about the existence of God.

Still, that's very far from being a trivial thesis, even from the atheist's point of view. If it is right, then theism is not a tenable position. And no doubt atheists would prefer a world in which all nonatheists were agnostics to a world in which some nonatheists were theists. In the sequel, I'll try to determine whether the superfluity argument can be used to show that one should *not* be a theist – even if it can't be used to show that one *should* be an atheist.

How good an argument for this conclusion is it? Let us examine it. One obvious question the argument raises is whether its premise is true: *can* science indeed explain everything we observe? Well, it is certainly not true that science can *at present* explain everything we observe. Perhaps the idea is that science will *one day* be able to explain everything we observe? This is far from evidently true. How can even a metaphysical naturalist be sure we human beings are intellectually capable of discovering scientific explanations for everything we observe? It is certainly conceivable that the observable world outruns our capacity to understand it. Is the idea then that science can *in principle* explain everything we observe – given world enough and sufficient time and brainpower? (Actually, there could be other barriers to our achieving a complete scientific understanding of the world than our having insufficient time or insufficient intellectual capacity. It is entirely possible that we cannot discover the correct laws of physics without employing some piece of experimental apparatus that it is physically impossible for us to construct – a linear accelerator many thousands of light-years long, for example.) A more plausible version of this thesis about scientific explanation would be this: there *exists* (in some Platonic sense) a purely scientific explanation for everything we observe, whether or not we human beings are able to discover it. Or, if it sounds strange to talk of a scientific explanation that can't be known by human beings (science being a human endeavor), let us say a purely *natural* explanation. By 'a purely natural explanation' I mean an explanation that involves only, refers only to, or appeals only to natural things. I will not attempt to say what the words *natural thing* mean; I will say only that whatever these words mean, they do not apply to supernatural beings like God or the archangel Michael, and they do not apply to nonnatural things, like moral properties as conceived by G. E. Moore.

Is it true that there exists a purely natural explanation for everything we observe? One important challenge to this thesis has been raised by some present-day philosophers of mind, who have presented various arguments for the conclusion that the subjective features of consciousness – the way pain feels or the way red things look to us – cannot be given a purely natural explanation. I propose simply to ignore the questions raised by this challenge, because they do not seem to be closely related to the question whether it is reasonable to believe in the existence of God. Leaving to one side, then, considerations about the subjective features of consciousness, is it true that there exists a purely natural explanation for everything we observe? I think that even the most committed naturalist should be suspicious of this principle. Consider the proposition that there exist natural things. This is a fact, and one easily verified by observation. Has it a purely natural explanation? That seems unlikely. How could facts about the properties of natural things and how they are related to one another (which are the only facts a purely natural explanation may appeal to) explain the existence of natural things? The difficulty of seeing how there could be an answer to this question suggests a general principle: To explain the existence of things of a certain type, we must somehow appeal to things that are not of that type. To explain the existence of human beings, for example, we must somehow appeal to things other than human beings. The explanation of the existence of human beings in Genesis appeals to God and the dust of the earth; modern scientific explanations of the existence of human beings appeal to the evolutionary precursors of human beings and the environments in which they lived – and, going further back, to the production of carbon and oxygen atoms in stellar cores, and their dispersal when some of the stars in which they were formed exploded. If this plausible principle about explaining the existence of things of a given type is correct, then there can be no natural explanation of the existence of natural things – for it implies that if there is an explanation of the fact that there are natural things, things other than natural things must figure in that explanation.

Reflection on the fact that there are natural things suggests that the best course for the proponents of the superfluity argument to take might be to say that they hadn't got their premise quite right, and to qualify it as follows: insofar as an observed fact *has* an explanation, this explanation is a purely natural one. That is, perhaps they should concede that some observed facts have no explanation at all, and go on to say that those observed facts that *do* have an explanation have a purely natural one. They *could* say that the proposition that there are natural things was a necessary truth, and thus had no explanation – at any rate, no causal explanation. But it doesn't seem very plausible to suppose that the proposition that there are natural things is a necessary truth. The friends of the superfluity argument would, I think, do better to maintain that the fact that there are natural things is a brute, contingent fact – a fact because there *are* natural things, contingent because there *might have been* no natural things, brute because there is no explanation whatever of there being natural things.

How plausible is the thesis that every fact has either a purely natural explanation or else no explanation at all? *Theists* will certainly not find this thesis plausible. Theists think that at least one observed fact, the fact that there are natural things, has an explanation and has no natural explanation – its explanation being, of course, that there are natural things because God created them. Doesn't the thesis that everything we observe either has no explanation whatever or else has a purely natural explanation simply assume the falsity of theism? Those who grant the truth of this thesis will not need the superfluity argument and its rather weak conclusion. They have available an argument whose conclusion is not simply the superiority of agnosticism to theism, but the nonexistence of God. Here is the argument:

Everything we observe either has no explanation whatever or else has a purely natural explanation;

If God exists, something we observe has an explanation but has no purely natural explanation (namely, the existence of natural things);

hence,

God does not exist.

But this is not a very impressive argument – and its weakness does not rest on its second premise, which is obviously true. Here is an only very slightly simplified version of this argument:

The world is uncreated;

If God exists, the world is created;

hence,

God does not exist.

Neither of these arguments is likely to embarrass the theist – any more than the following argument is likely to embarrass the atheist:

The world is created;

If the world is created, a Creator exists (or creators exist);

hence,

A Creator exists (or creators exist).

It is not always entirely clear to me what it means to accuse an argument of "begging the question," but one could hardly find arguments that more clearly deserved to be called question-begging than these.

But the justice of these reflections – *I* think they're just – does not imply that the superfluity argument is hopelessly flawed. If I were a defender of the superfluity argument, I think I would reply to them by saying something like the following:

I do not need the principle 'Everything we observe either has no explanation whatever or else has a purely natural explanation' in order to make a case for the explanatory superfluity of God. That is to say, I do not need to maintain that this principle is *true*. I need only maintain that it is *true for all anyone knows.* And surely the success of science establishes this? Repeatedly in the history of science, it has turned out that things people thought had personal explanations had impersonal explanations. The dethronement of the Design Argument by the Darwinian theory of evolution by random mutation and natural selection is only the most salient case of this. One could also cite, among many other examples, Newton's belief that the planetary orbits were unstable and required periodic correction by God – a belief that Laplace and Lagrange showed was false. Isn't it at least a very reasonable hypothesis, in the light of these examples, that no irreducibly personal explanation is required by any observed fact of nature, that every observed fact of nature either has an explanation that is ultimately impersonal – or else has no explanation? If the answer to this question is Yes, we should be agnostics (at least in the absence of a proof or disproof of the existence of God that was based on some consideration unrelated to explanation). No deep epistemological reflections are needed to establish this result. Here is a simple but exactly parallel case. Suppose Winifred has been accused of murdering Henry. And suppose that it is a very reasonable hypothesis – true for all you and I know – that Henry's death was an accident. Then (at least in the absence of some cogent demonstration that Winifred *didn't* murder Henry), we should suspend judgment about whether Winifred murdered Henry.

There is a good deal of rhetoric in this argument. Here are its bare bones:

For all anyone knows, everything we observe either has no explanation or a purely natural explanation. So, as far as anyone knows, everything we observe can in principle be explained without reference to God – if it has any explanation at all. In the absence of a cogent argument either for the existence or the nonexistence of God, therefore, we should suspend judgment about whether God exists.

But why should I concede, why should anyone concede, that for all anyone knows, everything we observe either has no explanation or a purely natural explanation? Remember that 'Everything we observe either has no explanation or a purely natural explanation' entails that God does not exist, for, if God exists, then at least one fact has an explanation that is not a natural explanation – to wit, the fact that there are natural things. The above argument is therefore no better than this one:

For all anyone knows, God does not exist;

If, for all anyone knows, God does not exist, then we should all suspend judgment about whether God exists;

hence,

We should all suspend judgment about whether God exists.

I say that the former argument is no better than the latter because I don't see any reason to accept 'For all anyone knows, everything we observe either has no explanation or a purely natural explanation' that would not be an equally good reason to accept 'For all anyone knows, God does not exist'. All the defenders of the first argument have given us, after all, are some reflections on the success of science in explaining observed phenomena in terms of natural objects and processes. They have given us no reason to suppose that the totality of natural objects and processes (that is, the natural world) has no explanation.

Suppose the defender of the superfluity argument again falls back a bit and makes a stand on the following ground:

We know of no consideration that forces us to believe that anything we observe requires a supernatural explanation of any sort. We should believe in God only if something we observe forces us to postulate a supernatural being. Hence, we should not believe in God.

Well, suppose some theist were to reply to this argument by pointing out that there was a well-known argument whose conclusion was that something we observe – namely, the existence of a natural world – forces us to postulate a supernatural being (or beings). (The argument, of course, is the cosmological argument in any of its various forms.) This theist will no doubt be told that plenty of philosophers who understand the cosmological argument perfectly do not accept its conclusion, owing to the fact that they see no reason to believe that there is an explanation of any sort for the existence of the natural world. Therefore (the theist will be told), nothing we observe *forces* us to postulate the existence of a supernatural being. This reply seems to be grounded on the following general principle: We should believe in supernatural beings only if some intellectual consideration *forces* us to. How could this principle be justified? Not, I think, by any appeal to the still more general principle that, for any proposition whatever, we should accept that proposition only if some intellectual consideration forces us to. For one thing, the objector will find that an appeal to this principle is self-defeating. It would imply that one should be an atheist (or an agnostic) only if some intellectual consideration *forced* one to believe that atheism (or agnosticism) was superior to any competing position concerning belief in God. And, obviously, no intellectual consideration has this power, owing to the fact that there are plenty of theists who are aware of all the intellectual considerations that have ever led anyone to be an atheist or an agnostic and who nevertheless remain theists. An atheist or agnostic might, of course, maintain that these theists are unreasonable, and that certain intellectual considerations should force any *reasonable* person who considered them carefully to abandon theism. But then, of course, those who find the cosmological argument convincing might maintain that those who say that there is no explanation for the existence of the natural world are being unreasonable, and that certain intellectual considerations should force any *reasonable* person who considered them carefully to reject the thesis that the natural world has no explanation.

In any case, it would seem that all human beings have beliefs that are not forced on them by the totality of the relevant intellectual considerations of which they are aware. Most of our philosophical beliefs are like that. Here are two of mine: that we have free will and that our thoughts and feelings are identical with certain physical processes in our brains. I believe these things, but many of my fellow philosophers do not, and at least some of the philosophers who do not believe these things are aware of every intellectual consideration that is relevant to the question whether we have free will or to the question whether mental events are physical events. And I'm not willing to say that these philosophers are obtuse or irrational. Not all of them, anyway. The point I have made can be made about kinds of beliefs other than philosophical beliefs; it can obviously be made about our political beliefs. But why should belief in God be held to stricter epistemic standards than beliefs of other sorts? It cannot be demonstrated that God exists; not, at least, in the sense that intellectual considerations can be adduced that would force any reasonable person who understood and carefully considered them to conclude that God exists. But it cannot, in this sense, be demonstrated that we have free will or that the country would be better off under one political party than another. If it's all right to believe, in the absence of conclusive demonstration, in the absence of what I have called a compelling argument, that we have free will or that the country would be better off under one political party than another, why isn't it all right to believe, in the absence of a compelling argument, that God exists?

Now here is one more argument of the "superfluity" sort. Suppose a defender of agnosticism argues in this fashion:

Agnosticism is the result of a straightforward application of Occam's Razor, that is, of the principle that postulated entities are not to be multiplied beyond necessity. You theists believe in what we agnostics believe in and more besides. You and we both believe in the world of natural things. *We* stop there. We don't deny that there *may* be more things in heaven and earth than are dreamt of in our philosophy, but we do not affirm the existence of anything outside the natural world. *You* don't stop there. You go on to believe in a supernatural Creator. But believing in the world of natural things is belief enough. To go on to postulate a Creator is to multiply entities beyond necessity – or at least to *add* one unnecessary entity.

I have in effect already considered the contention that to postulate a Creator is to multiply entities beyond necessity. I argued for the conclusion that this may be so, but that it has not been shown to be so. (And it's up to the defenders of agnosticism to show that it's so, because they're the ones who are trying to establish a conclusion – the conclusion that agnosticism is superior to theism. I'm not trying to establish anything, or at least I'm not trying to establish anything beyond the failure of the agnostics to make their case. I'm certainly not trying to establish the conclusion that theism is superior to agnosticism.) Let us leave this question, the question whether someone who postulates the existence of a Creator of the natural world is postulating entities beyond necessity, aside. And let us also leave aside another important question: whether I believe in just those things the agnostics believe in and more besides. (I think it's not implausible to suppose this is so, although I shouldn't be willing to say this in the case of atheists. I think atheists believe in things I don't believe in, most notably a world of natural things that can exist without a Creator, or, indeed, a cause of any sort.) I want to examine instead a presupposition of this (and probably of all) versions of the superfluity argument, viz, that belief in God is an explanatory hypothesis.

Compare this case. Bishop Berkeley says to me, "You believe in what I believe in and more besides. You and I both believe in minds (including the supreme Mind, God) and thoughts and sensations. *I* stop there. *You* don't stop there. You go on to believe in material things. But believing in minds and God and thoughts and sensations is belief enough. To go on to postulate material things is to postulate entities beyond necessity." Or let us suppose not that Berkeley himself says this (after all, Berkeley does not simply decline to accept the thesis that there are material things; he accepts its denial and he marshals an impressive array of arguments for its denial), but rather someone who has not been fully converted to Berkeley's immaterialism but who has been impressed by Berkeley's arguments to the extent of becoming an agnostic about the existence of material things. Suppose this person appeals to Occam's Razor in support of the conclusion that one should not believe in material things, should not have the belief that there are material things. Should we take this appeal to heart? Like almost everyone, I'm not willing to. I'm not going to allow an appeal to considerations of ontological economy to turn me into an agnostic about the existence of material objects, and I expect very few of my readers would allow such considerations to have that effect on *them*. But what is wrong with such an appeal? One thing that might be wrong with it is that the order and uniformity of my sensations can't be adequately accounted for without postulating the existence of material bodies. But this doesn't seem too plausible. I suppose God or a sufficiently able evil genius could produce any sequence of sensations whatever in an immaterial observer, and although I myself think I'm not an immaterial observer, my reasons for thinking this depend essentially on the assumption that there are material things. Why, then, do I persist in believing in material things despite the fact that the data of observation can be perfectly well accounted for without assuming that any such things exist? In my view, this question has a false presupposition, to wit, that one should not believe in things that exist independently of the mind unless the existence of such things is the explanatory hypothesis that best accounts for the order and uniformity of one's sensations. In my view, one does not need a reason, a reason of any sort, to believe in the existence of material things. I do not think that one, as it were, "starts with" one's sensations – the ultimate "data of observation" – and with nothing else except perhaps the fact of one's existence, and then somehow has to find within one's interior mental life a ground for believing in things that exist independently of the mind. In my view, if we were indeed in this epistemic position, we could never find any ground for believing in material things. (The landscape of modern philosophy is littered with the wrecks of attempts to find such grounds.) In my view, a belief in material things is simply a part of our physiological makeup. It is, as they say, "hardwired" into our brains by whatever is responsible for the design of those brains – God or evolution or both. I therefore have no reason (or at least no articulable reason, no reason that can be put into words) to think that there are material things, and yet I accept their existence and I do not see myself as thereby convicted of irrationality. If someone tells me that, if I can adduce no articulable reason for believing in material things, then my belief in material things must be irrational, I'll reply that my critic has a mistaken and impossibly demanding theory of rationality.

I want to say something similar about my belief in God. Why do I believe in God? Certainly not because I can write down some reason for believing in God that would force anyone who understood it to share my belief. There is no such reason. I can – I often do – set out reasons for believing in God, but these reasons are not *coercive*: a person who understands them and is unmoved by them is not, by that very fact, irrational. (This is only to say: every argument for the existence of God is a philosophical argument, and philosophical arguments are never coercive.) As far as I can see, the reason I believe in God is that belief in God is built into me – and, I would add, into everyone else. As Saint Paul says in the first chapter of his letter to the Romans (vv. 19, 20), "For that which may be known of God is manifest among human beings; indeed God himself has made it manifest. The invisible attributes of God, his eternal power and deity, have been perceived since the beginning of the world, being understood through created things." This is not, as some have maintained, a statement of the argument from design.[4] It is not a statement of an argument at all, any more than my observation (*I* call it an observation) that belief in material objects is "hardwired" into us is an argument.

The thesis that belief in God is hardwired into all human beings immediately raises a difficult and important question: If this is so, why does not everyone believe in God? I am not going to answer this difficult and important question; my excuse is that it does not really matter to my larger point whether belief in God is built into me, much less into everyone else. What does matter to my larger point is only my contention (or admission) that my belief in God is not based on – or is not based entirely on – statable reasons or publicly available arguments. In this, my belief in God is like my belief in a material world, my belief that the human figures with whom I daily interact have interior mental lives very much like my own, my belief in free will, and my belief in an objective truth and objective morality. And many of my beliefs that are too much concerned with the particularities of things to be called philosophical beliefs are likewise not based on statable reasons and publicly available arguments: my belief in the intellectual equality of the sexes, my belief that Marx and Freud have contributed nothing to intellectual history but rubbish, and my belief that it would be a grave mistake to legalize physician-assisted suicide are in this category. I repeat: it's not that I can't produce arguments in favor of or reasons that support these beliefs – I can, and with the least provocation will, argue interminably with anyone who disagrees with me about free will or physician-assisted suicide or any of the other matters I've mentioned. It's rather that my beliefs about these matters are not *based on* (or not based entirely on) the arguments I would, if provoked, bring in their defense. Here's an analogy I hope will make my position clear. I once met a man who believed that the moon did not exist, that it was a sort of optical illusion. Being unable to escape politely from the conversation he had forced on me, I asked him how he accounted for the tides. In my view, "If there were no moon, there would be no tides; There are tides; Hence, the moon exists" would be a good argument for the existence of the moon – if the person presenting the argument were in extraordinary circumstances, circumstances in which it was appropriate to present an argument for the existence of the moon. But my belief that the moon exists is not based on this argument. (I doubt whether it's even partly based on this argument.) Or consider my belief in "other minds," my belief that "the human figures with whom I daily interact have interior mental lives very much like my own." I think that the so-called analogical argument for the existence of other minds is a fairly good argument – as philosophical arguments go – but my belief that my wife has thoughts and sensations generally similar to my own is not based on this or any other argument. Not even partly.

Not only are my beliefs on the matters I've mentioned not based on the arguments I would use to defend them, but (in my view) someone who listened patiently to these arguments and was not convinced by them would not thereby convict himself or herself of irrationality. A philosopher who rejects the analogical argument is not *ipso facto* irrational. And *I* am not irrational in believing that the human figures with whom I daily interact have interior mental lives very much like my own.

I find this whole topic so fascinating (and so important) that I could easily be seduced into going on about it for another twenty pages or so. I must resist the temptation to do that, but I can't refrain from expanding on just one point. (And perhaps in the present ideological climate, it would be prudent to say something more about it.) The point has to do with the equality of the sexes. Does it follow from what I have said that it is epistemically permissible to believe in the inequality of the sexes – not to put too fine a point upon it, to believe that men are the intellectual superiors of women? Or does it follow from what I have said that it might be epistemically permissible to suspend judgment on the question whether men are intellectually superior to women? No: it follows only that it might be epistemically permissible to hear and understand all the arguments *I* could give for the equality of the sexes and either believe that men are intellectually superior to women or to suspend judgment on this question. An asexual Martian who had had no experience of human beings and who listened to a debate between me and a defender of male intellectual superiority might after listening to this debate believe that human males were intellectually superior to human females (or might suspend judgment on this question) and be guilty of no sin against reason. But this Martian would not be in the same epistemological position as a human being who was deciding what to believe about the intellectual capacities of men and women. Unlike the Martian, a human being has lived his or her whole life as a human being, interacting with other human beings, using the cognitive equipment supplied by human biology; and the human being will have been raised in a human culture and will be heir to the stored wisdom of that culture. My belief in the intellectual equality of the sexes is based on a lot more than what I am able to put into words, and the epistemic warrant it enjoys may be – I believe it is – due to many factors that cannot be put into words. But enough.

I maintain that my belief in God is in this respect like my belief in free will, my belief in other minds, and my belief in the intellectual equality of the sexes. It is not based on argument or on reasons I can put into words (I *hope* it and the other beliefs I have used as examples are based on reasons I have but which I can't put into words) despite the fact that I can give arguments for the existence of God that seem to me to be good arguments. (I don't, of course, claim that an atheist would agree with my judgment that these arguments were good arguments. An atheist would almost certainly say they were inconclusive – even that they were *bad* arguments that rested on long-exploded fallacies. But then I think the arguments I could give in support of the intellectual equality of the sexes are good arguments, but I would not expect someone who thought that women were intellectually inferior to men – or, for that matter, someone who thought that men were intellectually inferior to women – to agree with my judgment that they were good arguments.) You will misunderstand what I have been saying if you think I claim to have shown that my belief in God is rational; I have presented no argument for *that* thesis, and, indeed, I know of no plausible argument for it. To argue for the rationality of my or anyone's belief in God was not my project in the final part of this essay. My project was rather to defend the following conclusion: the fact that my belief in God is not based on statable or publicly available reasons is not a good reason for thinking that my belief in God is irrational. And this I have done. Whether the arguments I have used to defend this conclusion are good arguments is, of course, another question.

One thing, however, should be clear. One cannot show that these arguments are bad arguments by constructing parallel arguments for some absurd conclusion – a conclusion of the form that it is not irrational to believe that p, where p is some thesis that it obviously would be irrational to believe. (I'm led to make this remark by the popularity of the so-called Great Pumpkin objection to Plantinga's religious epistemology.) For such a *reductio ad absurdum* of my argument to be possible, there would have to be some thesis such that a person who accepted that thesis and had no cogent or compelling argument for it was irrational – and was irrational *simply because* that person accepted it without having a cogent or compelling argument for it. And there is no such thesis.[5]

My conclusion is this: that God exists is not an unnecessary hypothesis because it is not (not for us human beings at any rate) an hypothesis at all. A hardwired illusion, perhaps. For all I've said, it could be that. But not an hypothesis.

NOTES

1. See Antony Flew, *The Presumption of Atheism and Other Philosophical Essays on God, Freedom and Immortality* (New York: Harper & Row, 1976), chapter 1, "The Presumption of Atheism" (13–30); Michael Scriven, *Primary Philosophy* (New York: McGraw-Hill, 1966), 98–110. (Reports in the press suggest that Flew has recently abandoned atheism for some form of deism.)

2. The same *doesn't* go for the devil: *his* existence, unlike the existence of the other items in Scriven's list, is not disconfirmed by our everyday observations of the world around us or by anything science has discovered. Or so *I* say. From my point of view, therefore, belief in Satan is in an entirely different epistemological position from that of belief in Santa Claus or fairy godmothers. It may be that it is – I have said nothing inconsistent with this – as irrational to believe in the devil as it is to believe in Santa Claus, but even if it is, there is one extremely important *argument* for the irrationality of (adult) belief in Santa Claus that does not apply in the case of Satan: as I have pointed out, one can *show* that Santa Claus does not exist simply by staying awake throughout the appropriate night of the year. No such *experimentum crucis* is available in the matter of the existence of Satan. As I said a moment ago, the parts of the world observable by adults do not look the way they would look if Santa Claus existed. But the whole physical universe looks exactly the way it would look if Satan existed, and, a fortiori, the parts of the physical universe observable by adult human beings look exactly the way they would look if Satan existed.

3. A "negatively weighted" agnosticism perhaps – a negatively weighted agnostic is an agnostic who assigns a low probability to the existence of God – but agnosticism nonetheless. Negatively weighted agnosticism as regards the existence of God is comparable to my agnosticism about whether the card that is about to be drawn (in a random drawing from a standard deck of cards) will be the four of clubs. My doxastic relation to the proposition that the card will be the four of clubs is one of agnosticism because I do not accept the denial of that proposition (and, of course, I do not accept the proposition itself). My agnosticism about whether the card will be the four of

clubs is negatively weighted because I accept the proposition that the probability of the card's being the four of clubs is low – less than 0.02.

4. Then why does Paul say, "being understood through created things"? Compare this imaginary text with Paul's text: "The invisible interior lives of human beings other than myself, their thoughts and feelings, have been observed since the beginning of my life, being understood through their speech and facial expressions and bodily movements." If I imagine someone saying these words, it does not seem to me that I have imagined someone's presenting a philosophical argument for the existence of other minds. It seems to me, rather, that I have imagined someone's reporting the results of introspection. People do not believe that there are minds other than their own because they have examined various hypotheses each of which purports to explain the speech and facial expressions and bodily movements of the human figures around them, and have, upon reflection, concluded that, of all these hypotheses, the "other minds" hypothesis best explains those phenomena. (For all I know, it is *true* that the "other minds" hypothesis has this explanatory power – but this fact, if it is a fact, is not the explanation, is not a *part* of the explanation, of our beliefs about the thoughts and feelings of our fellow human beings.) As I understand Paul, his message can be stated in modern terms in words something like these: We perceive the invisible reality of God in the operations of created things – in a way analogous to the way in which we perceive the invisible mental lives of our fellows in their speech and facial expressions and bodily movements.

5. Many think there are such theses, but I have never seen a plausible example of one. The only supposed examples I am aware of are "Great Pumpkin" or "Santa Claus" examples.

7

∾

Direct Warrant Realism

KEITH DeROSE

DIRECT REALISM AND DIRECT WARRANT REALISM

Direct realism often emerges as a solution to a certain type of problem. Hume and, especially, Berkeley, wielding some of the most powerful arguments of eighteenth-century philosophy, forcefully attacked the notion that there could be good inferences from the occurrence of one's sensations to the existence of external, mind-independent bodies (material objects). Given the success of these attacks, and also given the assumption, made by Berkeley and arguably by Hume as well, that our knowledge of and rational belief in the existence of material objects would depend upon there being such good inferences, a problem arises: we cannot know of or rationally believe in the existence of material objects. Reid's Direct Realism then emerges as the solution to this problem. Reid admits the success of Berkeley's and Hume's attacks against the possibility of successfully grounding our material world beliefs on inferences from our sensations,[1] but claims that our belief in the existence of material objects can be perfectly rationally acceptable, and can amount to knowledge, despite the lack of such inferences. Though he did not use the terminology, it seems to be Reid's position – and it's this position that I will be referring to as his "Direct Realism" here – that certain perceptual beliefs whose content is such that they imply the existence of material objects are *properly basic*: they are rationally held, and if true, can amount to knowledge, without having to be based on any other beliefs, including, most notably, beliefs about one's own sensory experiences.

Direct Realism, so construed, is a thesis about the justification or rational acceptability of certain material object beliefs rather than a denial that we use sensations or images of sensations as representations when we conceive of material objects. Direct Realism, as I will be discussing it here, is opposed to Evidentialism, the thesis that we need to have good inferences from our sensations in order to rationally believe in the existence of material objects, though the term *Direct Realism* is also often used to describe a denial of Representationalism. Though Anti-Evidentialism and Anti-Representationalism often go together (as in the case of Reid), they are distinct, and it is Anti-Evidentialism that is required in order to solve the Berkeleyan problem just described.[2]

Inspired by Reid, late twentieth-century Christian philosophers, most notably William Alston, Alvin Plantinga, and Nicholas Wolterstorff, defended theistic belief by means of a form of Theological Direct Realism.[3] As in the case of Reid, this Direct Realism emerges as a response to an Evidentialist challenge[4] – this time the challenge that theistic beliefs are irrational because there is not sufficient evidence for them. And again, the challenge is met by denying the need for any such good evidence or inferences. Following Reid, but being more explicit about the matter, a key claim of this movement in religious epistemology is that certain theistic beliefs are properly basic.

In what follows, I will explore, and to an extent defend, in the case of sense perception, a view we will call "Direct Warrant Realism" (DWR), according to which the most basic material object beliefs are *not* properly basic.

Direct warrant, we will say, is warrant that a belief enjoys independently of the support it receives from others of one's beliefs. So, according to Direct Realism, on which our perceptual beliefs are properly basic, these beliefs have sufficient direct warrant to render them rationally acceptable – and also to make them count as knowledge, though I will in what follows now put such points only in terms of rationality.

On DWR, by contrast, the beliefs in question enjoy some direct warrant, but not enough to render them rationally acceptable. These "partially warranted" beliefs are then found to form a coherent picture of the physical world in which regularities are discovered and in which prediction is made possible, and this coherence enables the partially warranted perceptual beliefs to mutually support each other to the extent that most of them become rationally acceptable.

DWR, then, eschews the properly basic beliefs of Direct Realism. But it nevertheless delivers many of the advantages of Direct Realism. In particular, as we will see in the section The Argument by Elimination: Escaping Evidentialist Arguments, DWR provides an escape from the Evidentialist arguments that largely motivate Direct Realism. Direct Realists, in particular, then, should take DWR very seriously. I will argue in what follows that the main arguments that have been given for Direct Realism do not really favor Direct Realism over DWR, and will observe, along the way, some of the considerations that might make one prefer DWR over Direct Realism.

The next three sections will be a structural defense of DWR: I will defend the structural option in epistemology – which, following Laurence BonJour, we will call "Weak Foundationalism" – of which DWR is an instance. Having defended Weak Foundationalism as a structural option, we will then investigate, in the three sections that follow, the main reasons one might have for being a Direct Realist to see if they provide any reason for preferring Direct Realism over DWR. I will argue that they do not. In the last section, we will investigate what becomes of a certain claim of parity between sense experience and religious experience if we take a DWR, rather than a Direct Realist, approach to the former.

WEAK FOUNDATIONALISM

According to "foundationalism," as we will here use the term, there are certain privileged beliefs – the properly basic beliefs – that can be rationally held even if they are not based on others of one's beliefs. These properly basic beliefs do not depend for their justification upon the justification of any other beliefs. All other beliefs are rational only if they are (directly or indirectly) properly based on these properly basic beliefs. Direct Realism fits nicely into a foundationalist scheme: It is what results if you accept foundationalism, and hold that some perceptual beliefs about material objects are among the foundational, properly basic beliefs. DWR, by contrast, is not a foundationalist view, for according to DWR, there are rationally held beliefs that are neither properly basic nor are they based on properly basic beliefs. For recall that, according to DWR, simple perceptual beliefs are not properly basic but come to be rationally held in virtue of support they receive from other perceptual beliefs, which are not properly basic either. But neither is DWR a Coherentist view, for although the coherence of perceptual beliefs with one another plays a key role in DWR, it is, as we are about to see, a radically different role than it plays in Coherence theories.

DWR is a version of what Susan Haack has called "Foundherentism,"[5] and what Laurence BonJour (whose terminology we will follow here) has called "Weak Foundationalism" – where, we must remember, Weak Foundationalism is an alternative to, and not a form of, foundationalism, at least as we are here using the terms.[6] According to BonJour's description, Weak Foundationalism is the view on which "basic beliefs possess only a very low degree of epistemic justification on their own, a degree insufficient by itself... to satisfy the adequate-justification condition for knowledge.... Such beliefs are only 'initially credible,' rather than fully justified" (p. 28). We should modify BonJour's description a bit here: Weak Foundationalism need not demand that the amount of direct warrant perceptual beliefs be "very low"; all that's required is that this warrant be insufficient for knowledge or for rationally held belief. The Weak Foundationalist then attempts to:

augment the justification of both basic and nonbasic beliefs by appealing to the concept of coherence. Very roughly, if a suitably large, suitably coherent system can be built, containing reasonably high proportion of one's initially credible basic beliefs together with nonbasic beliefs, then it is claimed, the justification of all the beliefs in the system, basic and nonbasic, may be increased to the point of being adequate for knowledge, where achieving high enough degree of coherence may necessitate the rejection of some of one's basic beliefs. (pp. 28–9)

Is Weak Foundationalism a coherent structural option? In the following two sections, we'll briefly address that question. I will defend this structural option from its rivals on either side of it – from foundationalism and from Coherentism.

WEAK FOUNDATIONALISM AND FOUNDATIONALISM

According to most versions of foundationalism, warrant is transmitted among beliefs in a linear fashion: one or more beliefs that are all already fully justified form the basis for a new belief, which then, if all goes well, becomes fully justified, and is then available to base still further beliefs on. According to DWR, warrant is not always transmitted in this way. A group of beliefs, none of which is fully justified independently of the support it receives from the others, transmit warrant among themselves, and many of the beliefs in the group become fully justified as a result. A foundationalist may object to this mutual exchange of warrant among perceptual beliefs. But beliefs often do mutually support one another, as even such a staunch foundationalist as Alvin Plantinga recognizes here:

The supports relation, clearly enough, is not asymmetrical. Special relativity provides evidential support for muon decay phenomena, and muon decay phenomena also provide evidential support for relativity theory. A person could sensibly accept relativity theory on the evidential basis of muon decay phenomena, but it is also true that a person could sensibly accept muon decay phenomena on the basis of relativity. For one who is convinced of the Axiom of Choice, that axiom could serve as her evidence for the Hausdorff Maximal Principal; for the former entails the latter. But someone else already convinced of the latter could properly use it as his evidence for the former; for the latter entails the former.[7]

But, Plantinga insists, even though two beliefs may in fact mutually support each other, the rational person will not both believe the first on the basis of the second and the second on the basis of the first, nor, more generally, will there properly be any circles of beliefs based on one another – it cannot properly occur that one belief is based on another, which in turn is based on another, . . . , which is based on the original belief:

But even if the supports relation is not asymmetrical, the basis relation, in a proper noetic structure, *is* asymmetrical. If my belief that A is accepted on the evidential basis of my belief that B, then my belief that B must not be based on my belief that A. More exactly, suppose N is a proper noetic structure. Then if the belief that A (in N) is based upon $B_1 \ldots B_n$, none of the B_i will be based upon A. If my belief that life arose in antediluvian tide pools is based on, among others, my belief that the probability that life would arise in a given tide pool in a hundred-year period (under the conditions that then obtained) is $1/n$, then (if my noetic structure is proper) my belief that that probability is $1/n$ will not be based on the proposition that life arose in this way, and there were n tidepool/100 year pairs available. (p. 74)

Now, it is certainly true that if A is believed *solely* on the basis of B, then B had better not be believed on the basis of A, and that there cannot be any circles in the *believed* solely *on the basis* of relation. If that were Plantinga's point, he would be right. But according to DWR, perceptual beliefs do not receive all of their warrant from other beliefs; each belief starts out with a certain amount of direct warrant. In such a case, why could not the mutual support among the beliefs render them rationally acceptable, even though they are not rationally acceptable independent of this mutual support?

Consider a very simple system, consisting of just two beliefs, belief A and belief B. Suppose A and B each has a good deal of direct warrant for the subject in question, but that the amount of direct warrant each enjoys for her falls just short of what's needed for them to be sufficiently warranted. It's difficult to see how Plantinga could reject that such a situation, as so far described, could arise. Given that he, as a good foundationalist, believes in direct warrant, and given his views about how direct warrant is generated (and also on any plausible view about how direct warrant might be generated), I think he pretty well has to admit that beliefs can enjoy direct warrant just shy of the amount needed for knowledge. *Admit* might even be the wrong word; I suspect he'd happily accept this much.

But now suppose further that A and B are mutually supporting beliefs – a possibility that, as we've seen, Plantinga recognizes. Now suppose that our subject considers her two beliefs *together*, noticing that A supports B and that B supports A. Shouldn't she then feel more confident about both beliefs, and rationally so? And wouldn't each then transmit some warrant to the other? After all, each enjoys significant warrant and supports the other, and our subject has noticed this. When you have a (partially or sufficiently) warranted belief, like A, notice that it supports another belief (B, in this case), and, as a result, increases your level of confidence in that other belief; that seems a clear case in which warrant has transmitted from A to B. But likewise in reverse – from B to A. But then we would seem to have a violation of Plantinga's insistence that "the basis relation, in a proper noetic structure, *is* asymmetrical. If my belief that A is accepted on the evidential basis of my belief that B, then my belief that B must not be based on my belief that A" (p. 74).

However, Plantinga's arguments (see primarily the section entitled "Against Circles," pp. 74–77) seem suited only to establish the conclusion that the relation of *believes* solely *on the basis of* is asymmetrical (and noncircular) in a proper noetic structure, and have no power against our example, which, though it includes mutual *partial* basing, violates none of the intuitions Plantinga uses to rule out the propriety of circles. We may suppose that B was already a belief the subject held before it was "brought into contact" with her belief A; the result of that contact was perhaps just an increase in the level of confidence with which B was held. So B is not believed solely on the basis of A. Likewise, A is not believed solely on the basis of B.

Plantinga intuits that "Warrant does not increase just by virtue of warrant transfer."[8] Understood correctly, he's right about that. Of course, in an important sense, the warrant of one's whole system of beliefs not only can, but hopefully, often does increase by virtue of warrant transfer (or "warrant transmission," as I prefer to call it, for a reason given below): when one belief transmits warrant to another, and the second becomes more warranted without the first, thereby becoming less warranted, the warrant of one's whole system of beliefs has increased by virtue of warrant transfer. But what is true here is that the second belief cannot gain more warrant by the transfer than the first belief had to begin with. It's in that sense that warrant does not increase by virtue of warrant transfer. And that doesn't happen in my example. Rather, warrant that is direct to one belief is transmitted to the other, and vice versa, but we needn't, and I don't, suppose that either belief gains more by warrant transmission than the direct warrant that the other belief had to transmit. Indeed, though B is partially based on A and A is partially based on B, *no warrant moves in a circle*: the warrant A transmits to B was direct to A and did not come from B, and the warrant B transmits to A was direct to B and did not come from A. Of course, our subject *might* start getting *over*confident about her beliefs, treating B as if it were supported by a sufficiently warranted belief, because she loses track of the fact that A (B's partial basis) is sufficiently warranted only because of the support it received from B. If this happens, our subject's noetic structure will be defective. But we don't have to suppose that any such defect occurs, and I'm supposing that it does not.

And, of course, if both beliefs were very close to being sufficiently warranted just by virtue of their direct warrant, and each transmitted enough warrant to the other, then it will happen that each becomes sufficiently warranted by the partial mutual basing described above. So we get the result promised above: sufficiently warranted beliefs that are not properly basic, nor are they based upon properly basic beliefs. Here it's important not to be misled by the term Plantinga uses, *warrant transfer*, which to the ears of most of us suggests that the transferrer loses what it transfers to the receiver of the transfer. That's not how it works in warrant transfer among beliefs – which is why I prefer the term *warrant transmission*, because it doesn't carry as strong a suggestion of such a loss. Take a case of simple, one-way inference (the kind of basing foundationalists like): C is sufficiently warranted, you notice it implies D, and infer D from C. D becomes warranted (perhaps sufficiently so) by virtue of warrant transfer/transmission from C, but C's level of warrant is not thereby reduced (and *certainly* is not reduced by as much as D's level of warrant is increased). In our example of partial mutual basing, then, both beliefs will become sufficiently warranted, because they were almost so just by virtue of their direct warrant, and each received enough transmitted warrant from the other to make up the difference without losing the warrant it transmitted to the other.

In our two-belief case, I supposed both beliefs were initially (independently of any warrant transmission) just short of being sufficiently warranted. Notice, however, that this is inessential to the case, especially where you get a large system of beliefs, each of which has direct warrant, and enters into partial-basing relations with many of the others (so that each can receive warrant from several other beliefs). Here, the immediate warrant may fall well short of being sufficient, and yet the beliefs comprising the system may end up being sufficiently warranted, because of the warrant they transmit (without losing) to one another. And there doesn't seem to be anything incoherent in such a structural possibility. At least, I can't see how a foundationalist could have any good reason to reject Weak Foundationalism as a possibility.

WEAK FOUNDATIONALISM AND COHERENTISM

But could a Coherentist successfully attack Weak Foundationalism? From a Coherentist perspective (which he has since abandoned), BonJour writes:

The underlying logic of the weak foundationalist's account has never been made adequately clear. The basic idea is that an initially low degree of justification can somehow be magnified or amplified by coherence, to a degree adequate for knowledge. But how is this magnification or amplification supposed to work? How can coherence, not itself an independent source of justification on a foundationalist view, justify the rejection of some initially credible beliefs and enhance the justification of others? (p. 29)

Here BonJour points out an important difference in the role coherence plays in Coherentism and the role it plays in Weak Foundationalism. According to Coherentism, coherence is the ultimate source of warrant or justification – it is what has been called a principle of warrant *generation*. But, as BonJour points out, coherence is not such an ultimate source of warrant on a foundationalist view; on the Weak Foundationalist view, coherence is what we may call a principle of warrant *transmission*. And in the quotation indented above, BonJour seems to be baffled as to how coherence, construed as a method of warrant transmission, rather than as a vehicle of warrant generation (as itself an independent source of justification), could possibly work.

But at least to my thinking, it is easier, and not harder, to understand how coherence can facilitate warrant transmission than how it can account for warrant generation. The notion of (positive) coherence at play – a matter of the beliefs in question fitting in well with another or positively "dovetailing" with one another, rather than just failing to conflict – seems to be very close to, if it doesn't simply amount to, their mutually supporting one another.[9] And it seems that it is precisely when each of the cohering beliefs has something going for it independently of their relations of mutual support that this coherence will be of help in justifying the beliefs in question. Looked at the other way, it becomes harder, and not easier, to see what good the relations of mutual support among a group of beliefs can do if the beliefs in question do not have anything going for them already, independently of this mutual support.

This is closely related to some of the standard attacks on Coherentism. One objection, as BonJour puts it, is that:

no matter how high the standard of coherence is set, it seems clear that there will be many, probably infinitely many, systems of beliefs which will satisfy it and between which such a coherence theory will be unable to choose in an epistemically nonarbitrary way. (And *any* consistent empirical belief which is not internally incoherent will be a member of some of these systems.) (p. 25)

Another closely related objection that BonJour considers is that Coherentism:

seems to deprive empirical knowledge of any *input* from or contact with the nonconceptual world, making it extremely unlikely that it will accurately describe that world. (p. 25)

The idea behind these objections is that coherence, by itself, just doesn't seem to be enough to secure rational acceptability for our empirical beliefs. Our empirical beliefs have to be sensitive to the sensory input we are receiving in order for them to be epistemically acceptable. Thus, one's system of empirical beliefs, no matter how coherent, will not be rationally acceptable if it is not sensitive to sensory input. As far as coherence dictates, any of the infinitely many systems of beliefs of which BonJour writes in the first of the above two quotations will be equally acceptable. But not only are these systems not equally acceptable, some of them – those that are not at all in tune with the subject's sensory input – don't seem to be acceptable at all.[10]

The foundationalist view, Direct Realism, has the potential to avoid these problems by building into its account of when a perceptual belief can be properly basic some requirement to the effect that the belief be appropriately sensitive to one's sensory input. But the Weak Foundationalist view, DWR, can also avoid Coherentism's problem here, in much the same way. For on DWR, the direct warrant that perceptual beliefs enjoy is essential to their becoming rationally acceptable. Of course, working out an acceptable account of how either Direct Realism or DWR can require that basic perceptual beliefs be "appropriately sensitive" to sensory input in order to enjoy the direct warrant that either theory assigns to them in good cases is not an easy task. But at least there seems to be hope for requiring such sensitivity on such views.

Thus, as BonJour seems to recognize (p. 29), this Weak Foundationalist view has the ability to avoid Coherentism's problems by building into its account of when perceptual beliefs have significant direct warrant the same kind of condition that Direct Realism uses for when those beliefs can be properly basic. But DWR avoids these problems, then, precisely by treating coherence as facilitating warrant transmission, where warrant can only be transmitted if it first gets generated in some other way, rather than as itself underwriting warrant generation. It becomes puzzling then why BonJour finds it more problematic to suppose that coherence facilitates warrant transmission. As far as I can see, that is the less problematic of the two options.

I conclude that coherence is best construed as a principle of warrant transmission, and that therefore, Weak Foundationalism can withstand a general structural attack from Coherentism.

Having defended Weak Foundationalism as a coherent structural option, I should add that foundationalism seems a sound structural possibility as well. As I've noted, DWR isn't a foundationalist view, because it recognizes a class of rationally held beliefs – perceptual beliefs about material objects – that are neither properly basic nor based on properly basic beliefs. However, it is open to the DWR theorist (though not required of him or her) to hold that other beliefs – perhaps beliefs in self-evident necessary truths and/or beliefs about one's own sensory experiences – are properly basic, and that portions of our bodies of beliefs have a foundationalist structure.

THE ARGUMENT FROM PSYCHOLOGICAL IMMEDIACY AND THE DEMANDS OF COMMON SENSE

If DWR is structurally sound (if Weak Foundationalism is a coherent structural option), how might one choose between Direct Realism and DWR? In the next several sections, we will look at the main arguments given in support of Direct Realism to see if we can find in those arguments reason to prefer Direct Realism over DWR, starting with the argument that seems to me to have the most potential for providing such a reason.

The best reasons I know of for preferring Direct Realism over DWR are tied to a simple psychological observation about how we in fact form perceptual beliefs. We seem to form perceptual beliefs in a psychologically *immediate* way: we don't consciously *infer* them from other beliefs, and our coming to hold these beliefs doesn't seem to follow our consciously noticing how well they fit in with other beliefs. Rather, whether it's due to innate or to learned dispositions, we seem set up to just form the relevant beliefs upon the occasions of having appropriate patterns of sensory experiences – without having to entertain any thoughts about the relation of the belief we're forming to others of our beliefs. This psychological observation then combines with a piece of common sense – namely, that our perceptual beliefs are typically rational – to militate in favor of Direct Realism. As Robert M. Adams puts the point (which he goes on to dispute), Direct Realism:

seems initially plausible to common sense. If I perceive an object under favorable conditions – holding it in my hand, for example, and at the same time viewing it in good light – what need have I for reasoning or inference? Don't I just know directly that the object is there?[11]

Because these beliefs that are formed in a psychologically immediate way seem nevertheless to be rational, they do not seem to depend for their rationality on any support they might receive from other beliefs. This type of argument can be given by Direct Realists against various skeptical or Evidentialist rivals, but could also be marshaled against DWR. To accept DWR is to accept that perceptual beliefs are partially based on one another – they transmit warrant one to another that is essential to their being rationally held – though they are formed, and often maintained, in a way that involves no conscious thought about their relations to one another.

But I *still* find DWR to be a very attractive account of the warrant of perceptual beliefs. This is largely because I think it's wrong to require that a belief be
formed due to a conscious noticing of its relations of support to other beliefs
in order for those other beliefs to transmit warrant to it. Perhaps, though
we take no notice of a perceptual belief's relations of "coherence" (relations
of mutual support) to other perceptual beliefs as the belief in question is
formed and maintained, we are appropriately *sensitive* to its coherence with
these other beliefs, where such sensitivity consists in such facts as that we
wouldn't hold or continue to hold the belief in question, or at least wouldn't
continue to hold it to the degree that we do, were it not for its coherence
with our other beliefs. One could be in that way sensitive to the coherence of
one's beliefs even where one gives no conscious thought to the relations in
question, and yet it seems to me that warrant might very well be transmitted
among beliefs in virtue of the believer's sensitivity to the evidential relations
that hold among them, even where she gives no conscious thought to those
relations.

This is based on very general thoughts about the conditions under which
beliefs transmit warrant to one another. Foundationalists, too, should make
such a move, I think. The general advice I would give is: Don't require for warrant transmission a conscious noticing on the believer's part of the relations
among the beliefs involved in the transmission. The foundationalist, then,
should not require that an inference be consciously performed in order for
one belief to transmit warrant to another. Consciously performed inferences,
after all, seem fairly rare, whereas beliefs whose rationality depends on support
from other beliefs at least seem fairly common. On the other hand, it doesn't
seem sufficient for warrant transfer that one belief a subject holds, as a matter
of quasi-logical fact, happens to support another, if the subject is oblivious to
this quasi-logical fact. There must be some appropriate psychological relation
between the beliefs in question for such warrant transfer to take place, it seems.
But according to the advice I am here issuing, it is enough that the believer be
sensitive in his or her holding of the second belief to its evidential relations to
the first belief – that he or she wouldn't hold the second belief, or wouldn't
hold it as firmly, if it weren't supported by the first. Following such advice
is necessary, I think, to avoid an overly idealistic and overly intellectualized
picture of cognitive processing.

So, although common sense seems to demand that we usually don't have
to infer our perceptual beliefs from other beliefs or consciously base our
perceptual beliefs on other beliefs in order for them to be justified, or even
notice any relations of support between a given perceptual belief and other
beliefs, DWR can live up to this demand.

Does common sense demand anything more? Do any commonsense intuitions tell against DWR? I think the relevant test of intuitions for deciding between Direct Realism and DWR concern our reactions to situations in which our perceptual beliefs do not form a very coherent picture of the physical world – where the positive coherence we are so accustomed to is lacking, but there also is no real incoherence among our perceptual beliefs. So suppose that, for all our lives, we only had sense experiences very sporadically, maybe only a couple of times a day for about two seconds at a time (the rest of the time, we fill the time by thinking about pure mathematics, and wondering what our next sensory experience will be like). And suppose that these sense experiences produced in us (perhaps through innate dispositions) perceptual beliefs to the effect that we were perceiving material objects in various ways. Would these beliefs be rationally acceptable? My own inclination is to say no, and this may explain why I am a Direct Warrent Realist rather than a Direct Realist. But this "intuition" I have about this bizarre little thought experiment amounts to little more than my sense that relations of positive coherence among our perceptual beliefs are essential to their rational acceptability, and we are imagining a situation too far removed from our actual experience for our intuitions about the situation to be worth very much. And *any* imagined situation in which our beliefs about the physical world form neither a very positively coherent, nor a positively incoherent, view of the world will be too far removed from usual experience for us to be able to trust our intuitions about it. Certainly, there aren't any *commonsense* intuitions about such cases. Thus, I don't think that DWR goes against common sense – though I also think it isn't demanded by common sense. But we still have to see whether any of the other arguments for Direct Realism can give us a good reason for accepting Direct Realism over DWR.

THE ARGUMENT BY ELIMINATION: ESCAPING EVIDENTIALIST ARGUMENTS

In the introduction to what is perhaps the most prominent expression of Direct Realism in twentieth-century philosophy, *Perception and the Physical World*,[12] David Armstrong claims that "there is a triad of 'theories of perception' which compete for the allegiance of philosophers: Direct Realism, Representationalism, and Phenomenalism" (p. 7). His method of establishing Direct Realism is by arguing against its competitors, and then answering objections to Direct Realism. In chapters 5 and 6, Armstrong attempts a "Refutation of Phenomenalism," but we need not go into that for the purpose of deciding between Direct Realism and DWR, because both views, being realist theories of perception, would agree in rejecting phenomenalism. What's important to our comparative purposes is Armstrong's "Refutation of the Representative Theory of Perception" in chapter 3. What exactly is being refuted here?

Armstrong's main argument against the Representative theory is that "we have no reason to believe in the existence of the physical objects postulated by the Representative theory" (see pp. 29–30). He writes:

Now it is clear that an upholder of the Representative theory of perception will have to say that the perceiving of a physical object or event is *mediate* perception based on the *immediate* perception or awareness of a sense-impression. But then the question arises what warrant we have for believing in the existence of these mediate objects of perception.

Making heavy use of arguments from Berkeley and Hume, Armstrong concludes that there are no good inferences from our sense impressions to the existence of physical objects:

Now, if the Representative theory of perception is correct, we have no evidence at all for passing from the immediate perception of sense-impressions to the mediate perception of physical objects. The hypothesis that sense-impressions are caused by physical objects can never be suggested by immediate perception, nor can it be confirmed. This means that we have no good reasons for believing in the existence of physical objects. (p. 29)

As I already noted in the first section, Reid, the most prominent Direct Realist of the eighteenth-century, is also very fond of Berkeley's and Hume's arguments against there being any good inferences from the existence of our sensations to the existence of material objects (see the Reid quotation in footnote 1 of this paper). And Reid is inclined to think antirealist views of bodies or perception to be absurd; that certain principles or premises lead to such an antirealist view is considered by Reid to be a conclusive reason for rejecting those premises. Thus, although Reid does not use the term *Direct Realist* to describe himself, I think the argument by elimination is, to a great extent, behind Reid's Direct Realism. Indeed, this argument by elimination may deserve the title of the "master argument" for Direct Realism.

What this master argument amounts to, at least once the options of phenomenalism – and skepticism – are eliminated on some other grounds, is that Direct Realism provides an escape from the Evidentialist argument pressed most forcefully by Berkeley. We need not get involved in the dispute over whether there indeed are any good inferences of the type denied by Berkeley, Hume, Reid, and Armstrong.[13] The Direct Warrent Realist can simply grant the Direct Realist that there are none.

But DWR, like Direct Realism, obviates the need for the type of grounding in our sensations that we are now granting is impossible. The argument by elimination depends on construing the "Representational theory" as requiring that our sensation beliefs provide good evidence for our beliefs about physical objects (realistically conceived). But if the view that is being rejected or refuted when "Representative" (or perhaps "Evidential") Realism is attacked does require this, the Direct Warrent Realist can join in the attack. DWR, like Direct Realism, does not require that there be any such good inferences. According to DWR, perceptual beliefs about physical objects receive their direct warrant independently of any arguments from sensations to physical objects. They then receive further warrant, enough to secure rational acceptability, from support they receive *from each other* (as well as perhaps from other, higher-level physical object beliefs). Thus, perceptual beliefs do not depend for their justification upon sensation beliefs or inferences from sensation beliefs, according to DWR. On DWR, perceptual beliefs do depend on their relations of mutual support to one another to be rational, and this is not required by Direct Realism. But the arguments Direct Realists lean on in attacking Evidentialist Realists have no tendency to show that such mutual support does not exist.

If the attack against "Representationalism" (or what is perhaps better called "Evidentialist Realism") works, then the field of theories of perception is indeed significantly cut down, and the remaining theories do seem to be more probable because of the reduction of viable competing views, but *both* DWR and Direct Realism are left standing. And there is nothing involved in the argument by elimination that I can see that would favor one of them over the other. If realist theories of perception are put on a "Direct" – "Evidential" continuum, DWR is at least close enough to the Direct Realist end of the scale that it avoids falling prey to the standard attack on Evidential theories.

PARITY ARGUMENTS AND REIDIAN EPISTEMOLOGY

Reid faced opponents who accepted certain beliefs as properly basic, but who would not accept any material object beliefs as such. One of Reid's most provocative arguments is a *parity* argument directed at such an opponent: Reid argues that his opponent displays arbitrary partiality in accepting those other beliefs, but not his perceptual beliefs about material objects, as properly basic.[14] This argument was grounded in a general approach to epistemology, which Reid defended vigorously, on which one rationally trusts all of one's natural belief-forming mechanisms, or faculties, unless and until one has good reasons for thinking them unreliable (or for thinking that some particular beliefs resulting from a faculty are false).

The twentieth-century Reformed Epistemologists picked up on this Reidian approach to epistemology and, explicitly in the case of Alston, issued parity arguments of their own for the proper basicality of some theistic beliefs. Continuing our project of examining the grounds for Direct Realism to see if they provide reasons for preferring Direct Realism over DWR, we will in this section examine whether there is anything in these arguments that gives an edge to Direct Realism. Then, in the following section, we will look at what happens to parity arguments for the rationality of religious beliefs if perceptual beliefs are given a DWR, rather than a Direct Realist, treatment.

According to Reid's account of the perceptual process, human beings are, prior to any experience, set up in such a way that they will have certain "original perceptions" upon the occasions of having certain sensations. Thus, a particular type of tactile sensation, or particular patterns of tactile sensations, produce in a human being both the concept of hardness and the belief in the existence of a hard material object. Reid also recognizes a class of "acquired perceptions," in which certain sensations indicate the presence of a material object with certain qualities because we have learned by experience that the sensation is usually accompanied by the presence of such an object. Thus, a certain kind of visual sensation causes one to believe that there is a hard material object present because one has learned by experience of the connection between this type of visual sensation and the presence of hard objects. But in the case of original perceptions, we do not have to experience any constant conjunction before the sensation can produce the concept and belief; it produces them simply because that's the way we're wired.

But even if it is granted that there are such original perceptions, a skeptic with regard to the existence of material objects might ask how we know that the beliefs formed in cases of original perceptions are true. Reid responded to the immaterialism of Berkeley and Hume with a parity argument. Reid groups Berkeley and Hume together with many other philosophers in what Reid calls the "ideal system" of philosophy. (I am not concerned here with the accuracy of Reid's treatment of his predecessors.) The distinctive mark of an "ideal" philosopher is that, so far as contingent truths go, he will accept the existence of "our thoughts, our sensations, and every thing of which we are conscious," and what can be proven on the basis of these mental items by deductive reasoning, but will not accept the existence of anything else.[15] Thus, the ideal philosopher would not accept the belief in material objects, even if this belief were granted to be the result of a Reidian original perception. Reid's response is to argue that the ideal philosopher's belief in the existence of his sensations is on no better ground than is Reid's original perception belief: We cannot give any reason for accepting beliefs of either kind. We are set up in such a way that upon having a sensation, we believe in its existence, and our constitution is also such that upon having certain sensations, we believe in the existence of material objects having certain qualities. To, as Reid puts it in one place,[16] "pay homage" to one belief while rejecting the other because it is unfounded is to be guilty of arbitrary partiality.

In a similar way, in a parity argument we will examine in the next section, William P. Alston has argued that certain beliefs that entail the existence of God are on equal footing with perceptual beliefs and should therefore be accepted as rational. Reid's response to the "ideal" immaterialist is similar to Alston's response to the person who would accept perceptual beliefs as being rationally acceptable while refusing to grant the same status to the theistic beliefs in question. Both Reid and Alston find specific things accepted by their opponent and argue that in order to avoid arbitrary partiality, their opponent must also accept some other beliefs as rational.

These specific parity arguments are grounded in a "general perspective on epistemology" that Alston claims to share with Reid (1983, p. 119), and which provides for a general parity argument against any opponent who is not a complete skeptic. Reid admits that he has "nothing to say" against what he calls a "thorough and consistent skeptic" – that is, a skeptic who will not accept any belief until the belief-forming faculty by which it is formed is shown to be reliable.[17] Such a skeptic is invulnerable to attack because *nothing* can be proven or shown until *some* belief is accepted. So a thorough skeptic (if he *is* thorough and consistent) will end up not accepting *anything* (not even that Reid should not believe things), and it will be "impossible by argument to beat him out of this stronghold." Such a skeptic must "be left to enjoy his skepticism."[18]

But besides the thorough skeptic, there is the "semiskeptic" who chooses some of the sources of his beliefs to be acceptable before they are verified. All other sources must be verified by these favored sources. (Reid's "ideal" philosopher is a type of semiskeptic.) Such a semiskeptic, then, on the level of beliefs, will accept the beliefs that result from the favored faculties as properly basic, but the beliefs that result from the other faculties are not acceptable until the reliability of the faculties in question has been shown by means of the favored faculties. Reid's main complaint against the semiskeptic is that his choice of favored faculties is completely arbitrary. It seems arbitrary to Reid to pick out certain ultimate sources of belief to accept without having a reason for picking them over the other sources. And no reason can be given for anything until some source of belief is accepted. As Reid sees things, we have a choice among three options: (1) beginning with an attitude of trust toward all our faculties; (2) beginning with an attitude of distrust toward all our faculties; or (3) beginning by picking out certain faculties to be accepted as reliable in a completely arbitrary fashion. To escape complete arbitrariness and thorough skepticism, Reid thinks we must begin with an attitude of trust toward all our faculties.[19]

Alston cites Reid and follows Reid's argument fairly closely. He writes that we will never get anywhere if we require of all sources of beliefs that there be a noncircular argument for their reliability before it is rationally acceptable to trust them. Alston calls a belief-forming practice J_{ns} (justified in the strong normative sense) if and only if "one has adequate reasons for supposing it to be reliable." On the other hand, a practice is J_{nw} (justified in the weak normative sense) if and only if "one does not have adequate reasons for regarding it as unreliable" (1983, p. 116). If we require all practices to be J_{ns} in order to be rationally acceptable, if we treat them as guilty until proven innocent, then none of our belief-forming practices and none of our beliefs will be rationally acceptable. Alston concludes:

Thus, if we are to have any chance of acquiring knowledge, we must simply go along with our natural reactions of trust with respect to at least some basic sources of belief, provided we lack sufficient reason for regarding them as unreliable. In the above terms, we must be content with being J_{nw}. And if some, why not all? Of course we could, if we chose, accept some sources without any positive basis, such as intuition and reasoning, and then require that other candidates be certified by the former, that is, require J_{ns} for these latter. . . . But, as Reid points out, this is to be guilty of arbitrary partiality. (1983, p. 119)

Thus, Alston concludes that we should "simply go along with our natural reactions of trust" to all, and not only to some, of our "basic sources of belief," at least until we encounter reasons for withdrawing that trust. We may face vexing questions about the extension of our "basic sources of belief," especially, as we'll discuss briefly in the section, when we consider Alston's proposal to include practices of the formation of religious beliefs. But assuming that sense perception, by which we form perceptual beliefs about material objects, is among our "basic sources of belief," Alston's proposal here is that it, along with the rest of our basic sources of belief, be granted the status of innocent until proven guilty. And that would seem to imply that the perceptual beliefs that issue from this practice should be accepted as properly basic.

This result would be incompatible with DWR, because according to DWR, the direct warrant that a perceptual belief can have in virtue of being the result of a firmly entrenched J_{nw} practice (or in virtue of anything else) is not sufficient for rational acceptability. But the interesting thing is that, although the Direct Warrant Realist cannot accept Alston's Reidian conclusion, he or she can accept most of the argument that leads to the conclusion. Perhaps the conclusion that Alston draws is too strong for the argument he gives. The Direct Warrant Realist can agree that we cannot require that practices be J_{ns} for them to be rationally acceptable. The result of this, however, need not be that we must accept the beliefs emerging from all firmly entrenched J_{nw} practices as rationally acceptable. The most it could show is that all such practices (and their beliefs) derive *some* warrant from the fact that they are appropriately "basic" practices of ours. It is just not true that we must accept the output of all our basic J_{nw} practices as rationally acceptable if we are to have any hope of attaining knowledge while avoiding arbitrary partiality. There is no partiality involved in assigning a certain amount of direct warrant to the beliefs formed by *all* of these practices. And we are not giving up all hope of attaining knowledge if the amount of warrant so assigned is less than the amount needed for rational acceptability, for some of these beliefs may support each other to the extent that they are rationally acceptable. So I do not see anything in the general parity argument that favors Direct Realism over DWR. As with the argument by elimination, my purpose is not to assess the overall merits of the argument. This general parity argument, in particular, seems to need a lot more work before it can be convincing. (For instance, the question of which epistemic practices receive initial warrant just in case they are J_{nw} needs to be more fully addressed.) My purpose has been simply to show that there is nothing in these arguments to favor Direct Realism over DWR.

Even if the Reidian epistemologist is right in claiming that we must assign some beliefs some amount of warrant simply because they are the result of a firmly entrenched J_{nw} practice, this does not mean that we must conclude that the beliefs resulting from all firmly entrenched J_{nw} practices are rationally acceptable unless there is some reason for thinking them false. We are not faced with an either/or choice of a global policy of innocent until proven guilty or guilty until proven innocent. At most, the Reidian epistemologist has shown that certain of our epistemic practices have *something* going for them prior to our being able to have any reason for thinking them to be reliable. And this the Direct Warrant Realist can accept.

ALSTON'S PARITY ARGUMENT

As I've noted, William P. Alston has argued, in several places,[20] that certain beliefs that entail the existence of God are on equal footing with perceptual beliefs. The beliefs in question are what Alston calls "M-beliefs" (for *m*anifestation); they are beliefs a person gains through Christian experience "about what God is doing, or how God is 'situated' vis-à-vis that subject at that moment" (1986, p. 655). M-beliefs are supposed to be "the 'perceptual beliefs' of the theological sphere" (1986, p. 655). An example of an M-belief that Alston gives is *God is strengthening me*. Alston advances parity considerations to argue that it is "just as rational to take Christian experience to provide prima facie justification for M-beliefs as it is to take sense experience to provide prima facie justification for perceptual beliefs" (1983, p. 120).

In (1983), Alston at places seems to draw the conclusion that being J_{nw} is sufficient for the rational acceptability of *any* epistemic practice. He writes that "if we take it that being J_{nw} in engaging in [Sense Perception] is enough to make it reasonable for us to do so," then we should "generalize this to *all* epistemic practices" (p. 119). However, one might wonder about assigning an innocent-until-proven-guilty status to some conceivable epistemic practices – and the passage we looked at in the previous section does hint at assigning such a status to all of our "basic sources of belief." But what is meant by *basic* here? More generally, how shall we draw the line between those ways of forming beliefs that need only be J_{nw} to be rationally acceptable and those that don't receive this presumption?

In his later (1986), Alston lists several features shared by what he there abbreviates "RE" (for "Religious Experience," the practice by which M-beliefs are formed) and "SP" (for "Sense Perception," the practice by which perceptual beliefs are formed about the material world on the basis of sense experience):

A religious experiential doxastic practice like RE seems to me to be on all fours with SP and other universal practices. It too involves a distinctive range of inputs, a range of belief contents, and functions that map features of the former onto contents of the latter. It is socially established within a certain community. It involves higher-level procedures of correction and modification of its first-level beliefs. Though it *may* be acquired in a deliberate and self-conscious fashion, it is more typically acquired in a practical, prereflective form. Though it is obviously evitable in a way that SP, e.g., is not, for many of its practitioners it is just about as firmly entrenched. (p. 664)

I will need a simple way of referring to all of the similarities Alston mentions above, so henceforth, I will use *firmly entrenched* to describe a practice that has these features. In (1986), Alston seems to base his specific parity argument on the claims that RE, like SP, is J_{nw} *and*, in this sense, firmly entrenched. But one may wonder whether that's the right place to draw the line. Reid, Alston's inspiration, often appeals to the *naturalness* of sense perception, and that our "original perceptions" are the workings of "original principles of our constitution." Such appeals to naturalness issue quickly from Reid when he responds to "semiskeptics" by means of parity considerations, as, for instance, in this passage:

The sceptic asks me, Why do you believe the existence of the external object which you perceive? This belief, Sir, is none of my manufacture; it came from the mint of Nature; it bears her image and superscription; and, if it is not right, the fault is not mine: I even took it upon trust, and without suspicion. Reason, says the sceptic, is the only judge of truth, and you ought to throw off every opinion and every belief that is not grounded on reason. Why, Sir, should I believe the faculty of reason more than that of perception; they came both out of the same shop, and were made by the same artist; and if he puts one piece of false ware into my hands, what should hinder him from putting another?[21]

Alston's RE may not be, in the appropriate way, natural enough for Reid – which may perhaps explain why Reid himself wasn't a "Reidian" about religious beliefs.

But, having acknowledged the difficulties here, which I won't attempt to sort out, let us assume that Alston's RE is an appropriate recipient of the same initial status as SP. For I think that, if we take a DWR approach to the rationality of perceptual beliefs, which we have been given no reason not to do, this ruins Alston's parity argument.

One of the key moves in Alston's parity argument is to admit that the perceptual beliefs that result from our engaging in SP display stronger relations of positive coherence ("we discover regularities" in the physical world by means of perception to a greater extent than we discover regularities in God's behavior by means of religious experience), but to argue that this does not ruin the parity argument.[22] Briefly, according to Alston's argument, this is because, given God's "wholly other" nature and other facts, we *shouldn't expect* to discover regularities in God's behavior to the extent that we discover regularities in the physical world by means of perception – we shouldn't expect Christian beliefs to display as much coherence as do perceptual beliefs. And thus, that Christian beliefs don't cohere to the extent that perceptual beliefs do provides no reason to think "Christian Practice" unreliable. From Alston's perspective, a lack of positive coherence is relevant to the extent that one would expect positive coherence to be displayed, and thus to the extent that the lack provides reason for thinking the practice in question is not reliable.[23] But from the perspective of DWR, the coherence displayed by perceptual beliefs is crucial to their having sufficient warrant in the first place. Thus, if M-beliefs don't display the same level of coherence as the beliefs of sense perception, they may well not be warranted to the extent that perceptual beliefs are. From this perspective, if the entity or entities that an epistemic practice (allegedly) puts one in touch with is such that one wouldn't expect the beliefs that result to display much in the way of positive coherence, this will make us suspect that it may be harder for the beliefs resulting from such a practice to be warranted. And that seems the more rational attitude to take.

So, the prospects for a successful Alston-like parity argument are quite dim from the perspective of DWR, and seem to require that we instead take a stringent Direct Realist approach to the epistemology of sense perception, which we've seen no reason to do.

I should hasten to add, however, that a lack of parity with perceptual beliefs in the epistemic status of M-beliefs does not show that these theistic beliefs are unwarranted or even that they're not sufficiently warranted, especially if one, like me, thinks of perceptual beliefs as being *super*-warranted – as being warranted to an extent that far exceeds what's needed for knowledge.[24]

But it does mean that parity arguments like those tried by Alston in the 1980s won't work. To many, including many theists who, while presumably thinking theistic beliefs are rational, may nonetheless find implausible the suggestion that they are rationally on a par with our perceptual beliefs about the external world, this may be a selling point, rather than a drawback, for DWR.[25]

NOTES

1. For example, Reid writes, "I think it is evident, that we cannot, by reasoning from our sensations, collect the existence of bodies at all, far less any of their qualities. This hath been proved by unanswerable arguments by the Bishop of Cloyne, and by the author of the *Treatise of Human Nature*." *An Inquiry into the Human Mind on the Principles of Common Sense*, chapter 5, section 3, p. 61 of D. R. Brookes, ed. Critical Edition (Edinburgh: Edinburgh University Press, 1997); p. 44 of R. Beanblossom and K. Lehrer, eds., Thomas Reid, *Inquiry and Essays* (Indianapolis: Hackett Publishing, 1983).

2. Berkeley also raises problems for belief in matter from his representationalism, and Reid again responds with a form of direct realism, this time claiming that our thought of material objects is conceptually direct, in addition to being evidentially direct. I address Reid's response to this second Berkeleyan problem in my "Reid's Anti-Sensationalism and His Realism," *Philosophical Review* 98 (July 1989): 314–38.

3. This movement in religious epistemology is commonly referred to as "Reformed Epistemology" or as "that Alston-Plantinga-Wolterstorff stuff." Key papers by Alston, Plantinga, and Wolterstorff appeared in Plantinga and Wolterstorff, eds., *Faith and Rationality: Reason and Belief in God* (Notre Dame, IN: University of Notre Dame Press, 1983). Most recently, the movement has culminated in two books: Alston's *Perceiving God* (Ithaca, NY: Cornell University Press, 1991) and Plantinga's *Warranted Christian Belief* (New York: Oxford University Press, 2000).

4. On this, see especially pp. 5–7 of Wolterstorff's editor's introduction to *Faith and Rationality*.

5. Though Haack developed the view as well in earlier works, see especially Susan Haack, *Evidence and Inquiry: Towards Reconstruction in Epistemology* (Oxford: Blackwell Publishers, 1993).

6. Laurence BonJour, *The Structure of Empirical Knowledge* (Cambridge, MA: Harvard University Press, 1985), 28–9. According to BonJour, "Weak foundationalism is a version of foundationalism" (p. 28), but that is because BonJour is using the term "foundationalism" in such a way that a view qualifies as foundationalist so long as some beliefs have some warrant or justification that does not come from their coherence with other beliefs.

7. Alvin Plantinga, *Warrant: The Current Debate* (New York: Oxford University Press, 1993), 73–4.

8. This is Plantinga's foundationalist thesis VII, at p. 76.

9. Here is BonJour on the notion of coherence: "What, then, is coherence? Intuitively, coherence is a matter of how well a body of beliefs 'hangs together': how well its component beliefs fit together, agree or dovetail with each other, so as to produce an organized, tightly structured system of beliefs, rather than either a helter-skelter collection or a set of conflicting subsystems. It is reasonably clear that this 'hanging together' depends on the various sorts of inferential, evidential, and explanatory relations which obtain among the various members of a system of beliefs, and especially on the more holistic and systematic of these" (p. 93). For further characterization, see the rest of section 5.3 (pp. 93–101) of BonJour, though, as BonJour admits, there is a lot of work left to be done on characterizing this important notion.

   In the following passage, BonJour characterizes the relations of the cohering beliefs as one of mutual support: "According to the envisaged coherence theory, the relation between the various particular beliefs is correctly to be conceived, not as one of linear dependence, but rather as one of mutual or reciprocal support" (91).

10. In *The Structure of Empirical Knowledge*, BonJour tries to meet these objections by supplying a "recognizably coherentist" account of observation (p. 110). However, as most have judged, this attempt did not succeed. BonJour has since abandoned Coherentism.

11. Robert M. Adams, "Berkeley and Epistemology," in *Essays on the Philosophy of George Berkeley*, ed. E. Sosa (Dordrecht: D. Reidel Publishing Company, 1987): 143–61; p. 153.

12. David M. Armstrong, *Perception and the Physical World*, (London: Routledge & Kegan Paul, 1961).

13. For a helpful survey of the arguments on the issue of whether there are any such good inferences to the existence of material objects – a survey that reaches a largely negative conclusion that probably would please Berkeley, Hume, Reid, and Armstrong – see William P. Alston's *The Reliability of Sense Perception*, (Ithaca, NY: Cornell University Press, 1993).

14. On this, see especially the section entitled "The Skeptic's Injunction is Arbitrarily Discriminatory" (pp. 197–206) of Wolterstorff, *Thomas Reid and the Story of Epistemology* (New York: Cambridge University Press, 2001).

15. *Inquiry*, chapter 7; Brookes p. 210 = L&B p. 112.

16. *Inquiry*, chapter 5, section 7; Brookes p. 71 = L&B p. 57.

17. *Inquiry*, chapter 5, section 7; Brookes p. 71 = L&B p. 57.

18. Reid, *Essays on the Intellectual Powers of Man*, Essay 6, chapter 5; p. 480 of D. R. Brookes, ed. Critical Edition (Edinburgh: Edinburgh University Press, 2002) = L&B, p. 276.

19. For further discussion of this argument of Reid's, see Alston, "Thomas Reid on Epistemic Principles," *History of Philosophy Quarterly* 2 (1985): 435–52 and DeRose, "Reid's Anti-Sensationalism and His Realism."

20. See Alston, "Religious Experience and Religious Belief," *Nous* 16 (1982): 3–12; "Christian Experience and Christian Belief," *Faith and Rationality*, (1983): 103–134; and "Perceiving God," *Journal of Philosophy* 83, (1986): 655–65. This argument was a very prominent part of Alston's religious epistemology in the 1980s, but not in his very recent work. Still, it's worth trying to assess it.

21. *Inquiry*, chapter 6, section 20; Brookes, 168–9.

22. See "Religious Experience and Religious Belief," especially pp. 8–12.

23. In the terminology of his 1982 piece, whether a lack of positive coherence has the result that the practice fails to be J_{nw}, where that stands for "justified in the weak, normative sense" – i.e., there's not adequate reason to think the practice is unreliable. (J_{ns}, justified in the strong, normative sense, means for Alston that there is adequate reason to think the practice in question is reliable.)

24. To avoid issues extraneous to our current concerns, I here suppress my contextualist views about knowledge (or, more precisely, about knowledge attributions). Taking these contextualist views into account, I'd describe super-warranted beliefs as beliefs that are warranted to an extent that far exceeds what's needed to satisfy the standards for knowledge that are set by most ordinary contexts.

25. Of course, it may not be a *strong* selling point if one sees other ways of escaping Alston's parity argument.

PART THREE

☙

SOCIAL-POLITICAL PHILOSOPHY:

GOD, ETHICS, AND BELIEF

8

The Epistemic Authority of Testimony and the Ethics of Belief

ROBERT AUDI

The social aspects of knowledge and justification are an important dimension of epistemology, and in the history of the field they have often been neglected. Recent work in social epistemology has partially filled this gap,[1] and the literature of epistemology now contains much discussion of testimony and other aspects of the communication of knowledge and, if to a lesser extent, justification.[2] In the history of philosophy, Thomas Reid stands out among major philosophers both for his extensive treatment of testimony and for his distinctive conception of it. My aim is to extend my own account of testimony partly in the light of what we can learn from Reid and partly on the basis of comparing testimony with other major sources of knowledge. I begin with a short statement of some essential points in my account. I then proceed to describe some major elements in Reid's view of testimony and to compare the two positions. In that light, I make a number of points about how testimony works in yielding knowledge and justification, about its status as a source of each, and about some ethical dimensions of our reliance on it. The final section addresses an aspect of the importance of testimony for the philosophy of religion.

TESTIMONY-BASED BELIEF

When philosophers speak of testimony, they usually have in mind not the formal reporting of the court witness, nor even the self-conscious delivery of information in ordinary circumstances, but virtually any instance of someone's telling somebody something.[3] This is roughly a matter of saying the kind of thing from which we learn facts, however uninteresting or readily forgotten they may be. In this wide sense of 'testimony', the term applies to nearly everything we say to others. To be sure, there is the *expository saying* illustrated when, in setting out someone else's view, we drop ascriptive expressions like 'for her' and express the view from the inside. There is also the *theatrical saying* characteristic of acting and the *narrative saying* exemplified by reading a story aloud to others. What is said in these cases does not constitute testimony, or at least, testimony *simpliciter*, as opposed to testimony-in-fiction. For cases that do, the verb 'attest' often serves better than 'testify' (as do 'tell' and 'say', used with 'that'), and I will often speak of attesting, attesters, and so on, as well as of testimony.

If the philosophically interesting notion of testimony is immensely wide, the philosophically most important notion of testimony-based belief is much less so. I take this to be the kind of belief that arises naturally, non-inferentially, and usually unselfconsciously in response to what someone says to us. I ask you the time; you tell me it is nine o'clock; and straightaway, I believe this on the basis of your saying it. This basis relation that your testimony bears to my belief has a causal component, but that is not its only element. If I mishear you, your saying not that it is nine but that it is noon could cause me to believe it is nine; but my belief is not then based on your *testimony that it is noon*. It is in fact not, properly speaking, based on your testimony (as opposed to your testimonial act) at all. But I might still be said to believe it *because of*, and perhaps *from*, that testimony, as I certainly might believe that you have a cold from your attesting to this in a nasal voice, even when I do not understand what you have said and hence do not believe on the basis of your testimony that you have a cold.

Another case in which belief is produced by testimony, but not based on it, is this: Suppose I believe something on the basis of *premises* about your testimony, as where the content seems implausible by itself but I judge you to be both highly competent and unassailably sincere, and for that reason I believe what you say. Here I may also be said to believe it from your testimony and, if I come to know it, to know it *through* that testimony. But this is not belief or knowledge on the *basis* of your testimony. My basis is a combination of your testimony and my beliefs about you. To be sure, what is believed on the basis of testimony is also believed *from* it; but the converse does not hold.

Testimony is not the only case in which a mere causal relation between a source of knowledge and a belief based on that source is not sufficient to render that belief knowledge of the kind distinctive of the cognitive products of that source. A perceptual belief, for instance, is more than a belief caused by seeing, hearing, or otherwise perceiving a perceptible object. It must certainly be more if it is to constitute perceptual *knowledge* of the object. A machine that stimulates our brains in a certain way could cause us to believe (truly) that this machine is before us without providing us with any ground for believing this and without our perceiving it there or otherwise knowing that it is there.

Here, as in further respects, testimony is like other sources of knowledge and justification.

Perception provides more than a source of analogies (and disanalogies) with testimony. To yield a testimony-based belief, an attestation must figure as a perceptual object, say as heard. It must be appropriately received, and the appropriate reception requires that it be a perceptual as well as a semantic object. That is why the belief that someone has a cold, formed only through noting the nasal tone of an attestation, is not a testimony-based belief, but only a kind of belief *from testimony*. The content of what is said is irrelevant to the grounding of this belief. In a sense, then, testimony-based (or, equivalently, testimonially grounded) belief requires semantic interpretation or, at any rate, semantic construal. This is why misinterpreting an attestation can prevent the proper functioning of the testimony.

It would be a mistake, however, to think that some conscious activity of interpretation is generally required for testimony-based knowledge. Typically, we simply understand what is said and believe it. There may be a kind of interpretation process accomplished by the mind (or perhaps just by the brain). This certainly seems to occur where we avoid misinterpretation or see past an apparent ambiguity produced by syntax, intonation, multivocality, or some other source of potential misunderstanding. But no conscious activity of, say, parsing is automatically required for normal adults receiving testimony in their native language.

Even where one must think about what is said and laboriously interpret it, as with a complex message or an utterance by certain influent non-native speakers, it does not follow that one's belief arising from finally accepting the message one discerns is inferential. Indeed, testimony-based belief, as I construe it, and as I think it is normally understood, is never inferential. If, before taking your word for my student's having left a paper for me by yesterday's deadline, I must note that it could not have gotten in the mail room (which was locked at the end of the day) any later than the deadline, my belief is at most partly based on your testimony.

It is not easy to explicate such cases of two or more independent grounds for belief. Here both are necessary; but I can also have two independent sets of grounds, say one perceptual and the other testimonial, that are each sufficient for my knowing the proposition in question (p). There are other aspects of what we might call *mixed grounds*, but we may here set them aside. It is quite enough if we can understand belief based wholly on testimony, as much belief surely is.

One further point is needed before we can proceed to epistemological aspects of testimony. To say that testimony-based belief is not inferential is not to imply that it is "uncritical" or even requires a degree of credulity incompatible with a critical habit of mind. This seems to hold even for much testimony-based belief formed where one has no information about the attester beyond what the context provides, which is often very little. We all have background beliefs that constrain what we accept, for instance by preventing our accepting stock market forecasts without special evidence; and some people may have standards of plausibility that go beyond the constraints created by these beliefs. One might, for instance, be habituated to taking intonation and facial features into account. No specific beliefs need express fully the way these elements constrain one's acceptance. At least for non-skeptics, a critical stance is possible without reasoning from any of its standards to the acceptability of the testimony, and indeed without inference at all. Our critical habits and even our critical standards need not all reside in propositions we believe. Even active monitoring of testimony is possible without inference: if nothing is noticed that requires raising questions or drawing inferences, no questioning or inference need arise even from attentive monitoring by a critical listener.

Testimony as a Basis of Knowledge and Justification

If testimony-based belief is non-inferential, then if such belief can constitute knowledge, it might seem to follow that it constitutes non-inferential knowledge. This does not obviously follow, however. For perhaps it is possible for a belief's status as knowledge to *depend* on inference in certain ways even when the belief is not itself inferentially based on any other belief. From the perspective of a certain kind of epistemological coherentism, this is how it might be: even if I non-inferentially believe what you tell me, I do not know it except on the basis of either inferring it (perhaps unconsciously) from something else, or at least apart from having a set of suitable premises available to me and an appropriate readiness to infer it from them. Elsewhere I have argued against even the weaker of these inferentialist pictures of knowledge,[4] and I here assume the independently plausible view that we commonly acquire non-inferential knowledge from testimony.

I do not mean to deny that there is here (as elsewhere) a *negative* dependence on inference: our knowledge can be defeated if we draw certain inferences, for instance, infer from certain telltale signs that the attester is unreliable. But to treat testimony-based knowledge as inferential on that ground is rather like treating the absence of poisonous gas as a source of one's physical well-being because, if such gas were present, one would be ill. Vulnerability to defeat by inferences that could occur does not entail dependence on them in any positive sense. Quashing skeptical worries might require drawing certain self-protective inferences, but I take it that testimonially grounded knowledge is possible without the support of precautionary inference.[5]

It is one thing to say that testimony can be a source of non-inferential knowledge; it is quite another to say under what conditions it achieves this epistemic success in producing testimony-based belief. In earlier work, I have suggested that the attester must know that p, and that the recipient of testimony, in addition to acquiring a belief that is non-inferentially based on the testimony, must not have certain kinds of grounds for doubting or denying p. A great deal must be said to explicate all of these conditions, but much of that comes from general epistemology and can be presupposed here.[6]

I have also maintained that, although testimony is unlimited in the diversity of knowledge it can convey and in the ease with which it enables us to learn things "straightaway," it is, in two ways, limited. First, its success depends on the operation of another source of knowledge, namely perception, broadly conceived. Second, what is known through testimony must apparently be both known by the attester and, in addition, known (by the attester or someone earlier in the testimonial chain) at least in part on the basis of another source, such as perception or reflection. In order to receive your testimony about the time, I must hear you or otherwise perceive – in some perhaps very broad sense of 'perceive'[7] – what you say; and in order for me to know the time on the basis of your testimony, you or someone else must have read a clock or come to know the time on some other basis that is at least partly non-testimonial. If all this is right, testimony is, as a source of knowledge, *operationally dependent* on perception and *epistemically dependent* on at least one non-testimonial source of knowledge.

These points about epistemic limitations of testimony do nothing to undermine a special strength of testimonial sources: their combinatory capacity. It is true that, in relation to transmission of knowledge, a testimonial chain can be no stronger than its weakest link, so that if the attester fails to know the proposition avowed to the recipient, the latter does not thereby come to know it; and if the former has barely good enough grounds for knowledge, the recipient does not acquire any better grounded knowledge on the basis of the testimony. But – and this is a strength of testimony – in transmitting knowledge, a testimonial chain (a chain of attestations that p and beliefs based on them) need be no weaker than its weakest link. As long as each attester acquires knowledge that p from the previous one, it does not matter how many attesters there are. Testimony-based knowledge is indefinitely extendable. If it is in the first instance second-hand and may pass through limitlessly many hands, it need be none the worse for wear. This is not only epistemically

significant, but is important for the philosophy of religion. For in some religious communities, including Christianity, testimony of ancient origin is a
major element in the claims of religious knowledge.

To be sure, if we consider one person's *saying* that p to a second, the second's
saying it to a third, and so on, then the probability that a recipient knows that
p, given that the first attester does, tends to drop with the latter's distance
from the former in the chain. But this is a chain of attestations, not a chain of
testimony-based beliefs as just described.

The case with justification is different. Whereas I need to know that p in
order for someone else to know that p solely on the basis of my attesting to
it, I do not need any justification for believing p in order for my testimony
to provide others with ample justification for believing it. The credibility
of testimony may be objectively ill-grounded in this way without that fact's
providing any reason for the recipient to doubt either what is said or the
attester's credibility (where objective grounding of justification for a belief is
the kind that counts, as does normal perceptual grounding, toward the belief's
constituting knowledge). The crucial question here is whether my hearer is
justified in believing my testimony (something quite possible without the
hearer's having any actual *belief*, as opposed to dispositions to form beliefs,
concerning my credibility).

These points about justification bear on the status of testimonial chains
viewed in relation to justification. For one thing, one attester may be only
minimally credible to the recipient(s) in question, who is thereby only minimally justified in the resulting testimony-based belief that p, whereas further
down the line, an attester is highly credible and gives the last recipient much
better justification for p than that gained by the recipient of the minimally
credible testimony that p. It should be added, however, that for justification
(as most plausibly understood), the metaphor of a chain is less appropriate.
For regardless of how many links there are (with one person attesting to p
and the recipient passing on the attestation to someone else), the justification accruing to the last testimony-based belief in the chain depends only
on the justificatory basis the person in question has in that context. This
may be independent of how much justification anyone had earlier in the
chain.

There is a related contrast: whereas we can acquire testimony-based knowledge that p from testimony that p without having any knowledge of (or even
justification regarding) the credibility of the attester, we apparently cannot acquire justified testimony-based belief that p without having any justification
concerning that credibility. The former point is amply illustrated by the acquisition of such knowledge on the part of tiny children who are too conceptually

unsophisticated to have knowledge (or justification) concerning credibility. The latter point is controversial (and I return to it in the final section), but it is quite plausible once we note that *having* justification for a proposition does not entail believing it; hence, having justification regarding the attester's credibility does not entail the psychologically implausible requirement that the recipient must have *beliefs* about it. The point is still more plausible if we assume, as I do here, that the degree of justification required on the recipient's part is only that degree we normally have regarding ordinary attesters speaking within a domain concerning which we have no reason to think they are either misinformed or motivated to deceive us. I take the position (which I grant sets skepticism aside) that much of what people say to us and around us meets this condition. I view normal people as very commonly, and in many kinds of situations quite typically, both veracious and competent in the matters on which they give testimony.

I certainly do not wish to imply that, independently of the testimony, we need justification for *p* itself. This requirement would surely undermine our capacity to acquire much of the justification that, on a non-skeptical view, we gain from what we are told. Of both points – the common veracity and usual competence of attesters, and the absence of any need for justification regarding each attested item we are justified in believing – I consider Reid a persuasive proponent. Let us consider some of his main ideas concerning testimony.

SOME MAJOR ELEMENTS IN REID'S CONCEPTION OF TESTIMONY

Reid is well known to have taken humanity to have a 'natural credulity': "I believed by instinct whatever they [my parents] told me, long before I had the idea of a lie, or thought of the possibility of their deceiving me. Afterwards, upon reflection, I found that they had acted like fair and honest people."[8] Later, he includes a principle of credulity with one of veracity. Speaking of God as intending that "we should be social creatures" and as implanting "in our natures two principles that tally with each other," he says:

The first of these principles is, a propensity to speak truth.... Truth is always uppermost, and is the natural issue of the mind...

Another original principle implanted in us by the Supreme Being, is a disposition to confide in the veracity of others, and to believe what they tell us. This is the counterpart to the former; and, as that may be called *the principle of veracity*, we shall, for want of a more proper name, call this *the principle of credulity*. (pp. 94–5)

Developing the idea of credulity in relation to what he apparently views as reasonable belief formation in situations in which one receives testimony, he continues:

It is evident that, in the matter of testimony, the balance of human judgment is by nature inclined to the side of belief; and turns to that side of itself when there is nothing put into the opposite scale. If it was not so, no proposition that is uttered in discourse would be believed, until it was examined and tried by reason; and most men would be unable to find reasons for believing the thousandth part of what is told them. Such distrust and incredulity would . . . place us in a worse condition than that of savages. (p. 95)

If one is inclined to think of credulity as implying naïveté, one has the wrong picture of Reid's view. As he says in comparing the inductive principle with that of credulity, "This principle, like that of credulity, is unlimited in infancy, and gradually restrained and regulated as we grow up" (p. 102).

If, however, Reid finds important similarities between testimony and other sources of knowledge and belief, he also sees differences:

There is, no doubt, an analogy between the evidence of sense and the evidence of testimony. Hence, we find, in all languages, the analogical expressions of the *testimony of sense* . . . and the like. But there is a real difference . . . In believing upon testimony, we rely upon the authority of a person who testifies; but we have no such authority for believing our senses. (*Essays on the Intellectual Powers*, p. 203)

It is interesting that in comparing memory with perception Reid does not draw this contrast:

If we compare the evidence of sense with that of memory, we find a great resemblance, but still some difference. I remember distinctly to have dined yesterday with such a company. . . . I have a distinct conception and firm belief of this past event; not by reasoning, not by testimony, but from my constitution. And I give the name of memory to that part of my constitution by which I have this kind of conviction of past events.

I see a chair on my right hand. What is the meaning of this? It is, that I have, by my constitution, a distinct conception and firm belief of the present existence of the chair in such a place . . . (*Essays on the Intellectual Powers*, pp. 203–204)

Reid's view appears to be that whereas our reliance on testimony is instinctual initially and regulated as we mature, our reliance on memory, like our reliance on perception, is *constitutional*. (What is constitutional can also be instinctual, and Reid's contrast between testimony and, on the other hand, perception and memory, is consistent with our having to rely on God's design even in the latter cases, in the sense that – as Reid seemed to think – the reliability of all our faculties is dependent on the "Author of Nature.")

Our reliance on perception, moreover, is associated with its feeding directly into cognition: perception, for Reid, seems at least normally belief-entailing (a property he apparently does not attribute to memory impressions as such). Shortly after noting that "the perception of an object implies both a conception of its form, and a belief of its present existence" (*Inquiry*, p. 84) and that this belief "is the immediate effect of my constitution" (p. 84), he says, "My belief is carried along by perception, as irresistibly as my body by the earth" (p. 85).

The irresistibility of belief-formation given certain perceptions and perhaps certain memory impressions might seem to preclude the applicability of any standards expressing the ethics of belief, since the beliefs in question might seem beyond the reach of the will. But the kind of irresistibility in question does not preclude our regulating our responses to these two sources, say in how *strong* a belief we form or in our disposition to form related *higher-order* beliefs, such as the belief that we may be deceived. To be sure, for what one might call *basic perceptions*, as opposed to the "acquired" ones that we have when we have learned to see the three-dimensional roundness of a globe rather than just its circularity, Reid does not emphasize any regulation.[9] He seems, moreover, to treat memory and perception as playing roles in the development of our knowledge that are quite different from the role of testimony.

It would be a mistake to think, on the basis of Reid's contrast between testimony and memory, that he took the importance of testimony as a source of knowledge to be a secondary matter. He describes as a first principle of contingent truths "*That there is a certain regard due to human testimony in matters of fact, and even to human authority in matters of opinion*" (*Essays on the Intellectual Powers*, p. 281). It is noteworthy, however, that what immediately follows this is not (as I read it) mainly an indication of why testimony should be considered worthy of regard, but something quite different though certainly closely related. It is an affirmation of its necessity in developing human knowledge: "Before we are capable of reasoning about testimony or authority, there are many things which it concerns us to know, for which we can have no other evidence" (p. 281). Perhaps he took the unavailability of other evidence here to indicate worthiness of belief, if only through the good grace of God. But the concepts in question – certainly that of knowledge – are connected to the domain of reliability as well as with worthiness of regard, and in a way that implies the possibility of justification of testimony-based beliefs by reasons.[10] This possibility is consistent with Reid's view that we do not normally *need* reasons to believe testimony.

We might speculate regarding one reason why Reid might think testimony is worthy of regard. (I am taking it that there *can* be a reason for this and indeed that one can have it, even if the principle that testimony is due a "certain regard" is self-evident and one rightly thinks it is.[11]) Consider the principle he introduces just prior to setting forth the principle of testimony just quoted:

Another first principle I take to be, *That certain features of the countenance, sounds of the voice, and gestures of the body, indicate certain thoughts and dispositions of the mind.* (*Essays on the Intellectual Powers*, p. 279)

It is important to see that these features, sounds, gestures, and presumably other expressive aspects of human behavior are "natural signs": "It seems to me incredible, that the notions men have of the expression of features, voice, and gesture, are entirely the fruit of experience" (p. 280). Now, suppose Reid took testimony to be characteristically accompanied by natural signs of believing what is attested to (roughly, of conviction); he might have thought of testimony, if only in elementary or otherwise special cases, as naturally *indicating*, not as just *reporting*, or linguistically expressing, *belief*. In that case, it is easy to see how he could regard as so natural the kind of credulity that enables one to form testimony-based beliefs non-inferentially and without either screening for insincerity or seeking some premise to support what is attested to. Moreover, the recipient's ground for taking the attester to be sincere could be considered to be characteristically more "direct" than it would be if one needed to infer sincerity; there would normally be no liability to interference by deceitfulness or misspeaking, for instance. Misspeaking occurs, of course, but usually it is corrected before the recipient forms the relevant belief or at least before that becomes in any sense fixed.

We have seen that Reid thinks of belief as an inevitable product of perception (recall the passage quoted from p. 85 in the *Inquiry*), and it is plain that he takes perception as a major and reliable source of true belief. This is clear in connection with his principle 5, concerning perception; and the same holds for other major sources of belief as he sees them: he has "first principles" for consciousness and memory, for instance. Thus, even if, as it seems to me, he does not treat testimony as basic in the way perception, consciousness, and memory are – in part because we do not in those cases rely on someone else's authority – he may think of it as characteristically putting before us not just a verbal expression of a proposition but the attester's belief of it. We can sometimes "see that" one person believes another to be guilty of an offense, "feel" or sense a person's bigoted beliefs underlying a proposal, and the like.

Even apart from the possibility that belief can be somehow present in testimony, if my belief that *p* is directly (and "reliably") produced by your belief that p, is there any reason why it cannot inherit the strength, or at least a good proportion of the strength, of your own grounds? Those grounds might have to be ultimately at least in part non-testimonial, but that would not prevent my getting a kind of knowledge that is both non-inferential and not evidentially dependent on inductive grounds. (I return to this point in the last section.) My response to your belief is ultimately a response to your response to your grounds; and if, as seems plausible, the relevant knowledge-sustaining relation of *being a response to* is transitive, my belief is also a response to your grounds.[12] Such a chain may be long, either owing to the number of its essential links or to the length of some of them, say those constituted by memory connections. But here again it seems that if, in relation to transmitting knowledge, a testimonial chain can be no stronger than its weakest link, it also need not be weaker.

TESTIMONY AS AN EPISTEMICALLY ESSENTIAL SOURCE

It will be obvious that much of what Reid says about testimony is highly consonant with the sketch of its psychological and epistemological aspects I have presented on the basis of my own work on the topic. Indeed, I am aware of nothing he says that is clearly inconsistent with my conception of testimony. It may seem that my view that it is not a basic source of knowledge precludes treating it as an essential one, but this is not so. It need not be *basic*, in the sense that it can produce knowledge without the recipient's relying on some other source, even if it is *essential*, in the sense that what we think of as "our knowledge," in an overall sense, would collapse if the contribution to it made by testimony were eliminated: what remained would be at best fragmentary. Testimony is in this respect *globally essential* for human knowledge (and presumably also for our overall justification, which would also be fragmented if such elimination occurred). Indeed, I agree with Reid in the view that – in human life as we know it – one simply could not develop a body of knowledge at all apart from the instruction one receives in childhood, in which testimony is central.[13]

It is more difficult to see where Reid might stand on the matter of testimony-based justification. He speaks of reasons for believing testimony as well as of regard for it; both expressions suggest justification, however, and I think it is quite possible that he takes testimony to be a source of justified belief much as it is of knowledge (though the term 'justified belief' is not one he regularly uses). He notes, however, that most of us cannot give reasons for a "thousandth part of what we are told," and I take it that this is meant to indicate that for the vast majority of propositions we believe, we would also lack what might be called "independent evidence" (a justification, in one sense). He surely thought that for a huge proportion of these propositions that are objects of our knowledge, testimony, by contrast with the kinds of inductive grounds Hume took to be required for testimony-based knowledge and justification, is a (focally) essential basis of our knowledge of them as well as of our justification for believing them.

Would Reid think, then, that it is a mistake to maintain that in order to acquire testimony-based justification, one must have some justification either for taking the attester to be credible or for accepting *p*? I believe he need not. He *would* think that far more often than not we do not have independent sufficient reason for believing *p*; but that is utterly common in cases where we *do* have justification for taking the attester to be credible. Given his emphasis on the naturalness of veracity and on our utterly pervasive dependence on testimony in childhood, he at least leaves room for my view that – once we are mature enough to be candidates to have justification at all – we do have (prima facie) justification for believing normal testimony (the kind we typically get from family and friends).

Similarly, there is no reason to think that Reid must deny another point supporting my view that in order to obtain testimony-based justification for *p* one needs a measure of justification: apart from perceptual justification for believing something to the effect that you attested to *p*, I cannot acquire justification for believing *p* on the basis of your testimony. I need perceptually based justification for believing you said something and a related (semantic) justification for taking it to be *that p*; and again we find a contrast between testimony and an apparently more basic source. He says, for instance, that:

In artificial language [what is now called 'natural language'] the signs are articulate sounds, whose connection with the things signified by them, is established by the will of men; and in learning our mother tongue, we discover this connection by experience ... (*Inquiry*, p. 91)

He would presumably hold that one could culpably fail to have or exercise this knowledge of the relevant connection, whereas one would be deficient, but not necessarily culpable, if one lacked the innate power of perceptual belief-formation. Misinterpreting the words of one's language would tend to be avoidable and blameworthy in a way that being congenitally deaf is not.

In suggesting that Reid's view of testimony provides for its playing a role in knowledge (and presumably justification as well) that is less basic than the role of the standard basic sources, I may appear to undercut the point that testimony is (for Reid as for me) an essential source of knowledge and indeed of justification. But nothing I have said about testimony in comparison with other sources undermines the point that without testimony, we might not even acquire the concepts essential for so much as believing the propositions in question. In this way, it is globally essential in a genetic sense, as well as globally essential in the epistemic sense already noted: If we were deprived of all the knowledge and justification we have that arose from testimony, directly or indirectly, by inference (and is now memorially retained), we would be at best reduced to (as Reid put it) a condition worse than that of savages.

Moreover, everything I have said, and everything I am aware of in Reid's treatment of testimony, points to another aspect of the epistemological importance of testimony. It *is* a source of *basic knowledge*, that is, (propositional) knowledge not grounded in knowledge (or in justified belief) of some other proposition.[14] This is important. It distinguishes testimony from another non-basic source of knowledge – inference. Inferential knowledge is premise-dependent as well as dependent on at least one basic source; testimony-based knowledge has only the latter dependence. (Even in the case of knowledge by virtue of an inferential operation of reason, as with mathematical proofs, the conclusion is known or believed on the basis of a premise. Hence it is not basically known or basically justified, though it may still be a priori.)

It might seem that testimony cannot be a source of basic knowledge if I am right in thinking that although one need not believe that the attester is giving testimony that *p*, one must have grounds adequate *for* knowing or justifiedly believing this. But there is no inconsistency here: having grounds for believing this does not entail believing it. Even if it did, the belief in question would not necessarily be needed as a basis for believing the testimony, nor are the grounds a basis of the belief. We do not normally form such a belief. We may in some sense *presuppose* the proposition, but that is a quite different matter.

The point that testimony is a source of basic knowledge helps to explain why it is natural to hold the stronger view that testimony is a basic source of knowledge; for it is typical of such sources that they yield non-inferential knowledge, and it is necessary for a source's being basic at all that it do this with respect to the kind of knowledge for which it is a basic source. (It may seem that a basic source never yields *inferential* knowledge; but that is not clear, even if we leave out combined production of a belief from two sources, such as intuition and perception. Consider intuition as it operates in aesthetic experience: perhaps it might produce inferential knowledge constituting an interpretation of a poem, though it also produces non-inferential knowledge of such things as emotional tones in certain lines.)

TESTIMONY IN COMPARISON WITH OTHER SOURCES
OF KNOWLEDGE AND JUSTIFICATION

There are at least five further points that distinguish testimony from what I shall call the standard basic sources: perception, introspection, memory, and reflection (with intuition, in one sense, as a special case of the operation of reflection). I take these points in turn.

First, one cannot test the reliability of one of the basic sources or even confirm a deliverance of it without relying on that very source.[15] I refer here to *externally* testing for reliability – roughly, for reliability in yielding true beliefs in the appropriate domain *given* internal consistency. A source with inconsistent outputs is not a candidate for external reliability.[16] One can of course *internally* test for reliability by ascertaining whether there is inconsistency or probabilistic incoherence among the cognitive outputs of the source (though such testing would be only *negative* – aimed at ruling out *un*reliability, since consistency, and indeed even coherence, do not by themselves imply truth[17]). With perception, for instance, quite apart from any question of its overall reliability (which is not my concern here), one must, in a given case of mistrust, look again (or otherwise rely on perception). With memory, in order to overcome mistrust of a particular deliverance, one must try harder to recall or must consult other memories – and one must remember the original belief being examined, lest the target of confirmation be lost from view. With testimony, one can, in principle, check reliability using any of the standard basic sources.

The qualification 'in principle' is important. Even apart from the point that in normal human life one cannot acquire concepts without reliance on testimony, there may be facets of its reliability that one is in no position to check without dependence on its deliverances. Consider, for instance, testimony about technical matters on which, apart from relying on the testimony of colleagues or teachers, even experts do not know all one needs to know in order to understand these matters. It remains true, however, that important aspects of testimonial reliability can be checked without counting on specific knowledge grounded essentially in testimony, and the counterpart of this point does not seem to hold for the basic sources.

The second point about the standard basic sources in comparison with testimony concerns memory in particular and has already been suggested in that connection. Memory is central, in a way testimony is not, to both our retaining and our extending of knowledge at any given moment – at least if extension of knowledge, as where inference adds to what we know, is conceived as adding to knowledge we *retain*, as opposed to simply increasing the number of propositions we know. We could speak of *additive extension* to distinguish this (standard) case from *mere quantitative extension*, the case in which one simply gets new knowledge that increases the number of propositions one knows. That could occur where our brains are so affected that, without our memories' playing any role in the process, new knowledge of wider scope than our present knowledge (or of a larger number of propositions) supplants the knowledge we now have. But given the power of memory, even if knowledge could not be acquired at all without at least the amount and kind of testimony needed to learn a language (a process in which what parents or others attest to is crucial to acquiring a vocabulary), once we climb that linguistic ladder, we can discard it and still retain what we know.

Consider now the other standard basic sources. These I take to be basic with respect to knowledge as well as justification, whereas memory is basic only with respect to justification – assuming that what we *know* from memory we must have come to know on the basis of some other source. Reason in some minimal form is indispensable to possessing any knowledge (at least in protecting us from pervasive inconsistency), and certainly to inferential extension of knowledge, which depends on using deductive or inductive logic. Consciousness and perception are essential for development of new knowledge in their domains. There is, however, no domain (except possibly that of other minds) for which continued testimony is *in principle* needed for a significant increase of knowledge. Similar (but not entirely parallel) points hold for justification.

The third point is of a rather different sort. There is a sense in which testimony-based belief passes through the will – or at least through agency. There are at least two cases here. Consider the side of the attester. The attester must in *some* sense, though not necessarily by conscious choice, select what to attest to, and in doing so may also mislead or lie, in which case the testimony-based belief does not constitute knowledge[18] and the justification the recipient may get is, in a certain way we need not pursue here, objectively deficient in a sense that goes with the notion of misleading evidence. For the basic sources, there is no comparable analogue of such voluntary representation of information. Now consider the side of the recipient. The recipient commonly can withhold belief, if not at will, then by taking on a highly cautionary frame of mind. In many cases, then, testimonially grounded beliefs commonly pass through agency twice over. Their doing this does not entail an *exercise* of agency. The point is that testimony is subject to its power. The attester can falsify it and the recipient commonly has both a monitoring system and the voluntary capacity to withhold belief of a huge range of propositions, even if by no means just any proposition. To be sure, the contrast with the basic sources may be exaggerated; but we commonly can, and sometimes do, withhold belief from attested propositions in a way we cannot withhold belief from propositions strongly supported directly by experience or by reason.

What, then, of a case of double support, as where someone attests to a plainly self-evident proposition one had not thought of but intuitively sees to be true directly upon hearing it asserted? Here what is attested may be irresistibly obvious, so that withholding is not possible. It is also usually impossible where we already believe what we hear (though some people's attesting to certain propositions could even give us reason to *disbelieve* them).

I would also stress that the common possibility of withholding belief of what is attested to does not imply that in each case we must *consider* whether to believe the testimony, though we often do consider this. The point is that, commonly, whether we withhold is "up to us"; this is another place in which there is room for the application of an ethics of belief. For many cases, we may also have more voluntary control over how we *interpret* testimony than we have regarding normal deliverances of the standard basic sources. Laxity in exercising this control – or the unreasonable exercise of it – could yield a testimony-based belief that is either not justified or does not constitute knowledge.

In our (partial) voluntary control over our interpretation of testimony, as perhaps concerning withholdability of believing it, I grant that the contrast between testimony and the standard basic sources is probably more one of degree than of kind. But the degree of difference is significant, and it leaves room for the frequent application of standards of evidence that may properly limit one's natural credulity. Such standards are among those included in the ethics of belief. The phrase is appropriate because we can be intellectually – or even morally – irresponsible in not resisting belief where the attester is apparently insincere or the propositions averred are clearly implausible. A great deal can be said here (and I will return to the matter in the next section); my point now is that testimony is special among our essential sources of knowledge and justification. We tend to have greater control over belief-formation in testimonial cases; and the propositions in question can often be critically considered without dependence on that source, whereas (as already noted) deliverances of the basic sources cannot in general be so considered without reliance on the source in question.

It is, to be sure, a contingent matter when a person can withhold belief. Some people may be able to learn to withhold – even if not to reject as false – the natural belief that those speaking to them are people as opposed to robots.[19] Moreover, the possibility of withholding belief of what is plausibly and truly attested to would not show that testimony is not a basic source, but only that it is not an irresistible one. Still, it is significant that the normal level of control for the standard basic sources is different from that applicable to testimony. Reid seems to have been sensitive to this point. For one thing, he considered both receptivity to testimony and our use of induction to be "regulated" as we gain experience. He also contrasted testimony with memory and, especially, perception, on this score, as in the passage quoted above comparing memory and perception.

In addition, with respect to testimony, appraisal of credibility may always involve *both* the kinds of doubts we may have about basic sources and any we may have about the attester's response to them. To be sure, we sometimes speak of the "testimony of the senses." But this is metaphor, at least insofar as it suggests that the senses derive knowledge from another source, as attesters must ultimately do, since knowledge that *p* cannot derive from an infinite or circular testimonial chain in which *no* person giving testimony that *p* knows it even in part on a non-testimonial basis.[20]

One might think that the contrast between testimony and the standard basic sources as regards the will is important in part because testimony is less reliable than those other sources of justification and knowledge. Whether it is less so is a contingent matter. It is also a contingent matter whether testimony is less reliable in certain domains than in others. We normally take it to be highly reliable in matters concerning the attester's current mental states, with insincerity being the chief ground for doubting such attestations. By contrast, when it comes to religious phenomena, many are skeptical even when (as in the case of miracles) apparently independent reports concur. I doubt that Reid considered testimony intrinsically less reliable than the basic sources. In any case, the point would have limited significance. It would at best indicate a difference of degree rather than of kind and would allow the conclusion that, *given* adequate reliability, testimony, or some kind of testimony, functions as a basic source.[21] Moreover, for justification as opposed to knowledge, I do not see that actual reliability is the crucial ground (as I have argued elsewhere[22]), but that issue is too large to pursue here.

A fourth point of contrast between testimony and the standard basic sources has already been suggested. It concerns the need for grounds for the semantic construal of what is said on the basis of which it is taken to be *that p*. This is not a justificatory or epistemic burden intrinsic to the standard basic sources. In Reidian terms, we might say that apart from cases of what he called "natural language," testimony-based knowledge and justification must go *through convention*, since they depend on our understanding an artificial language; knowledge and justification grounded in the standard basic sources need only go *through nature*. I am not implying that no kind of interpretation is ever needed in order for (say) perception to yield knowledge or justification. My point is that testimony-based knowledge that *p* arises only when we have both perceptual justification for believing that the attester has affirmed something *and* semantic justification for believing that it is *the proposition that p* that is affirmed. This point illustrates both the operational dependence of testimony on perception and the epistemic dependence of testimony-based belief on semantic construal.

We might speculate that with Reidian natural language, such as the "threatening or angry tone of voice" by which "Children, almost as soon as born, may be frightened" (*Essays*, essay 6, chapter 5), what makes the language natural is that something about its oral expression is a criterion, in a Wittgensteinian sense, of some element it conveys. Here, however, we have knowledge *from* testimony rather than *testimony-based* knowledge; for just as we can know that people have a cold from their nasal tone regardless of what they attest to, a child can know that Father is angry quite apart from what he is saying.[23]

Granted, much a priori knowledge and justification is acquired *through* consideration of linguistic expressions of propositions. Still, on the most plausible account of the nature and basis of such knowledge and justification, its object is non-linguistic and, arguably, in principle accessible without reliance on semantic construal. In any case, the ground of justification or knowledge is a kind of understanding of the proposition in question or, perhaps more directly, the concepts figuring in or essential to it.

One might think that testimony could somehow convey propositional content directly to another mind without using any semantic "vehicle." If this is possible, it would surely require at least a *symbolic* vehicle, such as an image produced in my mind that I can see to come from some other mind. If someone simply causes me to have an image that produces a belief that *p* or, especially, simply causes me, in a direct way, to believe that *p*, then there is no testimony, but only some kind of cognitive product. Even where testimony is not verbal, then, if it retains its essential character, the fourth point of contrast with the basic sources seems unlikely to disappear, even if it becomes somewhat attenuated. But this speculative possibility is not what is normally in question in the epistemology of testimony, and it would, in any case, not affect the first three points of contrast.

It should also be granted that a lack of semantic understanding will normally restrict the range of propositions that are even candidates for one's a priori knowledge or justification, since one's comprehension of language will (for most of us, at least) limit the range of propositions we can get before our minds. Semantic *misunderstanding*–which is of course possible even in people of wide and deep semantic comprehension – may give us the wrong proposition or range of propositions. Nonetheless, neither of these defects need affect how good our grounds are once the right object is before us. To be sure, defeaters of knowledge or justification can come from semantically interpreted items and can afflict beliefs deriving from any of the standard sources; but none of those sources seems dependent on semantic grounds in the way that testimony is.

The fifth contrast I want to draw is of a quite different sort. It presupposes that testimony yields testimony-based knowledge in the recipient only if the attester knows that p; but although this point is controversial, any exceptions to it are at best rare and probably of special kinds that can be described in a way that enables us to set them to one side. In any case, given this presupposition, we can say that although testimony can increase the number of *knowers* in the world, it cannot increase the number of *propositions known*. Thus, in a sense, it cannot increase the amount of knowledge in the world. This is an important limitation. It does not, however, detract from the importance of testimony. Far from it: the indefinitely extensive testimonial communicability of knowledge is an incalculably valuable characteristic of testimony, and it is not paralleled by any of the standard basic sources. Moreover, in this limitation, testimony is like memory: it, too, cannot (by itself) increase the amount of knowledge in the world.

Testimony-based justification is a different matter. Testimony can *both* increase the number of justified beliefs in the world and contribute to the degree of their justification. It can thus add immensely to the amount of justification in the world. Indeed, as I have suggested already, there is much that we believe that we would not believe at all, much less justifiedly believe, apart from our reliance on testimony. Again, the comparison with memory is significant. For whereas testimony from many people can increase the justification of a single belief, memory impressions that p on the part of different people cannot – in the same way – increase the justification of a single belief. They can do so only indirectly, say by yielding testimony based on several people's memories; but this is quite different.

These contrasts between testimony and the basic sources are not meant to impugn the importance of testimony. In addition to being a source of basic knowledge and an essential source of our overall knowledge, it is apparently an essential source of much of our justified belief as well. Our overall knowledge depends on it in far-reaching ways, though not perhaps as much as, and certainly not in quite the same ways as, it depends on memory. The most important thing memory and testimony have in common may be that they do not generate knowledge (justification works differently here, since memory *is* a basic source of that). Memory preserves knowledge; testimony transmits it.

In one way, however, testimony is a more far-reaching source than memory: although they share unlimited epistemic breadth, in the sense that in principle anything that can be known can be known at least in part on the basis of them, we can *learn* from testimony in a way we cannot learn, as opposed to *recover*, from memory.[24] As to how testimony differs from both perception and memory, there is far more to say than can be said here. I have already stressed that the important differences are not a matter of reliability. No matter how reliable testimony in fact is, the acquisition of knowledge or even justified belief on the basis of testimony depends (as noted earlier) on the agency of another person. The attester must not lie, or seek to deceive, in attesting to *p* if we are to come to know that *p* on the basis of the testimony. By contrast, our responses to the deliverances of the basic sources is not normally mediated by anyone else's action. Testimony may be unreliable – or fail to justify one's accepting *p* – both because of a lack of some natural connection between the state(s) of affairs the testimony concerns and *p and* because of the attester's exercise of agency. This is not normally so for the testimony of the senses or of memory or of reason. The point is not that the exercise of agency cannot be a purely "natural" phenomenon – though philosophers who think that freedom is incompatible with determinism may argue that it cannot – but that the concepts of knowledge and justification apparently presuppose that if it is a natural phenomenon, it is nonetheless special.[25]

TESTIMONIAL AUTHORITY AND THE ETHICS OF BELIEF

Given how commonly testimony is a source of basic knowledge, and given that testimony-based beliefs are not only quite typically justified but very often *non-inferentially* justified, it is clear that testimony has an important kind of epistemic authority. It also might be said to have a high degree of such authority, particularly for children and, perhaps somewhat analogously, for people being introduced to the rules and goals of a new practice. For some people, testimony-based beliefs can be by and large better justified, and also more likely to constitute knowledge, than memory beliefs. This could also hold, in some people, even for perception. Even if only the basic sources have *basic* epistemic authority, *degree* of authority is a separable matter. One person's testimony may be more reliable than another's eyesight even at twenty feet.

A further question concerns the modality of the epistemic authority of a source. This authority may be either empirical or a priori. It might seem that if testimony is not a basic source of justification, then its justificatory authority must be entirely derivative and that one must have broadly inductive justification for believing it. But it has been plausibly argued that "We are a priori prima facie entitled to accept something that is prima facie intelligible and *presented* as true."[26] Developing the Reidian speculation offered earlier, we might rationalize this as follows. We might plausibly argue that undefeated normal testimony tends to express beliefs that are ultimately grounded in the standard basic sources: either produced by those sources or inferred from their cognitive products, and (apart from beliefs formed or re-formed at the time) retained by memory.[27] Assessing this thesis is beyond the scope of this paper (and I have undertaken it elsewhere).[28] But if we observe a certain distinction, we can identify a kind of a priori authority that it may be plausibly claimed to have. Let me explain.

It may not have escaped notice that I have spoken of the case for this authority in relation to belief, not *acceptance*. These are not always distinguished, but they differ significantly. I believe that 'accept' does not even seem natural for most of the normal, as opposed to, say, courtroom, cases of testimony. The model so natural for philosophers, of accepting what is said only after careful consideration, should not be allowed to intrude here: it is misleading to say that I *accept* the ordinary things my family and friends say to me. In the contexts in which *accept* is natural (for propositions), it contrasts with 'reject' and 'withhold'; and in that probably central use, acceptance does not entail belief. We can accept something while withholding – or simply not forming – belief.

Now I think that there *is* an a priori principle to the effect that if one needs to act and cannot do so without certain information, such as directions to a place one must get to, then in the absence of reasons to doubt testimony that provides such information, one should *accept* that testimony, for instance, act on it in appropriate ways, tentatively use it as a basis for inference, abstain from rejecting it if, merely from a general skeptical disposition or because of apparent uncertainty on the attester's part, one is tempted to do so, and so forth. Indeed, an even wider principle may be a priori: that in everyday life, one should accept testimony as prima facie credible unless one has reason to do otherwise. But – as is appropriate, given that the sort of acceptance in question is a kind of conduct – these principles are *practical*, not epistemic. They are nonetheless very important for seeking knowledge and justified belief. They are also good candidates to explain many of the major points that apply to the epistemological significance of testimony, including, I think, some denied by Hume and some important for the philosophy of religion. On the first point, these principles are not inductive; on the second, given the practical commitments of many religious people, acceptance of testimony handed down in scripture or tradition can be rational. This is not to imply that believing it cannot also be rational; but acceptance does not entail belief, and, in part for that reason, the conditions for its rationality may be weaker.

Talk of acceptance may call to mind other plausible practical principles in this range – *principles of epistemic regulation*, we might call them, by contrast with epistemic and justificational principles proper. The former are among the principles important in the ethics of belief.[29] They bear, for instance, on what we should take as a premise, even if only suppositionally, on what we should use to guide a search for evidence, and on what propositions we should use as guides to action or, on the other hand, withhold pending further information. It is essential to see that the soundness of such principles would not imply that testimony has the *kind* of a priori justificatory authority that has been claimed for it regarding belief. It is worth asking how much of the data supporting the justificatory autonomy of testimony can be accounted for by such practical principles.

Suppose, then, that the contrasts I have drawn between the standard basic sources and testimony are sound. It does not follow that testimony lacks a priori authority. The question whether testimony is a basic source must be distinguished from the question whether it has a priori justificatory authority. We must also distinguish between epistemic principles "proper" and epistemic regulation principles. This is important both for epistemology and for the philosophy of religion. For suppose (controversially) that, as many contemporary philosophers believe, much religious testimony, including testimony reporting miracles and many kinds of religious experiences, is either not initially credible or, at best, outweighed by counterevidence. This would not imply that related practical principles are false: specifically, even supposing no sound epistemic principles can be found that warrant believing religious testimony that seems implausible on what are commonly considered scientific grounds, there might be practical principles that warrant *accepting* it, in one or another way. Minimal acceptance would perhaps be acceptance for the sake of argument. But acceptance can have wide practical implications; it can also commit one to a wider range of actions than pursuit of arguments, including religious observances. Does any plausible "ethics of belief" preclude this?

One answer is that because acceptance does not entail belief, there is no opposition here. But if ethical standards above all concern conduct as distinct from belief – broadly, the practical as distinct from the theoretical – then we may plausibly take the kind of standards underlying a cogent ethics of belief to apply to acceptance as well. Given this wide construal of those standards, is there any bar in principle to the rationality of acceptance of testimony in religious matters? It might be argued that there is in the case of miracles, since there is so much inductive evidence against their possibility. This is a perennial issue that must be set aside.[30] But whatever one's judgment on this matter, one should grant that there is no comprehensive rational prohibition on accepting religious testimony. This is particularly clear where there is independent justification for the conduct that is to flow from the acceptance, as there is not only for a wide range of voluntary religious observances but also for the social conduct called for by many religious principles and ideals.[31] The epistemic authority of testimony may be in some ways less than that of the basic sources; but, like them, it has practical as well as epistemic authority.

Whether Reid could accept all these conclusions is not clear to me; but he does treat testimony differently from the standard basic sources, and I see no bar to his granting the specific differences I have noted. In any case, it should be plain that the contrasts I have drawn between testimony and the standard basic sources of knowledge and justification do not imply that testimony is inessential in a normal human life or that its authority in cognitive matters is only contingent and empirical. Testimony is both globally and focally essential in our lives; it is indeed of virtually unlimited breadth in its epistemic power: nearly anything that can be known firsthand can also be known on the basis of testimony. Testimony is a source of basic knowledge; it is normally the starting point of everyone's conceptual learning; it is, as Reid so vividly shows us, as natural a source of knowledge and justification as any of the others; it has a priori authority at least in the practical domain; and, for an indefinitely wide range of propositions in that domain, it can justify acceptance even if it does not justify belief.[32]

NOTES

1. See, e.g., Frederick Schmitt, ed., *Socializing Epistemology: The Social Dimensions of Knowledge* (Lanham, MD: Rowman and Littlefield, 1994); Alvin I. Goldman, *Knowledge in a Social World* (Oxford and New York: Oxford University Press, 1999); and J. Angelo Corlett, *Analyzing Social Knowledge* (Lanham, MD: Rowman and Littlefield, 1996).

2. Among the recent works on or treating testimony are C. A. J. Coady, *Testimony: A Philosophical Study* (Oxford: Clarendon Press, 1992); B. K. Matilal and A. Chakrabarti, eds., *Knowing from Words* (Dordrecht: Kluwer, 1994); Elizabeth Fricker, "The Epistemology of Testimony," *Proceedings of the Aristotelian Society* Supplementary Vol. 61 (1987): 57–83, "Against Gullibility," in Matilal and Chakrabarti, and "Trusting Others in the Sciences: A Priori or Empirical Warrant?" *Studies in History and Philosophy of Science* 33 (2002): 373–83; John Hardwig, "Epistemic Dependence," *Journal of Philosophy* 82 (1985): 335–49; Ernest Sosa, "Testimony and Coherence," in his *Knowledge in Perspective* (Cambridge: Cambridge University Press, 1991); Alvin Plantinga, *Warrant and Proper Function* (Oxford: Oxford University Press, 1993); Mark Owen Webb, "Why I Know About as Much as You," *Journal of Philosophy* 90 (1993): 260–70 (in part a critique of Hardwig); Jonathan E. Adler, "Testimony, Trust, Knowing," *Journal of*

Philosophy 91 (1994): 264–75 (in part a critique of Webb); Jennifer Lackey, "Testimonial Knowledge and Transmission," *Philosophical Quarterly* 49 (1999): 471–90; and Peter J. Graham, "Conveying Information," *Synthese* 123 (2000): 365–92, "The Reliability of Testimony," *Philosophy and Phenomenological Research* 61 (2000): 695–709, and "Transferring Knowledge," *Nôus* 34 (2000): 131–52.

3. Much space could be devoted to refining this idea, e.g., explaining why fictional cases do not count and ironic declarations can apparently tell us one thing when another is intended (in which case 'testimony' may be the wrong word for either reading, but certainly the former).

4. In, e.g., "The Foundationalism-Coherentism Controversy," chapter 4 in *The Structure of Justification* (Cambridge and New York: Cambridge University Press, 1993).

5. It might be argued, however, that apart from a certain level of critical reflection on the grounds of our beliefs, we cannot arrive at something plausibly called *reflective knowledge*. This concept, and the requirements it imposes, have been explicated in detail by Ernest Sosa. See, e.g., his *Knowledge in Perspective* and his forthcoming book, *Knowledge in Focus, Skepticism Resolved*.

6. For valuable recent discussion, see Lackey, "Testimonial Knowledge," and Graham, "Conveying Information." Both have attacked the view that the recipient of testimony that *p* can gain knowledge that *p* only if the attester knows that *p*. In "Testimony, Credulity, and Veracity" (in a collection edited by Jennifer Lackey and Ernest Sosa, forthcoming from Blackwell), I reply to some of their objections.

7. It may be that the sense is very broad indeed, since I might perhaps receive testimony by a telepathic reception of the attester's message. It may be that the relation between testimony and perception is such that as our inclination to treat reception of stated information as non-perceptual increases, our inclination to regard it as testimonial decreases.

8. See Thomas Reid, in *Thomas Reid's Inquiry and Essays*, eds. Ronald Beanblossom and Keith Lehrer (Indianapolis: Hackett, 1983), 87. Later references to Reid in this paper are to this edition.

9. Reid discusses acquired perceptions in Essay II, chapter 21 of the *Essays*, as well as in chapter 22. For discussion of his conception of such perception in relation to testimony, see Nicholas Wolterstorff's chapter on Reid's epistemological views on testimony in *Thomas Reid and the Story of Epistemology* (New York: Cambridge University Press, 2001).

10. Justification by reasons does not, of course, exhaust justification *by reason*, and Reid may take it that the worthiness in question is self-evident. For extensive critical discussion of how he conceived his first principles, see William P. Alston, "Thomas Reid on Epistemic Principles," *History of Philosophy Quarterly* 2 (1985): 435–52, and James Van Cleve, "Reid on the Principles of Contingent Truths," *Reid Studies* 3 (1999): 3–30, which explores the intriguing thesis that Reid's main first principles are not general epistemic principles such as those quoted, which are supposed to be self-evident indications of what conditions generate true belief (or knowledge or perhaps justification and knowledge) but the beliefs (of particular propositions) licensed by those propositions, say the belief that I just had Van Cleve's paper in my hands, grounded in my memory.

11. That the self-evident can be evidenced by something else, even though it does not stand in need of evidence, I have argued in some detail in "Self-Evidence,"

Philosophical Perspectives 13 (1999). Here, however, I depart from what Reid says in at least one place. At one point, he speaks of things that, "though they admit of illustration yet, being self-evident, do not admit of proof." (*Essays on the Intellectual Powers*, 153).

12. In *The Architecture of Reason* (New York: Oxford University Press, 2000), I stress this element of responsiveness to experience in explicating the nature of belief and treat its formation as a *discriminative* response because of the way in which it is "selective" and alters with alteration in the relevant stimuli. Cf. Fred Dretske's information-theoretical account of knowledge in his *Knowledge and the Flow of Information* (Cambridge, MA: MIT Press, 1981) and its application to testimony in the papers of Peter Graham cited above.

13. In "The Place of Testimony in the Fabric of Knowledge and Justification," *American Philosophical Quarterly* 34 (1997): 405–22, I have described conceptual learning in relation to propositional learning and emphasized the importance of both in the development of justification and knowledge.

14. For a detailed account of the epistemology of testimony that is in some ways inferentialist and in any event presupposes the formation of more beliefs on the part of the recipient as a condition for acquiring testimony-based knowledge, see Elizabeth Fricker, esp. "Against Gullibility," in Maitilal and Chakrabarti, op. cit., and (for a recent rounded statement of her position) "Testimony: Knowing through Being Told," in I. Niiniluoto, M. Sintonen, and J. Wolenski, eds., *Handbook of Epistemology* (Dordrecht: Kluwer, 2004).

15. I do not take this feature of untestability for reliability without dependence on the source in question to be essential to a basic source; but it does seem to hold for the basic sources I am comparing with testimony. (I leave open whether there can be other basic sources of knowledge, but on this question it is essential to bear in mind that the concept of perception does not require that it is possible only through the five senses.)

16. If a source has inconsistent outputs, how can it be a candidate for reliability *at all*? Perhaps it can if the inconsistencies cause no trouble, e.g., because the subject recognizes them and can isolate them for scrutiny and elimination. It is not at all easy to say under what conditions inconsistencies are innocuous; this is one reason the preface paradox is difficult to resolve.

17. I argue for this limitation on coherence in "The Foundationalism-Coherentism Controversy: Hardened Stereotypes and Overlapping Theories," in *The Structure of Justification*.

18. If we allow that a testimony-based belief may *also* be based on another source than the testimony in question – including other testimony – then lying testimony may not preclude knowing the proposition. I say 'may not' because it is not self-evident that a person is lying when attesting to a true proposition but *believing* the proposition false and intending to deceive the recipient in attesting to it. Unless otherwise indicated, however, I am making the natural assumption that calling a belief testimony-based implies that it is essentially based on the testimony in question, where this requires at least that the testimony is a necessary basis of it.

19. I discuss the issue of voluntary control of belief and cite much relevant literature in "Doxastic Voluntarism and the Ethics of Belief," *Facta Philosophica* 1, 1 (1999): 87–109.

20. This point is explained and defended in "The Place of Testimony."

21. Support for this point is provided in Peter Graham's informative (forthcoming) paper, "Testimony and Agency," in which he argues that the point that testimony (as I would put it) goes through the will does not favor either the reductionist view of testimony or the view that it is an irreducibly credible source.

22. For a detailed defense of a moderate internalism concerning justification, see my "An Internalist Theory of Normative Grounds," in *Philosophical Topics* 29, 1 and 2 (2002), 19–46.

23. It is noteworthy that the most relevant first principle is, "That certain features of the countenance, sounds of the voice, and gestures of the body, indicate certain thoughts and dispositions of the mind" (*Essays*, Essay 6, chapter 5). These natural signs do not even require making any assertions.

24. There are subtleties here that I cannot go into, but the need for 'at least in part' should be explained: for simple self-evident propositions, it may be possible to know them only in part on the basis of testimony because an understanding of them sufficient to come to know them on the basis of testimony at all is such that given even the minimal kind of entertaining of them required for receiving testimony that they are true, one must know them on the basis of that understanding. Some detailed discussion of knowledge on the basis of understanding is given in my "Self-Evidence," cited above.

25. This point may support my view, defended in "The Place of Testimony," that to acquire justification for p from testimony, one needs some degree of justification for taking the attester to be credible, though one can of course get it on the occasion of the testimony. (I do not think one needs a counterpart of this in order to acquire prima facie justification from one of the standard basic sources.)

26. See Tyler Burge, "Content Preservation," *Philosophical Review* 102 (1993): 472. His case for his view is lengthy and complex, and in rationalizing it, I suggest a different though prima facie compatible line of argument.

27. I do not find this thesis expressed in Burge, op. cit., but he says something akin to it and – for reasons I indicate shortly – different from his main a priori acceptability thesis: "It is not just the rationality of a source that marks an a priori prima facie connection to truth. The very content of an intelligible message does so as well. For content is constitutively dependent, in the first instance, on patterned connections to a subject matter, connections that insure in normal circumstances a baseline of true thought presentations" (471). The argument I have sketched is intended to yield a similar connection between testimony and truth, but without depending on Burge's externalist theory of content. (It is, however, consistent with that theory.)

28. In "The A Priori Authority of Testimony," *Philosophical Issues* (a *Nôus* supplementary volume) 14 (2004): 18–34.

29. For a related discussion of the ethics of belief, see my "Doxastic Voluntarism" (cited above); and, for an extensive historically informed treatment of many of its aspects, Nicholas Wolterstorff, *John Locke and the Ethics of Belief* (New York: Cambridge University Press, 1996).

30. For extensive discussion of the possibility of giving credence to testimony about miracles, including much criticism of the Humean view on this issue, See David Johnson, *Hume, Holism, and Miracles* (Ithaca, NY: Cornell University Press, 1999).

31. I have argued for this in *Religious Commitment and Secular Reason* (New York: Cambridge University Press, 2000), esp. chapters 5 and 6.

32. This paper was written in honor of Nicholas Wolterstorff, whose philosophical example and many writings – including his treatment of Thomas Reid among many other works of his – have been an inspiration to me. For comments on parts of the paper, I thank William P. Alston, Andrew Dole, Andrew Chignell, Peter Graham, and Jennifer Lackey. Conversations with Nicholas Wolterstorff have been of great value over many years.

9

∾

Kant on the Rational Instability of Atheism

JOHN HARE

This paper is about kant's view of people who are morally good but not theists.[1]
A Kant paper belongs in a collection about the ethics of belief because Kant's
central project is to deny (put limits on) knowledge so as to make room for
faith.[2] There has been a significant change in Kant scholarship over the last
ten or fifteen years. I would place as a key event the conference on Kant's
philosophy of religion that produced the volume *Kant's Philosophy of Religion Reconsidered* in 1991. As the editors of that book put it, they question
the commonly held view that Kant's account is "relentlessly reductionistic,
(seeking) to make religion – or at least those elements of religion which can
be critically justified – wholly identical with or reducible to morality."[3] This
change in Kant scholarship is part of a much larger movement in the interpretation of the great figures of modern philosophy, of Leibniz, for example, and
Descartes. The change is toward a greater emphasis on the vertical theme in
these philosophers, on the relation to God.[4] Kant's view, I am going to claim,
is that there is incoherence in the attempt to be morally good without being a
theist. But if this is right, it is even more important for us than it was for Kant
to add that it is possible to be both morally good and not a theist, because
we are likely to know many more such people, people who are both leading a
morally good life and are not theists.

Kant is a seminal figure in the subsequent history of theology. His views
about the relation of moral goodness and theism have, I think, been widely
misunderstood by both liberal and conservative theologians in the twentieth
century. In part, this is because some of the relevant texts have been very
little read. The title of my paper refers to one such text. Volckmann's notes
on Kant's lectures on Natural Theology report Kant as saying, "The condition
of the skeptical atheist is an unstable condition, in which one always deteriorates from hope into doubt and distrust."[5] The skeptical atheist, a character
Kant sometimes calls 'the speculative atheist,' accepts the possibility of God's

existence, and conducts himself as if there were indeed a God. But his condition is still unstable, Kant says, because he does not accept the actual existence of God. The liberal and conservative theologians I am thinking of unite in treating Kant as though he were himself what he calls in the passage I have just quoted a skeptical atheist.

An example of a liberal is Gordon Kaufman in his book *God the Problem*, which refers pervasively to Kant as the leader of the vanguard, in following whom we have to revise radically our traditional theology. Thus Kaufman says, "Our experience is of a unified and orderly world (Kant). In such a world, acts of God (in the traditional sense) are not merely improbable or difficult to believe: they are literally inconceivable. It is not a question of whether talk about such acts is true or false; it is, in the literal sense, meaningless; one cannot make the concept hang together consistently."[6] But this is *not* Kant's view. It is the view of those who extend Kant's restrictions on knowledge to the domain of meaning, as Kant himself did not. An example of a conservative is Henry Stob, who taught at Calvin College and Calvin Theological Seminary. He says of Kant, in a book roughly contemporary with Kaufman's, "he was not really removing theological support of ethics; he was merely altering the underlying theology by unseating the Christian God and placing Rational Law upon the empty throne. God was made subject to Law; and in that instant Law itself became a god and began to determine the Kantian ethic."[7] Here Kant is seen as the enemy, not the leader of the vanguard. But again, this is not really Kant's view that is being attacked. Kant did not want God off the throne. His system requires a divine person with a will as well as an intellect who can give us commands and intervene to accomplish in us the revolution of our wills, and who can coordinate the ends of all rational beings so as to form a kingdom of ends. This is why Kant says repeatedly, throughout the corpus, that we have to recognize our duties as God's commands.

My paper has three sections. In the first, I talk about Kant's view of morally good people who are not theists. In the second, I discuss his moral criticisms of atheism. The third section makes the distinction between Kant's use of the term 'religion', which is possible without believing that God exists, and Kant's view of the moral life, which does rationally require believing this. I will end by responding to two objections.[8]

MORALLY GOOD PEOPLE WHO ARE NOT THEISTS

I am going to start by discussing Kant's view that one can be a good person without believing in the existence of God, and that even someone who denies the existence of God can lead a virtuous life. Kant's prime example is Spinoza, whom he takes to be a conspicuously good person but not to believe in God in the way Kant approves of. The exegesis of Spinoza is not my purpose here; perhaps Kant is being unfair to him. My point is just that Kant *does* believe it is possible to be a good person without believing in God. He says, in one of his more purple passages,

Therefore, let us consider the case of a righteous man (Spinoza, for example) who actively reveres the moral law (but) who remains firmly persuaded that there is no God . . . and that there is also no future life. Deceit, violence, and envy will always be rife around him, even though he himself is honest, peaceable, and benevolent. Moreover, as concerns the other righteous people he meets: no matter how worthy of happiness they may be, nature, which pays no attention to that, will still subject them to all the evils of deprivation, disease, and untimely death, just like all the other animals on the earth. And they will stay subjected to these evils always, until one vast tomb engulfs them one and all (honest or not, that make no difference here) and hurls them, who managed to believe they were the final purpose of creation, back into the abyss of the purposeless chaos of matter from which they were taken. And so this well-meaning person would indeed have to give up as impossible the purpose that the moral laws obligated him to have before his eyes, and that in compliance with them he did have before his eyes.[9]

This purpose that the moral laws obligate us to have before our eyes is what Kant calls 'the highest good,' a world in which for all people their happiness is proportional to their virtue. Kant thinks this is the goal a moral person must try to realize as far as he or she can.

Before discussing this passage further, it will be useful to mention Kant's remark, recorded in Collins's notes, about people who are atheists in their theoretical beliefs, but are able to venerate God through their actions.[10] In this passage, the central example is again Spinoza. Kant's view of him is that his error extends to theology but not to religion. He "did what a man of religion should do. His heart was good, and could easily have been brought to rights; he merely had too much trust in speculative argument." By contrast, in a later passage in the same notes, Kant talks about a person "who *lives* in such a way that one would take him to maintain that there is no god. Those who live thus are called practical atheists, though that goes too far. The practical atheist is the godless man, for godlessness is a kind of shameless wickedness which bids defiance to the punishments that the idea of God inspires in us."[11] The distinction is that one kind of atheist has her heart right, like Spinoza. Even if, because of speculative mistakes or confusions, she ends up saying, "There is no God," this error can easily be remedied. She needs to be shown the limits of human understanding, and then the moral faith that she already has in germ will be free to express itself in terms of explicit belief in God. On the other hand, there is a person who does say he believes in God, but does not have moral faith. Such a person is in effect an atheist, though Kant admits it is a stretch to use the term, and Kant does not hold out hope for him.

Turning now to the passage about Spinoza in the Third Critique, Kant's point is that it *is* possible to be a good person and say, "There is no God"; but there is something rationally unstable about such a state. After describing the evils that Spinoza and indeed any good person will recognize in the world, Kant says (note the modality in this sentence), "And so, this well-meaning person *would* indeed *have to* give up as impossible (*müsste er als unmöglich allerdings aufgeben*) the purpose that the moral laws obligated him to have before his eyes, and that in compliance with them he did have before his eyes" (emphasis added). Kant does not say that Spinoza *did* this giving up, or that such a person *will* do it, but that he *would have to* do it. I think his point is that there is a dilemma that reason will present to such a person, and to resolve it requires either giving up the sense of the real possibility of the highest good or the refusal to believe in God. Given the passage from the Collins notes, I think we can suppose that Kant thinks that given the removal of his speculative confusions, Spinoza would actually be likely to resolve the dilemma in the direction of theism. Kant says a very similar thing about implicit belief in an afterlife.[12]

A nontheological analogy might be helpful here. Suppose you have two friends, James and Joanna, who are becoming increasingly fond of each other. At some point, you realize that in their hearts they have both made a commitment to spending the rest of their lives together. But James has not yet admitted this to himself, or declared himself to Joanna. What is holding him back is a certain exaggerated pride in his own intellect, which prevents him from acknowledging the validity of any impulse in himself that he cannot completely understand. You are sure that once James comes to see how misplaced this pride is, he will realize that he has in fact been committed to a life with Joanna for some time and that this commitment has been controlling the way he already lives his life and his decisions about where to spend his time and devote his energies. Now does James *believe* that he is going to get married to Joanna? You are not clear what to say. If you ask him to profess such a belief, he will probably say that he does not know, one way or the other. But his life choices indicate the condition of his heart, and in that sense, he does already have the belief. Another thing you do not know is how things are actually going to turn out for James. It all depends on which of the two dispositions prevails, his love for Joanna or his pride in his intellect.

To go back to Spinoza, suppose the speculative confusions remain. If he comes to see the dilemma he is in, he still has three options. One is to reject the pursuit of the highest good, one is to reject his atheism, and the third is to stay in the dilemma, unable to be happy with either alternative that presents itself. In the Third Critique passage, Kant goes on to say that if someone like Spinoza responds to the dilemma by refusing to give up the real possibility of the highest good, then he *must* assume (*so muss er annehmen*) the existence of a God. The modality is again significant. It is not that such a person will do this, but that he must. He must, that is to say, if he is to be rational. This is what I mean by saying that atheism is, for Kant, *rationally* unstable. It is unstable because there is a process that, if not artificially restrained (by pride of intellect), would lead to explicit faith.

To conclude this point, Kant is not saying that it is impossible to be a good person and disbelieve in God. He is saying there is a dilemma that such a state presents. Which way out of the dilemma a person takes will depend, first, on whether she has got rid of her speculative errors, and second on whether she is in fact committed to the moral law and the pursuit of the highest good. If she has and she is, then the atheism is easily corrected.

KANT'S MORAL CRITICISM OF ATHEISM

The atheism is easily corrected in these circumstances because there is, in Kant's view, a natural progression to theism from both moral experience and the experience of natural beauty, and there are also arguments covering the same ground. The natural progression is nicely described in a passage in the Third Critique that comes just before the passage about Spinoza that I quoted.[13] Kant says that our experience of beauty in nature, or of duty, or of guilt, already dispose us to think of a person to whom we are grateful, or to whom we have an obligation, or whom we have offended. The subsequent arguments can then be seen as an articulation of this already present inclination of the mind to widen its moral disposition (*Gesinnung*) so as to think of an object outside the world to which to be grateful or obedient or apologetic. I will mention three of these arguments, in the form of objections that Kant makes to atheism. First, atheism makes the moral life harder because it removes the ground for belief in the real possibility of being good.[14] Second, it changes our view of the system of rewards and punishments. Third, it leads to moral despair about the possibility of the highest good and thus corrupts moral character both individually and socially.

(a) In the preface to the second edition of *Religion within the Boundaries of Mere Reason*, Kant suggests that we think of revelation as two concentric circles, with the revelation to reason on the inside and historical revelation on the outside; and then he proposes the experiment of seeing how much of historical revelation he can translate into the terms of the inner circle. This experiment could result in various forms of atheism. We could find out that the translation fails, and then reject the outer circle as inconsistent with the inner. Or we could find that the outer circle was completely redundant after the translation, though still consistent with the inner circle. But Kant does not take either of these positions. Translating the doctrines of creation and fall, he talks of a predisposition to good and a propensity to evil. The predisposition to good is a predisposition we are born with toward reverence for the moral law that subordinates all our inclinations to our duty. But because we are also born under what he calls the evil maxim, we have the propensity to prefer our happiness to duty. We cannot reverse this ranking, because our fundamental maxim is already corrupt. So we have to believe in divine assistance to accomplish what Kant calls 'the revolution of the will.' The danger from atheism is that it might leave us without this kind of moral faith, "that God will have the means to remedy this imperfection."[15] As before, Kant has to be interpreted as presenting a rational dilemma here, not making a prediction. Which way the atheist will *in fact* resolve the dilemma depends on whether the atheist is in fact committed to the moral law. But it is going to be hard for an atheist to sustain belief in the real possibility of being good, given that we are social beings and given the social aspect of evil.[16] Kant's view is that the natural propensity to evil is activated in the social relations that we cannot dispense with, and divine assistance is the only way he sees that this propensity can be overcome. He says that we can suppose that God produces this revolution of the will by intellectual intuition, which is a kind of intuition that is productive rather than receptive.[17] An atheist can disagree with Kant about the propensity to evil. But an atheist who accepts Kant's views about the propensity but wants to lead a morally good life must find some substitute for divine assistance to fill the gap.

(b) Kant's second moral criticism of atheism relates to God's rewards and punishments. Kant goes through a certain development in his thought about this issue.[18] In *Religion*, Kant proposes that God has legislative, executive, and judicial functions within the kingdom of ends, of which God is the king and we are merely members. Actually, this is a theme that can be traced throughout Kant's *corpus*, including the *Groundwork*, but I will not try to do that here.[19] There are two problems about coordinating the ends of the members of the kingdom of ends. The first is that the agent has to believe not merely that *she* can be happy and virtuous, but that all the members of the kingdom can be; that rewarding is consistent across the kingdom. This is one central reason why we have to recognize our duties, Kant says, as God's commands. It is the higher moral being who is the head of the kingdom "through whose universal organization the forces of single individuals, insufficient on their own, are united for a common effect."[20] But there is a second important coordination constraint, and this is where God's sanctions come in. We have to be able to believe that those who are not motivated by reverence for the law can be motivated by the sanctions to at least external obedience. The role of the sanctions here is like what it is for an earthly kingdom, where, too, the ground of obedience is not supposed to be hope or fear but moral respect for freedom. The sanctions are, in Kant's phrase, "a hindrance to the hindrances to freedom."[21] Even nonvirtuous people can be motivated by the sanctions to refrain from interfering with the exercise of the moral freedom of others.

(c) The third of Kant's moral objections to atheism is already implicit in what I have said so far. Atheism makes it harder to believe in the real possibility of the highest good, and so tends toward a kind of despair, and thus a corruption of moral character, both individually and socially. In the passage about Spinoza in the Third Critique that I have already quoted, Kant talks about how the righteous atheist would have to give up as impossible the belief in the highest good, a final union of virtue and happiness, because all that is left is "the abyss of the purposeless chaos of matter from which we are taken."[22] The despair here is about whether the universe makes moral sense or is, as Sartre would say, absurd. It is not enough for avoiding absurdity to believe that we can individually have a revolution of the will (as discussed in relation to the first criticism I mentioned). If we were *all* virtuous, and we could believe that we were, perhaps what Kant calls in the First Critique 'self-rewarding morality' would be enough.[23] But as things are, we have to believe in the real possibility of the highest good *whether most other people are virtuous or not*, and this belief requires belief in some agency that is not merely human. As I said earlier in connection with the passage about Spinoza, Kant is optimistic about how Spinoza would in fact resolve this difficulty presented by his atheism, once the speculative errors of his philosophy were revealed. But it is nonetheless a good objection to atheism that it puts good people in this kind of difficulty.

It is a good objection *if* Kant is right that the moral life requires belief that virtue and happiness finally go together. He says that the final purpose of our compliance with the moral law is the highest good, "a happiness of rational beings that harmoniously accompanies their compliance with moral laws." I think Kant is here translating the picture of the kingdom of God in which justice and peace kiss each other (Psalm 85:10). There are moral philosophers who deny that the moral life requires such belief. Bernard Williams, for example, used to endorse the view that he attributed to Sophocles and Thucydides that "the world is not necessarily well adjusted to ethical aspirations."[24] But it is important to see if we can construct an argument that starts from a description of the moral life that even nontheists would accept and ends up with the postulation of a system in which virtue is made consistent with happiness even if we do not think we have the capacity to operate such a system ourselves. Suppose we find such an argument and it succeeds; what does it prove? Not that theism is true, but that if you want to reject theism, and you want to hold on to our traditional conception of morality, you will have to find a substitute to do the work in that traditional conception that God used to do.

Kant thinks there is a consequence for moral character of the failure to have hope in the highest good. He says in the passage about Spinoza that despair about that one ideal final purpose would "weaken his respect for the moral law," and "such weakening of his respect would inevitably impair his moral attitude."[25] This language sounds more like the kind of prediction that I have been saying Kant does not intend. But Kant does not say that Spinoza *will* reach this despair about the possibility of the highest good; only that if he *did* reach it, it would impair his moral attitude. If we think about atheism as a social phenomenon, however, something more like a prediction is available. I will call it a hypothesis. Kant thinks that Christianity has been the 'vehicle' by which his contemporaries in Europe have reached their appreciation of the moral law, and he thinks Christianity is destined to play this role for the whole world.[26] He thinks that atheism in its dogmatic form, if it became pervasive and destroyed this vehicle, would therefore be dangerous not just for the individual, and not just for the state, but for the whole human race. So we can look at the parts of the world like the one Kant himself lived in, now a detached part of Russia, and ask whether the decline of belief in the vehicle has in fact been accompanied by the decline of the attempt to lead the moral life. I am not saying such an enquiry would be easy, because, as Kant says, the heart is not open to our intuition; but we could try testing for significant correlations. Nietzsche suggested a similar hypothesis at the end of the nineteenth century, that the death of God would bring the death of guilt along with it.[27] There have indeed been various attempts, following the decline of theism in recent ethical theory, to reduce the moral demand. Certain sentiment-based theories, certain kinds of care theories but not others, certain kinds of communitarianism, and certain kinds of evolutionary ethics have all denied that we have the duty of impartial benevolence, to treat every human as one and none as more than one.[28] Certain outright skeptics have simply denied that this Kantian ethic makes sense in a post-Christian world. The question whether this theorized doubt about impartial benevolence has been accompanied by less actual impartial benevolence in popular practice is harder for a philosopher to answer with any confidence.[29]

'RELIGION' AND THE MORAL LIFE

Does Kant think religion and moral life in general require believing that God exists? On the one hand, the answer seems to be yes. After all, 'religion' is defined in terms of recognizing one's duties as God's commands.[30] How can a person who does not believe in God recognize her duties as God's commands? On the other hand, there are texts like the one about Spinoza from the Collins lecture notes: "Atheism can reside in mere speculation, while in practice such a person can be a theist or venerator of God, whose error extends to theology, but not to religion."[31] This implies that religion is consistent with some kinds of atheism. We need to separate here the question about whether Kant uses the term *religion* in such as way as to allow that skeptical atheists can be religious and the more important question whether he thinks *the moral life* rationally requires belief in the existence of God. On the first question, Kant is saying in this text and elsewhere that there is a kind of atheism that is consistent with venerating God, or with religion, namely the kind of atheism that "resides in mere speculation."

One example of this kind of atheist would be someone who thought she had to say "There is no God" if she did not have a good theoretical argument for the conclusion that God exists. She might refuse to say that she believed something when she did not understand it, and she might think she was obeying the demand of reason in this refusal. Moral philosophers in the twentieth century who were strongly influenced by the logical positivists like Carnap sometimes fell into this category. For example, R. M. Hare used to say the Apostles' Creed every Sunday in church a little ahead of the rest of the congregation, as though to express his distance from them. But his philosophical position (in the so-called University Discussion, reprinted in *New Essays in Philosophical Theology*[32]) was that we cannot make meaningful assertions about the existence of God, and that faith in God is properly construed as what he called a 'blik' (roughly, an attitude toward living in the world) rather than as making an assertion. "It seems, indeed, to be impossible," he said, "even to formulate as an assertion the normal *blik* about the world which makes me put my confidence in the future reliability of steel joints; . . . in my own continued well-being (in some sense of that word that I may not now fully understand) if I continue to do what is right according to my lights; in the general likelihood of people like Hitler coming to a bad end. But perhaps a formulation less inadequate than most is to be found in Psalm 75: 'The earth is weak and all the inhabiters thereof: I bear up the pillars of it.'"[33] R. M. Hare is here willing to use God's promises to express the attitude toward living in the world that R. M. Hare himself adopted, while at the same time denying that he could strictly speaking assert that God exists.

Later, R. M. Hare developed his position in the Nathanial Taylor lectures at Yale Divinity School, "What I am saying is that, granted that the good man wishes above all to realize the ends of morality – moral ideals – he can hardly pursue this object unless he has faith in the possibility, as things are, of realizing them. That is why faith and hope are virtues as well as charity. And I must confess that faith in the divine providence has always seemed to me to be one of the central features of the Christian religion, and one to which it is possible to cling even when much else is in doubt. This faith that all shall be well is matched by a feeling of thankfulness that all is well."[34] Here we have an example of a person who combines faith in divine providence with the refusal to assert that God exists. Kant's view of such a person is, "He did what a man of religion should do. His heart was good, and could easily have been brought to rights; he merely had too much trust in speculative argument."[35] In this case, the excessive trust in speculative argument is the excessive confidence that some form of the verifiability test can set limits on meaningful assertion. For Kant, there are constraints from the limits of sense experience on claims to have knowledge, but not on the meaningful statement of belief. I will say more about this later.

Kant uses the term 'religion' to include someone like R. M. Hare, who refuses to assent to the assertion, 'God exists,' even though Kant thinks this person's belief that God exists is rationally presupposed by this person's commitment to the moral life.[36] This usage of the term 'religion' was explicit in the quote from Volckmann's lecture notes that I started with. My analogy of James and Joanna was designed to illustrate a parallel case of a person who has a practical faith that is consistent with the refusal to assent theoretically or make public profession. But Kant's answer to the second question, about whether *the moral life* rationally requires belief in the existence of God, is that moral earnestness (or moral religiousness) does rationally presuppose belief that God exists. Kant's reply to the person I have just been describing is that she needs to see the limits of the human understanding. Kant agrees that there is no compelling theistic proof within the theoretical use of reason, but he thinks that we are nonetheless rationally required to believe that God exists.

Kant expands on this distinction at the beginning of Part Four of *Religion*, where he connects religion and assertoric faith, that is, faith in the *existence* of the highest good. The passage comes in a footnote to Kant's statement that religion is (subjectively regarded) the recognition of all our duties as divine commands.[37] Kant does *not* in this passage discuss whether the moral agent has to believe in the existence of God. But he is interested in making two linked contrasts. The first is between belief based on theoretical cognition (where only a *hypothesis* about God's *possibility* is required, and not knowledge of God's existence) and, on the other hand, our morally legislative reason, where, Kant explicitly says, "what is presupposed is an *assertoric* faith" (namely faith in the *existence* of the highest good). Kant explains that faith in the existence of the highest good needs "only the *idea of God*, . . . without pretending to be able to secure objective reality for it through *theoretical* cognition." Here the contrast is between theoretical cognition and practice. Assertoric faith (in the existence of the highest good) has to make do with an *idea*, and cannot secure the kind of object-status for God that theoretical cognition can establish for what we can sense and so put under empirical concepts.[38] The second contrast is between a person's public profession, where he should not be required to say that any supersensible object exists, and a person's inner moral life, which does presuppose assertoric faith in order that she can believe in a result for her ultimate purpose, namely the achievement of the highest good. Kant says that human beings do not have a duty to *say* publicly that God exists, because putting people under such a duty results only in the profession of faith being "hypocritically feigned." No doubt he was thinking of his own experience at a pietist school.

These two contrasts do not address the question, however, of whether a belief in the existence of God is presupposed by the moral life and therefore rationally required for human beings. The passages that do address the question answer in the affirmative. For example, in the Second Critique, Kant says that our reason finds the possibility of the highest good thinkable "only on the presupposition of a supreme intelligence; to assume the existence of this supreme intelligence is thus connected with the consciousness of our duty."[39]

I will end by responding to two objections to the view of Kant I have proposed. The first is that this view is inconsistent with limits Kant himself puts elsewhere on legitimate belief.[40] I will take a representative text from each of the three Critiques. In each case, I want to say that Kant is making, explicitly or implicitly, a distinction between what he calls theoretical or speculative cognition and practical cognition. In the First Critique, in which Kant explicitly restricts what can be cognized about God (A696f = B724f), he says, "If the question is whether this being is substance, of the greatest reality, necessary etc., then I answer that this question has no significance at all. For all the categories through which I attempt to frame a concept of such an object are of none but an empirical use, and they have no sense at all when they are not applied to objects of possible experience, i.e. to the world of sense." But this passage comes in a section called "Critique of All Speculative Theology," and ends with the remark that reason in its *speculative* use can never get beyond the field of possible sense experience (A702 = B730). In the Second Critique (5:136–8),

Kant says about natural theologians that one can confidently challenge them "to cite (over and above the merely ontological predicates) even one property, say of understanding or the will, determining this object of theirs, of which it could not be shown incontestably that if everything anthropomorphic is separated from it, nothing would remain to us but the mere word." But then Kant goes on to restrict this point explicitly to *theoretical* cognition, and to allow that with respect to the practical, objective reality is given to the idea of God, including the properties of God's understanding and will, though not, he repeats, for any speculative purpose. Finally, in the Third Critique, Kant says (5:456) "we can *think* these properties of the supreme being only by an analogy. For how could we investigate its nature, in view of the fact that experience can show us nothing similar? Second, this analogy allows us only to think the supreme being, not to *cognize* it."[41] But the book ends (5:484–5) with the claim that "we can have, through properties and attributes of God's causality that we think in him merely by analogy, a cognition of God and his existence (a theology)."

In all three cases, the passages at first look as though they are denying cognition of God and God's attributes, but in fact, they are only denying theoretical or speculative cognition. We have to hear always the contrast with practical cognition, though it is a topic for another paper to analyze what practical cognition is. My point is just that Kant does not put limits on meaning that would prevent practical cognition from issuing legitimately in belief. There is an irony in all of this. Kant's whole project, as I understand it, is to make room for moral faith by laying bare the limits of reason in its speculative employment. The objector has interpreted these limits as limits on *all* sense-making and so on *all* significant belief, and thereby has deprived Kant of the very moral faith that was his main objective all along.

A second objection is that Kant himself gives us a way to escape the position that atheism is rationally unstable, by proposing a 'historical conception' of the highest good, in which the historical conception *does not depend on divine agency.*[42] On this conception, humans simply make themselves happy by progressively becoming more virtuous as history proceeds. But this is not Kant's conception.[43] He does indeed believe in moral progress. But throughout his published work, he thinks of this progress as dependent upon divine assistance.[44] This is true also of the historical and political treatises, such as *Perpetual Peace*, which have to be understood as framed within the familiar Kantian ethical and religious framework, not as suggesting a replacement for it.[45] Not only is this nontheist historical conception not Kant's conception; it is also implausible on its own merits.[46] A conspicuous exponent of the historical conception is John Dewey, one of the original signatories of the humanist manifesto of 1933, which stated that "Man is at last becoming aware that he alone is responsible for the realization of the world of his dreams, that he has within himself the power for its achievement." It is significant that the statement was written in 1933. We need to ask the question whether the statement is true, and whether it is supported by our experience of the world run by the people who believed it. The historical conception is one of moral progress by human efforts alone. The 'progress' part of this is common to Kant and Dewey. The 'human effort alone' part has been more or less unique in our tradition to the last century and a half. This has been at once the most educated and the most brutal period of human history. Kant had a kind of modesty about what humans, given the propensity for evil, can accomplish on their own. If we lose the Kantian kind of modesty, we have shown that we open ourselves to horrendous evil. It is a hypothesis worth investigating that when people stop believing that there is divine authority over them, political systems evolve that overestimate the human power to change the human condition, and these systems lead to unspeakable miseries.

The key question about atheism, as Kant saw, is whether a person is already committed to the moral law and has reverence for it. If a person does have reverence for the moral law, then without God and God's assistance, she is in what I call 'the moral gap.' If she cannot produce a working alternative to theism in bridging this gap, her position will be rationally unstable in just the way Kant said Spinoza's position was. She will not be able to make consistent her beliefs about what she can do and what she should.

NOTES

1. This paper was first delivered at Yale Divinity School, as part of my candidacy to succeed Nick Wolterstorff, whom I had followed to Calvin fourteen years before. I have found that following him chronologically is possible, but not replacing him.
2. KrV B xxx, 3:18. My references will use the volume number of the academy edition, and I have used the translation (where available) of the *Cambridge Edition of the Works of Immanuel Kant*, eds. Allen Wood and Paul Guyer (New York: Cambridge University Press, 1989).
3. Philip J. Rossi and Michael Wreen, eds., *Kant's Philosophy of Religion Reconsidered* (Bloomington, IN: Indiana University Press, 1991), ix. Nicholas Wolterstorff has a paper in the volume, called "Conundrums in Kant's Rational Religion."
4. *The Books of Nature and Scripture: Recent Essays on Natural Philosophy, Theology and Biblical Criticism in the Netherlands of Spinoza's Time and the British Isles of Newton's Time*, eds. James E. Force and Richard H. Popkin (Boston: Kluwer Academic, 1994). Also J. B. Schneewind, *The Invention of Autonomy* (Cambridge: Cambridge University Press, 1998), Donald Rutherford, *Leibniz and the Rational Order of Nature* (New York: Cambridge University Press, 1995), Robert M. Adams, *Leibniz: Determinist, Theist, Idealist* (New York: Oxford University Press, 1994).

5. The passage begins, "The skeptical atheist denies all certain knowledge of God's existence. The question is whether the skeptical atheist can have religion? By all means. He accepts the possibility of God's existence; thus, he must conduct himself as if there were indeed a God, and this is religion. He can make room for the moral grounds [for God's existence], even when he does not accept the speculative ones; since he cannot prove the impossibility of a God." I owe reference to this passage to Patrick Kain.

6. Gordon D. Kaufman, *God the Problem* (Cambridge, MA: Harvard University Press, 1972), 134–5. See also the discussion of God as symbol, again referring to Kant, 109–116.

7. Henry Stob, *Ethical Reflections* (Grand Rapids, MI: Eerdmans, 1978), 37.

8. The initial version of this paper was a reply to a paper by Lara Denis, at the Pacific Division of the American Philosophical Association in 2001. I learned much from her paper, and some of the descriptions of Kant's moral criticisms of atheism in the second section of my paper are drawn from her. Fred Beiser was the other commentator. His view was that Kant's conception of practical faith (which Beiser concedes to be essentially theistic) "is a boil, a tumor, a cancer within the critical philosophy, which it is necessary to remove surgically." I have learned a great deal from Patrick Kain's unpublished paper, "Interpreting Kant's Theory of Divine Commands: Three Proposals," and in particular he pointed me to the reference in Volckmann's lecture notes.

9. *Critique of Judgment* 5:452.

10. Collins, 27:312. See also footnote 38 of the present paper.

11. Collins, 27:327, emphasis added.

12. At *Religion* 6:126, Kant attributes a kind of implicit faith in immortality to Jews in general: "It can also hardly be doubted that the Jews subsequently produced, each for himself, some sort of religious faith" (even though Kant thinks this was not part of statutory Judaism).

13. *Critique of Judgment* 5:445–7. I am grateful to Lee Hardy for discussion of this point. See also KrV A623 = B651, and A829 = B827, "The belief in a God and another world is so interwoven with my moral disposition (*Gesinnung*) that I am in as little danger of ever surrendering the former as I am worried that the latter can ever be torn away from me."

14. See Lewis White Beck, *A Commentary on Kant's Critique of Practical Reason* (Chicago: University of Chicago Press, 1960), 272: "To be really possible is to be (a) logically possible and (b) related necessarily to some other fact (viz. the moral) whose reality is given."

15. Collins, 27:317.

16. See *Religion* 6:94. Allen Wood emphasizes this point in his article "Religion, Ethical Community and the Struggle against Evil," in *Faith and Philosophy*, 17, 4 (2000): 498–511.

17. *Religion* 6:67. There are unresolved problems here about the extent to which we and God cooperate in the revolution of the will, and about how the revolution is supposed to relate to temporality.

18. In the First Critique, Kant puts this in a way that is not completely consistent with his mature ethical writing. He says, "Without a God and a world that is not now visible but is hoped for, the majestic ideas of morality are, to be sure, objects of approbation and admiration but not incentives for resolve and realization." (*KrV* A813 = B841. It

is clear in the rest of the passage that it is the highest good as a whole that is supposed to be the incentive, not merely the heavenly reward.) This suggests that we can only be motivated to *live* morally, as opposed to merely *admiring* the moral life, if the hope of heaven or the fear of hell is added to admiration for the moral law. This is not Kant's ultimate view. In his lectures on the philosophical doctrine of religion, Kant puts the point more carefully, "Natural morality must be so constituted that it can be thought independently of any concept of God, and obtain zealous reverence from us solely on account of its own inner dignity and excellence. But further it serves for this if, after we have taken an interest in morals itself (we) take an interest also in the existence of God, a being who can reward our good conduct; and then we obtain strong incentives which determine us to observe moral laws." (*Lectures on the Philosophical Doctrine of Religion*, 28:1003). Here Kant's point is that heaven gives us an *additional* incentive to that given by the moral law itself. See Sharon Anderson-Gold, "God and Community: An Inquiry into the Religious Implications of the Highest Good," in *Kant's Philosophy of Religion Reconsidered*, 113–31.

19. See *Groundwork* 4:433–4, "He belongs to (the kingdom) as a sovereign when, as lawgiving, he is not subject to the will of any other."
20. *Religion* 6:98.
21. *Metaphysics of Morals* 6:396. See also ibid. 231. I discuss this topic in "Kant on Recognizing Our Duties as God's Commands," *Faith and Philosophy*, 17:4 (2000), 459–78, especially pages 468–71.
22. *Critique of Judgment* 5:452.
23. *Critique of Pure Reason* A 809 = B 837. I have tried to retrieve and restate this argument in the third chapter of *The Moral Gap* (Oxford: Clarendon Press, 1996) and less formally in the fourth chapter of *Why Bother Being Good?* (Downers Grove, IL: InterVarsity Press, 2002).
24. Bernard Williams, *Shame and Necessity* (Berkeley: University of California Press, 1993), 163–4.
25. *Critique of Judgment* 5:453.
26. *Religion* 6:157–8
27. *On the Genealogy of Morals and Ecce Homo*, trans. Walter Kaufman (New York: Vintage Books, 1967), 90–1: "There is no small probability that with the irresistible decline of faith in the Christian God there is now also a considerable decline in mankind's feeling of guilt."
28. I am thinking, for example, of Nel Noddings, *Caring: A Feminine Approach to Ethics and Moral Education* (Berkeley: University of California Press, 1984), 86: "I am not obliged to care for starving children in Africa, because there is no way for this caring to be completed in the other unless I abandon the caring to which I am obligated." Another example is Larry Arnhart, *Darwinian Natural Right* (Albany, NY: State University of New York Press, 1998), 149: "When individuals or groups compete with one another we must either find some common ground of shared interests, or we must allow for an appeal to force or fraud to settle the dispute. The only alternative, which I do not regard as a realistic alternative, is to invoke some transcendental norm of impartial justice (such as Christian charity) that is beyond the order of nature."
29. But see Frank K. Prochaska, *The Death of Charity* (forthcoming) for a historian's account of Britain over the last century. As a side note, I have found this concern with the need for what Kant calls a vehicle of the moral life quite active in China. I

taught there briefly, and returned for a week's conference at Tsinghua University at their center for religion and ethics. I was struck both times by the affinity with Kant among the Chinese philosophers I spoke with. They knew Kant well, better than some of the American philosophers I was with, and they were especially interested in the connections he made between morality and religious faith. Several of them spoke of the need in China for some new way to think about the foundations of ethics, after the decline first of Confucianism and second of Marxism as an ideology. They spoke of the need for faith, and the transcendent, and even some of them the need for God. They have been engaging in an intense discussion with each other, into which we Westerners at the conference were invited to enter, about whether there is anything in Christianity that can be used in the Chinese context for this purpose.

30. *Religion* 6:154.

31. Collins, 27:312. There is a similar passage at Vigilantius, 27:531.

32. See *New Essays in Philosophical Theology*, eds. Anthony Flew and Alasdair MacIntyre (New York: Macmillan, 1955) 99–103.

33. See R. M. Hare, *Essays on Religion and Education* (Oxford: Clarendon Press, 1992), 37–9.

34. R. M. Hare, *Essays*, 1–36, especially 22–3.

35. Collins, 27:312.

36. I am indebted to Patrick Kain for some additional references here: Pölitz 28:998, "The mere possibility of such a being is sufficient to produce religion in the human being" (see also 28:1010); Refl. 6226 (18:515), "The mere possibility of God's existence is already sufficient for moral religion; yet not as much as faith." (I take it that the latter clause means that assertoric faith is better at producing and sustaining religion, even though it is not strictly necessary); Refl. 6244 (18:523), "It is possible that a God exists, is sufficient for religion, but not for *cultus*." Kant uses the term I have translated 'belief' (*Glaube*) more narrowly than the English term, and often 'faith' is a better translation.

37. The footnote reads as follows, "With this definition some erroneous interpretations of the concept of a religion in general are obviated. First, so far as theoretical cognition and profession of faith are concerned, no assertoric knowledge is required in religion (even of the existence of God), since with our lack of insight into supersensible objects any such profession can well be hypocritically feigned; speculatively, what is required is rather only a *problematic* assumption (hypothesis) concerning the supreme cause of things, whereas with respect to the object toward which our morally legislative reason bids us work, what is presupposed is an *assertoric* faith, practical and hence free, that promises a result for the final aim of religion; and this faith needs only *the idea of God* which must occur to every morally earnest (and therefore religious) pursuit of the good, without pretending to be able to secure objective reality for it through theoretical cognition." (*Religion* 6:154). Allen Wood has recently interpreted the passage to say that Kant's position is that neither religion nor the moral life requires that we believe in the existence of God (Wood, "Religion," 501). I will not discuss his interpretation here, as I have done so in an essay scheduled to appear in *Kant and the New Philosophy of Religion*, eds. Chris L. Firestone and Stephen R. Palmquist (Bloomington: Indiana University Press, 2005).

38. Kant continues, "subjectively, the *minimum* of cognition (it is possible that there is a God) must alone suffice for what can be made the duty of every human being."

This is a point Kant makes elsewhere about what kind of *duty* we have in our beliefs about God. In the Vigilantius notes on Kant's lectures on the Metaphysics of Morals, Kant makes a distinction between the dogmatic atheist and the skeptical atheist (Vigilantius, 27:531. The distinction is also found in *Lectures on the Philosophical Doctrine of Religion* 28:1010 and 1026. In the former passage, Kant says, "Hence a skeptic can still have religion," and goes on to say that the belief in a merely possible God as ruler of the world is the minimum of theology). The skeptical atheist cannot persuade himself of theism, or the reality of God, though he also cannot demonstrate that God is impossible. "It is therefore incumbent on him," says Kant, "merely to assume the possibility of a God." The dogmatic atheist, on the other hand, does not accept even the possibility. But then Kant goes on to say that whereas the dogmatic atheist is making a "wrong and even dangerous contention," the skeptical atheist is not punishable, for his doubts are guiltless.

39. *Critique of Practical Reason*, 5:126. Kant goes on, "although this assumption itself belongs to theoretical reason; with respect to theoretical reason alone, as a ground of explanation, it can be called a *hypothesis*; but in relation to the intelligibility of an object given us by the moral law (the highest good), and consequently if a need for practical purposes, it can be called *belief*." He insists, however, that the commitment to obey the moral law for its own sake must come before the belief. What he calls 'moral theology' gets this order right, *Lectures on the Philosophical Doctrine of Religion* 28:999. See *KrV* A632 = B661 and *Religion* 6:202.

40. I am grateful to Peter Byrne for making this objection at a conference in Oxford in 2003. I have taken the three representative texts from him.

41. The editor feels he has to add "theoretically," and to comment in a footnote, "We do cognize it practically by this analogy." Kant fails here, as in the other passages, to make this contrast explicit, though the passage goes on to limit the discussion to theoretical attribution of properties.

42. This was the proposal of Lara Denis in the original paper to which the present paper was a response. She referred to discussion by Andrews Reath, "Two Conceptions of the Highest Good in Kant," *Journal of the History of Philosophy*, 26:4 (1988): 593–619; Stephen Engstrom, "The Concept of the Highest Good in Kant's Moral Theory," *Philosophy and Phenomenological Research*, 52:4 (1992): 747–80; and Thomas Pogge, "Kant on Ends and the Meaning of Life," in *Reclaiming the History of Ethics: Essays for John Rawls* (New York: Cambridge University Press, 1997). I would add Fred Beiser, *Enlightenment, Revolution, and Romanticism*, (Cambridge, MA: Harvard University Press, 1992), e.g. p. 31, "The human will creates moral value."

43. I am uncertain about the *Opus Postumum*. See Eckart Förster, *Kant's Final Synthesis: An Essay on the Opus Postumum* (Cambridge, MA: Harvard University Press, 2000).

44. *Religion* 6:100. Wood stresses this point in the article already cited, p. 508: "Kant believes that (owing to a certain weakness of human nature) it is impossible for people directly to form a pure ethical community." See also *The Conflict of the Faculties*, 4:82.

45. *Perpetual Peace*, 8: 380.

46. I am being brief and dogmatic here, but I have given somewhat longer treatment to the topic in *The Moral Gap*, especially chapters 4–7, and in *Why Bother Being Good?*, especially chapter 2.

10

ॐ

Does Forgiveness Undermine Justice?

NICHOLAS WOLTERSTORFF

Prominent in the ethic of christianity is the declaration that God forgives and justifies the sinner who has faith, and the injunction that we are likewise to forgive those who have sinned against us. The issue I wish to consider in this essay is whether these teachings concerning forgiveness and justification undercut the moral order that Christianity itself affirms.

I

Jesus often declared to persons in his entourage that their sins were forgiven; his hearers took him to be speaking on behalf of God in doing so. The story of the healing of the paralytic is a good example. The episode is recorded in all four gospels. Here is how Mark tells the story.

When some people carrying a paralyzed man could not bring him to Jesus because of the crowd, they removed the roof above him; and after having dug through it, they let down the mat on which the paralytic lay. When Jesus saw their faith, he said to the paralytic, "Son, your sins are forgiven." Now some of the scribes were sitting there, questioning in their hearts, "Why does this fellow speak in this way? It is blasphemy! Who can forgive sins but God alone?" (Mark 2:4–7)[1]

And just as often as he pronounced God's forgiveness of some sinner, Jesus enjoined his followers to forgive those who had wronged them. Peter, apparently disturbed by the fact that Jesus set no clear limits on the scope of such forgiveness, posed what he regarded as a *reductio ad absurdum* question to Jesus: "Lord, how often should I forgive, as many as seven times?" Jesus first gave a hyperbolic answer: "Not seven times, but, I tell you, seventy-seven times." Then he told the parable about the king who, out of mercy, forgave the large debt owed him by one of his servants who, in turn, mercilessly refused to forgive the much smaller debt owed him by one of his fellow servants. The point of the story, in Jesus' words, is that you are to forgive your brother and sister out of mercy, "from your heart" (Matthew 18:21–35).

In his letter to the church at Rome, Saint Paul famously articulated and elaborated Jesus' point concerning God's forgiveness by the use of imagery taken from the courtroom. God, says Paul, "justifies" those sinners who have faith in order that there may be peace (*eirenê*) between God and them. What exactly Paul meant by "justification" has been much disputed. My own view, which I cannot take time to defend in this essay, is that by "justifying" someone, Paul has in mind dismissing or not pressing charges against him, not because he is not guilty of the charges – he is guilty – but for the sake of reconciliation between the wrongdoer and the judge, who in this case is also the lawgiver. Though the person has broken the law, his legal status as "justified" is that there are no charges pending against him.[2]

In the course of his discussion, Paul raised the worry that I want to discuss. Is not God's law "overthrown" by God's justification of the sinner? Paul's answer was an emphatic "By no means!" The law is not overthrown but upheld (Romans 3:31). The precise concern Paul had in mind becomes clear a few chapters later. Does not the teaching that sinners are justified on account of faith and not works encourage antinomianism and libertinism? When people hear about divine justification, won't they start to think "Should we [not] sin because we are not under law but under grace?" Won't they even start to think "Should we [not] *continue* in sin in order that grace may abound?" (6:15, 1). Paul's response is again the emphatic, "By no means."

II

In his discussion of justice in the *Nicomachean Ethics*, Aristotle distinguished between *distributive* justice and *rectifying* justice; the distinction has become a commonplace since then. Rectifying justice is present when the parties to an act of wrongdoing enjoy or undergo what is due them on account of that act of wrongdoing, when they enjoy or undergo what they deserve. Or to put it in yet another way: rectifying justice is present when the parties to a violation of justice enjoy what they have a right to, and undergo what is their desert, on account of that violation of justice. What Aristotle calls *distributive* justice is then that species of justice that has been violated.

I do not think that this latter species of justice is aptly called *distributive*; better simply to call it *primary* justice. For not all cases of primary justice consist of some form or other of maldistribution. Rape is an all-too-common example of the violation of a person's rights, thus an all-too-common example of the violation of primary justice. But what is wrong about rape is not that something or other has been maldistributed. The same is true for the violation of one's privacy for prurient reasons, and many other examples.

The relevance of these observations to the topic of forgiveness and Pauline justification is that these acts can occur only under certain conditions; one cannot dispense forgiveness hither and yon indiscriminately. Specifically, I can forgive you only if you have wronged me, and only *for* the wrong you have done me. The mere fact that you have failed to bring about one and another state or event in my life that would be a life-good for me is not sufficient for it to be possible for me to forgive you. If the life-good in question is not one to which I had a right, not one that was due me, then there is nothing for which I can forgive you. Forgiving you is not something I can do – though of course I may size up the situation incorrectly and *believe* that I can forgive you.

It follows that the person who never thinks about her fellow human beings in terms of primary justice and injustice cannot understand herself as forgiving them. To understand oneself as forgiving someone presupposes understanding oneself as having been wronged by the other; it presupposes understanding oneself as the victim of a breach of primary justice. The concept of forgiveness has the concept of primary justice as one of its components.

Might one nevertheless forgive someone without *understanding* oneself as doing so – in the way in which one might, say, kick someone without having the concept of kicking, and thus without understanding oneself as kicking him? More to the point: can one forgive someone without recognizing that he has treated one unjustly?

Surely not. To forgive someone requires not only that the person has wronged one but that one *recognize* that he has done so. Forgiveness can occur only in the objective context of the agent having a primary right that has been violated and in the conceptual and epistemic context of the agent recognizing that she has been wronged, such recognition presupposing employment of the concept of being wronged, that is, of being deprived of a primary right.

Take a further step. I hold that to forgive the person who has wronged one is to forego claiming or exercising certain of one's rights as a victim. Let me immediately add, lest there be any misunderstanding, that one can forego claiming or exercising the rights one has acquired as a victim without forgiving; forgiving is just one species of such foregoing. Sometimes we forego claiming or exercising our victim rights because we do not want to be bothered; such foregoing is not forgiveness. Yes, you have wronged me. But the wrong was too slight to bother with, or I have more pressing things to tend to, or I regard you as beneath my notice.

If this understanding of forgiveness, as the foregoing of certain of one's victim rights, is correct, then not only must the person who understands herself as forgiving employ the concept of primary justice and injustice; she must employ the concept of rectifying justice as well. I will not contend that one cannot forgive without understanding oneself as forgiving; perhaps it is possible to forego exercising or claiming one's rights to rectifying justice in a way that counts as forgiving without understanding oneself as doing so. But even if that is a possibility, what remains true is that the concept of forgiveness has the concept of rectifying justice as one of its components.

In short, though forgiveness, by its very nature, is a case of not claiming or exercising one's rights, nonetheless, if there were no such thing as primary justice and violations thereof, there could be no such thing as rectifying justice; and if there were no such thing as rectifying justice, there could be no such thing as forgiveness. Or given the fact that rectifying justice may include not only what is due the victim but also what is due the victimizer, the more precise thing to say is that the possibility of forgiveness presupposes the existence of *victim* rights. Where there are no victim rights, forgiveness cannot occur; and without the recognition of one's victim rights, one cannot understand oneself as forgiving. Similar things are true for Pauline justification. Justification presupposes primary and rectifying justice and the concepts thereof.

I can now put more precisely the question I wish to consider. The question is not whether forgiveness and Pauline justification undermine some dimension or other of the moral vision of Christianity. The question is whether they undermine a dimension that they themselves presuppose, namely, the existence of requirements of primary justice. In foregoing claiming our victim rights, do we not imperil the primary justice that the existence of those same rights presupposes? Is there not, in that way, a fundamental incoherence in forgiveness and Pauline justification?

III

In his *Proslogion*, Anselm asked a related but slightly different question from the one that I will be considering. He asked how God's merciful forgiveness and justification of the sinner is compatible with God's character as just. Addressing God, he asked in Chapter 9,

How do you spare the wicked if You are all-just and supremely just? For how does the all-just and supremely just One do something that is unjust? Or what kind of justice is it to give everlasting life to him who merits eternal death? How then, O good God, good to the good and to the wicked, how do You save the wicked if this is not just and You do not do anything which is not just? Or, since Your goodness is beyond comprehension, is this hidden in the inaccessible light in which You dwell?[3]

After a number of tentative probes, Anselm settled on the following solution. In speaking of God as just, we must distinguish between God's being just relative to us and God's being just relative to himself. God is just relative to us when God renders to us what is due us, including what is retributively due us; God is just relative to himself when God does what befits his nature as the supreme good. In sparing the wicked "You are just," says Anselm to God, "not because you give us our due, but because You do what befits You as the supreme good" (*Proslogion* 10). "In sparing the wicked You are just in relation to Yourself and not in relation to us" (ibid.).

Anselm's argument, that relative to himself, God is just both in pardoning the wrongdoer and in punishing him, goes as follows: whatever God does that accords with his will befits his goodness, since God's will is itself good. Accordingly, "that alone is just which You will, and that is not just which You do not will" (*Proslogion* 11). Now God wills to save some and to damn others. Accordingly, the salvation of the former and the damnation of the latter are both just. "It is just in relation to You, O just and benevolent God, both when You punish and when You pardon" (ibid.). Indeed, "it [would not be] just for those to be saved whom You will to punish, and it [would not be] just for those to be damned whom You will to pardon" (ibid.). Thus the relation of God's mercy to God's justice is that "Your mercy is derived from Your justice, since it is just that You are so good that You are good even in forgiving" (ibid.).

I submit that this is not Anselm at his best. Distinguish, he says, between God's being just relative to us and God's being just relative to himself. Understand the former as grounded in God's rendering to us what is due us, and understand the latter as grounded in God's acting in accord with his good will. Observe, next, that it is in accord with the will of the supremely good God that some wrongdoers be saved and some be damned. Conclude that whereas God is not just relative to us, on account of the fact that God does not always render to us what is retributively due us, God is always just relative to himself, since God's forgiveness and damnation of the wrongdoer are equally in accord with his good will.

We wanted to understand how it is that God is just even though, in mercifully forgiving wrongdoers, God does not act in accord with the requirements of retributive justice. We are now told that though God is indeed unjust relative to us, nonetheless it remains the case that whatever God does is done in accord with his good will. But this does not remove our perplexity; it merely reminds us of what we knew anyway, namely, that whatever God does is good, and concedes the point that worried us at the beginning, after rephrasing it in a slightly more complicated form. What worried us is that, in forgiving wrongdoers, God is unjust. Our worry rephrased is this: in forgiving wrong-doers, God is unjust relative to us. These moves yield no insight; our perplexity remains. Using the conceptuality Anselm proposes, the question to press is how it can be good for God to fail to render to us what is due us. That question receives no answer.

IV

My own solution to Anselm's perplexity is to deny one of the theses that produced the perplexity. Wronging someone typically engenders a variety of rights and deserts. The party wronged typically has a right, for example, to be angry at what was done to her. Among all the rights and deserts engendered by wronging, Anselm focuses entirely on punishment. And about punishment, he assumes that if the wrongdoer is not punished, justice has been violated; someone or other has been deprived of some right or desert. Absent this assumption, Anselm's perplexity never arises.

I hold that the assumption is mistaken. The rights that victims acquire on account of having been wronged are such that often nobody's rights or deserts are violated should the victim forego claiming those rights. In particular, the victim can often waive his right to the *punishment* of the wrongdoer without thereby violating the rights or deserts of either party. Hence there is no puzzle over how it can be that the mercy of forgiveness does not violate the principles of rectifying justice. The mercy of forgiveness constitutes waiving one's retributive rights, not violating one's retributive duties.

I know, of course, that Anselm is far from alone among Christian theologians in assuming that it would be a violation of rectifying justice were God to forego punishment for human wrongdoing. It is this assumption, in conjunction with those New Testament passages that speak of Christ as "representing" humankind and those that speak of Christ as taking onto himself our sorrows, that has engendered punitive theories of the atonement. God punished us by punishing our representative, Christ; divine forgiveness consists of God's taking that punishment of our representative as sufficient punishment of us. Or using a somewhat different conceptuality, Christ paid the penalty for us, in the way that one person sometimes pays a fine for another; and divine forgiveness consists of God's regarding Christ's payment of the penalty for our wrongdoing as sufficient payment.

It is my judgment that the Christian scriptures neither teach nor imply Anselm's assumption. To the contrary: one of the most distinctive teachings of Judaism and Christianity, constituting a striking difference between their moral vision on the one hand and the moral vision of pagan antiquity on the other, is that forgiving by foregoing punishment of the wrongdoer is not a violation of the principles of retributive justice. Only if we bring to our interpretation of Scripture the prior and extraneous conviction that retributive punishment is a duty and not merely a right will the texts be thought to support punitive theories of the atonement. It is worth adding that even those theologians who adopt one or another of such theories do not, so far as I can discern, hold a counterpart theory for human forgiveness and pardon. Be ready to forgive your brother seventy-seven times, said Jesus. Nobody postulates a theory of surrogate punishment hovering in the wings.

In a very interesting essay, "Equity and Mercy," Martha Nussbaum traces the intellectual and linguistic history that led up to Aristotle's explication of justice as equity – *epieikeia* – in the *Nicomachean Ethics*.[4] She argues that in Greek literature, *dikê* in moral and religious affairs originally meant paying back in kind; and originally the consensus was that *dikê* is required. If you have blinded me, then justice requires that you be blinded in turn so as thereby to restore the balance that your action upset. Human life, she says, was seen as something "that can be invaded, wounded, or violated by another's act in many ways. For this penetration, the only remedy that seems appropriate is a counterinvasion.... And to right the balance truly, the retribution must be exactly, strictly proportional to the original encroachment" (p. 89).

Such justice, since it paid no attention to the particular circumstances of the wrongdoing, was seen as often harsh in its workings; no consideration was given to whether or not the initial blinding was intentional, whether, if intentional, it was done under duress or with false information, and the like. But slowly, alongside this notion of *dikê* and its requirements, there emerged the idea of treating the other with equity (*epieikeia*), that is, of paying attention to all the particulars of the action and determining punishment in accord with those particulars. "*Epieikeia* is a gentle art of particular perception, a temper of mind that refuses to demand retribution without understanding the whole story" (p. 92). And once the whole story is understood, *epieikeia* will often recommend mitigating, or even foregoing, the punishment determined by *dikê*. Of course it is possible that when one understands the whole story, one will conclude that the wrongdoer should be punished more severely than *dikê* would suggest; but for reasons that Nussbaum explores, it will usually turn out that equity recommends more gentle treatment.

Equity came to be praised in a good deal of classical Greek literature. Yet *dikê* remained, in Nussbaum's words, "a venerated moral norm" (p. 92). The tension is noted, and then more or less definitively resolved, by Aristotle, when he says that equity is itself a kind of justice, a kind that in many situations is opposed to strict legal justice and, where opposed, is superior to legal justice. The reason for the conflict is that the law has no choice but to speak in generalities; it cannot take account of all the particulars that equity takes into account. Here is Aristotle's conclusion:

It is also clear from this [account of the equitable] what sort of person the equitable person is. For a person who chooses and does such things, and who is not zealous for strict judgment in the direction of the worse, but is inclined to mitigation, even though he can invoke the law on his side – such a person is equitable and this trait of character is equity, being a kind of justice and not a distinct trait of character. (*Nicomachean Ethics* 1137b34–1138a3)

Nussbaum traces this Aristotelian line of thought forward into the Latin Stoics, especially Seneca. Whereas the Greek Stoics were ardent defenders of *dikê* as opposed to *epieikeia*, Seneca, in his treatises *De Ira* and *De Clementia*, eloquently insists on the importance of paying attention to the particulars in order to make the proper decisions concerning punishment. This stance, or practice, "he now calls by the name of mercy, translating Greek *epieikeia* with the Latin word *clementia*" (Nussbaum, p. 102). *Clementia*, says Seneca, is "an inclination of the soul to mildness in exacting penalties"; alternatively expressed, it is "that which turns its course away this side of that which could be justly determined" (*De Clementia* II.3).

Nussbaum notes that Senecan clemency "does not fail to pass judgment on wrongdoing. . . . Seneca does not hold that the circumstances of human life remove moral and legal responsibility for bad acts. We may still convict defendants who fulfill some basic conditions of rationality in action. But, looking at the circumstances of human life, one comes to understand how such things have happened, and this 'medical' understanding leads to mercy" (Nussbaum, p. 102). Proper punishment is equitable punishment, merciful punishment, clemential punishment.

In short, mercy (clemency, *clementia*) is not understood by Seneca as *forgoing* imposing the punishment that true equity requires; it is understood as *imposing* the punishment that true equity requires. Compared with the punishment that the law would impose, given law's incapacity for dealing with all relevant particulars, the punishment of equity or clemency is often more gentle, less harsh. But nobody in pagan antiquity proposed that it is right sometimes to forgo imposing the appropriate penalty. Some were dubious about equity as opposed to abstract *dikê* in determining proper punishment; nobody was in favor of forgoing the proper punishment.

That, however, is the implication of Paul's teaching that God justifies the wrongdoer, and of Jesus' declaration on behalf of God that "Your sins are forgiven." God forgoes the fully equitable punishment. Determine first the truly equitable punishment. God forgoes imposing that punishment. Contra Seneca's equation of mercy with equity, mercy is pulled loose from equity. Mercy enters after equitable justice is determined. It is not required that we receive our "just deserts." Punishment is not a duty, not even equitable punishment.

But may it be the case that failure to punish the wrongdoer, and more generally, failure to exercise our victim rights, in some way undermines the very thing it presupposes, namely, primary justice – not rectifying justice but *primary* justice? That is my question.

V

The reason the Christian teaching concerning the forgoing of our victim rights, and especially the forgoing of our right to punishment of the wrongdoer, would have been seen by the philosophers of pagan antiquity as morally and socially dangerous, rather than an interesting new idea, was well expressed by Kant in a provocative passage:

Even if a civil society were to dissolve itself by common agreement of all its members (for example if the people inhabiting an island decided to separate and disperse themselves around the world), the last murderer remaining in prison must first be executed, so that everyone will duly receive what his actions are worth and so that the bloodguilt thereof will not be fixed on the people because they failed to insist on carrying out the punishment; for if they fail to do so, they may be regarded as accomplices in this public violation of legal justice.[5]

What reasons might there be for thinking that Kant is right about this? Or to be more specific, do plausible theories of retributive justice have Kant's thesis among their implications – the thesis, namely, that failure to punish a wrongdoer is to be an accomplice in his crime? Of course *accomplice* is used metaphorically here. What Kant means, presumably, is that to fail to punish a wrongdoer is to condone or endorse his wrongdoing.

The most plausible theory of retributive justice currently available seems to me to be the so-called expressive theory of punishment, first articulated with care in a seminal article by Joel Feinberg, "The Expressive Function of Punishment." Feinberg opens his discussion by exploring the difference between a punishment and a penalty – examples of penalties being a parking ticket, a library fine, an offside penalty in soccer, and disqualification from some competition. Both penalties and punishments belong to the genus "infliction of hard treatment by an authority on a person for his prior failing in some respect (usually an infraction of a rule or command)" (p. 95). So what differentiates punishments from penalties within this genus?

Feinberg's answer is that punishment has a certain expressive function that the infliction of a penalty lacks. Specifically, "punishment is a conventional device for the expression of attitudes of resentment and indignation, and of judgments of disapproval and reprobation, on the part either of the punishing authority himself or of those 'in whose name' the punishment is inflicted. Punishment, in short, has a *symbolic significance....*" (p. 98).

Not only *can* the imposition of hard treatment and reprobation – by the latter of which Feinberg means "the stern judgment of disapproval" (p. 101) – occur separately from each other; often they do occur separately. Penalties are sometimes hard treatment, as are, for example, the procedures undergone by those who enroll in drug rehabilitation programs; but in neither of these cases does the hard treatment express an attitude of resentment and indignation, or a judgment of disapproval and reprobation. And conversely: though a verbal denunciation is a reprobative judgment, and often expresses a feeling of resentment or indignation, the uttering of the words whereby the denunciation is issued is thoroughly harmless. The mere uttering of words in somebody's presence is as far from hard treatment as anything could be, unless, of course, it is done at painfully high volume. "Sticks and stones may break my bones but words can never harm me."

What is unique to punishment is that the hard treatment has gotten connected in some intimate way with the disapproving and reprobative judgment and with the indignant and resentful feelings. Specifically, the hard treatment *counts as* a stern judgment of disapproval. To use the language of speech-act theory: the illocutionary act of denouncing the wrongful act is accomplished by way of subjecting the wrongdoer to hard treatment; and the performance of the illocutionary act in turn expresses feelings of resentment, indignation, and the like. "To say that the very physical treatment itself expresses condemnation is to say simply that certain forms of hard treatment have become the conventional symbols of public reprobation. This is neither more nor less paradoxical than to say that certain words have become conventional vehicles in our language for the expression of certain attitudes, or that champagne is the alcoholic beverage traditionally used in celebration of great events, or that black is the color of mourning" (p. 100).[6]

Feinberg notes that some of the social functions standardly ascribed to punishment, such as deterrence and rehabilitation, have at best a loose connection with its nature as the pronouncement of public condemnation and the expression of resentment or indignation. Others of its social functions, however, are intrinsically connected with its nature. For example, punishment sometimes serves the function of an organization's disavowal of certain actions on the part of its employees; it could not serve that function were it not, in its nature, an act of public condemnation.

The social function most relevant to our inquiry is what Feinberg calls "symbolic nonacquiescence" (p. 102). Punishment communicates to those who have ears to hear that society does not acquiesce in, does not condone, what was done. Referring to paramour killings, which until rather recently were allowed in Texas, Feinberg argues that the demand that such killings be punished, whatever else it may be, is "the demand that . . . the state *go on record* against paramour killings and the law *testify to the recognition* that such killings are wrongful." He observes that "punishment no doubt would also help deter killers," and "this too is a desideratum." But deterrence "is not to be identified with reprobation; for deterrence might be achieved by a dozen other techniques from simple penalties and forfeitures to exhortation and propaganda." By contrast, "effective public denunciation and, through it, symbolic nonacquiescence in the crime seem virtually to require punishment" (p. 103).

I find this expressive understanding of punishment compelling. But before I consider whether or not it carries the implication that punishment of the wrongdoer is a duty and not merely a right that one can justly forgo claiming, let me add to Feinberg's statement of the theory Jean Hampton's elaboration in her essay "The Retributive Idea"[7] – elaboration in the sense that Hampton goes beyond Feinberg in specifying what she sees as the precise nature of the condemnation expressed by punishment. In Feinberg's version of the expressive theory, there is no note of the traditional idea of punishment as setting things right again, restoring the balance; Hampton's version adds this note.

Those who wrong others, she says, "objectively demean them. They incorrectly believe or else fail to realize that others' value rules out the treatment their actions have accorded the others, and they incorrectly believe or implicitly assume that their own value is high enough to make this treatment possible. So, implicit in their wrongdoings is a message about their value relative to that of their victims" (p. 124). Punishment, by *subjecting* the wrongdoer to hard treatment, sends a countermessage to the wrongdoer's message, a countermessage to the effect that the message of relative worth implicit in the wrongdoer's action was mistaken. Punishment is thus the assertion of:

moral truth in the face of its denial. If I have value equal to that of my assailant, then that must be made manifest after I have been victimized. By victimizing me, the wrongdoer has declared himself elevated with respect to me, acting as a superior who is permitted to use me for his purposes. A false moral claim has been made. Moral reality has been denied. The retributivist demands that the false claim be corrected. The lord must be humbled to show that he isn't the lord of the victim. If I cause the wrongdoer to suffer in proportion to my suffering at his hands, his elevation over me is denied, and moral reality is reaffirmed. I master the purported master, showing that he is my peer. (p. 125)

In short, "retributive punishment is the defeat of the wrongdoer at the hands of the victim (either directly or indirectly through an agent of the victim's, e.g., the state) that symbolizes the correct relative value of wrongdoer and victim. It is a symbol that is conceptually required to reaffirm a victim's equal worth in the face of a challenge to it. . . . [Its] *telos* is not so much to produce good as it is to establish goodness" (pp. 125–6). Punishment strikes "a blow for morality." It "plants the flag of morality" (p. 130).

Hampton then quotes the passage from Kant that I quoted earlier and comments: "I agree with Kant that we would be accomplices in the crime if we failed to punish its perpetrator, because we would be condoning the evidence it gave us of the relative worth of victim and offender, or to put it another way, because we would be acquiescing in the message it sent about the victim's inferiority. Kant takes it as fundamental that to be committed to morality is to be committed to asserting and defending it no matter what the consequences. Hence it is morally required that we send an annulling message after a crime so that the victim's value receives its proper defense" (p. 131).

Hampton explicitly concedes (as Feinberg does not) that mercy may sometimes be appropriate, understanding mercy as "the suspension or mitigation of a punishment that would otherwise be deserved as retribution . . . granted out of pity and compassion for the wrongdoer" (p. 158). Her thought seems to be that the obligation "to annul the wrongdoer's immoral message" (p. 159) may sometimes conflict with other and weightier obligations, "in particular, to the wrongdoer as a human being" (p. 158). But it is clear that her heart is not in this concession. The discussion is brief, and it closes not with an affirmation of the value of mercy but with a warning against it; mercy "risks undermining both the deterrent message and the expression of the value the wrongdoer has transgressed" (p. 159).

VI

Are Feinberg and Hampton right in their claim that, on the expressive theory of punishment, to decline to punish the wrongdoer is to condone what he or she did and to send a message to that effect? Is it true that to decline to send punishment's signal of symbolic nonacquiescence is to send a signal of acquiescence?

I fail to see that it is. For one thing, nobody issues condemnations of everything he does not condone. It is true, for the most part, that if one condemns something, one does not condone it, exceptions being those cases in which one speaks insincerely, under duress, and the like; but there are all sorts of reasons why we do not always condemn what we do not condone. For one thing, condemning would take up too much of our time, and sour all our relationships. Hence not only is it the case that not condemning does not imply condoning; but not condemning does not, in general, send the message that one condones. Whether or not in a given case it does send that message depends on features of the context.

More important is the fact that though it is true, on the expressive theory, that punishing is condemning, it is by no means the case that punishment is the only means of issuing a condemnation. If a person in authority makes clear by his speech that he firmly condemns the action performed, but then goes on to declare that, out of mercy for the offender, or for the sake of the common good or reconciliation with the offender, he will forgo punishing the guilty person, why would that forgoing constitute condoning, or why would it send the message that the action was condoned? Be it granted that mutely declining to punish can easily be construed as condoning – though that interpretation will in some cases be mistaken. But declaring that the person before one is guilty, and then announcing that out of mercy, or for the sake of reconciliation or the common good, one is going to forgo punishment – surely the forgoing of punishment in that context cannot be interpreting as condoning, endorsing, or anything else of the sort.

So far, then, we have uncovered no reason to agree with Feinberg and Hampton that to decline to punish the wrongdoer is to condone what he or she did and to send a message to that effect. But what about the following consideration? Feinberg and Hampton both argue that if we adopt the expressive theory of punishment, then the proportioning of punishment to crime that we demand of retributive justice should be understood along the following lines. Take as a given that denunciation is the sort of speech act that comes in degrees of emphaticness, and add the thesis that, in general, the worse the crime, the more emphatic should be the denunciation. The way this general principle gets implemented, when denunciation takes the form of punishment, is that the worse the crime, the harder the treatment imposed on the criminal.

Now suppose that the authority, after firmly denouncing what the person before him has done, announces that out of mercy, or for the sake of reconciliation or the common good, he will forgo applying the specified punishment.

Let our previous point be conceded, that this entire package does not amount to condoning what the person has done, nor does it send a message to that effect; it is in fact a condemnation. Nonetheless, this total package is surely a weak denunciation compared with that pronounced on someone else who committed the same crime and is sentenced, say, to twenty years of imprisonment. So does the whole package not send the message that this person's wrongdoing is less odious than the other person's? That would be a message that undermines morality, since in fact the crime was of the same category. If there is a system in place for expressing judgments as to the relative severity of crimes – worse crime, harder treatment – then to break with the system and give some crime a less hard treatment than the system specifies, or no hard treatment at all, is to send a wrong message about morality. Talk as loudly as one will, one's actions carry the message that it was not such a bad crime after all.

Again, I do not see it. Suppose that the criminal code has a variety of words to indicate the relative severity of crimes – as in fact our criminal code does: "first-degree murder," "second-degree murder," "manslaughter," and so forth. Suppose that the jury convicts the person in the dock of second-degree murder, that the judge gives a speech about the heinousness of such a crime and sentences him in accord with the criminal code, but that the executive then steps in and out of mercy for the plight of the offender and his family pardons him. Why would it be thought that this whole package carries the message that it was not such a bad crime after all? Why would any reasonable person interpret the whole package that way? Why would not any reasonable person conclude that the jury and judge had determined that he had committed a terrible crime for which severe punishment was appropriate, but that the executive had decided out of mercy to waive the punishment?

Of course, if someone who committed a crime was pardoned because he was white, or male, or wealthy, or socially prominent, or of a certain religion or nationality, that would send a wrong message about morality. But on the face of it, pardoning on the basis of such features is significantly different from pardoning out of mercy, as it is from pardoning for the sake of the common good or for the sake of reconciliation between offender and victim.

VII

Suppose that this response to the worries of Feinberg and Hampton, about the message sent by forgoing punishment, is conceded to be correct. The response does not yet address the specific question that Saint Paul raised, about the message sent by God's justification of wrongdoers on account of their faith. Paul was not raising the general question, whether waiving punishment sends a justice-undermining message. He was raising the specific question, whether that message is sent by God's waiver of punishment in justifying persons of faith.

A tacit assumption in my argument has been that forgoing punishment out of mercy, or for the sake of the common good or reconciliation of victim and offender, will be relatively uncommon. If the executive dispenses pardons hither and yon with abandon because he is a soft touch for the pitiful plight of the convicted, or because he is always worrying about the effects on the common good of the carrying through of punishment, then it will be hard not to interpret his actions as carrying a justice-undermining message. But Paul in Romans gives the impression that he believes God's justification of wrongdoers on the basis of faith will not be rare. His argument is that the requisite condition, namely faith, is available to all; and he gives the impression of believing that there are many who have faith. In this case, then, the worry that waiving punishment will undermine justice seems reasonable. The problem is not with justification as such. The problem is with the apparent ease of acquiring the ground for justification, and thus with God's apparent profligacy in dispensing it.

In Paul's thought, there are two, quite distinct, responses to this worry. Uncovering these responses will require some exegesis of Scripture that is considerably more careful and detailed than is customary among philosophers; philosophers exegete Aristotle and Kant with great care, but usually not Christian Scripture. But because our question is whether Christianity, in what it teaches concerning divine and human forgiveness and divine justification, undermines primary justice, we had better be sure we know what that teaching is. We will see that, all things considered, God's forgoing of punishment is not quite so profligate as it would appear to be if we considered only what Paul says about justification and ignored the relevant context.

In the opening verses of Romans 13, Paul offers an account of governmental justice. Most discussions of Paul on divine justification ignore what he says about governmental justice, and most discussions of what he says about governmental justice ignore what he says about justification. I suggest that the two belong together as parts of one integrated pattern of thought.

The concluding verses of the twelfth chapter of Romans are an introduction to what Paul has to say about governmental justice. If one skips the introduction, one is all too likely to misunderstand the main text. Here is the introduction:

Bless those who persecute you, bless and do not curse them. Rejoice with those who rejoice, weep with those who weep. . . . Do not repay anyone evil for evil, but take thought for what is noble in the sight of all. If it is possible, so far as it depends on you, live peaceably with all. Beloved, never avenge (*ekdikeô*) yourselves, but leave room for the wrath (*orgê*) of God; for it is written, "Vengeance (*ekdikêsis*) is mine, I will repay, says the Lord." No, "if your enemies are hungry, feed them; if they are thirsty, give them something to drink; for by doing this you will heap burning coals on their heads." Do not be overcome by evil but overcome evil with good. (12:14–21)[8]

Here then is the passage about governmental justice:

Let every person be subject to the governing authorities; for there is no authority except from God, and those authorities that exist have been instituted by God. Therefore whoever resists authority resists what God has appointed, and those who resist will incur judgment (*krima*). For rulers are not a terror to good conduct, but to bad. Do you wish to have no fear of the authority? Then do what is good, and you will receive its approval; for it is God's servant (*diakonos*) for your good. But if you do what is wrong, you should be afraid, for the authority does not bear the sword in vain! It is the servant (*diakonos*) of God to execute wrath (*orgê*) on the wrongdoer. Therefore one must be subject, not only because of wrath (*orgê*) but also because of conscience. (13:1–5)

Among the many bottles of ink spent over the centuries in arguing about this passage are those spent in arguing whether Paul is talking descriptively about government as he found it (and as we find it), or talking normatively about properly functioning government. To me, it seems too obvious to be worth argument that he is speaking normatively. Paul was intimately acquainted with local flesh-and-blood rulers of the first century who were more a terror to good conduct than to bad. Of course, if he had thought that the empire as a whole was so badly malformed as to be completely malevolent, he would presumably have spoken differently. He would have spoken of the menace of government more than of its proper function. And in fact a complete discourse about any actual government will always have to employ both ways of speaking: government is meant to put its stamp of approval on good conduct and to be a terror to bad; in every case, to varying degrees, government puts its stamp of approval on bad conduct and is a terror to good conduct.

When Paul says to his readers in the church at Rome – in the NRSV translation – that they are not to "avenge" themselves but are to leave "wrath" to God, and then quotes Deuteronomy 32:35 to the effect that "vengeance" belongs to God, what is it that he is saying must be left to God and not to be taken by his readers into their own hands?[9]

One clue to the answer lies in the fact that, in his introduction, he treats "wrath" and "vengeance" as synonyms of each other; and that then, in his

description of government's proper function, he says that governmental officials are servants (deacons) of God to execute wrath on wrongdoers. So what
is it that well-functioning governments do, and that his readers should not
do, that might be described as "avenging" or as "exercising vengeance" – or
to introduce other possible meanings of the Greek terms, as "punishing," or
as "exercising retribution"? Well, in case any of us are at a loss to answer this
question on our own, Paul gives a few hints: wrongdoers "incur judgment" at
the hands of good rulers, good rulers are a "terror" to bad conduct. The answer
is pretty obvious: good government subjects those convicted of wrongdoing
to retributive punishment. Paul's readers are not to do that. They are not to
take punishment into their own hands; in particular, they are to renounce the
old vengeance system. Another clue that leads to the same conclusion is the
fact that the full passage in Deuteronomy from which Paul quotes speaks of
God's *judgment*, and of his rendering recompense and vengeance.

The conclusion has to be that Paul is instructing his readers not to "get even"
with each other, not to take vengeance on each other. Punishment, retributive
punishment, is to be left to God. And government, when functioning as it
ought to function, is among the means God uses to exercise his retributive
punishment. Governmental officials are deacons, liturgetes (13:6) of God for
this purpose.

What would be a reasonable appropriation in our own day of Paul's teaching
on what governmental authorities may do and what his readers may not do?
In arriving at an answer to this question, an important fact to consider is that
authority is highly dispersed in our societies. When a person who is an official
in a nonpublic university acts in his official capacity, he is not acting as a
private citizen; but neither is he acting as a governmental functionary. So also
for those who are church officials; when acting in their official capacity, they
are neither private citizens nor functionaries of the government. Such people
fall between the cracks of Paul's distinction, as do many others. So should we
say that, since they are not government officials, they should not be allowed
to exercise retributive punishment?

Any attempt to implement such a view would of course be socially revo-
lutionary, since among us officials of multiple sorts – school officials, church
officials, parents, and the like – do in fact exercise retributive punishment.
The implementation of such a view would require that all such people either cease exercising retributive punishment or become functionaries of the
government.

I think the far more reasonable appropriation of Paul's line of thought
to our societies, characterized as they are by wide dispersal of authority, is
that retributive punishment is to be reserved to those "in authority," but

that authority is not to be understood as limited to governmental authority. Though the expression of disapprobation by means of hard treatment of the wrongdoer is to be confined to official acts, it is not to be confined to official acts of *government*. And retributive punishment, when properly exercised by legitimate authorities, be they governmental or not, is to be seen as a medium whereby God's retributive justice is exercised on earth. Legitimate authorities are servants (deacons, liturgetes) of God in his cause of securing justice for victims.

The other question of appropriation concerns who is to be regarded as forbidden to exercise retributive punishment. Might it be that Paul is enjoining Christians to refrain from exercising retributive punishment but leaving it open for others to do so? That would be a bizarre interpretation. If we do what I have just suggested, namely, extrapolate from Paul's words to the conclusion that retributive punishment is to be reserved to legitimate authorities acting in their official capacity, then the natural contrast will not be between authorities and Christians, but between authorities and private citizens. It is not just Christians who must refrain from retributive punishment; all private citizens must refrain. Naturally this does not imply that nothing Paul says, in what I have called his introduction to the topic of governmental justice, is meant to apply specially to Christians; some of it quite clearly does.

Now notice that Paul says nothing about the forgoing of punishment by authorities, and so, in particular, nothing about the forgoing of punishment on account of the wrongdoer's faith in God. Apparently he does not regard it as out of the question that one or another of his addressees, first-century Roman Christians, would engage in illegal activity; why else would he bother to issue to them the injunctions that he does issue? Nonetheless, he does not say that, should that happen, the well-functioning government will pardon them on account of their faith.

Within human society in this present era, retributive punishment is to be an official act exercised by authorities; the old vengeance system, of private parties getting even with each other, is forbidden. And when retributive punishment is rightly exercised by legitimate authorities, it is to be seen as an instrument of God's retributive punishment. It seems highly unlikely that Paul would be opposed to all official acts of waiving or mitigating punishment of wrongdoers. But this is a matter of speculation; he says nothing about the matter.

Now for the question: when we place divine justification within its larger context, this larger context including Paul's teaching that legitimate authority is a medium of God's retributive punishment, can it be said that in justifying wrongdoers, God is sending the message that wrongdoing does not matter? Surely not. If the entire picture consisted of God's profligate generosity in justifying those wrongdoers who have faith in him, that would be a different matter – or *might well* be a different matter. But that is not the entire picture, only part of it.

VIII

I mentioned that Paul had two responses to the worry that the generosity of God's justification of wrongdoers sends the message that fulfilling the requirements of justice is not important. The response we have so far considered – not offered by Paul himself *as* a response but certainly constituting a response – is that the God-ordained function of governmental authority is to remind us forcibly that wrongdoing does matter. To understand his other response, we must look at what he says in chapters five through eight of Romans, where he articulates his answer to the charge that his teaching about divine justification encourages antinomianism. Paul clearly thinks that even without bringing governmental justice into the picture, it would be a profound mistake to conclude that God's profligate generosity in justifying wrongdoers "overthrows the law." What are his reasons?

A good way to get into this part of Paul's thought is to ask what is the rationale for God's justifying wrongdoers on account of their *faith*. It is not difficult to understand why authorities sometimes waive or mitigate punishment of wrongdoers on account of the plight of the wrongdoer. It is also not difficult to understand why authorities sometimes issue pardons, and dismiss or forgo pressing charges, for the sake of the common good; Ford halted the proceedings against Nixon for the sake of the common good. But why would God forgo punishing someone on account of his or her faith? How is that relevant? Is it just arbitrary whimsy on God's part to settle on faith as the ground for justification? Might God just as well have latched onto something else?

Paul declares that because "we are justified by faith, we have peace with God" (5:1); by virtue of justification, we are "reconciled to God" (5:10). Justification is for the sake of peace with God, for the sake of divine–human reconciliation, for the sake of restoration of fellowship between God and human beings. The concepts Paul uses in the first chapter of Romans, namely, honoring and acknowledging God as God, are perhaps more illuminating of his thought than is our English word *faith*.[10] When the wrongdoer honors and acknowledges God as God, then no matter how badly he has acted, there remains the possibility of reconciliation between the two. Conversely, if that acknowledgment is lacking, then even though the wrongdoing is minor, there can be no reconciliation. To acknowledge God as God is to acknowledge God's right to ask obedience of us and his right to waive such rights as he acquires by our lack of obedience. How could there be reconciliation in the absence of such acknowledgment? Were God to offer justification, the recipient would reject it. If you request or command something of me and I neither do what you ask nor acknowledge your right to ask it of me, then if you offer to waive your victim rights so as to be reconciled with me, I will reject your offer out of hand. Rather than achieving reconciliation, your offer will anger me; I will see myself as insulted by it, wronged. Something like that, so I suggest, lies behind Paul's teaching that God justifies those who acknowledge him as God – those who have faith in him, who put their trust in him.

Those were preparatory comments. Now for Paul's answer to the worry. The *telos* of God's justification of sinners is that there be peace between God and the wrongdoer. God justifies those who acknowledge God as God and hence are willing to be reconciled. But Paul is clear that justification is not sufficient by itself to secure reconciliation. It is neither true in this case, nor is it true in general, that forgoing one's right to the retributive punishment of the one who has wronged one is sufficient to achieve reconciliation between oneself and the wrongdoer. What remains to be dealt with in this case is God's *orgê* – translated by the NRSV as 'wrath'.

In what way is God's *orgê* a problem? To explain, let me introduce an important and helpful distinction that Jean Hampton makes in those articles of hers that I referred to earlier. Distinguish, she says, between *anger* and *hatred*. Anger is the emotional correlate of the judgment that one has been wronged; its object is the action or inaction that one judges to have wronged one. It comes in various forms, resentment and indignation over the action or inaction being prominent among them. Hatred, by contrast, is aversion for someone or something. (In my judgment "hatred" is a rather poor choice of words here; though aversion sometimes takes the form of hatred, often it comes in less intense forms than that.) The opposite of aversion is attraction for someone or something, such attraction being one of the several different things that we call *love*.

Rather often, anger over what one judges to be the wronging of one gives rise to animosity toward the wrongdoer; one holds it against him that he did what he did. But one may feel animosity toward some person for reasons other than that one judges one has been wronged by him; and, more relevant to our purposes here, one may judge oneself to have been wronged by someone without feeling aversion toward him. The parent loves the child in spite of the child's wrongdoing.

The Greek word *orgê*, as Paul uses it, covers both what Hampton calls *anger* and what she calls *hatred* – and more besides. As we saw earlier, it also covers the exercise of retributive punishment. Sometimes the context makes clear which of these distinct phenomena Paul has in mind when he speaks of God's *orgê*, sometimes it does not. In Romans 1:18, Paul says that "the *orgê* of God is revealed from heaven against all ungodliness and wickedness"; in this case, it is clearly what Hampton calls *anger* that Paul is referring to.

So when Paul indicates that God's *orgê* must somehow be dealt with, what does he have in mind, God's animosity toward the justified believer or God's indignation over the wrongdoing?

Not the former. We can set to the side whether God once felt animosity toward the wrongdoer. Toward the justified believer God feels no animosity. If he felt animosity, why would he justify him with the aim of achieving reconciliation? We do not have to content ourselves with inferences here, however. Paul himself says that "God proves his love for us in that while we still were sinners, Christ died for us" (Romans 5:8).

God's indignation over the justified believer's wrongdoing appears, then, to be the problem. But what exactly is the problem? Reconciliation with the one who has wronged one does not await giving up one's judgment that one has been wronged and the indignation that accompanies that judgment; if it did, reconciliation would require more forgetfulness than most of us can manage, and certainly more than is possible for God. So once again, what is the problem?

There are two possibilities. One thing that often blocks reconciliation with the one who has wronged one is that he refuses to acknowledge that he has done so, and hence refuses to distance himself from what he did. Such denial is a source of friction between the two parties as long as it endures; the wrongdoer refuses to accept the offer of reconciliation because doing so implies that he was in the wrong. So far as I can see, Paul takes no explicit cognizance of this possibility. Perhaps he assumes that it is not a *live* possibility. The person who acknowledges God as God will not adopt such a stance of denial.

To see the other possibility, consider the abusive husband who, each time after flying into a rage, offers effusive apologies and expansive professions of repentance, but then later does the same thing over again. The apologies and protestations need not be insincere, nor need his wife perceive them as insincere. And she may feel no animosity toward him; she may in fact love him deeply. But if he cannot control his temper, there can be no genuine reconciliation. They will have to part ways. What reconciliation requires is not just apology and repentance for episodes of abuse, but reformation of character.

Paul thinks of human beings in general as like the abusive spouse. We need a reformation of the moral dynamics of the self, so that "the just requirement (*dikaiôma*) of the law might be fulfilled in us" (8:4). Only then will we be fully pleasing to God (8:8), only then can we be fully reconciled.

To understand how Paul thinks this reformation occurs, we must bring into the picture his conviction that our predicament as human beings is that we are *impelled* into wrongdoing by forces within and without us – usually not irresistibly impelled, but nonetheless impelled. Bodily passions impel us. Negative emotions impel us – hatred, fear, jealousy, insecurity. And all the many ideologies into which we have been inducted impel us to trample on the rights of others: nationalism, militarism, materialism, racism, sexism, communism, capitalism, you name it.[11] Paul employs the language of enslavement to make the point. He says to his readers that they were "enslaved to sin" (6:6), that they were "slaves of sin" (6:20). To understand his point, I think it best not to think in terms of the social system of slavery but in terms of the enslavement of the drug addict to his drugs and the alcoholic to his booze.

One can anticipate what comes next. If we are to become well-pleasing to God,[12] we must be released from subjection to those forces that impel us into wrongdoing – from those forces that impel us into violating God's law. Given Paul's picture of the dynamics of the human self, what such release requires is that there be an alternative force at work within us that impels us toward honoring rather than violating the requirements of justice. We need an alternative "enslavement." That is what Paul sees God as bestowing on those in whom God finds faith and whom he justifies. "God's love has been poured into our hearts through the Holy Spirit" (5:5) so that "we might no longer be enslaved to sin" (6:6). We have been set "free from the law of sin and of death" (8:2) so that "we might walk in newness of life" (6:4).

If you present yourselves to anyone as obedient slaves, you are slaves of the one whom you obey, either of sin, which leads to death, or of obedience, which leads to *dikaiosunê*. But thanks be to God that you, having once been slaves of sin, have become obedient from the heart to the form of teaching to which you were entrusted, and that you, having been set free from sin, have become slaves of justice (*dikaiosunê*). . . . For just as you once presented your members as slaves to impurity and to greater and greater iniquity, so now present your members as slaves to justice (*dikaiosunê*) for sanctification. (6:16–19)

Paul is not of the view – how could he be? – that the forces that impel toward wrongdoing have lost all grip on the justified believer. Instead the believer "groans" for full deliverance from those forces, and awaits that full deliverance with "eager longing" (8:18–27). In the meanwhile, injunctions are in place. Paul enjoins his readers not to "let sin exercise dominion in your mortal bodies, to make you obey their passions" (6:12).

I said that Paul had two responses to the worry that God's justification of those wrongdoers who acknowledge God as God sends the message that wrongdoing does not matter. One response consists of his account of the proper function of government. The other consists of what we have just now been looking into, namely, what he says about God's strategy for bringing about the reconciliation that is the *telos* of justification.

Now for the question. Does this second response constitute good reason for Paul's claim that justification, when seen in context, does not overthrow the requirements of justice but upholds them? It seems to me that it does. Divine justification in context cannot be construed as God's condoning of wrongdoing nor as sending a message to that effect. As we noted earlier, whether forgoing punishment of the wrongdoer constitutes condoning his wrongdoing and sending a message to that effect depends very much on context; in some contexts it does, in other contexts it does not. I see no reason to dispute Paul's claim that God's justification, seen in context, does not send that message.

IX

Be it granted that God's justification of human beings does not undermine primary justice. May it be the case, however, that the forgiveness Christ enjoined on his followers does that?

Earlier I remarked that a fundamental distinction of the moral vision of Judaism and Christianity is that retributive punishment of the wrongdoer is a right but not in general a duty; often it is appropriate to waive the right. Another distinction, closely related, is that willingness to forgive is regarded as a virtue, and actually forgiving as often a duty. Forgiveness nowhere appears in Aristotle's catalog of the virtues. What he says instead is that "people who do not get retributively angry at those at whom they should look like fools.... For they seem to have no perception and no feeling of pain ... and to allow oneself and one's loved ones to be kicked around, and overlook it, is slavish" (*Nicomachean Ethics* 1126a4–8).[13] And because the Stoic sage never perceives himself as wronged by another, the issue of forgiveness never arises for him.

What exactly was it that Jesus enjoined his followers to do when he enjoined them to forgive those who had wronged them? A good many times in the course of my discussion I have said that forgiveness consists of forgoing rights that one has as a victim. But there are many such forgoings: condoning, pardoning, declaring amnesty, dismissing charges, not pressing charges: all consist of an individual or social institution forgoing certain of its victim rights. Where in this panoply is forgiveness to be found? What is it that one forgoes when one forgives?

A review of the twentieth century philosophical and theological literature on forgiveness makes clear that there is no agreement on the nature of forgiveness.[14] "Forgiveness is primarily a matter of how I *feel* about you (not how I treat you)," says Jeffrie Murphy; "thus I may forgive you in my heart of hearts or even after you are dead."[15] Richard Swinburne disagrees. For you to forgive me is to undertake "that in future you will not treat me as the originator of an act by which I wronged you." "Feelings need not be involved."[16] Forgiveness is the overcoming of feelings of resentment and indignation, says Murphy, this time citing Bishop Butler. Jean Hampton insists on a distinction. Though forgiveness is the overcoming of hatred for the wrongdoer, it is not the overcoming of feelings of indignation over what was done to one.[17]

My own view of the matter, which here I cannot take time to articulate and defend, is the following. Distinguish first between forgiving as an official act of some sort and forgiving as an engagement between private parties. The forgiveness Jesus had in mind was often of the former sort; the model he often used in speaking of forgiveness is that of someone forgiving a contracted financial debt. In Matthew's version of The Lord's Prayer, Jesus instructs his hearers to pray, "forgive us our debts, as we also have forgiven our debtors" (6:12). And as we saw earlier, the story he told, when Peter asked how often he ought to forgive a "brother" who keeps on wronging him, is about a king forgiving the debt of one of his subjects who refuses to forgive, in turn, the debt of his fellow servant. Thus when Jesus speaks of God forgiving us, and when, speaking on behalf of God, he forgives the sins of various people in the crowds around him, it is God in his "office" as judge who is doing the forgiving; and the forgiveness includes the waiver of retributive punishment. (Because God is not only the judge but also the one to whom obedience is owed, there is always a personal dimension as well; God himself has been wronged.) The forgiveness we are now to consider is not forgiveness as an official act but forgiveness as an engagement among "private parties."

The *telos* of such forgiveness is reconciliation between wronged and wrongdoer – reconciliation of such a sort that the victim no longer feels animosity toward the wrongdoer on account of the wrongdoing and such that the wrongdoing no longer influences how the victim interacts with the wrongdoer. "I won't hold it against you. Bygones are bygones."

All too often that *telos* cannot be achieved, no matter how much good will there is on the part of the victim. We took note of some of the reasons earlier: the wrongdoer is dead, or he refuses in any way to acknowledge his wrongdoing and to distance himself from it, or he does acknowledge that and distance himself from it but then he keeps on doing the same thing over again.[18] Forgiveness itself, then (in distinction from its *telos*), is the overcoming of feelings of animosity toward the one who wronged one plus the *willingness* to be reconciled, that is, the willingness to engage with the wrongdoer as if the deed had not been done. It is not the overcoming of the belief that one was wronged, nor is it the overcoming of the emotional correlate of that belief, namely anger. What typically happens, however, is that when there is genuine reconciliation, the memory of the wrongdoing fades; because both parties acknowledge the wrongdoing, it is not a bone of contention between them.

Though forgiveness, in the Christian scheme of things, is often (perhaps always) a duty on the part of human beings, being forgiven is not a right on the part of the wrongdoer, not even if he repents.[19] If it comes, it comes as gift. Neither by God nor by our fellows do we have a claim-right to be forgiven. It is by virtue of God's command that we human beings are obligated to forgive, not by virtue of the wrongdoer's right to be forgiven. It follows that, unlike us, God is not obligated to forgive.

One might ask how I can have a right to feel animosity toward the one who wronged me on account of his wrongdoing – to hold his wrongdoing against him – while having a duty not to feel such animosity toward him. Are these not in flat contradiction with each other? The answer is that, in general, one can have the freedom-right to do something while being under obligation not to exercise that right. To say that I have the freedom-right to do A is to say that were others to try to prevent me from doing A, they would be wronging me. I might have a right of that sort to do A even though I ought not to exercise that right – that is, even though I ought not to do A.

How can we proceed from here without mounting a full articulation and defense of the view that I have just now presented as my own? Fortunately, that will not be necessary. A striking feature of the contemporary literature on forgiveness is that, in spite of the many points of disagreement, all participants in the discussion agree that a condition for an adequate account of forgiveness is that forgiveness neither imply condoning of the wrongdoing nor send a message to that effect. Different analyses offer different ways of satisfying the condition; but all participants in the discussion accept the condition.

What Swinburne mainly insists on is that, unless the wrongdoing was trivial, it is wrong for the victim "in the absence of some atonement at least in the form of apology" to treat the [act] as not having been done" (pp. 85–6). If I have murdered your wife and you decide to overlook my offense and interact with me as if it had never happened, your attitude "trivializes human life, your love for your wife, and the importance of right action. And it involves your failing to treat me seriously, to take seriously my attitude towards you expressed in my action. Thereby it trivializes human relationships, for it supposes that good human relations can exist when we do not take each other seriously" (p. 86).

What Murphy and Hampton mainly insist on is that, whatever its nature and conditions, forgiveness does not imply giving up one's anger or indignation over what was done to one; nor does it imply, Hampton insists, forgoing punishment. What it implies is a change of heart toward the wrongdoer – on Hampton's analysis, giving up one's hatred or animosity for *the person* who did the wrong while retaining one's indignation over *the wrong done.* "Hate the sin but love the sinner." And both Murphy and Hampton are of the view that that becomes possible when and only when one believes that the wrongdoer has separated himself from his act. Forgiveness, says Murphy, "may indeed restore relationships, but to seek restoration at all cost – even at the cost of one's very human dignity – can hardly be a virtue. . . . If I count morally as much as anyone else (as surely I do), a failure to resent moral injuries done to me is a failure to care about the moral value incarnate in my own person (that I am, in Kantian language, an end in myself) and thus a failure to care about the very rules of morality" (pp. 17–18).[20]

The question before us, then, is whether these analyses yield the desired result, that to forgive is not to condone. Clearly they do. One is to forgive only if the wrongdoer repents of his action, says Swinburne. The forgiver retains her feelings of indignation over the wrong done her, say Murphy, Hampton, and I. On none of these analyses does forgiveness constitute condoning or send the *message* that the wrongdoing is condoned.

In the course of my discussion, I have offered a solution to the so-called paradox of forgiveness that one finds mentioned in the literature every now and then.[21] If the wrongdoer repents, then he has a right to be forgiven and I ought to forgive him; forgiving him is what justice requires. But if he has not repented, then forgiving him would be an act of wrongdoing; it would amount to condoning the act. So forgiveness dissolves into either mere justice or the condoning of injustice. A counterpart "paradox of mercy" is ready at hand. If mercy fits the punishment to the particularities of the wrongdoing, as general law cannot do, then mercy is nothing more than justice. But if mercy waives the punishment required by true justice, then mercy is itself an act of wrongdoing. So mercy dissolves into either mere justice or the perpetration of injustice.[22]

The heart of my response to the latter "paradox" is to insist that retributive punishment of the wrongdoer is a right on the part of the victim but not in general a duty. The heart of my response to the former "paradox" is to insist, first, that to overcome one's animosity toward the wrongdoer and be open to treating bygones as bygones does not require giving up one's judgment that he wronged one and the anger that is the emotional correlate of that judgment; and to insist, second, that though forgiveness of the wrongdoer may be a duty on the part of the victim, it is not a right on the part of the wrongdoer, not even if he repents.

X

Anselm expresses a second ground of perplexity over the justice of God's mercy in the following remarkable sentence: "But if it can in some way be grasped why You can will to save the wicked, it certainly cannot be understood by any reason why from those who are alike in wickedness You save some rather than others through Your supreme goodness, and damn some rather than others through Your supreme justice" (*Proslogion* 11). What is remarkable about the sentence is that in stating the problem, Anselm throws up his hands in despair over solving it.

This second perplexity of Anselm is a special case of a more general problem: pardoning, declaring amnesty, dismissing charges, not pressing charges, and the like, often raise issues of fairness. When the president issues an executive pardon out of mercy for the plight of the convicted person, is it not unfair of him, and hence unjust, not to pardon all who are in a similar plight? Discussion of this perplexity will have to await another occasion.

NOTES

1. I use the translation of the New Revised Standard Version in all my quotations from the Bible.
2. I defend this interpretation in my forthcoming *Justice: Divine and Human*.
3. Translation by M. J. Charlesworth, in Brian Davies and G. R. Evans, *Anselm of Canterbury: The Major Works* (New York: Oxford University Press, 1998).
4. Nussbaum, "Equity and Mercy," *Philosophy and Public Affairs* 22:2 (spring 1993): 83–125.
5. Immanuel Kant, *The Metaphysical Elements of Justice*, trans. John Ladd (Indianapolis: Bobbs-Merrill, 1965), 102.
6. Emphasizing a point already made, Feinberg adds that "punishment generally expresses more than judgments of disapproval; it is also a symbolic way of getting back at the criminal, of expressing a kind of vindictive resentment" (100).
7. The essay is Chapter 4 in the book for which she and Jeffrie G. Murphy each wrote distinct chapters, titled *Forgiveness and Mercy* (New York: Cambridge University Press, 1988). Murphy contributed the first, third, and fifth chapters, Hampton the second and fourth.
8. The first embedded quotation is from Deuteronomy 32:35; the second is from Proverbs 25:21–2.
9. The passage from Deuteronomy reads thus as follows; God is speaking.

> Vengeance is mine, and recompense, . . .
> because the day of their calamity is at hand
> their doom comes swiftly.

10. Speaking of the "ungodly," Paul says that "though they knew God, they did not honor him as God or give thanks to him. . . . They did not see fit to acknowledge God" (Romans 1:21, 28).

11. The Latin Stoics had a strikingly similar outlook. In her discussion of Seneca in the article mentioned earlier in this chapter, Nussbaum speaks of him as regarding his fellow human beings as in the "grip" of "cultural forces." "Before a child is capable of the critical exercise of reason, he or she has internalized a socially taught scheme of values that is in many ways diseased, giving rise to similarly diseased passions. . . . " Where Paul differs sharply from the Stoics is not in the diagnosis but in the prescribed cure. It was the Stoic view that the forces that "take over the soul . . . can be eradicated, if at all, only by a lifetime of zealous and obsessive self-examination." All quotations from p. 100 of Nussbaum, "Equity and Mercy."

12. I mean the term 'well-pleasing' both to pick up what Paul says in Romans 8:8 ("those who are in the flesh cannot please God") and to carry echoes of Kant's discussion, in *Religion within the Boundaries of Mere Reason*, of how we become well-pleasing to God. It would be fascinating to discuss the similarities and differences between Kant's account and Paul's account. It is obvious from Kant's discussion that he was acquainted with Paul's account, though for him it was filtered through the lens of Lutheran and Pietist theological interpretations.

13. I am adopting Martha Nussbaum's translation of this passage in "Equity and Mercy," 97.

14. For an excellent review of this literature, see the essay by Nigel Biggar, "Forgiveness in the Twentieth Century: A Review of the Literature, 1901–2001," in Alistair McFadyen and Marcel Sarot, *Forgiveness and Truth* (Edinburgh & New York: T & T Clark, 2001).

15. "Forgiveness and Resentment" in *Forgiveness and Mercy*, 21.

16. *Responsibility and Atonement* (Oxford: Oxford University Press, 1989) 85, and 87 fn. 8.

17. See Murphy's and Hampton's essays in *Forgiveness and Mercy*.

18. It is presumably this hard reality that Paul has in mind when he says to his Roman Christian readers, "so far as it depends on you, live peaceably with all" (12:18).

19. On this last point, I disagree with Swinburne in *Responsibility and Atonement*.

20. Murphy appears to believe that it would be wrong to forgive in the absence of evidence of repentance. Hampton explicitly disagrees. She believes that it is psychologically impossible to give up one's animosity toward the wrongdoer while retaining one's indignation over what he did if one believes that he remains fully identified with what he did. But she interprets Jesus as telling us that no matter how "rotten" (her word) the wrongdoer may appear to be, we nonetheless ought to forgive. That requires, on her analysis, believing that he is not fully identified with what he did, even though sometimes all the evidence points in the opposite direction.

I find this view implausible. I am dubious in general about obligations to believe. But be that as it may, I think that sometimes the evidence makes it "morally certain" that the wrongdoer has not distanced himself from his act, and that one could not believe otherwise no matter how hard one tries. I think the better way to go is to deny the linkage Hampton sees between overcoming one's animosity toward the person and believing he has distanced himself from what he did. It seems to me possible to feel no animosity toward a person – to love him, in fact – while yet believing that he has not distanced himself from his wrongdoing. One's love in such a case is tinged with sorrow; but it may be love nonetheless.

21. The first to formulate it as a paradox was apparently Aurel Kolnai in "Forgiveness," *Proceedings of the Aristotelian Society, 1973–4*. Reprinted in his collection of essays, *Ethics, Value, and Reality* (Indianapolis: Hackett, 1978).

22. Jeffrie Murphy presents this "paradox of mercy" as what he calls a "gloss" on Anselm's perplexity. His formulation is worth quoting: "if we simply use the term 'mercy' to refer to certain of the demands of justice (e.g., the demand for individuation), then mercy ceases to be an autonomous virtue and instead becomes a part of (is reducible to a part of) justice. It thus becomes obligatory, and all the talk about gifts, acts of grace, supererogation, and compassion becomes quite beside the point. If, on the other hand, mercy is totally different from justice and actually requires (or permits) that justice sometimes be set aside, it then counsels injustice. In short, mercy is either a vice (injustice) or redundant (a part of justice)" (*Forgiveness and Mercy*, 169).

ↄ

Can Good Christians Be Good Liberals?

PHILIP L. QUINN

It is clear that there are hard times ahead for liberalism in the United States. In the immediate aftermath of the attacks on the World Trade Center and the Pentagon on September 11, 2001, some Muslims, or people taken to be Muslims, were victims of sporadic incidents of religiously intolerant behavior. American habits of religious toleration are now under more intense pressure than they have been at any other time in recent memory. American citizens have, understandably, become fearful and preoccupied with issues of national and personal safety. Many of them seem willing to sacrifice civil liberties or due process of law for the sake of homeland security. Playing to such fears, the Bush administration has adopted policies that are serious threats to liberal values, backing off from their worst features only in the face of domestic or international political pressure.[1] Puffed up by a quick and easy military victory over the Taliban regime in Afghanistan and the Baathist regime in Iraq, it has also become increasingly wrapped up in the arrogance of power. Its threat to liberal political arrangements may be expected to continue for the indefinite future. Liberals will be required to engage in a defensive political struggle in order to limit the damage to the institutions they cherish.

It is in this context that the question of whether good Christians can be good liberals assumes special urgency. Christianity is the most powerful religious force in American life. If Christians were solidly behind liberal institutions and values in politics, the prospects for successfully resisting currently foreseeable threats to them would be greatly enhanced. But they are not. In a recent paper, Nicholas Wolterstorff offers a terse assessment of the situation he encounters among his fellow Christians. He says: "I find many of them skeptical of the liberal polity. They tolerate it without embracing it. Some even look for openings to subvert it."[2] My findings on this matter are in complete accord with his. So we agree that many Christians will not come to the defense of liberal political institutions unless they are given reasons sufficient to persuade them to do so. Wolterstorff himself is firmly committed to fundamental liberal values. The final paragraph of his book *John Locke and the Ethics of Belief* provides a particularly eloquent statement of his commitment. There he says this:

Yet we must live together. It is to politics and not to epistemology that we shall have to look for an answer as to how to do that. "Liberal" politics has fallen on bad days recently. But to its animating vision of a society in which persons of diverse traditions live together in justice and friendship, conversing with each other and slowly altering their traditions in response to their conversation – to that, there is no viable alternative.[3]

So Wolterstorff accepts liberalism's animating vision; he thinks there is no viable alternative to endeavoring to realize and live in accord with it. We might therefore expect him to give a straightforward, positive answer to the question of whether good Christians can be good liberals. And we might also hope to discover in his writings in the area of political philosophy resources that could help to persuade reluctant Christians to support liberalism. Of course, we should not be under any illusions about the extent to which arguments by academic philosophers are likely to influence public opinion. But philosophers must do what they can and then hope for the best.

However, when we turn to Wolterstorff's discussions of liberalism, we do not find a straightforward answer to our question. Wolterstorff's attitude toward liberalism is ambivalent. On the one hand, he is a tenacious critic of liberal political theory or, more precisely as we shall see later, of a certain strand in the complex tradition of liberal theory. In two bold and forceful papers, "Why We Should Reject What Liberalism Tells Us about Speaking and Acting in Public for Religious Reasons" and "The Role of Religion in Decision and Discussion of Political Issues," he has argued against the liberal theories of John Locke and John Rawls.[4] According to Wolterstorff, many Christians cannot be good liberals if being a good liberal involves accepting the practical consequences of these theories. I have criticized his arguments against Johannine liberal theory elsewhere.[5] I shall not repeat all the details here, but I shall briefly rehearse what I take to be his most serious objection to this kind of liberal theory and my response. On the other hand, Wolterstorff has offered an independent argument to support liberal political arrangements. In a more recent paper, "Do Christians Have Good Reason for Supporting Liberal Democracy?," he sets forth an argument for liberal political arrangements that is explicitly addressed to Christians. It is an argument meant to show, I take it, that good Christians can indeed be good liberals if being a good liberal involves only endorsing liberal political arrangements for reasons of their own. I devote the bulk of this paper to a critical examination of this argument because it seems to me to show promise of being a valuable resource for the project of trying to persuade otherwise reluctant Christians to rally round in defense of liberal political arrangements. First I lay out the argument with some care, and then I subject it to critical pressure from two directions. My aim is to support two conclusions. One is that, though Wolterstorff's argument is independent of the Johannine liberal theories he rejects, it is actually continuous with a venerable tradition of liberal political thought and is therefore appropriately viewed as itself a specimen of liberal theory. The other is that his argument captures only part of the strongest case Christians can mobilize in support of liberal political arrangements. If I am right about these two things, Christians should appropriate Wolterstorff's argument, acknowledge its place within the tradition of liberal theory to which it belongs, and then move on to strengthen the Christian case for liberalism with other arguments.

But before moving on to my main task, I shall make a few remarks about how the debate with Wolterstorff to which I contribute in this essay fits into the renaissance of philosophy of religion in the final third of the twentieth century. During the preceding dark ages, American philosophy was under the spell of various forms of empiricism and positivism that inhibited constructive work in philosophy of religion. Defenses had to be mounted against challenges from empiricists, who argued that traditional religious belief is irrational, and from positivists, whose verificationist doctrines imply that a great deal of religious discourse is meaningless. Though these defensive efforts yielded interesting ideas about the nature of religious language, they were narrowly focused on issues in epistemology and philosophy of language. Only when the spell was broken were philosophical energies liberated to address anew many of the metaphysical problems that had preoccupied philosophers of religion in the more remote past. Thus during the earlier parts of the renaissance, important work was done on such topics as the divine nature and the problem of divine foreknowledge and human freedom, but not much attention was devoted to the relations of religion and politics.

It seems to me not difficult to understand, at least in broad outline, why this was the case. Normative political theory too had suffered an eclipse during the dark ages, and it was just beginning to emerge again into the light of intellectual respectability. It was harder then to find political philosophers who could serve as conversation partners for philosophers of religion. In addition, liberals were then inclined to welcome the contributions religious arguments made to public political discourse because they tended to support liberal causes. The religious arguments of Martin Luther King, Jr., served to motivate the Civil Rights movement, and many prominent members of the clergy spoke out against America's brutal war in Southeast Asia. Things changed dramatically, of course, when the dominant religious voices in the public square ceased to be liberal. During the last two decades of the twentieth century, the Religious Right, in the form of movements such as the Moral Majority and the Christian Coalition, became increasingly influential in American politics. The reaction was predictable. Secular liberal thinkers constructed theories that called for the exclusion of the religious from public political discourse on certain issues. A second predictable reaction soon followed. Philosophers of religion with religious commitments of their own began to challenge these theories. And so by the end of the twentieth century, debates about religion and politics had come to play an important part in the renaissance of philosophy of religion.

At the turn of the century, Wolterstorff had earned the reputation of being one of the most effective critics of religiously exclusionary liberal political theories. I side with him in opposing this trend in recent liberal theorizing. In philosophy, however, we often dispute as sharply with our allies as we do with our adversaries. In this essay, I find myself in the position of subjecting to critical scrutiny and then trying to improve on some of his recent reflections on liberalism.

WOLTERSTORFF'S MAIN COMPLAINT ABOUT JOHANNINE LIBERAL THEORY

Wolterstorff has several quarrels with Johannine liberal theory. Some of them turn on the details of particular theories or the epistemologies they rely on. But his main complaint, which should, in my opinion, strike a responsive chord in the breasts of good liberals, is moral and rather general: it is that liberal theories are unfair to religion and religious citizens. In the case of Rawls, the complaint is directed against the claim that political liberalism involves a moral duty of civility that requires citizens, under ideal conditions, to conduct debate on matters of basic justice and constitutional essentials within limits of public reason and so without appeal to religious or nonreligious comprehensive doctrines meant to regulate the whole of life.[6] And even though Rawls has relaxed this constraint somewhat as his view has developed, he is only willing to admit the religious reasons of comprehensive doctrines into public debate on fundamental questions subject to a proviso that makes it clear that religious reasons should, according to his brand of liberalism, ultimately be redeemed in terms of nonreligious considerations drawn from public reason.[7] Robert Audi has also proposed moral principles that would under certain conditions have the effect of excluding religious reasons from the public square in liberal democracies. As he sees things, liberal democratic citizens have prima facie obligations to abstain from advocacy or support of laws or public policies that

restrict human conduct unless they have, are willing to offer, and are sufficiently motivated by adequate secular reasons for such advocacy or support.[8]
Like Wolterstorff, I reject the view that, under the conditions of pluralism
currently holding in the United States, democratic citizens have such duties
of self-limitation or obligations of abstinence. I have argued against the positions of Rawls and Audi on this issue elsewhere.[9] However, I also believe that,
when it is construed as an objection to the Johannine liberal theory of Rawls,
Wolterstorff's main complaint is not justified by the argument he offers for it.

Wolterstorff spells out that argument in a passage that deserves to be quoted
in full. He sees a common pattern in the attempts by liberal theorists to exclude
religion from public life:

That common pattern is this: The liberal assumes that requiring religious persons
to debate and act politically for reasons other than religious reasons is not in
violation of their *religious* convictions; likewise he assumes that an educational
program which makes no reference to religion is not in violation of any parent's
religious convictions. He assumes, in other words, that though religious people
may not be in the *habit of* dividing their life into a religious component and a
nonreligious component, and though some might be *unhappy* doing so, nonetheless, their doing so would not be in violation of anybody's religion. But he's wrong
about this. It's when we bring into the picture persons for whom it is a matter of religious conviction that they ought to strive for a religiously integrated existence –
it's then, especially, though not only then, that the unfairness of liberalism to
religion comes to light.[10]

I think this passage touches on an important issue, but it will take some work
to get clear about exactly what it is. It is not, I shall argue, that Rawlsian
liberalism is, as charged, unfair to religion.

In one way, of course, it is modernity itself that works against people who
strive for a religiously integrated existence. It is a commonplace of sociological
grand theory in the tradition of Max Weber and Talcott Parsons that modern societies are composed of various social spheres or systems, such as the
economy, politics, religion, and so forth. Such spheres or systems are func-
tionally differentiated, relatively autonomous, and more or less self-contained.
Wolterstorff is aware of this tradition and the modern social order it endeavors
to comprehend. However, he prefers to discard the assumption that societies
are the basic units of analysis and the other spheres are subsystems of society.
On his view, "what characterizes the social world of modernity is the emer-
gence of economies which do not coincide with, but overlap, distinct states;
indeed, there is in general a striking lack of coincidence among economies,
states, nations, and religious groupings in the modern world."[11] But he does

not deny the relative autonomy and self-containment of such systems. It is this feature of the modern world that makes a separation of politics and religion a realistic social possibility; such a separation is not feasible in a traditional society that is religiously homogeneous and tightly integrated by its shared religion. To be sure, it remains possible for small religious groups such as Amish farming communities to preserve local religious integration by deliberately locating themselves at the margins of the modern social order and trying to keep its products and values at arm's length. But people who yearn for a religiously integrated existence outside of such special contexts are, so to speak, swimming against powerful social tides of modern life. Yet the presupposition of Wolterstorff's line of the thought that there are religious people of this sort is no doubt correct.

Wolterstorff seems to think his argument shows that liberalism is unfair to religion as such or to religious people generally. However, it is not strong enough to do that. Although there certainly are some religious people for whom it is a matter of religious conviction that they ought to strive for a religiously integrated existence, there are others for whom it is not. Some devoutly religious people find themselves at home in the differentiated social order to which modernity has given birth. They are content to separate their lives into religious and nonreligious spheres; acting politically on considerations other than religious reasons does not violate their religious convictions. So even if Wolterstorff's argument were otherwise flawless, its conclusion would apply only to some and not to all religious citizens in modern societies. In addition, there are in such societies nonreligious people whose comprehensive doctrines make it a matter of conviction for them that they ought to strive for lives integrated around those doctrines. Examples include some secular Millian liberals and Marxist socialists. Hence if the argument were otherwise free of defects, a parallel argument would show that liberalism is also unfair to nonreligious citizens of such persuasions. The question we ought to be asking, therefore, is not whether liberalism is unfair to religion but whether it is unfair to a group of people, some of whose members are religious whereas others are not, but all of whom as a matter of conviction want to live lives tightly integrated by their comprehensive doctrines. For the sake of convenience, let us call members of this group "integralists."[12]

It is entirely appropriate to address to Rawlsian political liberalism the question of whether it is unfair to integralists. Its ideal of public reason asks citizens generally to work up and be prepared to defend a political conception of justice, which is a conception whose values are to be derived from the public political culture of a liberal democracy and whose application is meant to be restricted to the political sphere. According to Rawls, "it is central to political liberalism that free and equal citizens affirm both a comprehensive doctrine and a political conception."¹³ What's more, this ideal also asks them to argue politically on issues of basic justice and constitutional essentials from their political conceptions rather than directly from their comprehensive doctrines. Of course the ideal asks these two things of all free and equal citizens. Yet compliance is likely to be a heavier burden for integralists than for others, since they would prefer to argue directly from their comprehensive doctrines, around which they wish to integrate their entire lives. So they are apt to be skeptical about the value of working up a political conception that is to be interposed, as it were, between their comprehensive doctrines and the public political forum. They may also fear, with some reason, that people of their sort are bound to decline in numbers and influence in a liberal democratic society in which the Rawlsian ideal of public reason takes hold and becomes more fully realized over time.

It should be granted to Wolterstorff, then, that Rawlsian political liberalism does impose special burdens on integralists. It may well in the long run, to the extent that it comes to prevail in a society, reinforce the threat to integralist forms of life, religious and nonreligious, already posed by the differentiated social order of modernity. Indeed, it may even contribute to dooming integralist forms of life to decline or extinction. But should it also be granted that Rawlsian political liberalism is, on that account, unfair to integralists? I think not. It seems to me Wolterstorff's argument for this conclusion is flawed. Along with Rawls, who attributes this thought to Isaiah Berlin, I believe "there is no social world without loss."¹⁴ I acknowledge that social worlds in which integralists can flourish realize some important values. The fact, should it turn out to be a fact, that integralists cannot, as a matter of social necessity, reproduce themselves over time in a society well ordered by Rawlsian political liberalism would no doubt be cause for regret. However, as Rawls insists, such social necessities "are not to be taken for arbitrary bias or injustice."¹⁵ Even the relatively capacious culture and institutions of liberal democracy are bound to prove uncongenial to some valuable forms of life, and integralism of various stripes may be among them. As Robert M. Adams notes, "some social arrangements seem to have few advantages, but all have disadvantages."¹⁶ Of course I do not really expect integralism to disappear from the American scene any time soon. Nevertheless, we must, with Rawls, reject the notion that "only unworthy forms of life lose out in a just constitutional regime."¹⁷ Once that has been done, there remains no good reason to suppose that integralists have been unfairly treated merely because their forms of life fail to endure and gain adherents, should such a failure occur in the history of a liberal democracy. Nor is there good reason to suppose that they have been unfairly treated merely because they bear burdens others do not. So I conclude that Wolterstorff has not shown that Rawlsian political liberalism is unfair to integralist religion, much less to religion as such or to religious citizens generally. The Rawlsian version of Johannine liberal theory can therefore be successfully defended against Wolterstorff's main complaint.

Perhaps a brief discussion of the issue of religious education to which Wolterstorff refers in the long passage quoted above will help to drive my point home. He correctly observes that there are in the United States religious parents for whom it is a matter of conviction that their children should receive a religiously integrated education. According to American constitutional law, the state can do very little to support religious schools. Of course religious parents are not forbidden by law to establish schools that provide religiously integrated education. However, Wolterstorff thinks parents who bear the burden of supporting their own schools suffer from a form of economic discrimination. He says:

If they are not legally forbidden to establish such schools, then the discrimination is located in the economics of the matter. Were those parents to establish schools which teach in accord with their convictions, they would have to pay for those schools out of their own pockets while yet contributing to the general tax fund for schools.[18]

It seems clear that Wolterstorff uses the word *discrimination* in this context precisely in order to exploit its negative moral connotations; he is suggesting that the economic burden such parents would have to bear would be a kind of unfair discrimination.

Obviously such religious parents would bear a special economic burden. It does not follow, however, that it would be an unfair burden. And it should be kept in mind that, under American law, religious institutions also enjoy the benefit of tax exemptions. So religious citizens in the United States operate under a distribution of benefits and burdens that has at most a small direct impact on nonreligious citizens. But this does not suffice to show that it is an unfair distribution. In some other liberal democracies, the state does more to support religious schools than is permitted by American law. Hence some religious parents might be better off economically if they were citizens of such democracies rather than of the United States. However, even this falls short of being sufficient to establish the conclusion that such parents suffer from unfairness or injustice under American liberal democracy.

Rawls addresses another issue that may trouble religious parents. They may wonder what requirements his political liberalism would have the state impose on religious schools. According to Rawlsian political liberalism, education in religious schools should prepare children to be cooperating members of society and to be self-supporting, and it should encourage in them political virtues. In addition, political liberalism "will ask that children's education include such things as knowledge of their constitutional and civic rights so that, for example, they know that liberty of conscience exists in their society and that apostasy is not a legal crime, all this to insure that their continued [religious] membership when they come of age is not based simply on ignorance of their basic rights or fear of punishment for offenses that do not exist."[19] Some religious parents may object that even this minimal exposure to liberalism is unwanted, because children may then of their own accord go on to adopt liberal comprehensive doctrines. Rawls grants that this may indeed happen in some cases. He points out, however, that his political liberalism does not insist that children in religious schools be educated to value traits such as autonomy or individuality that are endorsed by liberal comprehensive doctrines. It asks only that they be instructed in the rudiments of citizenship in a liberal democracy. I think it is reasonable to require all schools in a liberal democracy to do this much. But, as Rawls goes on to say, "the unavoidable consequences of reasonable requirements for children's education may have to be accepted, often with regret."[20] I agree. This is a specific instance in which social necessity must not be confused with unfairness or injustice. So my view is that Rawlsian political liberalism can mobilize an adequate response to the objection.

In sum, Rawlsian political liberalism would not be unfair to religion as such, because it would impose no special burdens on all and only religious citizens. It would impose special burdens on, and might pose a threat to, some religious citizens, namely, those who happen to be integralists. However, Wolterstorff's arguments fail to show that such burdens or threats would be unfair or in any other way unjust to integralists in general or to the religious among them.

Yet even when charges of unfairness have been successfully disposed of, the fact remains that religious citizens are asked by Johannine liberal theories to bear special burdens. And some of the burdens religious citizens of the United States must bear are not imposed by all liberal democracies on their religious citizens. Given this situation, it is quite understandable that some religious citizens of the United States have reservations about their own liberal democracy. They may acquiesce in its political arrangements for lack of a feasible alternative they regard as clearly preferable. But convincing them that those arrangements are not unfair to them should not be expected to persuade them to embrace or be willing to defend the liberal democratic polity in which they live. A stronger argument seems needed for that purpose, and the particular argument Wolterstorff has recently constructed may be a good candidate for this job of persuasion. It is addressed to Christians, but I see no obstacle to adapting it for use in addressing audiences of Jews and Muslims. My next task is to set forth that argument.

Christian Reasons for Supporting Liberal Democracy

In "Do Christians Have Good Reasons for Supporting Liberal Democracy?," Wolterstorff sets the stage for his argument with a distinction and a question. The distinction is between liberal polities and liberal political theories. Examples of liberal polities are "the members of the European Union, Canada, the United States, Australia, and New Zealand" (p. 229). Examples of liberal political theories are the Johannine theories of Locke and Rawls. This distinction is important for his purpose because of "the possibility that one might have good reasons for accepting the liberal polity while nonetheless rejecting liberal theory" (p. 230). His question is "whether Christian thought provides good reasons for people *in our sort of situation* to support the liberal polity" (p. 230). The feature of our situation that looms especially large in his deliberations is that it involves a diversity of comprehensive perspectives on God and the good within a single polity.

Seeking to come as close to neutral description as he can, Wolterstorff characterizes the liberal polity in terms of a list of its guarantees. A liberal polity is one "in which there is a constitutional-legal framework which guarantees to all its sane adult citizens due process of law along with the so-called 'civil liberties,' foremost among those liberties being these: freedom of conscience, freedom of religious practice, freedom of speech, freedom of assembly, freedom from search and seizure without warrant, freedom from cruel and unusual punishment, and freedom from intrusions into one's private life" (p. 232). According to Wolterstorff's reading of liberal theory, it understands the most fundamental component of the idea behind such a list to be that "a liberal polity is one in which each sane adult enjoys the freedom to choose a comprehensive perspective on God and the good and to live out the perspective chosen" (p. 234). In our situation of diversity, of course, a liberal polity must operate under a rule of law that regulates the interactions among citizens. For Rawlsian political liberalism, as Wolterstorff notes, its rules of engagement should ideally be acceptable to all reasonable citizens, no matter what their comprehensive perspective may be. Wolterstorff thinks the liberal theorist judges that "the highest good which it lies within the power of the state to secure is the good of each sane adult citizen freely choosing her own perspective on God and the good and freely acting thereon" (p. 238). As he sees it, liberal theory's rationale for the liberal polity is that it is the only polity that fully honors that judgment of value. It does so precisely because its rule of law guarantees due process and the civil liberties on the list.

Wolterstorff's view that liberal theory's rationale for the liberal polity appeals to the great good of each citizen freely choosing and acting on a comprehensive doctrine needs some qualification. It is not part of the project of the austere political liberalism of Rawls to justify liberal institutions in terms of goods they promote or secure. However, the comprehensive liberal doctrines of Kant and Mill do hold that freedom to choose and act on one's own perspective on God and the good is itself very valuable. The tradition in liberal theory from which Wolterstorff dissents does emphasize the idea that the political freedom secured by liberal arrangements is a great good. So I shall henceforth follow him in speaking of that tradition without mentioning qualifications that would be required in a more precise discussion of individual figures within it.

Wolterstorff argues that liberal theory so construed comes to grief on an educational issue. Because it attributes to sane adults the capacity to choose a comprehensive perspective on God and the good, and holds that infringing on the free exercise of that capacity is bad, it is hard to see how liberal theory could coherently deny that such things are also the case for sane children out of infancy. On his view, "part of the response of Mill, Rawls, and others to these facts is to insist that the education of children, by whomever conducted, ought to aim at producing 'autonomous' individuals rather than aiming at inducting them into some comprehensive perspective" (p. 237). But this response, according to Wolterstorff, leaves those liberal theorists open to a devastating objection. He puts it as follows:

It would be both implausible and contradictory, however, to argue that education for autonomy belongs to the essence of the liberal polity. Implausible, because every liberal democracy on the face of the earth allows parents to induct their children into their own comprehensive perspective. It's open to the liberal theorist to reply that, in this respect, every actual polity is far from being a liberal polity. But then contradictory, because forcing all children into education for autonomy would be a flamboyant example of discriminating against the comprehensive perspectives of most parents in present-day liberal democracies. Are all such to be dismissed as "unreasonable" in this regard? (p. 237)

In my opinion, though this line of argument has some merit as criticism of Mill, it misses the mark when Rawls is its target.

Wolterstorff offers no textual evidence at all to support his attribution to Rawls of the view that the education of children, by whomever conducted, ought to aim at producing autonomous individuals rather than aiming at inducting them into some comprehensive perspective. As has been shown above, Rawls does not subscribe to this view. Indeed, he explicitly distances himself from Mill on precisely this point. Rawls says: "The liberalisms of Kant and Mill may lead to requirements designed to foster the values of autonomy and individuality as ideals to govern much if not the whole of life. But political liberalism has a different aim and requires far less."[21] Rawls does not make the implausible claim that the education of all children for autonomy belongs to the essence of the liberal polity. Nor does he hold that any children in a liberal polity may be forced by public authorities into education for autonomy. And he does not dismiss as unreasonable parents who wish to induct children into their own comprehensive perspectives. He insists only that all children in a liberal polity be instructed in the rudiments of liberal democratic citizenship. And so he would regard as unreasonable only parents who were opposed to even this minimal educational requirement. Wolterstorff's argument therefore fails to undermine Rawlsian political liberalism. It falls short of the goal of discrediting all Johannine liberal theories, and a fortiori it does not show that liberal theory as such is defective.

Wolterstorff next claims that every Christian writer before the modern era would have disputed the view that the highest good it is within the power of the state to secure is the good of each individual being free to choose and act on an understanding of God and the good. In other words, premodern Christian writers would have affirmed "the merely moderate worth of political liberty as such" (p. 242). In what I take to be a reconstruction of the sort of reasoning such writers might have used to support this affirmation, Wolterstorff argues from examples. He declares: "Being free to form racist beliefs doesn't have much going for it by way of excellence; neither does being free to make a living at merchandising pornography" (p. 239). He then observes that, though the state does not have at its disposal methods that will guarantee the elimination of racist beliefs and the merchandising of pornography, there are available to it techniques that will promote the elimination of such beliefs and conduct and will reduce their frequency. And he concludes thus: "So in the case of racist beliefs and the merchandising of pornography, there are higher goods which lie within the power of the state to promote than that of securing the freedom to form such beliefs and to conduct such merchandising; the state can promote the elimination of such convictions and actions, and the replacement of such beliefs and actions with better beliefs and actions" (p. 239). What are we to make of this argument? It seems to me that, before we can evaluate it, we must do some work to unpack it.

Wolterstorff wishes to conclude that promoting the elimination of the formation of racist beliefs and the merchandising of pornography is a greater good than securing the freedom to form such beliefs and perform such actions. So his argument needs to make the assumption, which seems to me correct, that promoting the elimination of such things is a great good. From this assumption, we may suppose, he is entitled to conclude that forming racist beliefs and merchandising pornography are great evils. Indeed, I am prepared to grant that doing such things freely is worse than merely doing them. For it seems to me that forming racist beliefs under compulsion from social pressure is not as bad as forming them freely and merchandising pornography under a tyrant's lash is not as bad as doing it freely. In order to get his conclusion from these assumptions, however, Wolterstorff needs to show that securing the freedom to form racist beliefs and merchandise pornography is only a small good, and we may suppose that he can get this conclusion from the claim that possession of the freedom to do such things is only a small good. It is clear that Wolterstorff accepts this claim when he maintains that being free to form racist beliefs and merchandise pornography does not have much going for it by way of excellence. But he cannot make it a premise of his argument without begging the question against his liberal opponents. So he may assume only that being free to form racist beliefs and merchandise pornography is a good, and the argument must bear the burden of showing that being free to do these things is no more than a small good.

For simplicity of exposition, let us restrict our attention to the example of pornography. It seems to me useful to represent the axiological core of the argument in the following way: (1) Promoting the elimination of merchandising pornography is a great good; (2) hence, merchandising pornography is a great evil; (3) freely merchandising pornography is worse than merchandising pornography; (4) being free to merchandise pornography is a good; (5) thus, being free to merchandise pornography is only a small good; (6) so, securing the freedom to merchandise pornography is only a small good; (7) therefore, promoting the elimination of merchandising pornography is a greater good than securing the freedom to merchandise pornography. I think traditional Christian writers might well have accepted all seven of these statements. Obviously (7) follows from (1) and (6), and it is fairly clear that (2) follows from (1). I shall not challenge the claim that (6) follows from (5). Moreover, I shall, for the sake of argument, grant that the argument's premises, which are (1), (3), and (4), are all true. Even so, I shall try to show, it is doubtful that (5) follows from the conjunction of (2), (3), and (4).

It might be objected that because the conjunction of (2), (3), and (4) is inconsistent, (5) and anything else one cares to mention follows from it. It seems to me, however, that reflection on organic unities of value allows this objection to be turned aside. In the following hedonistic example, analogues

of (2), (3), (4), and (5) all appear to be true: (i) Smith suffering terrible undeserved pain is a great evil; (ii) Jones feeling mild pleasure at Smith suffering
terrible undeserved pain is worse than Smith suffering terrible undeserved
pain; (iii) Jones feeling mild pleasure is a good; and (iv) Jones feeling mild
pleasure is only a small good. So I consider it quite legitimate to grant that
all the argument's premises are true. The trouble, as I see it, is that other
cases of organic unities of value cast doubt on the validity of the inference from the conjunction of (2), (3), and (4) to (5). In the following example, it seems that the analogues of (2), (3), and (4) and the negation of
(5) are all true: (v) Brown suffering terrible undeserved pain is a great evil;
(vi) Black feeling immense pleasure at Brown suffering terrible undeserved
pain is worse than Brown suffering terrible undeserved pain; (vii) Black feeling immense pleasure is a good; and (viii) it is not the case that Black feeling
immense pleasure is only a small good. So even when we grant that merchandising pornography is a great evil and we go further by saying that doing so
freely only makes the situation worse, I think it remains reasonable to affirm
that being free to merchandise pornography is a great good. And I think the
same thing is true in the case of forming racist beliefs and in countless other
examples.

I have invested a good deal of effort in spelling this point out because I
shall want to appeal to it later in the discussion. I am going to argue that
Christians can and should hold that the possession of political liberties of the
sort liberals favor is a great good. When I do, I wish to have in place a case
for saying that this does not commit me to denying the traditional Christian
claim that some exercises of those liberties are great evils or even the claim
that some evil actions are worse than they would otherwise be in virtue of
being exercises of such liberties.

Wolterstorff looks in a different direction to find a basis for Christian allegiance to the liberal polity. He says: "To spy the theme in Christian thought
which does, in my judgment, yield a powerful argument in support of the
inherent worth of the liberal polity, we must turn our attention from goods to
evils, and from the nature of well-being to the nature of the person" (p. 242).
Because he does not think Christian thought contains a powerful argument
that liberal freedoms are a great good, he focuses on the great evil of violating
persons. According to Wolterstorff, Christians especially should be sensitive
to violations of persons because they hold that "we bear God's image; we are
icons of the Holy One" (p. 243). And it seems to me that the thought of persons being images of God, which comes from the Hebrew Bible, also provides
for Jews and Muslims a reason for regarding violations of persons as great
evils. Wolterstorff proposes that a violation of a person occurs when someone

carries out a direct and serious attack on or an unwanted intrusion into "that person's body, that person's inner life, that person's deep moral and religious convictions, that person's deep investment in the world" (p. 245). He urges adoption of the view that the idea behind the civil liberties characteristic of the liberal polity "is not so much the *great good* of being free to form and act on one's convictions, whatever those happen to be, but (in part at least) the *great evil* of having one's personhood seriously attacked or invaded by such actions as not being allowed to practice one's religion, not being allowed to gather with others of one's choice, not being allowed to speak of important matters, and not being free from surveillance and eavesdropping" (pp. 246–7). In short, the idea behind the liberal polity is preventing a great evil rather than securing a great good.

In urging that this is the idea behind the liberal polity, Wolterstorff means to suggest two things. One is that this understanding of matters provides a better account of the actual practices of existing liberal polities than does liberal theory. In support of this suggestion, he offers two considerations. First, everyone would agree that certain sorts of surveillance are not to be allowed in a liberal polity, even though they do not constrict anyone's freedom of conviction and action, because they are intrusions that violate personhood. The example he gives is the surveillance J. Edgar Hoover ordered of Martin Luther King, Jr.'s private life, when Hoover was head of the FBI. Second, liberal polities find it acceptable to enact certain forms of coercive legislation by majority vote, even though such legislation does constrict the freedom of action of some people, because this process and its results do not violate anyone's personhood. I suppose an example of this would be more or less just tax legislation.

Wolterstorff's second suggestion is that his understanding of the idea behind the liberal polity makes possible a better account of the historical origins of liberal polities than does liberal theory. Appealing to what he describes as historical speculation, Wolterstorff conjectures that "the origins of the liberal polity lie in the people of Western Europe, in the sixteenth and seventeenth centuries, slowly giving ever greater weight to the evil of violating a human being's personhood, slowly coming to a more expansive view as to when this evil occurs, and slowly coming to acknowledge that the religious pluralization of their societies meant that forcibly cultivating in others their own understanding of human well-being would require more and more pervasive violation of persons" (p. 248). To concentrate all this in a single striking image, the decisive change in early modern Europeans was that they became increasingly "horrified by the violation of the person which occurs in, for example, burning people at the stake for their religious convictions" (p. 248).

One might wonder whether Wolterstorff's attempt to elucidate the distinction between the liberal tradition he opposes and the liberal tradition with which he sympathizes in terms of a contrast between securing a great good and preventing a great evil gets to the heart of the matter. It seems that the idea behind the Johannine liberal tradition can be redescribed as preventing the great evil of not being free to choose and act on a comprehensive doctrine of one's own. And it also appears that Wolterstorff's idea of liberalism can be redescribed in terms of securing the great good of being free from violations of personhood. If this is correct, the contrast on which he relies does not mark a deep logical distinction. As I see it, however, his way of contrasting two liberal traditions is useful, even if it is not logically deep, because it reflects an important historical reality. For as I argue in the next section, Wolterstorff's variety of liberalism belongs to a tradition that arose in early modernity as a direct response to great evils produced by religious warfare in Europe and European colonialism elsewhere in the world. By contrast, the liberal tradition from which he dissents flourished in the more secularized intellectual climate of later modernity in which individual autonomy was coming to be perceived as a great good and liberal theorists emphasized the hope that political institutions would nurture it. So I am content to go along with Wolterstorff's way of stating the contrast between two liberal traditions, even though I am prepared to grant that there may be logically equivalent alternatives to it.

Wolterstorff's argument for the inherent worth of the liberal polity seems to me to contain elements of great value. I agree that violating persons is a great evil. I also agree that the liberal polity helps to prevent such violations in our situation of diversity of religious and nonreligious comprehensive doctrines. And I think Christians can and should support liberal polities for this reason. But I also think it is a mistake to suppose, as Wolterstorff does, that his line of argument is an alternative to liberal theory. As I shall next try to show, that line of argument is best seen as an attempt to appropriate, for Christian purposes, the fundamental political ideas of a venerable tradition within modern liberal theory. I also contend that it would be dangerous to rest the whole Christian case for the liberal polity on these ideas alone.

WOLTERSTORFF'S LIBERALISM AND THE LIBERALISM OF FEAR

Boiling Wolterstorff's liberalism down to its simplest terms, we may say that it places most of the weight in the argument for the liberal polity on its ability to prevent, or at least to mitigate, the great evil of violations of personhood. It counts the liberal polity's ability to secure the freedom to choose a comprehensive doctrine of the good and to act upon it once chosen as a small

good. For these reasons, his liberalism's thrust presses in a different direction from that of the Johannine strand of liberal theory. That strand extends
historically back to the work of John Locke, and its most distinguished contemporary exponent is John Rawls. And it is these two philosophers who are
the chief targets when Wolterstorff criticizes and rejects what he regards as
liberal theory. But Johannine theory is not the only strand of liberal theory;
there is another strand with an even more impressive pedigree. Its historical
roots go all the way back to Michel de Montaigne; and his disciple, Charles de
Montesquieu, greatly influenced some of the American Founding Fathers. In
honor of its French antecedents, we might think of it as the Gallic strand of
liberal theory. I reckon that Judith Shklar is its most eloquent contemporary
exponent. And the thrust of Wolterstorff's liberalism presses in a direction
parallel to the Gallic strand of liberal theory.

In her provocative book, *Ordinary Vices*, Shklar distinguishes between the
liberalism of rights, which she associates with the Lockean tradition, and the
liberalism of fear, which is the liberal tradition whose heroes are Montaigne
and Montesquieu. On her view, the ordinary vices are cruelty, hypocrisy,
snobbery, betrayal, and misanthropy, and it is the defining feature of the
liberalism of fear that it puts cruelty first among the vices. Shklar spells out
the connection between putting cruelty first and the liberalism of fear in the
following dramatic passage:

> To put cruelty first is not the same thing as just objecting to it intensely. When
> one puts it first one responds, as Montaigne did, to the acknowledgment that
> one fears nothing more than fear. The fear of fear does not require any further
> justification, because it is irreducible. It can be both the beginning and an end of
> political institutions such as rights. The first right is to be protected against the
> fear of cruelty. People have rights as a shield against this greatest of public vices.
> This is the evil, the threat to be avoided at all costs.[22]

Like Wolterstorff's liberalism, the liberalism of fear argues for the liberal polity,
not from some great good it aims to secure for citizens, but from a great evil
against which it shows promise of protecting citizens.

As Shklar reads Montaigne, he took cruelty to be the ubiquitous moral
disease of the Europe of his time. She declares: "He put it first among the vices
because it had become the most conspicuous and the least reformed evil, especially in the course of the then-current wars of religion" (p. 10). What's more,
"putting cruelty first exacerbated his antagonism to an established religiosity
that seemed to him hypocritical at best, and actively cruel at worst" (p. 11). For
both Montaigne and Montesquieu, the Spanish colonizers of the Americas
provided the most salient instances of cruel behavior carried out in the name

of religion. Shklar observes: "Montaigne regarded them as the supreme example of the failure of Christianity. It preached a purer doctrine than any other religion but had less influence on human conduct. Mohammedans and pagans tended to behave better than Christians" (p. 11). So the liberalism of fear originated in fear of the evils perpetrated or threatened by organized religion. And even today, the attitudes of many liberal theorists are shaped by fear of religious conflict. Robert Audi, for example, motivates his proposed exclusion of religious reasons from politics by an appeal to fear. Unless we discipline ourselves to abide within the limits of a secularized politics, he says, "there is a special problem: a clash of Gods vying for social control. Such uncompromising absolutes easily lead to destruction and death."[23] And, invoking again the image of warfare in the heavens, Audi insists that "religious polarization is uniquely serious. A clash of Gods – or even of clerical authorities – easily becomes a battle to the death."[24]

It is Shklar's judgment that the liberalism of fear "contributed as much to American liberal democracy as did the 'great Mr. Locke,' powerful as his influence was" (p. 237). On her view, "the unique position of cruelty was indeed fully recognized by Montesquieu's and Locke's most distinguished heirs. The Eighth Amendment to the United States Constitution prohibits, among other things, the infliction of 'cruel and unusual punishment'" (p. 238). Thus in the United States, the liberalism of fear came to be integrated with the liberalism of rights. However, Shklar contends, "the difference remains, and Montesquieu did not speak the language of rights" (p. 239). Wolterstorff's idea that the liberal polity should protect its citizens against great evils is not alien to American traditions.

And much has changed since the days of Montaigne. The cruelest regimes of the twentieth century were totalitarian polities that persecuted Christians (among others), and contemporary Christians do not regard the Spanish *conquistadores* as models of how to spread the good news of the gospel stories. Yet it seems to me Christians will not wish to take on board all the baggage of the historical tradition of the liberalism of fear. They will instead appropriate it selectively.

Some of the selectivity that is called for strikes me as fairly unproblematic. After all, contemporary philosophers who use Aristotle's virtue ethics as a resource for their own projects usually find ways to ignore or dismiss his views about slaves and many of his remarks about women. Advocates of religious toleration who see themselves as standing in a Lockean tradition consider his views about Catholics and atheists an embarrassment from which they take care to distance themselves. Similarly, most Christians who wish to appropriate Montesquieu's liberalism will no doubt reject his relativism, though perhaps they will also wish to honor him for being a pioneer in the use of comparative methods. And Christians may be divided in their attitudes toward Montaigne. Some will contest his skepticism, whereas others will feel comfortable locating him in a tradition of skeptical fideism that leads forward from him through Pascal to Kierkegaard.

But part of the portrait Shklar paints must, I think, be challenged by Christians who are interested in appropriating the liberalism of fear. In a passage that trades in contrasts drawn in the sharpest of terms, she argues in the following way:

To put cruelty first is to disregard the idea of sin as it is understood by revealed religion. Sins are transgressions of a divine rule and offenses against God; pride – the rejection of God – must always be the worst one, which gives rise to all the others. However, cruelty – the willful inflicting of physical pain on a weaker being in order to cause anguish and fear – is a wrong done entirely to *another creature.* When it is marked as the supreme evil it is judged so in and of itself, and not because it signifies a denial of God or any other higher norm. It is a judgment made from within the world in which cruelty occurs as part of our normal private life and our daily public practices. By putting it unconditionally first, with nothing above us to excuse or to forgive acts of cruelty, one closes off any appeal to any order other than that of actuality. To hate cruelty with utmost intensity is perfectly compatible with Biblical religiosity, but to put it *first* does place one irrevocably outside the sphere of revealed religion. (pp. 8–9)

So Shklar offers us what she takes to be a forced choice. Either you put cruelty first, in which case you are automatically placed outside revealed religion, or you take your stand inside revealed religion, in which case you are precluded from really putting cruelty first. Forced to make this choice, traditional Christians will, of course, opt to stand within the sphere of revealed religion and, if they are lucid, refuse to put cruelty first.

It seems to me, however, that it is Shklar's rhetoric, rather than any argument she offers, that creates the appearance that the choice is forced. I think she is correct in assuming that one could not really be putting cruelty first if one hated it only because it is offensive to God or violates a divine law. In order to put cruelty first, one must hate it because of what acts of cruelty do to their victims or because they are wrongs done to their victims. But Christians of Wolterstorff's stripe can hate cruelty for those reasons. Of course, they will also think that acts of cruelty to human beings are violations of the divine image in persons, since they discern images of God in persons. They will thus have reason to believe that such acts are offensive to God precisely because they are assaults on divine images. It will therefore be natural for such Christians to hold that cruel acts are both sins, because they offend God, and grave moral wrongs, because they inflict serious damage on their victims. They can have all the reasons for hating cruelty that liberals who put it first do. Above and beyond that, however, they will have an independent theological reason for hating cruelty.

I also believe that something can be done to soften Shklar's contrast between pride and cruelty. Traditional Christians may wish to insist that, because it bespeaks rebellion against God, pride is the worst vice when things are viewed from a comprehensive, and hence in part otherworldly, perspective. But even if they do, it remains open to them to think that pride is no worse than cruelty when we restrict ourselves to a this-worldly point of view. Cruelty could still be the worst of what Shklar considers the ordinary vices – worse than hypocrisy, snobbery, betrayal, and misanthropy. On behalf of Shklar, it might be objected that this would not really be to put cruelty unconditionally first. I agree. But I reckon ranking cruelty first among the ordinary vices and second only to pride among all the vices would be good enough to underpin a robust commitment to the core values of the liberalism of fear. And, speaking personally, I have never been able to see any strain between Christian commitment and giving Amnesty International the highest priority among the secular organizations to which I make financial contributions precisely because, more than any other organization I know, Amnesty works effectively toward the goal of eliminating torture from the face of the earth. So I am convinced that Shklar's portrait can easily be altered to make the basic ideas of the liberalism of fear hospitable to contemporary Christians. I see Wolterstorff's argument for the liberal polity as fitting comfortably with the tradition of the liberalism of fear, broadly construed.

We must construe the tradition broadly if we take Shklar's remark that cruelty is the willful inflicting of physical pain on a weaker being in order to cause anguish and fear as definitive of the worst of evils on a narrow construal. Clearly the violations of personhood Wolterstorff finds repugnant are not all cases of inflicting physical pain. Hoover's surveillance of King caused neither physical nor psychological pain, since King did not even know about it. It was therefore neither physically nor psychologically cruel in a narrow sense. Those who oppose the full range of violations of personhood described by Wolterstorff will oppose more than physical or psychological cruelty. Perhaps we should say that their target is cruelty and various analogical extensions of it, or maybe we should continue to speak of cruelty but understand our speech metaphorically.

If I am right about this, then, invoking a third Frenchman whose name begins with the letter *M*, I would say that Wolterstorff is a liberal theorist (of a certain sort) *malgré lui*. I am prepared to grant, however, that it may come as a surprise to him to be told that he has been speaking within the discourse of a venerable tradition of liberal theory, just as the character in Molière's play was surprised to learn that he had been speaking prose all along.

RELIGIOUS LIBERTY AND THE LIBERALISM OF RIGHTS

Like Shklar, Wolterstorff seems to think we are faced with a forced choice. Either Christians support the liberal polity solely because of the great evils against which it protects us, in which case they cannot support it because it secures great goods for us; or Christians support the liberal polity only because of the great goods it secures for us, in which case they cannot support it because it protects us against great evils. Wolterstorff betrays his tendency to frame the issue in such dichotomous, either/or terms in a footnote in which he acknowledges his indebtedness to the work of Robert M. Adams. In the chapter of his book *Finite and Infinite Goods* devoted to politics and the good, Adams reflects on the freedoms that most deserve protection by political arrangements because they are most closely connected with our personhood and the meaning of our lives. His claim is that "the greatest values in human life depend on people being able, and allowed, to make their own decisions in these matters, so that an interference with *freedom* to make such choices is apt to be a violation of something sacred, whether the actual choice will be a good one or not."[25] Wolterstorff chides Adams for making this comment. He declares: "This last comment seems to me to bring Adams perilously close to the liberal theorist's analysis of the governing Idea of the liberal polity, according to which what accounts for our prizing of civil liberties is not that infringing them typically involves the great evil of violating a person, whether or not coercion is involved, but that infringing them typically involves interfering with the great value of people being able and allowed to make their own decisions" (p. 246, footnote). As we are now in a position to see, the liberal theorist Wolterstorff has in mind is the Johannine theorist of the liberalism of rights, not the Gallic theorist of the liberalism of fear.

But why should we go along with Wolterstorff's supposition that Adams imperils himself by making the comment in question? Wolterstorff attributes to the liberal theorist, and does not himself dispute, the view that if we prize civil liberties because infringing them involves interfering with the great good of people being allowed to make their own decisions, we cannot also prize them because infringing them involves the great evil of violating persons. Because he thinks Christians ought to prize them for the latter reason, it is not surprising to find him thinking that it is perilous for Christians to prize them for the former reason, because, by his lights, Christians should not be doing this. There seems, however, to be a more integrative, both/and approach to the issue available to us. It seems possible to prize civil liberties *both because* infringing them involves the great evil of violating the personhood of human beings *and because* it involves interfering with the great good of allowing people to make their own decisions. And once it has become clear that Wolterstorff's arguments against Johannine liberal theory are flawed, Christians who accept his view that civil liberties protect us against the great evil of violations of personhood will have open before them the possibility of also holding that civil liberties secure the great good of being allowed to make important decisions for ourselves.

In my opinion, Christians ought to take this possibility very seriously, for I fear that an argument for the liberal polity focused exclusively on protection from the great evil of violations of personhood may fall short of justifying the extensive religious liberty Christians currently enjoy in the United States. The reason is that contemporary religious groups and institutions are not entirely free from complicity in the practice of cruelty and violations of personhood. To be sure, their cruelty is no longer directed outward to the extent it was at the time of the Spanish conquest of the New World; now it is instead directed inward toward their own members. In making this grave charge, I have in mind above all the sexual abuse of children by Catholic priests and particularly the scandal of pedophile priests in the Boston area.[26] Such actions are obviously instances of cruelty and violations of the personhood of their victims. A powerful religious institution engaged in a cover-up that spanned decades. And at their June 2002 meeting, the U.S. Catholic bishops, two-thirds of whom have transferred offending priests into unsuspecting parishes, failed to resolve the issue of how to hold such members of their own ranks accountable for this abuse of power.[27]

But Catholicism does not have a monopoly on inwardly directed cruelty for which Christian groups are accountable. Other examples are reported in Margaret P. Battin's book *Ethics in the Sanctuary*. In this book, Battin develops the promising idea of applying to religious professionals the analytic techniques philosophers have created in order to scrutinize the conduct of health care professionals, legal professionals, business persons, and others. Much of the theoretical interest of Battin's work lies in the methodological problems generated by the attempt to transfer to organized religion techniques of applied ethics developed in other contexts. For my purposes, however, her book is useful chiefly because of the large number of case studies it contains. Battin summarizes one case as follows:

In 1981 in Collinsville, Oklahoma, a rumor reached the elders of the Church of Christ that one of their members, a divorcee named Marian Guinn, was having an affair with the former town mayor, Pat Sharp. The elders summoned Guinn, insisted that she terminate the affair, and warned her that if she did not do so they would "tell it to the church." Guinn refused. She sent the church a letter of resignation and forbade the elders to mention her name in church except to say that she had withdrawn. Nevertheless, the following Sunday, the elders denounced Guinn's "sins of fornication" to the entire congregation in the church.[28]

According to Battin's analysis, "the extraordinary violation of Guinn's privacy – no light matter in a small town – could be subjected to criticism under the norms of ordinary morality and professional ethics – especially those of nonmaleficence and autonomy."[29] I think the elders' violation of her privacy was also an unwanted intrusion that violated Guinn's personhood. The elders, I submit, acted cruelly. Yet it is clear that they acted in the name of Christianity. They cited Matthew 18:15–17 as scriptural warrant for their conduct; the phrase "tell it to the church," which is quoted in Battin's summary, is drawn from Matthew 18:17.

These examples, and others like them, of cruel acts performed in the name of religion or by religious professionals suggest that we might do better at prevention of or protection against the great evil of violation of personhood if we imposed on religious groups and institutions more legal restrictions than the present liberal order's doctrine of religious freedom allows. There are, of course, objections to this suggestion worth considering. It might be objected, for example, that additional restrictions on religious liberty would produce greater evils than the evil they were aimed at preventing. But it is far from obvious that this counterfactual hypothesis is true. Or, it might be objected that the victims of such cruelty already have available to them legal remedies. Marian Guinn sued the Collinsville Church of Christ. Though the Oklahoma Supreme Court later remanded the case to the trial court with directions to award damages to Guinn only for things she suffered after she had notified the church of her withdrawal, the trial court jury initially awarded her $205,000 in actual damages and $185,000 in punitive damages.[30] Estimates of the amount the Catholic Church has paid out since the 1980s to settle cases of sexual abuse of children are in the hundreds of millions of dollars.[31] And in February 2002, a priest in the Boston area was sentenced to a prison term after being convicted of indecent assault on a boy who was only ten years old at the time.[32] But the effects of such legal remedies are mainly retributive or compensatory. Whether they have significant preventive or deterrent effects is uncertain. So there is room to doubt that the extensive religious liberty that Christian groups and institutions currently enjoy in the United States rests on firm ground if the only thing that Christians can say to support it is that it is a safeguard against the great evil of violations of personhood.

In my view, Christians can and should say more. They should support religious liberty and other liberal freedoms with arguments that also appeal to great goods these freedoms secure or promote. In making this point, I do remain aware that Christians will differ among themselves on such questions. Addressing the topic of disagreement among Christians, Wolterstorff says this: "I do not propose just sinking passively into this diversity, however; at various points I will defend certain theses as those which, in my judgment, Christians *ought to* accept" (p. 232). I shall follow his lead in this respect.

Speaking of the main religious traditions, Adams observes that "to the extent that these religious traditions stress, as in general they do, that the main thing of real worth in religious observance is sincere and willing adherence, devotion, loyalty, worship, and service, they cannot see value in coerced religious conformity."[33] I concur with his view. In a footnote to this remark, Adams cites to support it not only Locke's *A Letter concerning Toleration* but also the Second Vatican Council's *Declaration on Religious Liberty (Dignitatis Humanae)*. I think this declaration insightfully portrays a great good which religious liberty aims to promote in a way that Christians ought to find attractive. That good is the search for religious truth.

Dignitatis Humanae's first chapter begins with a ringing declaration that "the human person has a right to religious freedom."[34] Its definition of religious freedom is that "all men [*sic*] should be immune from coercion on the part of individuals, social groups and every human power so that, within due limits, nobody is forced to act against his convictions nor is anyone to be restrained from acting in accordance with his convictions in religious matters in private or in public, alone or in associations with others" (p. 800). It asserts that the right to religious freedom is based on the dignity of the human person. The connection between human dignity and the right to religious freedom is established by means of a moral obligation to search for truth. The *Declaration* argues as follows: "It is in accordance with their dignity that all men, because they are persons, that is, beings endowed with reason and free will and therefore bearing personal responsibility, are both impelled by their nature and bound by a moral obligation to seek the truth, especially religious truth" (p. 801). Because human persons are by nature free and reasonable beings, they cannot carry out the project of seeking religious truth in a way that is in keeping with their nature unless they enjoy freedom of religion. Hence, exercise of the right to religious freedom is necessary for satisfying the obligation to search for religious truth in a way that is consonant with human nature itself. Moreover, possession of the right is not contingent upon satisfaction of the obligation for beings endowed with such a nature. Hence, "the right to this immunity continues to exist even in those who do not live up to their obligation of seeking the truth and adhering to it" (p. 801). Those who fail to find or adhere to religious truth and even those who flout the obligation to search for it do not forfeit their right to religious freedom.

Dignitatis Humanae goes on to weave a tight web binding the right to religious freedom to some of the other rights that are marks of the liberal polity. For example, freedom of speech is important because the search for truth "must be carried out in a manner that is appropriate to the dignity of the human person and his social nature, namely, by free enquiry with the help of teaching or instruction, communication and dialogue" (p. 801). And freedom of assembly is important because human nature has a social dimension that is expressed in religious communities, and so "the freedom or immunity from coercion in religious matters which is the right of individuals must also be accorded to men when they act in community" (p. 802).

For my purposes, however, the idea that deserves emphasis is the *Declaration*'s assertion that the search for religious truth, rather than its possession, is a great good protected by the right to religious freedom. If we cared only about insuring orthodoxy of religious belief, we would welcome more coercion in religious matters than the liberal polity permits. Coercion may not be a perfect instrument for the enforcement of orthodoxy, but it surely can both swell the numbers of the orthodox and limit defections from orthodoxy. Wolterstorff says: "Attempts at indoctrination sometimes backfire; but often they work. If that were not the case, states wouldn't bother engaging in it" (p. 241). He is right about this. And we would also welcome more coercion of the religious than the liberal polity permits if we cared only about preventing the violations of personhood religious individuals or groups too frequently engage in. But liberty is better than coercion, other things being equal, when it comes to fostering or promoting the search for religious truth by the methods of free inquiry consonant with the nature of human beings.

As I see it, Christians have two special reasons for endorsing the claim that searching freely for religious truth is a great good. First, doing so would enable them to appreciate at its proper worth their own unending quest for religious truth. Christians, we may suppose, are entitled to believe that they already possess a good deal of religious truth, but it would be foolhardy of them to think that they now have in their possession the whole truth about religious matters or even all the religious truth God wants to share with Christians.[35] So they would do well to see the right to religious liberty as well as other civil liberties as protecting their own search for additional religious truth. Second, endorsing this claim would provide them with a firm basis of respect for the religious endeavors of practitioners of religions other than Christianity. For many such people satisfy the obligation to seek religious truth in a way that is in accord with human nature. Christians who acknowledge that doing this is a great good can extend due respect to these people for their efforts while holding that their search has been less than fully successful. So just as Wolterstorff takes it to be a signal achievement of modernity to give the great evil of violating a human being's personhood the weight proper to it, I take it to be a significant accomplishment of modernity, reflected in *Dignitatis Humanae*, to give the great good of freely searching for religious truth the weight proper to it. I think Christians can and should appropriate both of these modern discoveries.

Let me emphasize, however, that I do not claim that freely searching for religious truth is the only great good promoted by the practice of religion. Even when oppressive conditions do not allow for the free quest for religious truth, religious people can successfully pursue other great goods, such as growth in moral and spiritual virtue. Nor do I claim that freely searching for religious truth is the greatest good promoted by the practice of religion in the life of every religious person. Though it might be the greatest good in the lives of a few religious intellectuals, it is surely not the greatest good promoted by religious practice in the lives of most religious people. Nevertheless, freely searching for religious truth is a great good.

In conclusion, let me briefly summarize my argument: (1) Christians should, as Wolterstorff has maintained, regard protection against the great evil of violations of personhood as a good reason for supporting the liberal polity; (2) but it is doubtful that this reason alone is sufficient to justify the extensive religious liberty Christians enjoy in contemporary liberal democracies; (3) so Christians should want to find additional reasons for supporting the liberal polity; (4) Wolterstorff's arguments fail to show that such reasons are not provided, as Johannine liberal theorists contend, by great goods the liberal polity promotes; (5) Christians should also, as I have argued, regard promotion of the great good of freely searching for religious truth as a good reason for supporting the liberal polity; (6) hence Christians should support the liberal polity both because it offers protection against the great evil of violations of personhood and because it serves to promote the great good of freely seeking truth, especially religious truth; (7) therefore, just as the liberalism of rights and the liberalism of fear have been integrated in liberal American political institutions, so also should they be integrated in a complete Christian case for the institutions of American liberal democracy.

I began with the thought that liberal democracy in America will urgently need the support of Christian citizens in the years ahead. I end with the hope that my attempts to strengthen Wolterstorff's Christian case for the liberal polity may help to secure that support.[36]

NOTES

1. See Aryeh Neier, "The Military Tribunals on Trial," *New York Review of Books* 49.2 (February 14, 2002): 11–15.
2. Nicholas Wolterstorff, "Do Christians Have Good Reasons for Supporting Liberal Democracy?," *The Modern Schoolman* 78 (2001): 231. Subsequent page references to this paper will be made parenthetically in the body of my text.
3. Nicholas Wolterstorff, *John Locke and the Ethics of Belief* (New York: Cambridge University Press, 1996), 246.
4. See Nicholas Wolterstorff, "Why We Should Reject What Liberalism Tells Us about Speaking and Acting in Public for Religious Reasons," in Paul J. Weithman, ed., *Religion and Contemporary Liberalism* (Notre Dame, IN: University of Notre Dame Press, 1997): 162–81, and Nicholas Wolterstorff, "The Role of Religion in Decision and Discussion of Political Issues," in Robert Audi and Nicholas Wolterstorff, *Religion in the Public Square* (Lanham, MD: Rowman and Littlefield, 1997): 67–120.
5. Philip L. Quinn, "Religious Citizens within the Limits of Public Reason," *The Modern Schoolman* 78 (2001): 105–24.
6. See John Rawls, *Political Liberalism* (New York: Columbia University Press, 1993), especially Lecture VI.
7. See John Rawls, "The Idea of Public Reason Revisited," in John Rawls, *The Law of Peoples* (Cambridge, MA: Harvard University Press, 1999): 129–80.
8. Robert Audi, *Religious Commitment and Secular Reason* (New York: Cambridge University Press, 2000), especially chapters 4 and 5.
9. See Philip L. Quinn, "Political Liberalisms and Their Exclusions of the Religious," in *Religion and Contemporary Liberalism*, ed. Paul J. Weithman (Notre Dame, IN: University of Notre Dame Press, 1997): 138–61.
10. Wolterstorff, "Why We Should Reject What Liberalism Tells Us," 176–77. Wolterstorff seems to be very fond of this argument, for he repeats it almost word for word in "The Role of Religion." There (p. 116) he says: "The common pattern is this: the liberal assumes that requiring religious people to debate and act politically for reasons other than religious reasons is not in violation of their *religious* convictions; likewise he assumes that an educational program that makes no reference to religion is not in violation of any parent's *religious* convictions. He assumes, in other words, that though religious people may not be in the *habit* of dividing their lives into a religious component and a nonreligious component, and though some might not be *happy* doing so, nonetheless, their doing so would in no case be in violation of their religion. But he is wrong about this. It is when we bring into the picture people for whom it is a matter of religious conviction that they ought to strive for a religiously integrated existence – then especially, though not only then, does the unfairness of the liberal position come to light."
11. Wolterstorff, *John Locke*, 244.
12. After I had used the term "integralists" in the paper cited in note 5 above and in the first draft of this paper, I discovered that Nancy L. Rosenblum had independently picked up on Wolterstorff's phrase "religiously integrated existence" and defined what she calls "integralism." However, we do not have exactly the same thing in mind despite the terminological coincidence. For me, integralists are people, some

but not all of whom are religious, but all of whom want to live lives tightly integrated by their comprehensive doctrines. For Rosenblum, integralism is a set of challenges to democratic government in the name of religious faith. So she views integralism as an exclusively religious phenomenon, whereas I do not. See Nancy L. Rosenblum, "Pluralism, Integralism, and Political Theories of Religious Accommodation," in Nancy L. Rosenblum, ed., *Obligations of Citizenship and Demands of Faith* (Princeton, NJ: Princeton University Press, 2000): 3–31.

13. Rawls, "The Idea of Public Reason," 172.
14. Rawls, *Political Liberalism*, 197.
15. Ibid., 197.
16. Robert M. Adams, *Finite and Infinite Goods* (Oxford: Oxford University Press, 1999), 334.
17. Rawls, *Political Liberalism*, 198, footnote.
18. Wolterstorff, "Why We Should Reject What Liberalism Tells Us," 176.
19. Rawls, *Political Liberalism*, 199.
20. Ibid., 200.
21. Ibid., 199.
22. Judith N. Shklar, *Ordinary Vices* (Cambridge, MA: Harvard University Press, 1984), 237. Subsequent page references to this book will be made parenthetically in the body of my text.
23. Audi, *Religious Commitment*, 103.
24. Ibid., 174.
25. Adams, *Finite and Infinite Goods*, 328.
26. See Lisa Miller and David France, "Sins of the Fathers," *Newsweek* (March 4, 2002): 42–52. A more detailed account of the scandal is contained in The Investigative Staff of the *Boston Globe*, *Betrayal: The Crisis in the Catholic Church* (Boston: Little, Brown and Company, 2002).
27. David France, "Day of Atonement," *Newsweek* (June 24, 2002): 80–1.
28. Margaret P. Battin, *Ethics in the Sanctuary* (New Haven, CT: Yale University Press, 1990), 21–2.
29. Ibid., 67.
30. Ibid., 65.
31. Miller and France, "Sins of the Fathers," 49.
32. Ibid., 44. In August 2003, this priest became a homicide victim while in prison. See Daniel McGinn, "Preying on the Predator," *Newsweek* (September 8, 2003): 34–5.
33. Adams, *Finite and Infinite Goods*, 336.
34. *Declaration on Religious Liberty*, in Austin Flannery, O. P., ed., *Vatican Council II: Vol. 1, The Conciliar and Postconciliar Documents*, Newly Revised Edition (Northport, NY: Costello, 1996), 800. Subsequent page references to this document will be made parenthetically in the body of my text. In this discussion, I focus on the *Declaration*'s treatment of the search for religious truth in chapter 1, sections 2, 3, and 4; Adams highlights its emphasis on free faith in chapter 2, section 10.
35. On epistemic entitlement to religious belief, see Nicholas Wolterstorff, *Divine Discourse* (Cambridge: Cambridge University Press, 1995), chapter 15, and my criticism of Wolterstorff on some points of detail in Philip L. Quinn, "Can God Speak? Does God Speak?," *Religious Studies* 37 (2001): 259–69.

36. I read a version of this paper at the Conference on God and the Ethics of Belief, honoring Nicholas Wolterstorff on the occasion of his retirement, at Yale University on April 18–20, 2002. I presented another version to the University of Notre Dame Philosophy Department Colloquium on October 4, 2002. I am grateful to members of the audience on both these occasions for comments that helped me in making revisions. I am also grateful to Andrew Chignell and Andrew Dole for useful editorial suggestions.

Index